A Glossary of Literature and Composition

A Glossary of Literature and Composition

Arnold Lazarus
formerly, Department of English
Purdue University

H. Wendell Smith
Department of English
Santa Monica College

National Council of Teachers of English
1111 Kenyon Road, Urbana, Illinois 61801

The original edition of this work was published in 1971 by Grosset and Dunlap. Subsequently, the rights were ceded to the authors when the work went out of print. With thanks to the authors, the National Council of Teachers of English is happy to make this revised and updated edition available to its members.

Book Design: Tom Kovacs for TDK Design

NCTE Stock Number 18526

Library of Congress Cataloging in Publication Data

Lazarus, Arnold Leslie.
    A glossary of literature and composition.

    Includes bibliographical references.
    1. English philology—Dictionaries. 2. Literature
—Dictionaries.   I. Smith, H. Wendell, 1923–
II. Title.
PE31.L28   1983   803   83-4053
ISBN 0-8141-1852-6

Acknowledgments

We wish to thank our many friends and colleagues who have given us their advice during the preparation of this book, especially those in the English Departments at Purdue University and Santa Monica College. We are gratefully indebted to Professors John Block Friedman and J.N. Hook of the University of Illinois; Robert Hapgood of the University of New Hampshire; and James Runnels of Minneapolis, Minnesota. Librarians who have helped us include Mary Anne Black, Mary Gibbs, Margo Hayes, Amy Johnson, Norma Nyquist, Barbara Pinzelik, Elaine Puckett, Helen Schroyer, Pat Vann, Kathy Walker, and Reta Weintraut.

We would also like to thank the following publishers for their courtesy in granting permission to reprint from copyrighted material:

Brandt and Brandt: From "John Brown's Body," in *The Selected Works of Stephen Vincent Benét.* Published by Holt, Rinehart and Winston, Inc. Copyright 1927, 1928, by Stephen Vincent Benét. Copyright renewed 1955, by Rosemary Carr Benét. Reprinted by permission of Brandt and Brandt.

Jonathan Cape: From *The Bestiary,* by T. H. White. Copyright 1952 by T. H. White.

J. M. Dent and Sons, Ltd.: "Song of the Open Road." From *Family Reunion,* by Ogden Nash. Copyright 1950 by Ogden Nash.

Faber and Faber, Ltd.: From *Murder in the Cathedral,* by T. S. Eliot. Reprinted by permission of Faber and Faber Ltd. Copyright 1935 by T. S. Eliot.

————: "Paysage Moralise," by W. H. Auden. Reprinted by permission of Faber and Faber, Ltd. from *Collected Poems 1927–1957.* Copyright 1958 by W. H. Auden.

————: "Langue d'Oc," by Ezra Pound. Reprinted by permission of Faber and Faber, Ltd. from *Personae.* Copyright 1909 by Ezra Pound.

Angel Flores: From "Correspondences," by C. Baudelaire, translated by Kate Flores, in *The Anchor Anthology of French Poetry from Nerval to Valéry,* edited by Angel Flores (Garden City: Doubleday, 1958).

Harcourt, Brace and World, Inc.: From *The Meaning of Meaning,* by I. A. Richards and C. K. Ogden. Copyright 1945 by Harcourt, Brace and World.

Holt, Rinehart and Winston, Inc.: From a letter from Robert Frost to Louis Untermeyer, reprinted from *Selected Letters of Robert Frost,* edited by Lawrance Thompson. By permission of the Estate of Robert Frost and Holt, Rinehart and Winston, Inc.

v

Little, Brown and Company: "Song of the Open Road." From *Verses from 1929 On,* by Ogden Nash. Copyright 1932 by Ogden Nash.

MIT Acoustics Laboratory: From *Preliminaries to Speech Analysis,* by R. Jakobson, C. G. M. Fant, and M. Halle (Cambridge: MIT Acoustics Laboratory, 1952).

National Council of Teachers of English: For "Decorations on a Japanese Fan," by Arnold Lazarus. Reprinted from *College English* (May, 1965) by permission of the National Council of Teachers of English.

Prentice-Hall, Inc.: From *Thinking Straight,* second edition, by Monroe Beardsley. Copyright 1956 by Prentice-Hall, Inc.

Princeton University Press: From *Anatomy of Criticism,* by Northrop Frye. Copyright © 1957 Princeton University Press.

———: From *The Anatomy of Satire,* by Gilbert Highet. Copyright © 1962 by Gilbert Highet (Princeton: Princeton University Press, 1962).

Random House, Inc.: "Hearing of Harvests Rotting in the Valleys," by W. H. Auden. Copyright 1937 and renewed 1965 by W. H. Auden. Reprinted from *Collected Shorter Poems 1927–1957,* by W. H. Auden, by permission of Random House, Inc.

———: From the Introduction to The Modern Library Edition *Complete Poetry and Selected Prose of Milton,* edited by Cleanth Brooks. Copyright © 1950 Cleanth Brooks. Reprinted by permission of Random House, Inc.

Martin Secker and Warburg, Ltd.: From *A Grammar of Metaphor,* by Christine Brook-Rose. Copyright 1958 by Secker and Warburg.

The University of Texas Press: From *The Regional Vocabulary of Texas,* by E. Bagby Atwood (Austin: The University of Texas Press, 1962).

Preface

This book provides a useful index to concepts that writers, critics, and scholars have used to describe and discuss the language and its literature. We offer this glossary not as a last word but as a tool that teachers, writers, and anyone who uses English may find helpful and up to date.

The revised edition of the glossary concentrates on three major branches of English studies: literature (including criticism), rhetorical theory, and composition. Each of these branches during the last few years has developed scores of new concepts and has brought new significance to many old ones. We have included as many terms as our own scholarship embraces, seeking as much depth as is permitted by a glossary that does not try to be encyclopedic.

In line with "what's happening" in modern rhetoric and literature studies this book adopts a "now" approach to English. Wherever contemporary practice conflicts with the traditional, we have moved intrepidly toward the contemporary. Yet we are aware that *now* has grown out of *then,* that the scholarship of the '80s and '90s must blend the traditional with the new, the normative with the permissive, the analytic with the intuitive, emphasizing each as may be appropriate. In short, we have tried to put the language and its literature in contemporary perspective without forsaking those traditions that remain valid—and we have tried to do so without making our book a hodgepodge of all things to all readers.

Since the first appearance of this glossary a decade ago, many teachers have written to thank us for the unique feature of bibliographies at ends of entries. We are pleased that these references have proved useful. In this edition we retain most of the original references, and we update many entries with contemporary references.

Properly, this glossary belongs not on the reference shelf but at the elbow, ready for instant use. Its aim is to aid in what is essentially a private but ultimately a social enterprise—the sharpening of both zest and competence in reading, writing, talking, listening, and reasoning.

Arnold Lazarus
H. Wendell Smith

A Glossary of Literature and Composition

A

abbreviation   Brevity and conciseness are virtues in composition, but the needless abbreviation of words is a form of discourtesy to the reader and should be avoided. In a reference book, where the intention is to convey the most information in the least space, abbreviation is freely used; in the Armed Forces and in businesses a stringent abbreviation, almost to the point of shorthand, is also used; and in the sciences and in technical writing the conciseness of abbreviation and the precision of symbols speed communication. But in standard prose abbreviation should be used only when it is customary or conventional. Deciding what is customary or conventional is the crux of the writer's problem. The answer almost always depends on context, but a general solution is never to abbreviate if the reader will be puzzled or stymied in discovering the intended meaning.

Since abbreviation is an aspect of spelling, deciding the literal appearance of an abbreviation is easily done: a good dictionary usually provides lists of abbreviations. But decisions about the *form* of an abbreviation pose greater difficulties: (1) Should the initial letter, or all the letters, be capitalized? (2) Should the abbreviation be italicized? (3) Should the abbreviation be writter with or without period or periods? General answers, which are helpful but not invariable, are (1) Capitalize an abbreviation that would be capitalized when spelled out. Thus *Mr., Dr., St.,* when used as titles preceding names; *U.S.A., AFL-CIO,* and similar all-initial abbreviations. (2) Italicize an abbreviation if the spelled-out word or words would be italicized. (3a) Punctuate any abbreviation that is pronounced in full, as if the complete spelling were present, with the appropriate number of periods: *Mr.* (read *mister*); *n.d.* (read *no date*); *e.g.* (read *for example*). (3b) An all-initial abbreviation should be punctuated if the letters are pronounced individually—*U.S.A., C.O.D., A.D., B.C.*—but to this there are many exceptions. (3c) Any abbreviation that is read as a complete word (thus, an ACRONYM) should not be punctuated: *NATO, UNESCO, CORE, SNCC. Note:* Words like *don't* and *we'll* are contractions, not abbreviations; they never take periods.

Standard American English does use the following abbreviations:

1. For titles before names: *Mr., Mrs., Ms., Dr., St.* (sometimes the more formal *M., Messrs., Mlle., Mlles., Mme., Mmes.,* and *Monsig.*).

2. For certain designations after names: *Jr., Sr., M.P.* (Member of Parliament), *B.A.* (Bachelor of Arts), *M.A.* (Master of Arts), *Ph.D.* (Doctor of Philosophy), *M.D.* (Doctor of Medicine), *D.D.S.* (Doctor of Dental Surgery), *LL.D.* (Doctor of Laws), and for all other academic degrees.

3. For initialized terms more widely used in speech than their full forms: A.D. and B.C. (with dates), *C.O.D.* (the periods usually retained), *D.C.* (for District of Columbia), *f.o.b., P.S., R.S.V.P.* (the periods usually retained), *SOS, FCC, NAM, AMA, UN, UNESCO, CIO, YMCA, FBI, UCLA, NBC, TVA, TV, FM, AP.*

4. For names of radio and television stations: *WGN, KCBS, KTLA.*

5. For certain terms used in DOCUMENTATION or in parenthetical reference to such documentation: *p.* (*page*), *pp.* (*pages*), *ch.* (*chapter*), *col.* (*column*), *No.* (*number*), *Nos.* (*numbers*), *sec.* (*section*), *supp.* (*supplement*), *et al.* (*et alii*—"and others"), *etc.* (*et cetera*), *ca.* (*circa*—"about"), *cf.* (*confer*—"compare"), *f.* ("and the following page"), *loc. cit.* (*loco citato*—"in the place cited"), *MS* (*manuscript*), *n.d.* ("no date"), *op. cit.* (*opere citato*—"in the work cited"), *passim* ("throughout"), *q.v.* (*quod vide*—"which see"), *viz.* (*videlicet*—"namely").

Currently, the trend in scholarly work is toward less Latin, more English—and thus fewer abbreviations even in footnotes and scholarly asides. Such terms as *op. cit.* and *loc. cit.* are being dropped altogether in contemporary scholarship; *q.v.* and *viz.* are appearing as "see ..." and "namely."

6. For certain address designations *after* names of streets, avenues, boulevards, drives: *St., Ave., Blvd., Dr.* (But these are giving way to spelled-out forms—even in business offices and newspapers.)

7. For certain commercial terms after names of companies and corporations: *Co., Corp., Inc., Ltd.* (These, too, are giving way to spelled-out forms, and should be written only when a firm itself uses the abbreviation on its letterhead.)

8. For initials in names: *T. S. Eliot, H. G. Wells, Winston S. Churchill.* (Names should be written as their owners prefer—always *W. Somerset Maugham,* never *William S. Maugham;* always *George Bernard Shaw* or *G. B. S.,* never *George B. Shaw.*) When an initial is strictly a letter and stands for no name in particular, it usually is written without a period: *Harry S Truman.* No periods are used after nicknames or foreshortened names like *Jim Sam, Fred,* or *Al,* for those are not abbreviations.

In standard American usage the names of days, months, states, cities, and countries (except *U.S.A., USSR, UK* and certain other special designations) are spelled out rather than abbreviated.

abecedarian   1. A beginner. 2. A learner or teacher of the alphabet or of the elements of any discipline. 3. In a derogatory sense, a writer who spells out the obvious.

abridgment   A condensed version of an originally larger work. Well-known examples of abridged books, both fiction and nonfiction, appear regularly in *Reader's Digest.* Claims for advantages and disadvantages of abridgments remain controversial. A social advantage is that one who reads while running, so to speak, acquires at least a handle acquaintance with a few popular books among a welter that one could read only if one had "world enough and time." A disadvantage is that readers of abridged novels miss rich details of RENDERING. Indeed, aesthetes—more than historians—tend to condemn abridgments of good novels. By the same token, historians and biographers often disapprove of abridgments of nonfiction—for example, of the one-volume abridgment of Arnold Toynbee's twelve-volume *A Study of History.* Perhaps even among biographers, however, the one-volume version of Edgar Johnson's two-volume life of Dickens is more acceptable than would be an abridgment, say, of Leon Edel's five-volume life of Henry James.

abstract   See PRECIS.

abstraction   The process of separating attributes from their physical structures or "referents." As a device of semantics, abstractions name classes of things rather than individual things. The semanticist imagines an "abstraction ladder" upon which the successively higher rungs are the more and more general terms. An abstraction is a word whose referents are many (the more referents, the more abstract the word). An example is *animal,* which has such referents as cats, dogs, impalas, monkeys, and so on. See SEMANTICS.

abstraction ladder   See SEMANTICS 3.

academic drama   See CLOSET DRAMA.

accentual verse   Verse measured by a set number of accents (heavily stressed syllables) in each line, rather than, as in other poetry, a regular alternation of accented and unaccented syllables. The unstressed syllables vary in number and placement from one line to the next. Anglo-Saxon poetry (for example, *Beowulf* or "The Seafarer") was not only accentual but also ALLITERATIVE and provided the model for subsequent poetry that followed the same rhythmical pattern. Thus poetry of the Middle English alliterative revival was at the same time accentual; for example, the anonymous *Gawain and the Green Knight,* William Langland's *Piers Plowman,* and *Morte d'Arthur.* Frequently the alliterative consonants fall on the stressed syllables, as in a typical line from *Piers Plowman* (slightly modernized): "Wives and widows wool and flax spinneth." By and large, accentual verse is unrhymed, but some Middle English examples —notably *Gawain* and the York CRAFT CYCLE PLAYS—employ rhyme in addition to alliteration, showing the influence of French literature. Among the modern poets who have written accentual verse, Gerard Manley Hopkins is perhaps the best known (see SPRUNG RHYTHM).

REFERENCE: J. C. Pope, *The Rhythm of Beowulf.*

acronym   A word in which each letter stands for another word. In the acronym "laser," the *l* stands for *light,* the *a* for *amplification,* the *s* for *stimulated,* the *e* for *emission,* and the *r* for *radiation.* In acronyms, articles, conjunctions, and prepositions are usually not assigned letters. Thus a fuller "translation" of "laser" would read: "light amplification *by* stimulated emission *of* radiation." Compare PORTMANTEAU WORDS.

acrostic   A kind of poem, puzzle, or word game in which beginning and other letters form a word or phrase. Acrostics were regular features of the *Saturday Review.*

act   **1.** In a play, a major division in action or story-line, in a theater usually marked by the drawing of a curtain, but in printed copy simply by the words "Act One," "Act Two," and so on. (Divisions within an act are SCENES.) Sixteenth-, seventeenth-, and eighteenth-century plays, following Roman models, had five acts. According to Renaissance commentators on Aristotle's *Poetics,* the five acts were supposed to correspond to five divisions of the action—*introduction, rising action, climax, falling action,* and *catastrophe* (see DRAMATIC STRUCTURE). Except for Ben Jonson, the Elizabethans did not pay much attention to acts in that sense. Shakespeare's plays, for example, were originally produced in scenes and were posthumously divided into five acts in a thorough way by the editor Nicholas Rowe (1674–1718). Rowe was a product of the age of NEO-CLASSICISM, in which dramatists were very much concerned with the problems of the classical UNITIES. Nineteenth-century plays (especially those of Barrie, Ibsen, and Shaw) consist usually of four acts. Contemporary plays tend to consist of two or three acts. The one-act play, which developed with the Abbey Players of Dublin, Ireland, and with the Provincetown (Massachusetts) Players (and also with the early twentieth-century little theater movement), is a genre of its own, corresponding to the SHORT STORY in unity of impression and brevity of time-span. **2.** One of the key terms in Burke's pentad (see DRAMATISM).

REFERENCES: Richard Corbin and Miriam Balf, "How to Read a Play," *Twelve American Plays 1920–1960;* Eric Bentley, *In Search of Theater;* Gustav Freytag's "Graph" in Jackson Barry, *Dramatic Structure.*

adage   An old and supposedly wise saying, like the proverb and APHORISM. Adages are brief and memorable ("A stitch in time saves nine") and have thus become a part of folklore, transmitted orally and in writing. The adages or "morals" at the ends of Aesop's *Fables* (sixth century B.C.) are generally believed to have had oral currency in one form or another before he used them. About 1500 A.D. there appeared a collection of adages and proverbs, *Adagia,* by the Dutch humanist Erasmus. There is little definable difference between an adage and a proverb, though the latter label has a more reputable connotation. If pointlessly used too often, either may become little more than an old *saw.* A MAXIM is usually literary in origin.

REFERENCES: Desiderius Erasmus, *Adagia;* Funk & Wagnalls *Standard Dictionary of Folklore, Mythology, and Legend.* For distinctions between *adage, proverb, aphorism,* etc., see *Webster's Dictionary of Synonyms.*

adaptation   A rewriting of a work for presentation in a distinctly different GENRE or with a different style, setting, or time-frame. For example, in Greek mythology a sculptor who hated women fell in love with his own statue and, when she turned into a real woman, married her. That myth was retold in verse by Ovid and was adapted in several different genres by John Marston (1598), William Morris (1868), and W. S. Gilbert (1871). George Bernard Shaw adapted William Morris's story, turning it into the play *Pygmalion* (1913). Shaw's play was adapted by Lerner and Loewe as *My Fair Lady,* a musical comedy (1956) and a film (1964).

ad captandum or **ad captandum vulgus**   The deliberate use of unsound reasoning in an attempt to deceive the crowd. Using this device, an advertiser says, "More people buy Poofy—so Poofy is the best buy." The lack of connection between the two statements will probably not be noticed by more than a few. Compare BANDWAGON.

ad hominem   In ARGUMENTATION, any appeal to the personal feelings and prejudices of the reader or audience (the Latin phrase means "to the man"). The device may also be used to refute an opponent's argument by reasoning through propositions already accepted. This sort of argument was the technique of Clarence Darrow in the Scopes trial of 1925, when he called his opponent, William Jennings Bryan, to the stand. Starting with Bryan's belief in the Bible as absolute truth, Darrow led Bryan to untenable positions; that is, he used Bryan's own beliefs to humiliate him.

Argument *ad hominem* is not the same thing as ARGUMENT AGAINST THE MAN, which attempts to discredit a proposition on the grounds that it is asserted by a discredited person. Compare NAME-CALLING.

ad ignorantiam   In ARGUMENTATION, the contention that a proposition is true because an opponent (or the audience) can offer no evidence to the contrary. The device takes advantage of the ignorance of the audience. The arguer may, for example, assert that there is no such thing as infinity, and offer as "proof" that the opponent cannot prove otherwise.

ad misericordiam   An appeal to the sense of pity or to the sympathy of an audience. An example is the use of photos of a crippled child to inspire gifts to research funds; another, the "send an underprivileged boy to camp" appeal to sell newspaper subscriptions. These appeals may often be justified, of course.

ad populum   In ARGUMENTATION, an appeal to the emotions of the masses. The device is exemplified by the rabble-rouser who avoids presenting rational evidence against a proposition and shouts instead, "Are we going to let them do that to us?"

ad verecundiam   Snob appeal or an appeal to one's sense of prestige. Advertisers use this device when they suggest that their product is the one to "step up" to "when you can afford the best." In ARGUMENTATION, the appeal is to pride, rank, sense of status.

aesthetic distance   The theory that once an author has created a piece, it goes forth on its own and is to be understood on its own terms. In its extreme form, the theory holds that any reference to the author's intentions or to cultural and historical backgrounds is irrelevant.

REFERENCES: W. K. Wimsatt, "The Intentional Fallacy," *The Verbal Icon;* Meyer Abrams, *The Mirror and the Lamp;* René Wellek, "The Mode of Existence of a Literary Work of Art," *The Southern Review* (Spring, 1942). Gordon Thompson, "Authorial Detachment ... *Ring and the Book,*" *Studies in English Literature* (Autumn, 1970); Morse Peckham, *Man's Rage for Chaos.*

aestheticism, Aesthetic Movement   See DECADENTS and FIN DE SIÈCLE.

affective fallacy   Judging a work solely by how one feels about it.

Age of Reason   See RATIONALISM.

agent   **1.** In Burke's rhetoric, the third term of DRAMATISM. **2.** In conventional rhetoric, the performer of an action. This performer may be subject of a predication ("That *newspaper* misled us") or object in a prepositional phrase ("We were misled by that *newspaper*"). Notice that both examples identify the agent, so that the distinction between "active" and "passive" is not here in question, although the first example emphasizes "newspaper" while the second emphasizes "we." When a reader or listener must ask, "Who is doing what?" the writer had better recast. A vague utterance, like "There will be a visitation tonight," for example, prompts the reader to ask, "Who is going to do the visiting?" An agent-verb statement, like "The inspector will be visiting," is clearer and more direct, unless the writer deliberately intends for "visitation" to connote "plague." Finally, agent-verb constructions clarify and refine ambiguous strings of -ations and -icities, strings known as "NOUNIFICATIONS." For example, an ambiguous phrase like "the correction of the administration" leaves the reader asking, "Who corrected whom?" An agent-verb-object pattern can rescue the meaning here: "The administrators corrected the voters" or "The voters corrected the administrators." Compare REIFICATION.

agon   **1.** One of the national game festivals of ancient Greece. **2.** In Greek drama, the conflict between the protagonist and the antagonist(s). See DRAMATIC STRUCTURE.

agrarianism   See SENSIBILITY and IDEALISM.

agreement   In English syntax, the principle of consistency in number or case between verbs and their subjects, between pronouns and their referents.

1. Verb agreement is a problem only in the present tense, where English has a special form for the third-person singular verb. These rules are standard:

(*a*) Third-person singular subject demands singular verb: "She *wins.*"

(*b*) Two singular subjects joined by *and* demand plural verb (unless the two are considered as one unit or each is considered separate): "Coffee and tea *are* served" (but "Ham and eggs *is* his favorite dish"). If the two subjects are modified by *each* or *every,* each is considered separate: "*Each* man and woman *has* an account"; "*every* city and town *is* on the map."

(*c*) Two subjects joined by *or* demand a verb that agrees with the nearer subject: "The sparkplugs *or* the carburetor *needs* cleaning"; "the carburetor *or* the sparkplugs *need* cleaning."

(*d*) If one subject is negative, the verb agrees with the affirmative: "The captain, not the men, *is* responsible."

(*e*) The phrase beginning "along with" does not affect the subject-verb agreement. "The captain, along with his men, *is* responsible."

(*f*) A noun clause as subject demands a singular verb: "What we want *is* lower interest rates."

Verbs agree with subjects, not with noun complements: "Our disgrace *is* the slums of great cities"; "The slums of great cities *are* a disgrace." The expletive *there* is not a subject, and the verb should agree with the subject that follows: "There *are* a panda and her cubs in our zoo."

2. Pronoun agreement requires that a pronoun have the same number and the same case as the noun it stands for.

(a) The pronouns *everyone, everybody, someone, somebody, either, neither,* and *each* are singulars. A later pronoun that refers to such words must be singular: "*Everybody* does *her or his* own laundry"; "*neither* of the delegates *has* voted"; "*each* of us *deserves* recognition."

(b) Pronouns used in pairs or series must be consistent in case: "Mother and *I* went shopping," not "Mother and *me*"; "They gave the award to Tom and *me*," not "to Tom and *I*." (You would not say "to I.")

REFERENCE: H. Wendell Smith, *On Paper.*

alazon   In Greek drama, a braggart—not necessarily a braggart soldier, as is the miles gloriosus in Roman comedy. See DRAMATIC STRUCTURE and IRONY 2.

Alcaic stanza   A stanza developed by the Greek poet Alcaeus, who flourished in the late seventh and early sixth century B.C. The Roman poet Horace (65–8 B.C.) also wrote many of his poems in "alcaics." The alcaic stanza consists of four lines, the first two containing eleven syllables each; the third line, nine syllables; and the fourth line, ten syllables. In these lines, the distribution of light (˘) and of heavy (⸍) stresses, sometimes with slight variation, is as follows:

1. ˘ ⸍˘ ⸍˘ ⸍˘˘ ⸍˘˘
2. ˘ ⸍˘ ⸍˘ ⸍˘˘ ⸍˘˘
3. ⸍ ⸍˘ ⸍˘ ⸍˘ ⸍˘
4. ⸍˘˘ ⸍˘˘ ⸍˘ ⸍˘

Among the best known alcaic poems in English is Tennyson's "Milton":

O mighty-mouthed inventor of harmonies,
O skilled to sing of Time or Eternity,
   God-gifted organ-voice of England,
   Milton, a name to resound for ages;
Whose Titan angels, Gabriel, Abdiel,
Starred from Jehovah's gorgeous armories,
   Tower, as the deep-domed empyrean
   Rings to the roar of an angel onset!
Me rather all that bowery loneliness,
The brooks of Eden mazily murmuring,
   And bloom profuse and cedar arches
   Charm, as a wanderer out in ocean,
Where some refulgent sunset of India
Streams o'er a rich ambrosial ocean isle,
   And crimson-hued the stately palm-woods
   Whisper in odorous heights of even.

REFERENCES: Richmond Lattimore, *Greek Lyrics;* Gilbert Highet, *The Classical Tradition;* Alex Preminger and others, *Princeton Encyclopedia of Poetry and Poetics.*

Alexandrine   In English poetry, an iambic hexameter line, usually in a stanza of iambic pentameter lines; for example, the last line of the SPENSERIAN STANZA. The term derives from the *Roman d'Alexandre,* a twelfth-century French romance that used the twelve-syllable line. Since its use by the poet Ronsard (sixteenth century) and by the playwrights Corneille and Racine (seventeenth century) the Alexandrine has been standard in French poetry as the dactylic hexameter in Latin and the iambic pentameter in English. But whereas the French Alexandrine, especially that of the nineteenth-century poet Verlaine, can be measured in syllables, the English Alexandrine is more accurately measured in metrical feet. A classic example of the English six-foot line is Alexander Pope's "Thăt líke / ă wóund / ĕd snăke / drăgs ĭts / slŏw léngth / ă lóng," which pokes fun at the form. (Pope regarded as freakish any line longer than five feet.) But the Alexandrine need not drag: it may be an artistic triumph, as it is in certain lines of W. H. Auden's poem "In Memory of W. B. Yeats"—notably the line "Now Ireland has her madness and her weather still." In oral interpretation, the Alexandrine, like other six-beat lines, tends to break into three-beat lines, as John Hollander observes in "Metrics," in Edward Gordon, ed., *Writing and Literature.*

alienation   **1.** A condition in which a person is rejected or feels cut off from friends, community, or society. **2.** An archetypal theme in literature (see ARCHETYPE), especially in such works as Dostoevsky's *Notes from Underground,* Kafka's *Metamorphosis,* Joyce's *A Portrait of the Artist as a Young Man,* Camus' *The Stranger,* Guerard's *The Exiles,* Baldwin's *Another Country,* and most of Brecht's plays.

REFERENCES: Hannah Arendt, *The Human Condition;* Timothy O'Keeffe, ed., *Alienation;* Gerald Sykes, ed., *Alienation: The Cultural Climate of Our Times;* Ned Hoopes, ed., *Who Am I?*

allegorical level   See LEVELS OF MEANING.

allegory   A kind of extended metaphor in which characters or PERSONIFICATIONS represent something other than themselves—virtues, vices, causes, issues. There are two main kinds of allegory: those that use personifications, as in Bunyan's *Pilgrim's Progress;* and those that use a special kind of symbolism, as in Dante's *Divine Comedy.* In *The Pilgrim's Progress* the main character, Christian, who "trudged through the Slough of Despond," represents the Christian soul on its pilgrimage through the world. Christian is not a real person, of course, nor is the Slough of Despond a real place; they are rather concretizations of abstract ideas made real and vital to the reader by their dramatic presentation. In *The Divine Comedy* a real man, Dante, meets the ghost of a real person, the Roman poet Vergil, who serves him as a guide through Hell. Aside from their literal roles as pilgrim and guide, Dante and Vergil represent humanity led by human reason to an understanding of the nature of evil and the spiritual consequences of sin. Such a representation is *symbolic allegory.*

Allegorical writing was quite common in early didactic literature (see DI-DACTICISM), as reflected in numerous FABLES and PARABLES. Some major works that are allegorical in one respect or another are *Everyman* (a morality play), *Piers Plowman, The Parliament of Fowls* (Chaucer), *The Faerie Queene* (Spenser), and *A Tale of a Tub* (Swift). In modern literature, allegorical LEVELS OF MEANING tend to be more veiled and thus less susceptible to explicit interpretation, as in *Moby Dick* (Melville), *Animal Farm* (George Orwell), and *Tiny Alice* (Edward Albee). There is, in fact, some controversy over whether such works should be called allegorical at all.

REFERENCES: C. S. Lewis, *The Allegory of Love;* R. W. Frank, Jr., "The Art of Reading Medieval Personification Allegory," *E*[nglish] *L*[iterary] *H*[istory] (December, 1953); Edwin Honig, *Dark Conceit: The Making of Allegory;* Don Cameron Allen, *Mysteriously Meant* ... ; Michael Murrin, *The Veil of Allegory;* Anne Skura, "Revisions and Rereadings in Dreams and Allegories," in J. H. Smith, ed., *The Literary Freud;* Maureen Quilligan, *The Language of Allegory;* Jane Vogel, *Allegory in Dickens.*

alliteration (Also called **head rhyme**)   The close-order repetition of initial consonants in a series of words, as in Poe's "While I nodded, nearly napping, ..." Alliteration deftly used may contribute to EUPHONY; but excessive use of alliteration can degenerate into EUPHUISM. Alliteration also serves as a MNEMONIC device; advertising copywriters often use it to catch attention and impress the memory. Our heritage abounds in alliterative utterances: "Fifty-four forty or fight," "Tippecanoe and Tyler too," "right as rain," "kith and kin," "time and tide," "might and main." Compare CONSONANCE and ASSONANCE.

alliterative verse   The unrhymed ACCENTUAL VERSE of Old English poetry, especially of *Beowulf:*

> There was laughter of heroes, the heroes high,
> Words were winsome. Waltheow went forth,
> Hrothgar's queen, in courtly costume ...
> Then there came forth from the moors under the mists,
> Grendel creeping; he bore God's anger;
> The dreadful serpent drew near the sires....

Old English poetry relied on ALLITERATION and on a certain number of accented syllables to each line. The line was broken into two HEMISTICHS with a CAESURA in between.

An alliterative revival took place in the fourteenth century, as evidenced in *Sir Gawain and the Green Knight* and *Piers Plowman.* Certain of the York CRAFT CYCLE PLAYS (ca. 1340) are also written in alliterative verse; for example, the first one, on the creation and fall of Lucifer. But these plays also use rhyme, perhaps reflecting a French influence.

REFERENCES: Margaret Williams, ed., *Word Hoard: A Treasury of Old English Literature;* Neil Isaacs, *Structural Principles in Old English Poetry.*

allusion   Loosely, any reference—direct or indirect; strictly, an allusion is an *indirect* reference to anything the writer feels should be well known in literature, history, and the arts. By tapping the reader's memory, the writer or speaker brings the import of an experience—with all its associations—to bear upon a present meaning. Thus, much is said in few words, allusion being a striking device for economy, as Reuben Brower observes in *Alexander Pope: The Poetry of Allusion.*

Allusions may range from the universal to the obscure and momentary. What is necessary is that they be recognized by the audience. How much does the reader or listener know of the culture—of history, of art, of science, of yesterday's headlines, of philosophy, of great men and women, of great books and poems and plays? The more one knows of all these, the more one will derive from current reading and listening, as Ronald Christ suggests in *The Narrow Act: Borges' Art of Allusion.*

If a speaker or writer mentions "a visit to England in the cruellest month," the line would mean much to those in the audience familiar with the opening line of T. S. Eliot's *The Waste Land:* "April is the cruellest month, ..." Those familiar with the Eliot poem know that he, in turn, alludes "to England in April"—and they also understand that the whole background of Eliot's poem bears upon the present "visit to England." For some the reference will take on still further implications because they recall another line of poetry—Browning's "Oh, to be in England / Now that April's there!" Note the contrast of attitudes between the pleasurable April and the cruel April.

What happens in the mind of the reader or listener who does not "pick up" those allusions? The full sense of the line as well as the delight of "getting it" is missed. Allusions are truly successful only when the audience does share the knowledge. The wider the audience, the more universally known must be the thing alluded to. Literature (as well as daily speech) abounds with allusions to the Bible and to Shakespeare, perhaps the two most widely assumed literary experiences of English-speaking people. If the audience is small and local, however, an allusion may call up specific knowledge of something very immediate—something, let us say, that would be unknown to those who had not attended a certain baseball game or read a certain news story yesterday. Local or ephemeral allusions obviously do not make good material for the writer who hopes to appeal to the wider, general audience.

REFERENCES: Most dictionaries, collegiate or larger, identify proper name (i.e., direct) references. For identifying a quotation or an allusion to one, even when only a few key words are given, the following dictionaries can be useful: (1) *Bartlett's Familiar Quotations,* (2) *The Oxford Dictionary of Quotations,* (3) Bergen Evans, *Dictionary of Quotations,* and (4) Laurence J. Peter, *Peter's Quotations: Ideas for Our Time.* A celebrated work that identifies indirect as well as direct references is S. A. Allibone, *Critical Dictionary of English Literature and British and American Authors* (1899). Patricia Kane, "Reading Matter as a Clue to Dreiser's Characters," *South Dakota Review* (Winter, 1970); Howard German, "Range of Allusions in Iris Murdoch's Novels," *Journal of Modern Literature* (Fall, 1971); Helen Williams, *Allusion.*

alter ego   Literally, "other I." **1.** Another person, a close friend, who is very much like oneself; e.g., Damon's Pythias; Achilles' Patroclus; Gertrude Stein's Alice B. Toklas. **2.** Another side of oneself, as in a "split personality" or "schizophrenia"; e.g., Dr. Jekyll may be thought of as Mr. Hyde's alter ego. **3.** A character who shares another character's manifest or suppressed traits; e.g., in Conrad's *Secret Sharer* the narrator-Captain and Leggatt; and in

Hesse's *Demian* Demian and Emil. In that context the alter ego is close to the German *Doppelgänger* (literally, "doublegoer") since one of the two characters seems to be a ghostly manifestation or reincarnation of the other. (Strictly the German term refers to a pair of persons of whom one is flesh, the other spirit.)

REFERENCES: Otto Rank, *The Double;* Robert Rogers, *A Pschoanalytic Study of the Double in Literature;* Claire Rosenfield, "The Shadow Within ... The Double," *Daedalus* (Spring, 1963); William Gillis, "Doppelgänger," CEA *Critic* (February, 1969); C. E. Robinson, "Devil as Doppelgänger ... Byron's Unfinished Drama," *Bulletin NY Public Library* (March, 1970).

ambiguity   Multiple meaning. Whatever has more than one possible meaning is ambiguous. When ambiguity is not intended, it is usually considered a flaw. But intentional ambiguity may enhance.

1. In unintended ambiguity the uncertainty may be caused by careless syntax, spelling, punctuation, or word choice. Here are ambiguous statements: "We all know that woman is fickle." (Are *all* women fickle, or just *that* woman? Is *that* a connective or a demonstrative? In speech the proper stress would no doubt clarify the meaning.) "We boarded the *Elizabeth II* for our ocean voyage in New York." (The misplaced modifying phrase does the damage.) "The little valley made a perfect site." (Spelling trouble: was *sight* intended?) "We saw her play last night." (Did she play tennis? Did she act in a play? Did she write the play we saw?) "He's an old coin collector." (A hyphen might clarify things: though young, he's an old-coin collector.) Context often clarifies such ambiguities as those above, but careful speakers and writers know that the way into the minds of their audience is difficult at best, and that unintended ambiguity makes contact still more difficult. Among unintentional yet meaningful ambiguities is the FREUDIAN SLIP: "I was sure I heard a burglar downstairs, and I lay there wild awake."

2a. Occasionally, ambiguity is deliberate. EQUIVOCATION, giving "equal voice" to two meanings, is an intention to mislead or deceive. It may appear when the speaker wants to avoid taking either of two stands. Politician, diplomat, barrister, parent—almost anyone—may equivocate to avoid commitment; the student may equivocate in an essay examination, hoping to appear in agreement with whatever the teacher believes. Equivocation is considered at best unethical.

2b. Desirable ambiguity occurs when a context yields two or more meanings to enrich, rather than obscure. Most writers of poetry and other imaginative literature use such ambiguity. Cleanth Brooks says, "The tendency of science is necessarily to stabilize terms, to freeze them into strict denotations; the poet's tendency is by contrast disruptive." The poet consciously "disrupts" the normal uses of words, both to pack much meaning into a few words and to startle the reader into a sharper attention to a turn of thought. Shakespeare often boldly directs our attention to the double-flip that words may take. Says Othello as he enters Desdemona's bedchamber with intent to kill her: "Put out the light, and then put out the light." He extinguishes the lamplight—and then Desdemona's life. PUNS and other sorts of DOUBLE-ENTENDRE are common in everyday speech but are especially useful to the poet, as is virtually "any verbal nuance, however slight, which gives room for alternative reactions to the same piece of language," as William Empson puts it in *Seven Types of Ambiguity*. Laurence Perrine has said of desirable ambiguity: "The poet needs a multi-dimensional language, and creates it partly by using a multi-dimensional vocabulary.... The poet, we may say, plays on a many-stringed instrument. And he sounds more than one note at a time." Those who play the violin know that Perrine has in mind, here, something like the "double stop."

REFERENCES: Ruth Krauss, *There's a Little Ambiguity Over There Among the Blue Bells;* C. T. Samuels, *The Ambiguity of Henry James.*

ambivalence   1. In Freudian psychology, simultaneous love and hate. 2. In literature, especially fiction and drama, a pair of contrasting (often contradictory) characteristics within a single character. The classic example is Stevenson's Dr. Jekyll, who is also Mr. Hyde; the first good, the second evil. Freudian ambivalence is manifest in such characters as Melville's John Claggart (*Billy Budd*), Dostoevsky's Raskolnikov (*Crime and Punishment*), Conrad's Mr. Kurtz (*Heart of Darkness*), and Henry James's John Marcher (*The Beast in the Jungle*).

REFERENCES: W. Eugene Davis, "Tess . . . Some Ambiguities," *Nineteenth Century Fiction* (March, 1968); W. H. Gass, *Fiction and the Figures of Life.*

amphibole   An utterance that can be taken in opposite senses. For example, "Feed a cold and starve a fever" can mean *(a)* "If you have a cold, eat; if you have a fever, fast" and *(b)* "If you eat when you have a cold, you will get a fever." In Greek literature such ambiguous predictions were attributed to the Pythian priestesses and oracles at Delphi.

amphibrach   See METER.

anachronism   The use of any character, incident, artifact, or language at a time or place inconsistent with historical fact. The striking of a clock in Shakespeare's *Julius Caesar* is a case in point, since the Roman setting of the play antedates the invention of this kind of clock by hundreds of years. Such archaic language as "thee," "thou," "thy," and similar words in would-be contemporary poetry is quite anachronistic. Most anachronisms are unintentional. Occasionally, anachronisms may be deliberate, as they are in *A Connecticut Yankee in King Arthur's Court*. Here the comic IRONY emerges to a large degree from Twain's deliberate joining of modern with medieval language, customs, and technologies. Similarly, George Bernard Shaw has his Joan of Arc, his Cleopatra, and his Androcles speak in a modern idiom, the better to show the human characteristics they share with contemporary people.

anacoluthon   Failure to follow through a syntactical structure once begun. Some examples: "To tell the truth, I found the book rather dull and ends with an anticlimax"; "She couldn't find a parking place, had to run late to her exam, and which undoubtedly spoiled her performance." Anacoluthon is the term Fowler uses to castigate such befuddlements as FRAGMENTS, DANGLERS, and MISPLACED MODIFIERS. Anacoluthon is also a kind of slipping on such banana peels as FAULTY PARALLELISM, WHICHMIRES, SYLEPSIS, and ZEUGMA.

REFERENCE: George Starbuck, "Anacoluthon All Over Again," *Papers of the Midwest MLA* (1969).

Anacreontic   (After the Greek poet Anacreon, sixth century B.C.) A song celebrating wine and women as objects of pleasure. Anacreon used no rhymes, and his meters varied as widely as did those of his imitators. The TROCHAIC meter in Longfellow's *Hiawatha* ("By the shóre of Gítche Gúmee / By the shíning Bíg-Sea-Wáter") is said to resemble one of the anacreontic meters. Thomas Moore (whom Byron nicknamed "Anacreon Moore") and other modern poets have adapted anacreontics to quatrains rhyming *abab*.

REFERENCE: Alex Preminger and others, *The Princeton Encyclopedia of Poetry and Poetics.*

anacrusis   Literally, "upbeat." A kind of grace-note or extra unaccented syllable(s) at the beginning of a line of poetry. Longfellow's "The Reaper and the Flowers," for example, uses an anacrusis in the line-opener "There is a reaper." *Note:* The context of that poem does not call for a heavy finger-pointing stress on *there.*

anadiplosis   Deliberate repetition for emphasis, especially when the ending of an utterance is used to begin the next: "Spare me your *words; words* are not what I need." Compare ANAPHORA and EPANADIPLOSIS.

anagram   A word or phrase consisting of letters transposed from another word or phrase—for example, "Salt at last!" "Nedra" is an anagram of "Arden." Compare PALINDROME.

analects   Miscellaneous occasional observations, as in the *Analects of Confucius.*

analogue   In a literary work a theme, passage, scene, or episode similar to that in another literary work; for example, Lucas's betrayal of Lena in Faulkner's *Light in August* is an analogue of Alec's betrayal of Tess in Hardy's *Tess of the D'Urbervilles.* (For betrayal as an archetypal human experience, see STRUCTURALISM.)

analogy   A comparison of two things that are essentially unlike but which can be shown to have some similar properties. When construed loosely, analogy may cover all sorts of figurative comparisons—METAPHOR, SIMILE, ANTONOMASIA. But in its more restricted sense, analogy is a more fully developed comparison than any of the other sorts of similitude. Its use is among the most effective ways to explain, describe, or convince.

When used to describe or explain, an analogy clarifies some new concept by comparing it to a better-known one. Hobbes's *Leviathan,* for example, compares political governments to a great whale, showing that both have structure, organization, power. The comparison goes beyond metaphor and simile, for it points up a larger number of similarities between the two unlikes. The more points of similarity, the stronger the analogy. These points of similarity are made explicit, not left to the reader's imagination.

Alexander Pope used analogy to explain something about the variety of human opinion: " 'Tis with our judgments as with our watches; none go just alike, yet each believes his own." The figure is analogy rather than simile because Pope points explicitly to the ways in which the two things, judgments and watches, are alike. Without his clause of explanation, the clause of assertion would only puzzle us. A simile, on the other hand, deliberately leaves something to the imagination.

In ARGUMENTATION, analogy is both useful and dangerous. It is useful as a shortcut, for it draws upon accepted knowledge to establish new, and as yet unaccepted, theory. But reasoning by analogy is dangerous because it may claim or suggest fundamental similarity between two things whose similarities are only superficial. To say that "Cure-All is like a doctor's prescription because it contains multiple ingredients" is, of course, a FALSE ANALOGY—one that ignores differences in favor of superficial likenesses. See INDUCTIVE REASONING 4.

REFERENCES: Randall Decker, "Analogy as an Expository Device," *Patterns of Exposition;* Monroe Beardsley, "Analogies," *Practical Logic.*

anapest   In poetry, a unit of rhythm consisting of two lightly stressed syllables followed by one heavily stressed syllable. Here is an example from Alfred Noyes's "The Highwayman": "And he taps with his whip on the shutters, but all is locked and barred." Notice that the last three feet of this line are iambic and not anapestic. Verse that is purely anapestic tends to become monotonous. It is a mark of the skillful poet to use occasional substitutes interestingly and appropriately.

anaphora   1. Repetition (literally, "bringing back") of a word or word-group to begin successive phrases, clauses, sentences, or lines of poetry. A familiar example is found in Lincoln's Gettysburg Address: "But in a larger sense, we cannot dedicate—we cannot consecrate—we cannot hallow this ground." The device was much used by Shakespeare, as in John of Gaunt's lyrical lines on England: "This royal throne of kings, this sceptred isle, / This earth of majesty, this seat of Mars, / This other Eden." (*Richard II,* II, i). Also called EPANA-DIPLOSIS. Compare ANADIPLOSIS and EPANALEPSIS. 2. In linguistics, the use of words, especially pronouns, to refer to (or bring back to mind) other words already used.

REFERENCES: Alex Preminger and others, *Princeton Encyclopedia of Poetry and Poetics;* Noam Chomsky, *Language and Responsibility.*

anarchy   Radical hatred of governments (literally, "against government"). For details on some real-life anarchists see NIHILISM. Several fictive anarchists figure in Joseph Conrad's novel *The Secret Agent* (1907).

anastrophe   A wrenching of words from their normal or expected order, either to achieve emphasis or to meet the exigencies of meter. In *Hamlet* an example occurs in the words of Polonius: "[He] fell into a sadness, / ... and by this declension / Into the madness wherein now he raves / And *all we* mourn for." (II, ii.) And Hamlet himself: "When he himself might *his quietus make* / With a bare bodkin." (III, i.)

anecdote   Literally, "not for publication." 1. A confidential tale or bit of gossip. 2. An episode or event worked in as a kind of parenthesis to the main story-line in a work of fiction (as in Sterne's *Tristram Shandy* and Dickens's *Pickwick Papers*) or in a long narrative poem (as in *The Iliad* and *The*

Aeneid). The didactic anecdotes in Chaucer's "Nun's Priest's Tale" are a delightful parody of anecdotal digressions.

REFERENCES: Edmund Fuller, ed., *Thesaurus of Anecdotes;* Donald Hall, ed., *Literary Anecdotes.*

animism   1. Ancestor worship, in several Oriental cultures, whose assumption is that the spirits of ancestors live on in the universe. 2. The investing of animals and inanimate objects in nature with human characteristics. Thus, in several mythologies, trees and bodies of water, for example, have human personalities and even divine doubles (dryads, nymphs).

REFERENCES: James Frazer, *The Golden Bough;* Bronislaw Malinowski, *Magic, Science, and Religion;* Robert Redfield, *The Primitive World;* William G. Sumner, *Folkways;* William Butler Yeats, *The Celtic Twilight;* Marjorie Perloff, "... Animism in Sylvia Plath's Poetry," *Journal of Modern Literature* (Fall, 1970); "... Yeats' Poetry," *PMLA* (Oct., 1967); Ron Smith, *Mythologies of the World.*

annotated bibliography   See DOCUMENTATION.

antagonist   The villain or chief negative character in a plot; the one who opposes the protagonist. In Shakespeare's *Othello,* for example, Othello's chief antagonist is Iago. But Othello himself is also his own enemy. Thus, Othello's own "green-eyed jealousy"—his TRAGIC FLAW—may also be considered an antagonistic force. See DRAMATIC STRUCTURE.

anthology   A collection (literally, a "bouquet") of selected pieces;—e.g., Palgrave's *Golden Treasury.* The chief purpose of most anthologies is to delight or entertain. A secondary purpose, especially in school anthologies (e.g., *Adventures in Modern Literature*), is to whet the appetites of readers so that they will read more of a given author's works or more works of a certain literary type. In this sense an anthology is also called a *sampler* or a *reader.* *Note:* Just as appetizers are not intended as substitutes for complete meals, anthologies are not intended as substitutes for authors' whole books.

antibacchius   See METER.

anticlimax   1. Any event or scene (usually at the end of a play) that is less crucial than what precedes it; in classical drama and early fiction, the spelling out of minor details and the tying up of loose ends. See DÉNOUEMENT. The climax, or high point of a play or story, is at the end, so that the anticlimax, if any, which can come only after the climax, is very close indeed to the end. Anticlimax may be a blemish only when it is structurally irrelevant. Early popular fiction was usually marred by it, for writers tried to satisfy sentimental readers by explaining every last detail of the characters' "fates." 2. Anticlimax is also a stylistic device that may occur within as small a unit as the sentence: something trivial following something of importance: "As a serious young man, I loved Beethoven, Keats, and hot dogs." Intentional anticlimax can be first-rate humor. Advertising writers sometimes fall into anticlimax unintentionally by placing too much value on a product: "Look gay and beautiful! Let romance enter your life! Spray your hair with Sheen!" Intentional anticlimax is a favorite device of the satirist. It can be seen in Pope's title "The Rape of the Lock," for example, and in these two lines from Canto V: "'Now meet thy fate,' incensed Belinda cried, / And drew a deadly bodkin from her side...."

anti-closure   See CLOSURE.

anti-hero   In several modern novels and plays, a protagonist who lacks heroic virtues, especially courage and honesty. Unlike the PICARO, who is deliberately roguish, the anti-hero has ambivalent feelings, both conscious and unconscious, about traditional values. Examples of the anti-hero include Bloom in Joyce's *Ulysses,* Loman in Arthur Miller's play *Death of a Salesman,* Yossarian in Joseph Heller's novel *Catch 22,* and Billy Pilgrim in Kurt Vonnegut's novel *Slaughterhouse Five.* Compare ANTI-NOVEL.

REFERENCES: Raney Stanford, "When a Not-Hero Is a Hero," *Journal of Popular Culture* (Winter, 1967); Ihab Hassan, *Radical Innocence;* E. R. Steinberg, "James Joyce and the Critics Notwithstanding, Leopold Bloom Is Not Jewish," *Journal of Modern Literature,* IX-1 (1981–82); Laura Adams, *Will the Real Norman Mailer Please Stand Up?*

anti-masque   See MASQUE.

anti-metabole   Repetition of the same words in reverse order, as in "One for all and all for one" or "Eat to live; don't live to eat."

antinomies   **1.** Opposites traditionally juxtaposed in many genres of literature —for example, the material vs. the spiritual; the city vs. the countryside. In Blake's "The Marriage of Heaven and Hell," antinomies are referred to as "contraries": "Without contraries is no progression. Attraction and Repulsion, Reason and Energy, Love and Hate are necessary to Human existence." **2.** Apparent self-contradiction or PARADOX—for example, in Yeats's "Sailing to Byzantium" "The young . . . those dying generations." (*Note: antinomy,* the literary term, is to be distinguished from *antimony,* the metal.) Compare TENSION.

anti-novel   A kind of fiction that disregards or deemphasizes plot, and instead emphasizes psychological introspection into human motivations and feelings— into all the thousands of minutiae that fill time. (Compare STREAM OF CON-SCIOUSNESS.) Such works as Joyce's *Finnegans Wake,* Woolf's *Orlando,* Proust's *Remembrance of Things Past,* and William H. Gass's *Omensetter's Luck* may be called anti-novels. The term first gained prominence when it was used by Jean-Paul Sartre in his review of *Portrait of a Man Unknown* by Nathalie Sarraute, the Russian-born French novelist. Such writers as Robert Walser, Jorge Luis Borges, Samuel Beckett, and Donald Barthelme disregard plot (certainly the traditional well-made plot). Indeed, the revolt of contemporary novelists against traditional forms parallels the revolt of playwrights in the THEATER OF THE ABSURD.

REFERENCES: Jean-Paul Sartre, *Literary Essays;* Ruth Temple, *Nathalie Sarraute;* Alain Robbe-Grillet, *For a New Novel;* B. Gross, "Antinovels of John Barth," *Chicago Review,* xx-3 (1968); Louis Rubin, *Curious Death of the Novel;* Sallie Sears and G. W. Lord, eds., *The Discontinuous Universe;* Robert Scholes, "Metafiction," *Iowa Review* (Fall, 1970).

antiphrasis   Any use of a word in a sense contrary to its meaning; for example, "Let's slap a *mandate* on him" for "Let's slap an *injunction* on him." Compare MALAPROP and IRONY.

antistrophe   See ODE.

antithesis   **1.** An idea opposed to another idea or THESIS. **2.** The balancing of one thing against another opposing or contrasting thing. What is contrasted may be words, phrases, clauses, sentences—even paragraphs or whole sections of a literary work; but antithesis most often consists in the contrast between two parts of a sentence: "Art is long; life is short." The second clause of an antithesis may omit the verb if that verb can be assumed the same as the first: "The early writers are in possession of nature, and their followers of art."— Samuel Johnson. Antithesis, as one form of rhetorical balance, was used to extreme in the oratory of the Sophists of ancient Greece. In English it became almost an obsession of John Lyly, whose markedly artificial style became known as EUPHUISM. Antithesis also lent itself especially well to expression in the HEROIC COUPLET of the age of Dryden and Pope. Antithesis turns easily to the EPIGRAM. As a device of contrast, antithesis is related to IRONY, OXYMORON, PARADOX, AMBIVALENCE, FOILS, ANTAGONIST. See also DIALECTIC 3.

antonomasia   The substitution of the name of an individual for that of a class. Call a person an Izaak Walton and you have indirectly called him an expert fisherman. This device is a sort of METONYMY, or cross-naming: a lover becomes a *Romeo,* an orator a *Cicero,* a poet a *Milton.* For details of an intended antonomasia that proved disastrous see William F. Buckley, Jr., "A Journal," *The New Yorker* (Jan. 31, 1983).

apheresis   See CLIPPED FORM.

aphorism   Any terse statement of doctrine or of acknowledged principle. Examples include such pithy assertions as "Education is learning to take pleasure in the right things" (Aristotle), "Whatever is, is right" (Alexander Pope), and even the remark of a character in a modern cartoon, "Happiness is a warm puppy" ("Peanuts"). Like these examples, the brief attempt at defining the indefinable often becomes an aphorism. If it happens also to be startling or paradoxical, it may be called an *apothegm:* "History is bunk" (Henry Ford). When such a brief assertion is widely known and the author forgotten, it is called a *proverb:* "There's no fool like an old fool." If generally accepted as a truth, it becomes an ADAGE: "Handsome is as handsome does." If an aphorism turns to advice on how to live, it becomes a MAXIM: "Give every man thy ear, but few thy voice" (the advice of Polonius to Laertes in *Hamlet*). A maxim of ethical content or purpose is a *precept,* a term that may also apply to any instructional *adage:* "Don't change horses in mid-stream." Aphorisms, proverbs, and maxims in verse are known as GNOMIC poetry. Compare EPIGRAM.

REFERENCES: W. H. Auden and Louis Untermeyer, eds., *The Viking Book of Aphorisms;* "Prose Forms: Apothegms," in A. Eastman, *Norton Reader.*

apocalypse   From the Greek word meaning "that which is uncovered or revealed." **1.** A synonym for the Book of Revelation, the last book of the New Testament. In this work are found the Four Horsemen of the Apocalypse— Conquest, Slaughter, Famine, and Death. They ride white, red, black, and pale horses respectively. It is to Death that Katherine Anne Porter alludes in

Pale Horse, Pale Rider. The Four Horsemen of the Apocalypse, a novel by the Spaniard Vicente Blasco-Ibañez, was based on the horrors of World War I. **2.** Sometimes the word is used for any literary work or vision of experience which, like the classic Judaeo-Christian apocalypses, is cast in the form of a dream or several dreams in which a superior authority reveals the imminent end of the world. The apocalypse usually constitutes a warning to, and criticism of, contemporary society and hints that a chosen people (the Israelites, the Christians, and so on) will triumph over an oppressor. The imagery of the apocalypse is often rife with fires, floods, storms, mysterious signs, and symbolic portents. **3.** Viewed in a much more special "cosmic vision," the "apocalyptic world of the Bible" consists, according to Northrop Frye, of these equivalents:

Divine world   = *society of gods* = *One God*
Human world   = *society of men* = *One Man*
Animal world   = *sheepfold*   = *One Lamb*
Vegetable world = *garden or park* = *One Tree of Life*
Mineral world   = *the city*   = *One Building or Temple*

REFERENCES: Northrop Frye, "Archetypal Criticism," *Anatomy of Criticism;* Norman Cohn, *The Pursuit of the Millenium;* Frank Kermode, *Sense of an Ending;* Harold Bloom, *Blake's Apocalypse;* J. F. Stewart, "... Apocalypse in Faulkner's 'Wash,'" *Studies in Short Fiction* (Fall, 1969).

apocope   See CLIPPED FORM.

Apocrypha   A group of Old Testament books not entirely accepted from time to time as part of the CANON. The best known include Esdras, Tobit, Judith, Esther (in part), Wisdom of Solomon, Ecclesiasticus, Baruch, Maccabees, and Daniel (in part—usually not the part about Susanna's seduction by two elders and her rescue by Daniel). The Apocrypha were included in early printings of the King James Translation (1611), and most Jews consider them sacred—if not so sacred as the other books of the Old Testament. The Apocrypha were made a part of the Catholic Bible at the time of Saint Jerome's Translation (see VULGATE). In spite of their disputed authenticity or rejection for other reasons, they have inspired many poems and paintings and are frequently alluded to in Western art.

REFERENCES: R. H. Pfeiffer, *The Apocrypha;* B. H. Metzger, *Introduction to the Apocrypha;* Miller Burrows, *The Dead Sea Scrolls;* James Hastings, *Dictionary of the Bible;* Harold Watts, *Modern Reader's Guide to the Bible.*

Apollonian   Pertaining to **1.** Apollo, god of song and prophecy; **2.** Classical moderation as opposed to DIONYSIAN revelry.

apophasis   In rhetoric, the making of an assertion while pretending to deny it. A classic example is Antony's address in *Julius Caesar:* "... If I were dispos'd to stir / Your hearts and minds to mutiny and rage, / I should do Brutus wrong, and Cassius wrong, / Who, you all know, are honorable men." However annoying it may be to hear a tedious introduction to a speaker "who needs no introduction," the device of saying something by denying that you will say it has long been a staple of RHETORIC. Apophasis usually begins with such phrasing as "needless to say," "not to mention ... ," "I need not point out

... ," "Surely this audience need not be reminded ... ," or the timeworn "It goes without saying ...." Apophasis is often a means of informing an unknowing audience while at the same time complimenting that audience by courteously asserting that it already knows. It is essentially a device of IRONY, not to mention its kinship to the COUNTER WORD.

aposiopesis   From a Greek root meaning "to be silent." A sudden interruption of thought in mid-sentence, conveying emotion or irony. The device is common in dramatic literature; e.g., Lear addressing his daughters: "No, you unnatural hags, / I will have such revenges on you both / That all the world shall—I will do such things,— / What they are, yet I know not ..." (*King Lear,* II, iv). In writing, the sudden silence is usually marked by a dash.

a posteriori reasoning   Reasoning from effect to cause. See INDUCTIVE REASONING 3; compare A PRIORI REASONING.

apostrophe   1. In rhetoric, a brief turning aside to address a person who is not present or to address a personified object or abstraction: "Milton! thou shouldst be living at this hour." "Oh, Eden!" Ben Jonson apostrophizes his late contemporary:

> Yet must I not give nature all; thy art,
> My gentle Shakespeare, must enjoy a part.

George Peele, also a contemporary of Shakespeare, apostrophizes (in a PERSONIFICATION) his shadow:

> Shadow, my sweet nurse, keep me from burning.

2. In punctuation, the apostrophe (') was originally—and in some uses still is—a mark of elision: It takes the place of something that has been omitted. Its use to form the possessive of nouns, for example, perhaps developed through elision of a syllable, so that Chaucer's line "Our hoste seyde, and swoor by goddes bones" is now written, "Our host said, and swore by *God's* bones...." The Elizabethan habit of writing "his" for the possessive ("William Shakespeare his Tragedie of Macbeth") became, at least according to some historians of language, simply " 's" ("William Shakespeare's Tragedy of Macbeth"). But these historical matters are of small concern to anyone bent on learning how today's English uses the apostrophe. The system is almost entirely arbitrary, and therefore can be more readily learned if the learner accepts the arbitrary without too much chafing under illogic.

The apostrophe suffers widespread abuse by those who have neglected to learn the system, and the abuses tend somewhat to affect the system, though it is not likely that competent printers and editors will adopt such errors as "Book's for sale" or "Henrys Hamburger Haven." Recent practice has, however, tended to drop the possessive inflection from many words (*baby carriage* and *executive car*); if the trend continues (from *goat milk* to *boy shoes* and *driver license*), the apostrophe may become obsolete. So far, however, the trend seems to apply mostly to possessives in which there is no clear possession: The carriage does not really belong to the baby; the goat does not now own the milk. Apostrophes have already been declared officially obsolete in many institutional names: The Veterans Administration, the Lions Club, State Teachers College, Citizens National Bank. It is also disappearing from signs: Esquire Mens Wear, Ladies Shoes, and—Henrys Hamburger Haven. And the names of post offices, by administrative fiat, are uniformly spelled without the apostrophe: Snedens Landing, Harpers Ferry, Prides Crossing.

To form the possessive of plural nouns, observe the following rules:

1. If the noun does not end in *s*, add *'s*.

men : men's   children : children's

2. If the noun ends in *s*, add ' only.

Joneses : Joneses'   girls : girls'   citizens : citizens'

To form the possessive of singular nouns, observe the following rules:

3. If the noun does not end in an *s* or *z* sound, add *'s*.

cat : cat's   child : child's

4. If the noun ends in an *s* or *z* sound,

(a) and it has only one syllable, add *'s*.

James : James's   boss : boss's

(b) has two or more syllables, and the accent is on the last syllable, add *'s*.

Hortense : Hortense's

(c) has two or more syllables, and the last syllable is preceded by an *s* or *z* sound, add ' only.

Moses : Moses'   Jesus : Jesus'

(d) has two or more syllables, and the last syllable is *not* preceded by an *s* or *z* sound, add *'s*.

Thomas : Thomas's   Dickens : Dickens's

5. If the noun ends in an *ez* sound, and the accent is on the penultimate syllable, add ' only.

Achilles : Achilles'   Archimedes : Archimedes'

The apostrophe is also used to indicate the omission of letters, numbers, or sounds:

we'll   can't   o'clock   g'bye   'most (for almost)   *KO'd   '88* (for 1988)

The apostrophe is also used to form plurals of figures, abbreviations, and words used as words (although some writers prefer to omit the apostrophes in such cases):

6's   YMCA's   if's, and's, and but's   ABC's   p's and q's

If this style is followed, and two apostrophes are called for, because of a contraction and a plural, then omit the second apostrophe:

Roaring '20s   too many don'ts

Note: No apostrophe is used in forming the possessive of personal pronouns: yours, its, ours, theirs, whose. The possessive of indefinite pronouns is regularly formed with the apostrophe: everybody's, someone's.

apothegm   See APHORISM.

appropriateness of illustration   An inexperienced preacher, intent on illustrating the idea that we often hurt ourselves when we cast aspersions on our enemies, told this ANECDOTE: "A soldier walked into a room of an abandoned house, where he thought he saw an enemy soldier. He fired, but *only* shattered a mirror." What the preacher had intended to imply was that the killer is his own worst enemy, as reflected in the mirror. But the soldier's success in eliminating "only" the mirror all too readily suggests that he might have been more successful had he eliminated another soldier. Confronted with this ambiguity, the horrified preacher conceded that the illustration was not appropriate.

approximate rhyme   See RHYME.

a priori reasoning   Reasoning from cause to effect; also, reasoning from "fixed causes" or premises. See DEDUCTIVE REASONING; compare A POSTERIORI and INDUCTIVE REASONING 3.

Arcadian   **1.** Pertaining to Arcadia, a region of ancient Greece, whose inhabitants were known for their simple, nature-loving life styles. **2.** Pertaining to idyllic literature like Sir Philip Sidney's *Arcadia* (1590). Compare SENSIBILITY. (*Note:* Distinguish Arcadian from Acadian, pertaining to certain expelled Nova Scotians who migrated to Louisiana and whose hardships are described in Longfellow's *Evangeline.*)

archaism   **1.** An ancient expression, one older than just obsolete; for example, "Methinks" for "it seems to me." In *The Faerie Queene,* Spenser used archaisms deliberately. **2.** Conscious or unconscious imitation of the archaic or obsolete: "It behooves us to pay heed, as it were, to his every word."
REFERENCE: *The Shorter Oxford English Dictionary on Historical Principles.*

archetype   **1.** In mythology, the Bible, and imaginative literature, a character with whom readers readily identify because the character seems to reenact familiar experiences, especially ordeals. Thus Sisyphus, the mythological character condemned in Hades to roll uphill a boulder that always rolls down again, is an archetype. So is the biblical Job. When we read about such characters, we experience a kinship with their human condition, and we hear in their utterances echoes of our own. Among other archetypes are the stranger or outsider (Ruth), the hero who risks everything to bring progress to humanity (Prometheus), the initiate (young David), the scapegoat (Isaac), the sorceress (Circe). Some of the reader's identification may be unconscious—the collective racial unconscious described by Carl Jung. **2.** According to Northrop Frye, an archetype may be not only a character but also a MODE. In the "archetype of romance," for example, there are such myths and "myth-phases" as *dawn, spring,* and *birth; birth of the hero; revival and resurrection; defeat of the powers of darkness; winter and death.*

REFERENCES: Northrop Frye, "The Archetypes of Literature," *Fables of Identity;* Carl Jung, *Archetypes and the Collective Unconscious;* Maud Bodkin, *Archetypal Patterns in Poetry;* Joseph Campbell, *The Hero with a Thousand Faces;* J. B. Friedman, *Orpheus in the Middle Ages;* J. B. Vickery and J. M. Sellery, eds., *The Scapegoat;* Winston Weathers, *The Archetype and The Psyche.*

architectonics   Structural design in works of art and literature. See DRAMATIC STRUCTURE and STRUCTURALISM.

argument   **1.** In logic, an ordered series of statements including the premises (or "reasons") and a conclusion drawn from those premises. See LOGIC. **2.** In expository writing, a major reason in support of a THESIS. **3.** In literature, especially that before 1800, a SYNOPSIS prefixed to a canto or a section of a long poem (such as Milton's *Paradise Lost*) and intended to give the reader an overview of its story line.

argument against the man   Argument in which it is asserted that a proposition is false because a certain person says it is true. The validity of the assertion depends upon the person's being a "reliable anti-authority"; that is, one who is almost always wrong in statements on the topic at hand. See EMOTIONAL APPEALS and PROPAGANDA DEVICES. Compare NAME CALLING and GENETIC FALLACY.

argument from authority   A form of ARGUMENTATION in which it is asserted that A is true because a certain person says it is. Chaucer's Chauntecleer and Pertelote, in the *Nun's Priest's Tale,* parody this form of argument, each citing a long list of authorities to support them in their views that one should (or should not) put much stock in dreams.

argumentation   Presentation and support of a thesis or proposition; one of the traditional four forms of discourse. It may employ any or all of the other forms (EXPOSITION, DESCRIPTION, and NARRATION), but it subordinates them to its own purpose, to convince.

Since argumentation must support a proposition, its method is chiefly logical. Yet because its audience is the human mind and not a computer, argumentation often benefits from emotional warmth, as long as it does not fall into fallacy or unjustified appeals to emotion. See EMOTIONAL APPEALS.

Good argumentation has these virtues—and avoids the opposing dangers:

Economy: The writer uses no unnecessary words.

Clarity and order: Good argumentation makes its premises clear and its conclusion unmistakable. It avoids EQUIVOCATION and AMBIGUITY. An argument that confuses an issue with the unclear or irrelevant is a failure.

Validity and thoroughness: The writer of sound argumentation carefully observes the rules of reasoning (see LOGIC) and checks the premises for accuracy of fact. Opposing arguments are dealt with justly and with care not to overlook points that might invalidate one's own. An argument that draws an unjustified conclusion or ignores alternatives cannot stand against challenge.

Balance: Good argumentation does not overstate its case. It neither over-complicates an issue nor oversimplifies it. Its tone is temperate, not invidious—and though argumentation is usually based upon opinion, it is not merely opinionated.

REFERENCES: "Argument and Persuasion," in Francis Connolly and Gerald Levin, eds., *The Art of Rhetoric;* Lee A. Jacobus, ed., *Issues and Response.*

arrangement   See RHETORIC.

Arthurian romance   Any of the numerous legends, chiefly in verse, about King Arthur and the Knights of the Round Table. Among the most celebrated versions: Malory's *Morte d'Arthur* (prose version, 1471), Spenser's *Faerie Queene (1589–96),* and Tennyson's *Idylls of the King* (1859 ff.). Chief characters in these legends are the brave King Arthur (with his magic sword Excalibur and his wizard, Merlin); his beautiful but unfaithful wife, Queen Guinevere; the knight Sir Lancelot and his FOIL, Sir Galahad; and the lovers Tristan and Isolde.

REFERENCES: E. K. Chambers, *Arthur of Britain;* Roger S. Loomis, *The Development of Arthurian Romance* and *Arthurian Literature in the Middle Ages;* J. D. Bruce, *Evolution of the Arthurian Romance;* Madeleine Cosman, *The Education of the Hero in Arthurian Romance;* A. B. Ferguson, *The Indian Summer of English Chivalry;* William Matthews, *The Ill-Framed Knight;* Charles Moorman, *A Knyght There Was.*

article   A short prose piece that informs or persuades. See ESSAY.

aside   1. A digression or a parenthetical remark sometimes figuratively called "a footnote." 2. In drama, part of a character's dialogue intended for the audience only, and not for the play's other characters. Examples abound in William Wycherly's *Country Wife* (1675). At the beginning of the play, when Sir Jaspar Fidget asks Horner to "salute" (kiss) Lady Fidget, and the professed woman-hater Horner declines ("I have taken eternal leave, Sir, of the Sex"), Sir Jaspar in an aside to the audience says, "So the report is true . . . his coldness or aversion to the Sex; but I'll play the wag with him."

Most modern playwrights have abandoned the aside, although in Eugene O'Neill's *Strange Interlude* (1928) one or another of the characters reveals thoughts to the audience only (usually in ironic contrast with the spoken lines) by means of prerecorded lines electronically reproduced on a public address system concealed in the trappings over the stage. Such "interior monologue" is a combination of the aside and of the STREAM-OF-CONSCIOUSNESS technique used by certain novelists. Compare SOLILOQUY.

assertion   An affirmation or declaration; a positing (hence a positive statement). In LOGIC, either a PREMISE or a CONCLUSION may be an assertion, though in ordinary usage an assertion is presented without supporting evidence. Mere assertion is not evidence.

assonance   The repetition of internal vowel sounds usually for aesthetic effect— "*a rain-tiraded clay*"—or for humorous effect—"H*ow* n*ow,* br*ow*n c*ow!*" and "the r*ai*n in Sp*ai*n st*ay*s m*ai*nly in the pl*ai*n."

In poetry such sound effects as assonance, ALLITERATION, CONSONANCE, and ONOMATOPOEIA are associated with the works of Algernon Swinburne, Gerard Manley Hopkins, and Edith Sitwell in England; and with the works of Edgar Allan Poe, Sidney Lanier, and Vachel Lindsay in the United States. But poems that rely solely or mainly on these sound effects seem now to be going out of fashion, especially in poems that rhyme, in favor of the quieter and subtler effects of METAPHOR and PARADOX, as Henry Rago has observed.

assumptions   Ideas taken for granted. Practically every assertion a speaker or writer makes is based on one or another assumption. Such assumptions may be explicit or implicit, conscious or unconscious; they may be susceptible to logical and factual analysis or they may be explicable only in the context of a milieu or philosophical system or point of view. Assumptions about the purpose of humanity, the human condition or place in the universe, are least often clearly stated in a work, and a deep reading may be necessary to reveal them. Assumptions in this sense may be considered the equivalent of anschauung or VIEWPOINT.

Assumptions in the sense discussed here are usually amenable to logical and factual analysis. When a speaker says, "The study of grammar does not transfer to competence in writing," then "Throw grammar out" is implied. However, the speaker assumes that the study of grammar should contribute to competence in writing, an assumption not accepted by most linguists.

The thoughtful listener or reader tries to identify assumptions and to ask whether they are valid. Assumptions, when stated, are often qualified by words like *all* and *some*. "Most people are rational" does not mean "All people are rational." Furthermore, the *some*ness of a statement may lie hidden or obscured. To say, "Citizens are *often* voters" is practically the same as saying "*some* citizens are voters." Something tantamount to a *some*-statement is also made when, in place of *some*, there appears a verb modifier like *sometimes, usually, often,* or *seldom*.

Conversational English freely uses the pattern "All ... is not ..." even though precision would call for the pattern "Not all ... is ..." Consider, for example, the statement "All people are not voters." It is reasonably safe to assume that the speaker meant, "Some people do not vote," rather than "All people do not vote." See EVERY-ALL FALLACY. (*Note:* It is a good plan for the writer of an article or essay to level with readers immediately in the first paragraph, if possible, by stating one or two of the chief assumptions relating to the subject of the article.) Compare *illicit presumption* under BEGGING THE QUESTION 1.

asterisk   A mark shaped like a little star (*), used most often to draw attention to a footnote. In some printed works, especially in earlier centuries, the asterisk was used in series to indicate an ELLIPSIS or an omission from a text; today it is seldom used for that purpose, except in poetry when a complete line or more is omitted. Its use as a censoring ellipsis was satirized by Laurence Sterne in *Tristram Shandy* (1761): "and all the world as usual, gave credit to her evidence —'That the nursery window had not only * * * * * *; but that * * * * * * * * * * * *'s also.'"

asyndeton   The omission of conjunctions (chiefly *and*) between parts of a compound; literally, "lack of *and*'s." This form of ELLIPSIS, because it departs from the expected, often lends a sense of rapid movement. *Time* magazine, for example, adopted asyndeton as one of the marks of its famous Time style: "As a boy, he recalls, he tried to break up a fight, got a drubbing for his pains" (*Time,* March 20, 1964). The example omits *and* between the verbs of a compound predicate; but asyndeton can also result from omission of the conjunction between independent clauses ("I came, I saw, I conquered"). Where formal punctuation demands a semicolon, informal usage (especially that of journalists) prefers the comma. Thus asyndeton may sometimes produce what may look at first like a COMMA FAULT. Effective asyndeton is a mark of sophistication; overused, it may seem an annoying mannerism. See POLYSYNDETON.

atmosphere   A mood that dominates part or all of a literary work—for example, the hilarity that dominates John Barth's *The Sot-Weed Factor;* the brooding or sense of doom that dominates Emily Brontë's *Wuthering Heights* and several of Hardy's Wessex novels.

Attelan comedy   See COMMEDIA DELL'ARTE.

attic sentence   An urbane, conversational sentence.

attitude   1. The author's way of looking at a subject (material, content, topic, and so on); usually implicit in the mode—satire, comedy, tragedy, romance—and an essential clue to meaning. 2. The imagined speaker's or narrator's attitude toward unfolding experiences may be different from the author's attitude. See PERSONA.

REFERENCE: Walker Gibson, "Writing for Attitude," *Persona.*

aubade (also called **alba**)   Literally, "dawn song." A lyric poem dealing with the parting of lovers after a night spent together. The famous aubades of the Provençal TROUBADOURS contain these traditional elements: the watchman's song waking the lovers and telling of first light; the need for secrecy for fear of discovery by the lady's husband; chastisement of the sun for returning too soon; complaint at the need to part; the lovers' pledge of mutual fidelity. Here is Ezra Pound's "Alba" from *Langue D'Oc:*

> When the nightingale to his mate
> Sings day-long and night late
> My love and I keep state
> In bower,
> in flower
> 'till the watchman on the tower
> Cries:
>> 'Up! Thou rascal, Rise,
>> I see the white
>>> Light
>>> And the night
>>>> Flies.'

Other examples are Donne's "The Sunne Rising"; the "Hark, the lark, the herald of the dawn" speech in Shakespeare's *Romeo and Juliet;* and William Empson's "Aubade" with the refrain, "The heart of standing is you cannot fly."

audience   1. In communications theory, the intended receivers of the message and one of the three major polarities, the others being the "sender" and the message, or "signal." These three poles represent only the skeleton of the model, however, since rather complex processes of "encoding" take place on the sender's end and similarly complex processes of "decoding" take place on the receiver's end. To hear Marshall McLuhan, strongly influenced by the NEW CRITICS' tenet that in any literary work the manner is more significant than the matter, the "medium *is* the message." Critics of contemporary mass media have accused producers and publishers of irresponsible use of the media and of callous disregard of audiences. Nevertheless, publishers and disseminators of cinema and television productions do consider the preferences of the audiences, as reflected in sampling polls and in film ratings. In the end, the controversy comes down to the philosophical question of whether the audience should receive "what it wants" or whether its tastes should be constantly "elevated."

2. In SEMANTICS, a more or less mythical entity, on the general principle that most audiences are likely to share very few referents with the speaker; what the speaker says is usually a comment on the speaker. Careful speakers or writers, to avoid talking to themselves, will use concrete examples that are not only pertinent to the communication but also as close as possible to the experience of the audience. There is, of course, a limit to the practicability of that procedure; consider the classical writers' enthusiasm for EPIC SIMILE and, in "The Nun's Priest's Tale," Chaucer's satire of the exasperating narrator who proliferates his examples when he should be making a point or getting on with the story.

3. In literary criticism, certain contemporaries contend that the audience plays, or should play, an active role in "completing" any literary work; that just as a drama remains a mere "script" until experienced by a theater audience, so a poem or a narrative remains a mere script until experienced by readers in a kind of author-reader "transaction."

4. In rhetoric, the audience has long played an important role. One of the traditional guidelines of speakers and writers has been "Respect your audience." The writer who postures—"I write to please myself, and let the audience be damned"—is in the misguided minority. The novelist William Styron has said, "Look, there's only one person a writer should listen to, pay any attention to ... the reader. The writer must criticize his own work as a reader. Every day I pick up the story ... and read it through. If I enjoy it as a reader, I know I'm getting along all right." Admirable as this practice may be as a beginning, the final proving ground requires the receiver and the sender to be different persons. In modern studies of rhetoric and linguistics, especially works by Martin Joos and Walker Gibson, audience *size* has been identified as a controlling consideration in the speaker's or writer's choice, not only of vocabulary, but also of usage and PERSONA —with larger audiences eliciting more formal, smaller audiences more informal, choices.

5. In school and college composition classes an instructor may specify the audience (e.g., "myself," "your classmates," "the senior citizens of this community," "the men of this community," "the women of this community," and so on). It is obviously important to decide early upon the audience one intends to address. The writer may well ask, "Who will my audience be? How large will it be? What are my audience's ages, sexes, professions? What is its mood? What are its cultural biases?" The writer or speaker who asks these questions before writing will find several related problems comparatively easier to solve —for example, decisions about vocabulary, usage, ATTITUDE, and TONE. See PERSONA and SLANTING.

REFERENCES: Bernard Berelson and Morris Janovitz, eds., *A Reader in Public Opinion and Communication;* Marshall McLuhan, *Understanding Media;* S. I. Hayakawa, *Language in Thought and Action;* Louise Rosenblatt, *Literature as Exploration,* Second Edition; William Styron, [Interview in] *Writers at Work: Paris Review Interviews, 1958;* Walker Gibson, *Tough, Sweet, and Stuffy;* Martin Joos, *The Five Clocks;* William Riley Parker, "The Question of Audience," *MLA Style Sheet;* Robert Graves and Alan Hodge, *The Reader over Your Shoulder;* T. E. Pearsall, *Audience Analysis for Technical Writing;* Robert Hapgood, "Shakespeare and the Included Spectator," *Reinterpretations of Elizabethan Drama;* B. Morison and K. Fliehr, *In Search of an Audience;* Sara Lundsteen, *Listening;* James Hoetker, *Students as Audiences;* Douglas Park, "The Meaning of Audience," *College English* (March, 1982).

audience analysis   See AUDIENCE and SLANTING.

Augustan Age   1. Era of the Roman Emperor Augustus (27 B.C.–14 A.D.) and of the poets Vergil, Horace, and Ovid. 2. In England, the eighteenth century, especially the era of Queen Anne (reigned 1702–1714) and of such writers as Pope, Swift, Addison, and Steele. See CLASSICISM and NEO-CLASSICISM.

REFERENCES: G. Saintsbury, *The Peace of the Augustans;* B. A. Goldgar, *The Augustan Milieu.*

authorial voice   See VOICE and INDIRECT DISCOURSE.

autobiography   The story of the writer's life. The *Autobiography of Benjamin Franklin* and the *Autobiography of Lincoln Steffens* are two well-known examples. Notable experiments with this form are *The Education of Henry Adams,* in which the writer speaks of himself as "he" instead of "I"; James Joyce's *A Portrait of the Artist as a Young Man,* in which the autobiographer uses PSYCHOLOGICAL INTROSPECTION and occasionally some POLYPHONIC PROSE; and Gertrude Stein's *Autobiography of Alice B. Toklas,* in which the narrator, Miss Stein's companion for twenty-five years, reveals as much about Miss Stein as about Miss Toklas. See BIOGRAPHY.

REFERENCES: Maurianne Adams, ed., *Autobiography;* Roger Porter and H. R. Wolf, *The Voice Within: Reading and Writing Autobiography;* James Olney, *Metaphors of Self;* R. Sayre, *The Extended Self;* Roy Pascal, *Design and Truth in Autobiography;* A. E. Stone, "Autobiography and American Culture," *American Studies* (Winter, 1972); Louis Kaplan et al., *A Bibliography of American Autobiographies.* See also the journal *Biography, an International Quarterly* edited by George Simson; it is concerned as much with autobiography as with biography.

awards   See LITERARY PRIZES AND GRANTS.

B

babbittry   A term derived from the nonintellectual attitude exemplified by the leading character in Sinclair Lewis's novel *Babbitt;* materialistic "go-getting"; lack of sensitivity toward cultural values and things aesthetic. Compare PHILISTINISM.

bacchius   See METER.

balance   A symmetrical arrangement of ideas in which word matches word, phrase matches phrase, or clause matches clause. By its repetition of rhythms, as well as by its usual repetition of words and word-patterns, balance achieves a marked emphasis, and places two or more ideas in similar syntactical form. Balance occurs when the speaker or writer says *this is that, this and that, this or that,* or *this but not that;* in other words, balance may display two or more ideas as *parallels,* as *alternatives,* or as *contrasts.* To illustrate each: (1) balance of parallels: "As *ye sow,* so shall *ye reap*"; "*To be great* is *to be misunderstood*"; (2) balance of alternatives: "*Give me liberty,* or *give me death*!" "We must indeed all *hang together,* or, most assuredly, we shall all *hang separately*"; (3) balance of contrasts: "This nation cannot exist *half slave, half free*"; "Say *what you have to say,* not *what you ought.*" (For more on balance of contrasts, see ANTITHESIS.) Though balance appears most often as symmetry of clauses in a sentence, it may apply to larger elements: the parts of a paragraph or the sections of a whole work may balance one another. Like any artifice of discourse, balance may be overdone, as it was by the Greek Sophist orators and by certain Elizabethans. See EUPHUISM.

ballad   **1.** An anonymous narrative song transmitted orally; often called a *folk ballad.* The stories told by ballads are sometimes authentic historical events important to a clan or nation, sometimes adventures dealing with romantic love. A few are humorous, and many are concerned with the supernatural—seduction by supernatural figures, visitations by ghosts, detentions by evil persons or spirits, and the eruption of irrational evil into the world, as in the "demon lover" ballads where a young man takes his love for a walk and kills her for no evident reason. Whatever the subject, folk ballads are narrated with little comment or intrusion by the teller. The action and dialogue are presented for their own sake, the stress being on the situation rather than on the motivation behind it, character or development, or questions of morality. Indeed, a moral tag at the end of a folk ballad suggests a later reworking of the text.

The *ballad stanza* usually rhymes *abcb* and alternates a four-stress line (lines *a* and *c*) with a three-stress line (lines *b* and *d*). Here is an example from "Little Musgrave and Lady Barnard":

> She cast an eye on Little Musgrave,
>   As bright as the summer sun;
> And then bethought this Little Musgrave,
>   This lady's heart I have won.

Two frequently mentioned stylistic features of folk ballads are their "incremental repetition" and "leaping and lingering." The first takes place when a formula introduced in one stanza, perhaps in the form of a question, is repeated in the next, but with something added or changed. In "Little Musgrave," for example, Lord Barnard asks his foot-page:

> "What news, what news, my little foot-page,
>   What news do you bring to me?
> Oh are my castle walls torn down
>   Or are my towers three?

And the foot-page replies, repeating the formula:

> "Your castle walls are not torn down,
>   Nor are your towers three,
> But Little Musgrave is in your house,
>   In bed with your gay lady."

"Leaping and lingering" refers to the tendency of the ballad to omit details we might expect—for example, a description of an ocean voyage between two points where the action takes place—and to linger over seemingly unimportant matters, such as details of a dress or the food served at a banquet. Leaping is like TIGHTENING; lingering, like RENDERING.

The best-known English folk ballads include "Lord Randal," "Lord Lovel," "Sir Patrick Spens," "Barbara Allen," "King Orfeo," "Robin Hood and Maid Marian," "The Braes of Yarrow," and "Get Up and Bar the Door." The best-known American folk ballads include "Frankie and Johnny," "John Henry," "Jesse James," and "Shenandoah."

2. A literary poem written in the style of the folk ballad or in an adaptation. One of the best-known literary ballads is Coleridge's "Rime of the Ancient Mariner." Here is one of Coleridge's several different stanza forms:

> The western wave was all aflame.
> The day was well-nigh done!
> Almost upon the western wave
> Rested the broad bright Sun;
> When that strange shape drove suddenly
> Betwixt us and the Sun.

REFERENCES: G. H. Gerould, *The Ballad of Tradition;* Albert B. Friedman, *The Ballad Revival;* Matthew Hodgart, *The Ballad;* Francis J. Child, *English and Scottish Popular Ballads;* Bertrand H. Bronson, *The Traditional Tunes of the Child Ballads, with Their Texts according to the Extant Records of Great Britain and America* (as the subtitle implies, this work contains careful comparisons and discussions of variant texts, including recent American variants); Bartlett J. Whiting, ed., *Traditional British Ballads;* Arthur Quiller-Couch, ed., *Oxford Book of Ballads;* John and Alan Lomax, eds., *Folk Song U.S.A.: The 110 Best American Ballads* and *American Ballads and Folk Songs;* David Fowler, *Literary History of the Popular Ballad;* Bertrand Bronson, *The Ballad as Song; Harvard Catalogue of English and American Ballads.*

ballade   A French verse form consisting typically of three eight-line stanzas and a four-line *envoy,* all in four-beat iambics. Each of the first three stanzas rhymes *ababbcbc;* the envoy, *bcbc.* The envoy repeats the REFRAIN, which is introduced in the last line of the first stanza and repeated with or without variation in the last line or two of each of the other stanzas. As a general rule only three or four rhymes are used in the whole poem, with no rhyming-word repeated except in the refrain lines. A representative example is W. E. Henley's "Ballade of Dead Actors":

> Where are the passions they essayed,
> And where are the tears they made to flow?
> Where the wild humors they portrayed
> For laughing worlds to see and know?
> Othello's wrath and Juliet's woe?
> Sir Peter's whims and Timon's gall?
> And Millamant and Romeo?
> Into the night go one and all.
>
> Where are the braveries fresh or frayed?
> The plumes, the armors—friend and foe?
> The cloth of gold, the rare brocade,
> The mantles glittering to and fro?
> The pomp, the pride, the royal show?
> The cries of war and festival?
> The youth, the grace, the charm, the glow?
> Into the night go one and all.
>
> The curtain falls, the play is played:
> The Beggar packs beside the Beau;
> The Monarch troops, and troops the Maid;
> The Thunder huddles with the snow.
> Where are the revelers high and low?
> The clashing swords? The lover's call?
> The dancers gleaming row on row?
> Into the night go one and all.
>
> *Envoy*
> Prince, in one common overthrow
> The hero tumbles with the Thrall;
> As dust that drives, as straws that blow,
> Into the night go one and all.

REFERENCES: Nigel Wilkins, ed., *One Hundred Ballades, Rondeaux, and Virelais from the Late Middle Ages;* John H. Fisher, *John Gower.*

bandwagon   An appeal to the human readiness to "jump on the bandwagon"; that is, to approve what those around us seem to approve. This "Everybody's doing it" appeal is especially effective in PROPAGANDA. Advertisers use this device when they claim that their products are "the nation's best selling," "the most popular in the West," "the one all the kids are going for." Candidates use it when they hire opinion pollsters to establish that a majority of voters favors so-and-so. The purpose of the appeal, of course, is to attract customers or voters to do or think as "most" are said to do or think.

barbarism   **1.** A particular kind of SOLECISM reflecting an uncivilized or illiterate background—"the sort of thing one might expect from a foreigner,"
says Henry Fowler, somewhat snobbishly, in *Modern English Usage* (Second
Edition). The ancient Greek noun for foreigner was indeed *barbaros,* and
according to one theory of its origin (the onomatopoetic theory) the noun was
applied to outsiders (that is, to non-Athenians) who, to the Athenian ear,
could only babble "bar, bar, bar." From this early meaning—one who doesn't
know the language—*barbarism* came to mean the misuse or mistaken combination of roots and affixes from different languages (originally, Greek and
Latin languages) in the creation of new English words. Classical scholars, like
Fowler, who have abhorred such hybrid creations as *electrocute, bureaucracy,*
and *finalize,* have ceased to resist such coinages, regarding the process as
beyond their control. Many so-called barbarisms are well established in modern
English. **2.** By extension, barbarism has come to mean any expression that
indicates the user does not know how to use the language, or how to use it
gracefully; the use of grammatical structures not found in standard speech; the
use of words or phrases inappropriate to the tone, purpose, or audience. Many
barbarisms today result from pedantic or misguided attempts to observe what
is called "correctness" in language, such as the too rigorous avoidance of
PREPOSITION AT END. Still others have come into the language through anti-
sexist militarism (e.g., evasion of the generic masculine in *his or her, s/he,
chairperson,* and even *a person ... they*). See CATACHRESIS and SOLECISM.

REFERENCES: Roy H. Copperud, *American Usage and Style: The Consensus;* J. R.
Masterson and W. B. Phillips, *Federal Prose: How to Write in and/or for Washington;*
William Safire, *On Language.*

bard   **1.** A poet, especially one of the early itinerant Celtic poets. **2.** "The
Bard"—William Shakespeare.

REFERENCES: Marchette Chute, *Shakespeare of London;* Oscar James Campbell, ed.,
The Reader's Encyclopedia of Shakespeare; Marvin Spevack, *The Harvard Concor-
dance to Shakespeare.*

baroque   An ornate or grotesque style. Deriving from the name of a rough or
irregularly shaped pearl, the term has been used to describe certain kinds of
architecture, painting, music, and literature produced mainly in Europe during
the seventeenth and early eighteenth centuries. Things baroque are characterized by redundance, floridness, and sometimes distortion. In architecture a
baroque ceiling, for example, may be ornamented with small sculptured
cherubs, personified winds and seasons, figures from classical mythology, and
the like. In baroque (also Mannerist) painting, the artist strove to say something in an abnormal manner, preferring the artificial and the affected to the
plain and natural. An example of the baroque in music is Bach's Toccata and
Fugue in D Minor, in which the opening phrases suggest to some listeners the
bloodcurdling shriek of a Hunchback of Notre Dame about to jump from the
cathedral. A less prejudicial description would say that the toccata opens with
a startling treble, repeats it twice, then shifts down to the organ's lowest notes,
from whence it makes a return climb punctuated by heavy and grandiose

chords. Of baroque style Jorge Luis Borges has said, "It exhausts its possibilities and borders on its own caricature."

In the 1960s baroque artifacts, clothing, and decor constituted one aspect of the revolt against classical (i.e., Establishment) restraints. In contemporary criticism the epithet "baroque" remains derogatory. For baroque literature is characterized by startling or farfetched imagery, excessive ALLUSION, and contorted syntax. Such characteristics were often employed self-consciously in the GOTHIC NOVEL of the middle eighteenth and early nineteenth centuries. But it was perhaps in the prose and verse of the seventeenth century that baroque was most conspicuous. The prose of Milton and Sir Thomas Browne has often been called baroque, as have the sermons of John Donne and the verse of certain METAPHYSICAL POETS, especially Richard Crashaw. Here is the first stanza of Crashaw's "The Weeper," a poem in praise of Mary Magdalene:

> Hail, sister springs,
>   Parents of silver-footed rills,
> Ever bubbling things,
>   Thawing crystal, snowy hills!
>   Still spending, never spent; I mean
>   Thy fair eyes, sweet Magdalene.

REFERENCES: Wylie Sypher, *Rococo to Cubism in Art and Literature;* Rosemond Tuve, *Elizabethan and Metaphysical Imagery;* Gilbert Highet, "A Note on Baroque," "Baroque Prose," and "Baroque Tragedy," *The Classical Tradition;* Morris W. Croll, "The Baroque Style in Prose," *Studies in Honor of Frederick Klaeber;* René Wellek, "The Concept of Baroque in Literary Scholarship," *Journal of Aesthetics and Art Criticism,* V (1946); Frank Warnke, *Versions of Baroque;* Mark Bertonasco, *Crashaw and the Baroque.*

bathos   Literally, "depth." Unconscious humor; intended loftiness that has failed. A classic example is the couplet in which the speaker says, "Advance the fringed curtains of thy eyes / And tell who comes yonder." See Alexander Pope, "Peri Bathous." Compare ANTICLIMAX 2.

beast epic, beast fable   See BESTIARY.

Beat poets   Such poets as Allen Ginsberg (author of *Howl*), Lawrence Ferlinghetti (author of *A Coney Island of the Mind*), Gregory Corso, Gary Snyder, Paul Blackburn, Kenneth Rexroth, Brother Antoninus, and Jack Kerouac (who was better known as a novelist). Ginsberg is sometimes described as "neo-Whitmanesque"; Ferlinghetti, as "neo-surrealist"; and Corso, as "neoromanticist." The ideological forbearers of the Hippies, the Beat poets, with individual differences, subscribe to antimaterialism, radical Christianity ("Make love, not war"), and certain adaptations of ZEN Buddhism. They stress oral presentation of their poems, often to the accompaniment of jazz and Oriental percussion instruments. Beat poetry usually avoids rhyme and meter and relies heavily on confession, catalog, and radical graphics, including unusual punctuation or no punctuation at all.

"Beat," a shortened version of "beatific" or "beaten down," served to describe the state of mind which the social-economic-political Establishment had allegedly induced in the generation that came of age in the late 1940s and early

1950s. At least a part of this generation—the part Jack Kerouac depicted in
On the Road and *The Dharma Bums*—chose to disengage itself from the Cold
War, from the "Establishment's spiritual bankruptcy," and from conventional
society in general and to adopt its own conventions of dress, religion, sex, and
drugs.

REFERENCES: Lawrence Lipton, *The Holy Barbarians;* Elias Wilentz, ed., *The Beat
Scene;* W. B. Fleischman, "Those 'Beat' Writers," *America* (September 26, 1959);
Seymour Krim, ed., *The Beats, Evergreen Review* (No. 2, 1957); Donald M. Allen, ed.,
The New American Poetry (1945–1960); Stephen Berg and Robert Mezey, eds., *Naked
Poetry* (this anthology contains poems by almost all of the Beat poets); "Bang, Bong,
Bing," *Time* (September 7, 1959); Gene Feldman and Max Gartenberg, eds., *The Beat
Generation and the Angry Young Men;* Ann Charters, ed., *Scenes Along the Road.*

begging the question   An unsupported assumption of something that has yet
to be proved (also called *petitio principii*). It is also known as "arguing in a
circle," since it asserts (even if only by indirection) a premise and then returns
to the same premise as a conclusion. Such fruitless argument takes several
forms.

1. *Illicit presumption:* In arguing on one side of a question, the arguer
improperly uses words prejudicial to the other side, smuggling into the premises
an assumption of a particular conclusion. For example: "The ridiculous belief
that Jones is qualified for office should be questioned seriously." (The arguer
has asked us to question something—but has already labeled that something
"ridiculous" and so has prejudiced our questioning.)

2. *Circular reasoning* (or vicious circle): In attempting to establish conclusion A, the arguer supports it with premise B; but the evidence for B lies in, or
depends upon our acceptance of, conclusion A. For example: "My check is
perfectly good; you may ask my friend Jack to vouch for it—and I assure you
that Jack can be trusted."

3. *Tautological argument:* In the belief that proof of something is being
established, an arguer may actually only be restating that "proof" in different
words. For example: "This is the finest symphony Haydn ever wrote, because
none of his others approaches it in quality." (The arguer has not offered
evidence to support the statement that "none of his others approaches it in
quality"—which is really the same thing as saying that the symphony in
question is "the finest.")

In an interpretive essay on *Macbeth* a student, developing the thesis, "Lady
Macbeth functions less as a believable woman than as Macbeth's own evil
self," asked the question "How do we know this?" and answered, "Because she
seems more an evil spirit than a flesh-and-blood woman." But that was not an
answer to the thesis question, for it repeated the thesis, as in a tautology.

belles lettres   1. Imaginative literature. In the United States, usually, poetry,
drama, and fiction. 2. In England it includes items in (1) but extends to
literary criticism and to "familiar essays"—e.g., Lamb's *Essays of Elia* and
DeQuincey's *Confessions of an English Opium Eater.* In American usage the
latter are called simply "essays" or "nonfiction prose."

bestiary   A medieval work about animals, which mingles natural history with fables and Christian ALLEGORY. Bestiaries contained chapters of varying lengths, often illustrated, treating birds, animals, fish, and sometimes a few stones and plants. Among the animals described were many fabulous ones like the manticore, chimera, phoenix, yale, and unicorn. Here is an account of the unicorn from T. H. White's *Book of Beasts; Being a Translation from a Latin Bestiary of the Twelfth Century:*

> He is a very small animal like a kid, excessively swift, with one horn in the middle of his forehead, and no hunter can catch him. But he can be trapped by the following stratagem. A virgin girl is led to where he lurks, and there she is sent off by herself into the wood. He soon leaps into her lap when he sees her, and embraces her, and hence he gets caught.
>
> Our Lord Jesus Christ is also a Unicorn spiritually, about whom it is said: "And he was beloved like the Son of the Unicorns." . . . The fact that it has one horn on its head means what he himself said: "I and the Father are One." Also, according to the Apostle: "The head of Christ is the Lord." It says that he is very swift because neither Principalities, nor Powers, nor Thrones, nor Dominations could keep up with him, nor could Hell contain him, nor could the most subtle Devil prevail to catch or comprehend him; but, by the sole will of the Father, he came down into the virgin womb for our salvation. . . .
>
> The Unicorn often fights with elephants, and conquers them by wounding them in the belly.

REFERENCES: E. and J. Lehner, *A Fantastic Bestiary;* Peter Lum, *Fabulous Beasts;* Thomas Browne, *Pseudodoxia Epidemica;* Norman Douglas, *Birds and Beasts of the Greek Anthology;* J. B. Friedman, *The Monstrous Races in Medieval Art and Thought;* Merrill Boynton, *A Bestiary.*

bibliography   See DOCUMENTATION.

Bildungsroman   A novel depicting the spiritual growth or education of the hero —usually a young man—as he faces various moral and intellectual crises and meets characters representing different attitudes toward life. Some examples of the Bildungsroman are *Wilhelm Meister's Apprenticeship* (Goethe), *Joseph Andrews* (Henry Fielding), *Huckleberry Finn* (Mark Twain), *Look Homeward, Angel* (Thomas Wolfe), *The Catcher in the Rye* (J. D. Salinger), and *A Separate Peace* (John Knowles). A synonymous term is *Entwickelungsgeschichte.* Another synonym is *Kunstlerroman,* the development of the artist, as, for example, *A Portrait of the Artist as a Young Man* (James Joyce) and *Tropic of Capricorn* (Henry Miller). Compare DIDACTIC NOVEL.

REFERENCE: J. H. Buckley, *Season of Youth.*

billingsgate   Vulgar language (named for the Billingsgate fish market in London).

biographical fallacy   The interpretation of a literary work all too naively in the light of the author's life. While any author is in certain ways influenced by environment (MILIEU) and personal experiences, the literary piece has a life and logic of its own. Compare AESTHETIC DISTANCE. The NEW CRITICS and other contemporary critics tend to discredit literary interpretations and explications that rely too heavily on biography. See LEVELS OF MEANING.

REFERENCES: W. K. Wimsatt, "Genesis: A Fallacy Revisited," in Peter Demetz, ed., *The Disciplines of Criticism;* Lillian Gilkes, "Crane and the Biographical Fallacy," *Modern Fiction Studies* (Winter, 1970).

biography   An exposition of a person's life. Though primarily informational, certain biographies tend to support theories or teach moral lessons. Among the latter, "DIDACTIC" biographies are the biblical portraits of Ruth, David, and Joseph; the lives of the saints (*Acta Sanctorum*, written by the Bollandists); and the well-known Plutarch's *Lives* (of eminent Greeks and Romans). Plutarch's biographies were also called *The Parallel Lives*, for in attempting to prove his various ethical and political theories, he often compared pairs of prominent Greeks and Romans of the same calling (e.g., Demosthenes and Cicero, orators). Plutarch's biographies in Sir Thomas North's translations provided the bases for Shakespeare's *Julius Caesar, Antony and Cleopatra, Coriolanus,* and *Timon of Athens*. What makes Plutarch readable, if not always factually reliable, is his human touch and his use of ANECDOTE. He remains not only one of the most charming of biographers but also the pioneer of collective biography.

His example was followed in such collections as Suetonius' *Lives of the Caesars,* Giorgio Vasari's *Lives of the* [Renaissance] *Artists,* Thomas Fuller's *Lives of the Worthies of England,* Izaak Walton's *Lives,* Samuel Johnson's *Lives of the Poets,* Walter Scott's *Lives of the Novelists,* William Thackeray's *Four Georges,* Lytton Strachey's *Eminent Victorians,* Hendrik Van Loon's *Lives,* Paul de Kruif's *Microbe Hunters,* Louise Tharp's *Peabody Sisters,* Jacques Barzun's *Darwin, Marx, and Wagner,* and John F. Kennedy's *Profiles in Courage.*

Another kind of biography, one's life story written by oneself, is known variously as AUTOBIOGRAPHY, DIARY, JOURNAL, memoir, and the like. One of the earliest and best known, St. Augustine's *Confessions,* illustrates by content as well as by title one of the therapeutic purposes of this genre. But most autobiographers have admitted that they could not or would not confess everything. Among the most celebrated autobiographies have been those of Benvenuto Cellini, Samuel Pepys (*Diary*), Jean-Jacques Rousseau (*Confessions*), John Stuart Mill, John Woolman (*Journal*), J. W. von Goethe, Benjamin Franklin, John Henry Cardinal Newman, Mark Twain, Maxim Gorky, Booker T. Washington, T. E. Lawrence (of Arabia), Henry Adams (*The Education of Henry Adams*), William Butler Yeats, Anne Frank (*The Diary of Anne Frank*), Simone de Beauvoir (*Memoirs of a Dutiful Daughter, The Force of Age, The Force of Circumstances*); Jean-Paul Sartre (*The Words*); and André Malraux (*Anti-Memoirs*).

Biography has perhaps yet to win recognition as an art form in its own right. It is still classified for the most part as reportage or EXPOSITION rather than as BELLES LETTRES or imaginative literature. Yet if there is a single biography that comes close to the art of re-creating a subject in as well-rounded a portrait as possible, it is James Boswell's *Life of Samuel Johnson* (1791). Even though Boswell was not a close associate, and not always a friend, he nevertheless was able to capture at first hand an in-the-flesh portrait and to quote almost verbatim Johnson's most sententious and characteristic pronouncements. These the biographer took down either immediately (to Johnson's *professed* annoyance) or soon after their utterance. Boswell also introduced in his biography certain insights that, in a later age, were hailed as "psychological introspection."

Psychological introspection, which is after all more art than science, characterized nineteenth- and twentieth-century biographies, as reflected in such well-known works as those of Lytton Strachey (mentioned above), Ernest Renan's *Life of Jesus*, Gamaliel Bradford's *Lee the American* (and many another of Bradford's "psychographs"), Sigmund Freud's *Leonardo da Vinci*, Emil Ludwig's *Napoleon*, André Maurois' *Disraeli*, Amy Lowell's *John Keats*, Marchette Chute's *Ben Jonson of Westminster*, and A. L. Rowse's *William Shakespeare*.

Three modern biographies combining readability with scholarship are Carl Sandburg's *Abraham Lincoln*, Catherine Drinker Bowen's *Yankee from Olympus* [Justice Oliver Wendell Holmes], and Leon Edel's *Henry James*.

Biographical dictionaries, which make no claims to art but which are useful to students, are the multivolume (British) *Dictionary of National Biography* (the *DNB*), *The Dictionary of American Biography* (the *DAB*), and *Current Biography*, the latter being chronicles of prominent people who make the news. One-volume biographical reference works are *The Concise Dictionary of American Biography*, *Who's Who* (British), *Who's Who in America*, *Directory of American Scholars*, Webster's *Biographical Dictionary*, and *American Authors*.

The use of biography and autobiography as keys to interpreting literary works has been for the most part disparaged by the NEW CRITICS. See BIO-GRAPHICAL FALLACY. Viewed strictly as fact, biography and history may provide meaningful background, as reflected in Louis Bredvold's *Intellectual Milieu of John Dryden* and Leon Edel's life of Thoreau, which interprets *Walden* as an unreliable account of Thoreau's "trip."

REFERENCES: Catherine Drinker Bowen, *Biography: The Craft and the Calling;* John A. Garraty, *The Nature of Biography;* Louis Kaplan *et al., A Bibliography of American Autobiographies;* James Clifford, *Biography as an Art;* Philip Daghlian, ed., *Essays in Eighteenth-Century Biography;* R. H. Costa, "The Rashest Art: A Forum on Literary Biography," *Quartet* (Fall, 1969); Leon Edel, *Literary Biography;* Phyllis Riches, *An Analytical Bibliography of Universal Collected Biography;* Lynn Bloom, "Popular and Super-Pop Biographies: Definitions and Distinctions," *Biography* (Summer, 1980); D. J. Winslow, *Life-Writing: A Glossary of Terms in Biography, Autobiography, and Related Forms.*

black humor   1. Works that are superficially humorous but at bottom gruesome and terrifying. An example is Frederick Dürrenmatt's *Physicists*. 2. A comic treatment of events that might seem pathetic or painful to other writers. The hero of a novel using black humor is usually an ingenue figure, hopeless and helpless in the grip of events but still portrayed with much satire, as is the world that crushes the hero. Black humor can be found in Kafka's novels and stories, Nathaniel West's *Cool Million*, Evelyn Waugh's *Decline and Fall* and *The Loved One*, and in Terry Southern's *Candy*, to name only a few. Recent novels employing black humor are much dependent upon the topical and impermanent world of popular culture. Their authors strive to give scene, dialogue, and narrative structure a light, transitory, "throw-away" quality.

REFERENCE: B. J. Friedman, ed., *Black Humor.*

black literature   A term pertaining to literary works written by or about black people in the United States. It is generally conceded to refer to American as opposed to African works. (Thus Alan Paton's *Cry, the Beloved Country,* Leonard Joob's collection of poetry, and such fiction as that of Achebe, Senghor, and Tutuola would not be included.) Several writers of different skin colors (among them poet Robert Hayden and Novelist Mark Harris) question the logic and appropriateness, in America, of classifying literature along racial separatist lines. They argue that American literature consists, rather, of GENRES. It consists, they maintain, of fiction whether written by William Faulkner or Ralph Ellison; of poetry whether written by Robert Lowell or Langston Hughes; of essays whether written by Henry Thoreau or James Baldwin; of plays whether written by Arthur Miller or Amiri Baraka. This argument aside, it is a fact that, until the 1960s, the literature of black American authors was little known, and the Negro in literature was primarily the creation of white authors. Perhaps the best-known portrayals are in *Uncle Tom's Cabin* (Harriet Beecher Stowe), *Uncle Remus* (Joel Chandler Harris), *The Adventures of Huckleberry Finn* (Mark Twain), *Strange Fruit* (Lillian Smith), *Intruder in the Dust* (William Faulkner), and, more recently, *To Kill a Mockingbird* (Harper Lee), *Black Like Me* (John Howard Griffin), and *The Confessions of Nat Turner* (William Styron).

With the emergence of increased racial consciousness and of pride in the black cultural heritage, the situation has changed. Heretofore the black writer was heard mainly through small literary magazines. Now contemporary writers are finding a broader and better informed audience, as well as a more open market for their works, and earlier black authors are being rescued from oblivion. Many of these earlier works, in particular, are being reassessed and reissued, although it would seem that most will remain of interest primarily to scholars and historians. Among the most celebrated works by black authors are *Up from Slavery* (Booker T. Washington), *The Life and Times of Frederick Douglass, The Souls of Black Folk* (W. E. B. DuBois), *Autobiography of an Ex-Colored Man* (James Weldon Johnson), *Native Son* (Richard Wright), *Invisible Man* (Ralph Ellison), *The Fire Next Time* (James Baldwin), *A Raisin in the Sun* (Lorraine Hansberry), *The Autobiography of Malcolm X, Soul on Ice* (Eldridge Cleaver), and the poetry of Paul Lawrence Dunbar, James Weldon Johnson, Countee Cullen, Langston Hughes, Gwendolyn Brooks, Amiri Baraka, and Toni Morrison.

REFERENCES: Arna Bontemps, *Golden Slippers: An Anthology of Negro Poetry;* John Henrik Clarke, ed., *American Negro Short Stories;* James Emmanuel and Theodore Gross, eds., *Dark Symphony;* Milton Meltzer, ed., *In Their Own Words;* William L. Katz, ed., *Eye Witness;* Sterling Brown, "A Century of Negro Portraiture in American Literature," *Massachusetts Review* (Winter, 1966); Dorothy Sterling, "The Soul of Learning," *English Journal* (February, 1968); Charlemae Rollins, *We Build Together;* Abraham Chapman, *The Negro in American Literature;* Addison Gayle, ed., *Black Expression;* Robert Hayden, ed., *Kaleidoscope;* John Henrik Clarke, ed., *Ten Black Writers Reply to Styron's "Nat Turner";* Alan Lomax and Raoul Abdul, eds., *3000 Years of Black Poetry* [includes Africans]; Jean Yellin, *The Intricate Knot.*

blank verse   Unrhymed iambic pentameter. This verse form, used by Shakespeare in his plays (although the first English play to use it was Norton and Sackville's *Gorboduc*, 1561), was the most widely used verse form in the history of English poetry and drama up to the twentieth century. In 1557 Henry Howard, Earl of Surrey, published a blank verse translation of Vergil's *Aeneid* (the original Latin having used dactylic hexameters), and in the same year Surrey and his contemporary Sir Thomas Wyatt (who had imported the sonnet form—at least, the Petrarchan form—into England from Italy) published blank verse in *Tottel's Miscellany*. Wyatt and Surrey thus established the trend that modern English verse was to follow for more than four centuries. Here is an excerpt from Surrey's translation of Vergil:

> The Greeks' chieftains, all irkëd with the war
> Wherein they wasted had so many years,
> And oft repulsed by fatal destiny,
> A huge horse made, high raisëd like a hill, ...

In reading this blank verse, one tends to drop one's voice at the end of each line, a phenomenon that suggested the label "end-stopped" and George Saintsbury's "single moulded line," as distinguished from ENJAMBEMENT, the effect produced by the kind of line whose sense flows into the next line without a logical or phonological break. Such run-on lines in blank verse were to be developed first by Christopher Marlowe. Although a study of Marlowe's blank verse reveals that only about a fourth generates enjambement, most of his lines do demonstrate an ingenious variety of stresses within the line. Here, for example, is Marlowe's Mephistopheles in *The Tragical History of Doctor Faustus:*

> Hell has no limits, nor is circumscribed
> In one self place; for where we are is hell,
> And where hell is there must we ever be.

It was Shakespeare, however, who demonstrated a remarkable virtuosity with blank verse. A comparative study of his earlier plays, for example, *Two Gentlemen of Verona* and *Love's Labour's Lost,* with such later plays as *Macbeth* and *The Tempest* reveals an increased number of run-on lines. Compare these lines from *Two Gentlemen of Verona*

> Here can I sit alone, unseen of any,
> And to the nightingale's complaining notes
> Tune my distresses and record my woes.

with these lines from *The Tempest*

> Where should this music be? i' th'air or th'earth?
> It sounds no more! And sure it waits upon
> Some god o' th'island....

Notice, incidentally, the conventions and cliché statements in the *Verona* lines as contrasted with the disarming questions and the invention in the lines from *The Tempest.* Shakespeare has yet to be surpassed in blank verse.

The tradition of enjambement in blank verse was carried forward by John Milton in *Paradise Lost* (1667). Milton also demonstrated talent in varying the stresses within lines. In defending his use of blank verse, he called it

English Heroic Verse without Rime ... Rime being no necessary Adjunct or true Ornament of Poem or good Verse, in longer Works especially, but the Invention of a barbarous Age, to set off wretched matter and lame Meeter [sic]

but he also resorted to an artificially poetic line (see POETICISM), distorting modern English syntax and sound patterns while echoing Vergil:

> Of man's First Disobedience, and the Fruit
> Of that Forbidden Tree, whose mortal tast[e]
> Brought Death into the World, and all our woe,
> With loss of Eden, till one greater Man
> Restore us, and regain the blissful Seat,
> Sing Heavnly Muse....

Milton's laureate successor, John Dryden, deprecated blank verse (*Essay of Dramatic Poesy,* 1668), although he used it himself in the play *All for Love* (1671). Dryden and Pope preferred to cultivate rhymed iambic pentameters, especially the HEROIC COUPLET, and their brilliance seems to have outshone even posthumously the blank verse of poets like James Thomson ("The Seasons," 1726), Edward Young ("Night Thoughts," 1742), and William Cowper ("The Task," 1785).

But with the publication of William Wordsworth's *Prelude* (1850) blank verse was once again vindicated, and all its most admirable possibilities revived. Aside from natural syntax and sound patterns Wordsworth accommodated it to an appropriate lexicon—"a selection of language really used by men," as he observed in the Preface to the second edition of *Lyrical Ballads* (1800). (Although *The Prelude* was not published until 1850, he had been working on it since the turn of the century and had practically completed it by 1805.) Here is a representative passage from *School-Time,* Book Two:

> We ran a boisterous course; the year span round
> With giddy motion. But the time approached
> That brought with it a regular desire
> For calmer pleasures, when the winning forms
> Of Nature were collaterally attached
> To every scheme of holiday delight
> And every boyish sport....

Almost every major poet of the nineteenth century—among them Keats, Tennyson, and Browning—used blank verse, especially in such longer poems as *Hyperion* (1820), *Idylls of the King* (1859), and *The Ring and the Book* (1868). In the twentieth century, blank verse was used by T. S. Eliot (notably in *The Waste Land,* 1922), by Robert Frost, and by W. H. Auden. But even these poets used less blank verse than FREE VERSE and rhymed forms. After 1950 blank verse suffered a decline, and it now seems to be giving way to free verse and to more experimental forms.

REFERENCES: Alex Preminger and others, *Encyclopedia of Poetry and Poetics;* George Saintsbury, *A History of English Prosody;* John Thompson, *The Founding of English Metre;* Roy Harvey Pearce, *The Continuity of American Poetry.*

Bloomsbury Group   A group of brilliant writers and artists—among them, Virginia and Leonard Woolf, Vanessa and Clive Bell, Lytton Strachey, Roger Fry, Duncan Grant, Desmond MacCarthy, E. M. Forster, Maynard Keynes, and Bertrand Russell—who met irregularly during the early 1900s in a house in Bloomsbury, a Bohemian artists' section of London. They discussed aesthetic and philosophic issues and responded critically to one another's works.

REFERENCES: Leon Edel, *Bloomsbury, a House of Lions;* Quentin Bell, *Virginia Woolf;* Michael Holroyd, *Lytton Strachey;* Virginia Woolf, *Roger Fry.*

bluestocking   An eighteenth-century term for an intellectual woman; for example, Fanny Burney, author of *Evelina,* and Lady Mary Wortley Montague, who introduced smallpox inoculation into England.

bombast   Pompous language. Derived from the French for "cotton stuffing," bombast is a style overstuffed with pretentiousness. It is "rhetorical" in the worst sense (see RHETORIC). Its chief marks are long words (when short ones would do), circumlocution, EUPHEMISM, and stock EPITHETS. When learned men use bombast, it is pedantic; when unlearned men use it, it tends to be full of MALAPROPISM and MIXED METAPHOR. A blight on plays of the early 1700s, bombast was parodied in Fielding's *Tom Thumb* (1730).

bon mot   A witty remark.

book review   A brief invitation to read a book that the reviewer has, usually, enjoyed. By "brief" is meant anywhere from a hundred to five hundred words, depending on space limitations of the newspaper or magazine that will look at, and perhaps publish, the piece. One reviewer's enjoyment of the book is indispensable, for more often than not the newspaper or magazine that will print a review prefers *(a)* to educate, if possible elevate, its reader's tastes; and *(b)* to avoid, if possible, attacking a shoddy book, to say nothing of even reviewing it. An adequate review gives only such factual elements as will suffice to identify the book—not such factual elements as may tend to substitute for a reading of the book itself (not, that is, the whole plot of a novel). The reviewer should settle on one interesting aspect that may whet the reader's curiosity or appetite. One of the best ways to do this—assuming a first-rate book—is to quote a key short passage, then suggest how this quoted piece reflects a major theme, characterization, issue, or even the writer's style. One caution: a reviewer must check with the publisher on how many words may be quoted.

REFERENCES: L. B. Cebik, "A Note on Reviewing," *Georgia Review* (Spring, 1970); Anne Davis, "The ABC's of Book Reviewing," in A. S. Burack, ed., *The Writer's Handbook; The Book Review Digest; Publishers' Weekly; The New York Review of Books; The Saturday Review; American Book Review.*

bourgeois tragedy   See SENTIMENTALISM 3.

bowdlerized   Expurgated or "cleaned up"; after Thomas Bowdler (1754–1825), editor of *The Family Shakespeare* (1818), from which he deleted certain words that he felt were "unfit to be read by a gentleman in the company of ladies."

REFERENCES: Noel Perrin, *Dr. Bowdler's Legacy: A History of Expurgated Books in England and America;* Bertrand Russell, "Mr. Bowdler's Nightmare," *Nightmares of Eminent Persons;* Marvin Rosenberg, Appendix: "A Kind Word for Bowdler," *The Masks of Othello.*

brackets   The pairs of square-cornered marks, [ ], that are easily confused with PARENTHESES. Their uses are almost entirely scholarly:

1. To enclose editorial addition or comment within matter being quoted: "You may observe [said Sir Arthur Wardour, speaking of Jonathan Oldbuck] that he never has any advantage of me in dispute. . . ."—Sir Walter Scott. "To err is humane [*sic*]; to forgive, divine."

2. To enclose the correction of an error in matter being quoted: "The Roosevelt inauguration on January 20 [March 4], 1933, launched a whirlwind program."

3. To enclose information supplied by the editor: "He was a lifelong admirer of [Teddy] Roosevelt's."

4. To enclose parenthetical matter within parentheses: "An age of scientific discovery gave rise to defenders of literature (including John Stuart Mill [see p. 90] and Matthew Arnold)."

5. To enclose symbols in phonetic transcription: "By assimilation, [ŋ] has become [n] in *congress* [kɑngrəs]."

braggadocio   Language of a braggart. (Braggadochio was a boastful character in Spenser's *Faerie Queene*.)

Brahmin   1. Also Brahman, a member of one of the highest castes in India. 2. An aristocrat, sometimes an intellectual snob; often associated with nineteenth-century Boston.

brief   An abridged statement, summary, or abstract of the content of a written work. See PRÉCIS. In law, a brief is either a short statement of a legal argument or a formal, documented outline of the argument.

broadside ballads   The most popular of all ballads and songs during the Tudor and Stuart reigns. These ballads were usually of anonymous authorship, especially when politically risky. They were printed on one side of a printer's unfolded sheet and introduced with a large title and sometimes an attractive woodcut. Purchasers used them not only for entertainment, very much as purchasers used sheet music during the early 1900s, but also for decoration of walls, much as people today decorate walls with posters. One of the most popular in its day, and well known even today, was the broadside ballad "Greensleeves" (1580), whose chief repeated stanza went (in a slightly modernized spelling):

> Greensleeves was all my joy,
> Greensleeves was my delight;
> Greensleeves was my heart of gold,
> And who but my Lady Greensleeves?

The royal court intrigue reflected here, if any, is now for the most part lost to us. But consider the possibilities of veiled meanings in this broadside ballad that was hawked in the streets, possibly in alleys, of London during the reign of Henry VIII (occasionally married, occasionally divorced, occasionally a widower):

> The hunt is up, the hunt is up,
> And it is well-nigh day;
> And Harry our king is gone hunting
> To bring his deer to bay!

Among the subjects of ballads—besides politics, court intrigue, and gossip—were current events, personal feuds, and the last words of criminals before execution.

REFERENCES: Charles H. Firth, "Ballads and Broadsides," *Shakespeare's England;* "Broadside Ballads," in J. William Hebel and Hoyt H. Hudson, eds., *Poetry of the English Renaissance (1509–1660);* Herbert Coleman, ed., *Ballads and Broadsides.*

bromide   A dull, stereotyped remark offered as if it were an original thought. "It isn't *what* you know—it's *whom* you know," says the spouter of bromides. The bromide may be obviously true (see TRUISM) or open to question; in either case it lacks originality. See CLICHÉ, PLATITUDE, STEREOTYPE, and TRITENESS.

Brook Farm   A commune or co-operative ("Institute of Agriculture and Education") founded in West Roxbury, Massachusetts, about 1840, by George and Sophia Ripley and other new England intellectuals devoted to TRANSCENDENTALISM. Each member agreed to do an equal share of chores to make the venture economically successful and to leave time for cultural amenities. Among the best-known members were Charles Dana and Nathaniel Hawthorne. Celebrated visitors were Margaret Fuller, Elizabeth Peabody, Charles Brownson, Bronson Alcott, William Channing, Theodore Parker, Horace Mann, Washington Allston, and Ralph Waldo Emerson.

REFERENCES: Lindsay Swift, *Brook Farm: Its Members, Scholars, and Visitors;* Odell Shepard, *Pedlar's Progress;* Henry Sams, ed., *Autobiography of Brook Farm;* E. R. Curtis, *A Season in Utopia;* Henry Thoreau, "Paradise (To Be) Regained," *Miscellanies;* Katherine Burton, *Paradise Planters;* Van Wyck Brooks, Chapter XII, *The Flowering of New England;* Nathaniel Hawthorne, *The Blithedale Romance* [fiction].

bucolic poetry   See ECLOGUE.

burlesque   1. A form of "strip-tease vaudeville" or "follies" popular in English and American music halls before the era of television. 2. In literature, an extended farce or take-off, usually an extravaganza in which the characters are caricatures (persons with exaggerated features) of fictional or real-life counterparts. By its use of exaggeration, burlesque resembles PARODY; but the two forms differ, since burlesque has to do with subject or character and parody with form or manner of expression. In a burlesque, hilarity usually exceeds bitterness, if any. The operettas of Gilbert and Sullivan, for example, are burlesques of several nineteenth-century empire-builders. Among the most celebrated burlesques is John Gay's *Beggar's Opera* (1728), in which the vices of certain public officials under England's King George I (d. 1727) are ridiculed, as are the follies of a society that idolized highwaymen and other criminals even when it punished them with hanging. Distinctions between "high burlesque" and "low burlesque" remain controversial even after one defines the first as "serious treatment of the trivial" and the second as "low-comic treatment of the serious." A synonym for "low burlesque" is Hudibrastic, after Samuel Butler's *Hudibras* (1663), a verse narrative that ridicules with jingles the adventures of a Puritan knight and that does not try to conceal its indebtedness to Spenser's *Faerie Queene* (in which Hudibras is Elissa's lover) and to Cervantes's *Don Quixote.*

REFERENCES: Richmond Bond, *English Burlesque Poetry;* Edmund Gosse, "Burlesque," *Selected Essays;* Simon Trussler, ed., *Burlesque Plays . . . 18th Century.*

Burns stanza   A six-line stanza rhyming *aaabab,* with two IAMBS in lines 4 and 6; four iambs, in each of the other lines. Here for example, is the first stanza of Robert Burns's "To a Louse":

> Ha! whare ye gaun, ye crowlie ferlie?
> Your impudence protects you sairly;
> I canna say but ye strunt rarely
>   owre gauze and lace;
> Tho' faith! I fear ye dine but sparely
>   on sic a place.

buskin   In ancient Greece, the bootlike footwear of actors in a tragedy. Compare SOCK.

Byronic hero   1. A brooding young man attractive to women; a young man whose melancholy arouses the mothering instinct. 2. A Don Juan or dashing lady-killer.

C

cacophony   The result of a disagreeable combination of sounds, although its use is not always a flaw. Unintended cacophony, however, when not suited to the sense of its context, mars expression; but skilled writers often employ cacophony deliberately to emphasize a discordant idea or unpleasant image.

Whatever is difficult to pronounce is likely to be cacophonous—jawbreaking juxtaposition of sound. Jingles that use excessive ALLITERATION, hissing sibilants, unintended rhymes, or needless repetitions of a word may produce cacophony. Though no sounds in English are themselves essentially unpleasant, an insistence upon any one sound may tax the ear—especially a close piling-on of explosive *stops* (*p, t, k, b, d, g*) or of the harsher *fricatives* (*ch, j*). Cacophony consists in what Sir Walter Raleigh called the "unfit or untuneful phrase." Contrast EUPHONY.

cadence   The rise and fall of a person's voice while reading a passage aloud. Though most poets, in "counting syllables," assign either a heavy or a light stress to each syllable, they do not intend that the reader echo this counting; neither do they intend that the reader's voice drop automatically at the end of every line. Rather, the intention is that the oral reading be as natural and contextual as possible. In "Stopping by Woods on a Snowy Evening," for example, Frost may have counted out "He will not see me stopping here," but many a reader says, "HE will not see me sTOPping here." Similarly, the sensitive reader's voice does not drop at the end of the line "The only other sound's the sweep," but, rather, reads, "the sweep / of easy wind and downy flake."

As early as 1894, in a letter to editor Susan Hayes Ward, Robert Frost observed, "I have not succeeded in revising my poem ['My Butterfly'] ... the line, 'These were the unlearned things,' is wretched ... the would-be cadence may be incorrect also ... when once I doubt an idiom, my ear hesitates to vouch for it thereafter."

caesura   A pause taken by an oral interpreter in reading literature, especially poetry. Thus, in the line "This is the forest primaeval, the murmuring pines and the hemlocks," the comma marks the caesura. There is also a caesura, although a weaker one, after "pines." Caesura is essentially what linguists mean by "pause" or "juncture."

Calvinism   1. The system of theological thought expounded by the Frenchman John Calvin (born Jean Chauvin) in *The Institutes of the Christian Religion* (1536) and adopted by his Protestant followers. His doctrinal descendants in England, Scotland, Holland, and America were known variously as Puritans,

Presbyterians, Separatists, and Congregationalists. Departing from Luther, who believed in the subordination of church to state, Calvin argued for a theocratic state, the kind of society that came in fact to dominate Geneva (Switzerland), parts of Holland, and Puritan New England in the sixteenth and seventeenth centuries. The five chief tenets of Calvinism, along with their corollaries, were *(a)* total depravity of humanity ever since Adam's fall ("In Adam's fall / we sinned all," said the hornbook studied by seventeenth-century children in New England): even infants were subject to eternal damnation; *(b)* limited atonement: our hereditary corruption only partially atoned for by Christ; no automatic redemption; salvation only for those infused with the Holy Spirit; *(c)* irresistible grace: grace available only to the elect of God; *(d)* predestination: absolute power of the will of God, our own inability to exercise free will, and the superiority of faith over good deeds; *(e)* perseverance of saints by predestination, election, and conversion: even a saint might not recognize his or her good fortune (election) until a regeneration, an "inner light," was experienced.

Unlike the damned, who, unaided by God, were incapable of suppressing their evil natures, the elect by nature lived a righteous life. Nevertheless, to determine God's will on specific matters of daily existence, they had to consult God's revealed word, the Bible. And the correct interpretation of the scriptures required a literate and educated mind. Thus the fostering of education became a religious duty. Moreover, a deep concern for moral conduct and an earnestness about this life, the prelude for the next, encouraged a sense of thrift and hard work. The so-called Protestant ethic of perseverance and industry owes much to Calvinism. On the other hand, Calvinism could also give rise to a strait-laced, sanctimonious way of life and impelled some leaders to attempt what now would be considered an unwarranted control of the personal lives of others and a rigid suppression of various entertainments and fashions no longer considered evil. Although the Five Points comprised the main doctrine of Protestant reformed churches originally, their intractable austerity gradually gave way.

2. In English and American literature, Calvinism and anti-Calvinism have had a profound influence. Calvinistic puritanism outlawed the comic muse from the English stage and sent it underground from 1642 to 1660. In America Calvinism undergirded such theological and historical works as Michael Wigglesworth's *Day of Doom* (1662), Cotton Mather's *Magnalia Christi Americana* (1702), and Jonathan Edwards's *Sinners in the Hands of an Angry God* (1741). These works were faithful to the letter and spirit of the Five Points. Other works hazarded revisionist interpretations. Regeneration or conversion is a well-known example. Conversion—experiencing an inner light —could turn out in practice to be possible for ordinary parishioners, not just ministers and saints. Annie Bradstreet secular, for example, could become Mistress Anne Bradstreet the divine after she looked into her heart and versified her discoveries about "Flesh and the Spirit." Her collected poems, *The Tenth Muse Lately Sprung Up in America* (1650), echoed the sacred/profane conflicts and ambivalences in John Donne's poems, especially "The Extasie"

and "Of the Progress of the Soul," but hardly competed with his metaphysical wit and invention.

Meanwhile, back in the Mother Country, where the Colonists' archetypal poet was John Milton, the Fall of Man was being celebrated in *Paradise Lost,* the epic poem Milton published in 1667. But in justifying God's ways to Man, Milton argued for free will. (Milton—like Locke, Newton, and Franklin—was quite unorthodox in this respect.) Later, in *Samson Agonistes* (1671), Milton tried to reconcile in an almost autobiographical context (he had his own Delilah and his blindness) reformed Protestantism with certain antithetical orthodoxies, among them conflicting doctrines of backsliding, atonement, and redemption.

Mankind's precarious mission in this life—to shun evil, pray for grace, seek salvation—was graphically outlined in *The Pilgrim's Progress* (1678), perhaps the most popular allegory of all time. It was written by the Puritan preacher John Bunyan while he was imprisoned by the Stuart regime.

All Five Points, especially the practical consequences of their elaborations, their "laces and bows," were irreverently lampooned by Jonathan Swift in *A Tale of a Tub* (1704). Swift's *Tub* elicited a spate of essays pro and con, among them Anthony Ashley Cooper, Third Earl of Shaftesbury's *Characteristics of Men, Manners, Opinions, and Times* (1711, 1713). The 1713 edition contained the essay "An Enquiry Concerning Virtue," which in turn elicited from Bernard Mandeville *An Enquiry into the Origins of Moral Virtue, the Fable of the Bees, or Private Vices, Public Benefits* (1714). In the *Fable of the Bees,* Mandeville downgraded do-goodism and "good works," as had Calvin, but went on to discourage all virtue and religious restraints as delusions. In fact, he satanically championed selfishness as responsible for all human progress and nationalistic empire building.

If England was to lose its American colonies in one sense, however, nobody could ever take away the contributions made by the English Dissenters to colonial and early national culture—especially the impact made by such families as the Cottons, the Mathers, the Edwardses, and their descendants. For example, Timothy Dwight (1752–1817), the grandson of Jonathan Edwards, was one of the most prominent Calvinists in America during the beginning decades of the United States. Aside from serving as pastor of the Congregational Church at Greenfield Hill, Connecticut, he collaborated with John Trumbull and other "Connecticut Wits" in introducing contemporary English literature into the Latinate curriculum of Yale College, of which he eventually became president. One of his famous sermons, later published as the pamphlet *Folly, Guilt, and Mischief of Duelling* (1805), was inspired by the duel between his cousin Aaron Burr and Alexander Hamilton. But Dwight is remembered most for his Calvinist convictions on theocracy and federalism, as expounded in *The True Means of Establishing Public Happiness* (1798).

Public vs. private happiness was a major issue and theme in the prose and poetry of the late 1700s and early 1800s, especially of three such romanticists as Percy Bysshe Shelley (1792–1822), author of *Prometheus Unbound* (1820); his father-in-law William Godwin, a Calvinist minister who later defected and who, in *An Inquiry Concerning Political Justice and Its Influence on General Virtue and Happiness,* denied the whole notion of innate depravity; and the Godwins' and Shelleys' friend and relative (through marital ties without benefit of clergy) George Gordon, Lord Byron (1788-1824). Byron is not generally associated with Calvinism, although often with Satan and Satanic themes. *Don Juan,* an uncompleted satirical poem which he began in 1818, is full of guilt-ridden intrigues that the hero undertakes after his mother banishes him from Seville because of liberties he has taken with Donna Julia. The legendary libertine Don Juan, incidentally, appears in a dream of Tanner's in George Bernard Shaw's play *Man and Superman* and insists, with typical Calvinist misogyny, that far from pursuing women, *he* is the pursued. Byron, whose mother was a strict Calvinist, never outgrew the Calvinistic influences of his childhood.

But perhaps the most unmistakable Calvinist influences in the nineteenth century are reflected in the stories and novels of Nathaniel Hawthorne and Herman Melville. Hawthorne's stories "The Minister's Black Veil" (1836) and "Young Goodman Brown" (1856) and his novels *The Scarlet Letter* (1850) and *The House of the Seven Gables* (1851) are exhibits in point. The brooding dark guilt feelings of Hawthorne's Reverend Mr. Hooper, Goodman Brown, and the Reverend Mr. Dimmesdale are matched only by the depraved obsessions of Melville's Captain Ahab in *Moby Dick* (1851) and Petty Officer Claggart in *Billy Budd* (written in the late 1800s; published 1924). Of Hawthorne, Melville wrote: "This great power of blackness in him derives its force from its appeals to that Calvinistic sense of Innate Depravity and Original Sin." But perhaps Hawthorne was less critical of Puritanism than of the Puritans who failed to practice what they preached. Of Melville, F. O. Matthiessen wrote: "Though deeply impressed by the ... Puritans' conception of evil, his mind moved away from a fixed system of theology." (As for Hawthorne's and Melville's contemporary Edgar Allan Poe, his macabre tales about murderers, ghouls, and graves are not rooted in Calvinism but rather in the kind of ROMANTICISM that undergirds the GOTHIC NOVEL.)

A nineteenth-century American dropout from Calvinism was Harriet Beecher Stowe (1811-96), daughter of the celebrated Calvinist minister Lyman Beecher. She gained fame for her novel *Uncle Tom's Cabin* (1852), which aroused millions of readers against slavery although paradoxically enough she herself was not an Abolitionist. But in a less well-known novel, *The Minister's Wooing* (1859), she attacked the injustices of Calvinism and thus obliquely explained her eventual apostasy.

As for Total Depravity—that motif has been subject and object of hundreds of novels, plays, poems, and essays. The depravity of the human heart and that "moral sense" which somehow accommodates tortures, hypocrisies, inequalities, and other inhumanities, are depicted not only in the works of Hawthorne and Melville but also in such well-known works as Mark Twain's *Adventures of Huckleberry Finn* (1884) and "The Mysterious Stranger" (1916); Henry James's "Beast in the Jungle" (1903); Joseph Conrad's "Heart of Darkness" (1905); Ford Maddox Ford's *Good Soldier* (1915); Theodore Dreiser's

American Tragedy (1925); Sinclair Lewis's *Elmer Gantry* (1927); and George Santayana's *Last Puritan* (1928).

But to this power of blackness certain American and Scottish-American Calvinists in the late 1800s (among them, Andrew Carnegie and Anthony Comstock) opposed the powerful light of industry and perseverance, reviving the ethos that had enabled Puritan and Pilgrim to endure and prevail. Carnegie, for example wrote *The Gospel of Wealth* (1889) and founded the Carnegie public libraries. Comstock, a self-appointed censor, as reflected in *Traps for the Young* (1883), policed what went into those libraries, organized YMCA cultural improvement groups and the New York Society for the Suppression of Vice. This Protestant Ethic became the staple of many dime novels, especially those of Horatio Alger, Jr. (1834–99).

Over the years "perseverance of saints" has been dramatized in novels and plays (to say nothing of melodramas), notably in versions of the sainthood of the Maid of Orleans. Mark Twain's fictionalized Joan of Arc (1896), in which the heroine is a kind of impeccable maiden school-teacher, is much less credible than George Bernard Shaw's *Saint Joan* (1923). Shaw's Joan is a real saint complete with Irresistible Grace. Although the historical Joan was born a Catholic a century before Calvin, she was in many respects "one of the first Protestant martyrs and one of the first apostles of nationalism," as Shaw observed in the Preface to this play. Nor was Shaw as ironic about Joan's Irresistible Voices as he was about her enemies, the corrupt cartel of Feudal Lords and Organization Bishops. Both Shaw and Clemens thus personified in Joan some of the nobler aspects of Calvinistic Protestantism, notably the rights and responsibilities of the individual.

But the Perseverance of Saints was not minted without an obverse side— the reality of Satan. Just as saints were the elect of God, so witches and heretics were the chosen representatives of Satan. As such, they were not to be spared for Hell-fire if they could be burned at the stake in the upper world. (Calvin himself had set the example by putting the torch to the heretical Dr. Michael Servetus in 1553.) It is a witches' sabbath, a veritable WALPURGIS-NACHT, that lures Hawthorne's Goodman Brown away from home; and in *The House of the Seven Gables,* the atmosphere is permeated with the curse pronounced on the narrator's family, the Pyncheons, when his great grandfather was a judge in the salem witchcraft trials. Witch-hunting, by no means the exclusive preserve of the Salem orgies and Calvinist New England, has been the subject of many literary works, among them Arthur Miller's play *The Crucible* (1953). Other modern plays that have grappled with Calvinist, anti-Calvinist, and existentialist issues are Samuel Beckett's *Waiting for Godot* (1954) and Archibald MacLeish's *J.B.* (1958).

REFERENCES: J. T. McNeill, *The History and Character of Calvinism;* James Holly Hanford and James W. Taaffe, *A Milton Handbook;* F. M. Krouse, *Milton's Samson and the Christian Tradition;* F. R. Leavis, "John Bunyan," *The Common Pursuit;* George Lyman Kittredge, *Witchcraft in Old and New England;* Vernon L. Parrington, *The Colonial Mind;* John Berryman, *Homage to Mistress Bradstreet;* Ralph Barton

Perry, *Puritanism and Democracy;* Howard Mumford Jones, *O Strange New World;* A. T. Davies, *John Calvin and the Influences of Protestantism on National Life and Character;* Leslie Stephen, "Godwin and Shelley," *Hours in a Library;* Bertrand Russell, "Byron," *History of Western Philosophy;* Herman Melville, "Hawthorne and His Mosses," in Jay Leyda, ed., *The Viking Portable Melville;* T. Walter Herbert, "Calvinism and Cosmic Evil in Moby Dick," *PMLA* (October, 1969); F. O. Matthiessen, "The Vision of Evil," *American Renaissance;* Harry Levin, *The Power of Blackness;* Van Wyck Brooks, "New England at Large," *The Flowering of New England;* C. H. Foster, *Rungless Ladder: Harriet Beecher Stowe and New England Puritanism;* James M. Cox, "The Muse of Samuel Clemens," in Justin Kaplan, ed., *Mark Twain, a Profile;* Lionel Trilling, "Huckleberry Finn," *The Liberal Imagination;* Mark Twain, "Andrew Carnegie," in Bernard De Voto, ed., *Mark Twain in Eruption;* Richard Henry Tawney, *Religion and the Rise of Capitalism;* Heywood Broun and Margaret Leech, *Anthony Comstock, Roundsman of the Lord;* Herbert Mayes, *Alger, a Biography Without a Hero;* Norman O. Brown, "The Protestant Era," *Life Against Death.*

camp   A cult name for a style characterized by elegant artifice, extravagance, theatricality, outlandishness, dandyism, hedonism, and innocent revolt against stereotyped sex patterns, high seriousness, and boredom. One of the first camp utterances was Mae West's "Peel me a grape, Beulah!" (1930). In the 1960s camp was observable in certain clothing, furniture, movies, plays, novels, and rock 'n' roll music. The term first appeared in Christopher Isherwood's novel *The World in the Evening* (1954) and gained popularity after its discussion by Susan Sontag in a *Partisan Review* article in 1964. Miss Sontag listed, among other examples of camp, Tiffany lamps, lighting fixtures shaped like flowering plants, Scopitone films, Gaudi's architecture, Aubrey Beardsley's drawings, Oscar Wilde himself, Greta Garbo and Mae West, *King Kong, Vanessa, Zuleika Dobson,* Jean Cocteau's plays, beaded dresses, long hair on men, and trousers on women. Compare BAROQUE.

REFERENCE: Susan Sontag, "Notes on Camp," *Against Interpretation.*

canon   1. A critical standard. 2. The authorized books of the Bible. 3. A catalogue or official list of an author's works. The Shakespeare canon, for example, consists of *(a)* works verified to be Shakespeare's, *(b)* works verified to be those on which he collaborated, and *(c)* works ascribed to him but not verified as his. Compare APOCRYPHA.

REFERENCES: David V. Erdman, ed., *Evidence for Authorship Essays on Problems of Attribution, with an Annotated Bibliography of Selected Readings;* Richard Altick, *The Art of Literary Research.*

cant   1. The special vocabulary used by a group to conceal meaning from outsiders; e.g., thieves' cant. 2. The use of stock words or phrases that produce an affectedly pious, insincere tone; the hypocritical use of religious or moralistic JARGON.

canto   From *cantus,* "song." A book or a section of a book written in verse; a major division of a long poem, as in Dante's *Divine Comedy,* Scott's *Lady of the Lake,* and Pound's *Pisan Cantos.*

capa y espada   See CLOAK AND SWORD.

capitalizing   Capital letters developed from two aims: to beautify and to emphasize. The first capitals, or head letters, were the ornamental initials of hand-lettered books. All letters other than the first of a page or chapter were of the same size and were unadorned; indeed, in such manuscripts almost no punctuation was used, and spacing between words was rare. Reading became easier when punctuation was added to mark stops—and easier again when capital letters came to be used to begin each new sentence.

Desire for emphasis led to the use of capitals to begin proper names, in some places the device being extended to all nouns. Common nouns have seldom been capitalized in English, however, except during the eighteenth and nineteenth centuries—and then not by all writers. The heavy capitalizing by Samuel Johnson and Thomas Carlyle was never consistent.

Generally, lower-case letters are easier to read than capitals, except such a short and thin letter as *i*. The use of capital *I* for the first-person pronoun in English developed because of the tendency of the single *i* to get lost on the printed page.

Currently, the trend, particularly in newspapers, is toward a "downstyle," the use of fewer capitals. Some newspaper stylebooks call for lower-case letters even in such things as Main *street,* Presbyterian *church,* and U.S. *army.* Standard usage, however, still dominates the printing industry as well as the schools, and the most-used forms are Main *Street,* Presbyterian *Church,* and U.S. *Army.*

The use of capitals for special emphasis is now quite unpopular and is confined almost entirely to PERSONIFICATION, as in, "We quail when Politics speaks, for its voice is the voice of Taxation."

In Standard American usage capitals are used:

1. To begin utterances:

   (a) full sentences: They say that a stitch in time saves nine.

   (b) minor sentences: Why not? In a minute.

   (c) full sentences after a colon: We have one complaint: The air in here is stifling.

   (d) full sentences used as complements of verbs: The difficulty is, How does one find the time for writing?

   (e) full sentences following item-markers: By definition: (1) Method is the order to be observed in any series of operation. (2) Demonstration is the deducing of a new truth from two known truths.

   (f) full or minor quoted sentences: He asked, "Where is my book?"

2. To begin each line of formal poetry, although some poets use lower-case letters to produce a special effect.

3. To begin a formal resolution or question: *Resolved,* That this organization acknowledge....

4. To begin proper names:

   (a) persons: Abraham Lincoln, Ernest Hemingway

   (b) places and special geographical features: Europe, Brazil, the South, New York, Fifth Avenue, Rocky Mountains, Grand Canyon, Pacific Ocean, Missouri River, Yosemite National Park, the Orient

(c) organizations and institutions: University of Chicago, American Legion, Lutheran Church, General Motors

(d) buildings, ships, aircraft, trains, and brand names: Chrysler Building, Eiffel Tower, Ile de France, Starjet, Super Chief, Pennzoil

(e) special time designations: Monday, Tuesday, May, September, Memorial Day, Hallowe'en, Stone Age, Renaissance, Christian Era (but not seasons—fall, summer)

(f) special events, historical or other: Reign of Terror, Reconstruction, Battle of the Bulge, Olympic Games, World Series

(g) special documents and treaties: Magna Carta, Declaration of Independence, Alliance for Progress

(h) languages: German, Latin, Russian, Sanskrit

5. To begin adjectives derived from proper names: American, Chinese, Legionnaire, Shakespearean, Californian, Democratic. Certain other adjectives are not capitalized: oriental, southern, italic, platonic. Names that have become common nouns by METONYMY are *not* capitalized: quisling, java, martini, gerrymander, boycott

6. To begin nouns or abbreviations that are followed by numerals: Room 24, Chapter 10, Psalm 23, Article V, No. 6. Minor literary subdivisions are not capitalized: p. 123, ll. 12–14, verse 12

7. To begin titles before proper names: Mr. Danley, Dr. Carruthers, Senator Towne, Professor James, Captain Ellis. Such titles are not capitalized when used appositively after names, except in reference to the President of the United States: Daniel Moynihan, senator from New York; Ronald Reagan, President of the United States

8. To begin first and last and all principal words in titles except short conjunctions, short prepositions, and *a, an,* and *the: How Thinking Is Written, The Way of All Flesh, War and Peace, Il Trovatore,* "Stopping by Woods on a Snowy Evening," *Los Angeles Times, The New York Review of Books*

9. To name language courses and numbered or lettered courses, and courses with special titles: Greek, French, History 7A, Philosophy 21, The Age of Pope and Dryden, Contemporary Economics. Names of studies are not otherwise capitalized: "She's taking history, philosophy, biology, and literature."

10. For the pronoun *I* and the interjection *O:* O when will I listen to experience!

11. To begin the name of the Deity and all nouns and pronouns referring to Him: God, the Father, the Source of all creation; and the names of sacred books: Bible, Koran, Talmud; of religions: Judaism, Buddhism, Christianity; of persons belonging to religions or denominations: Jews, Buddhists, Christians, Mohammedans, Unitarians; and of all deities other than the pagan: Jehovah, the Prophet

12. To begin words of family relationship when they do not follow a possessive: "What did Mother say?" "This is Father." *But* "This is my father."

13. To begin abbreviations of titles, academic degrees, eras, and proper nouns: Mrs., Dr., Ph.D., B.C., A.D., Wash., Calif.; and for all-initial abbreviations: TVA, UCLA, UN, JFK

14. To begin nouns used as PERSONIFICATIONS: How firmly Virtue replies to the error of Vice; how Faith overcomes Despair!

15. To begin EPITHETS that substitute for or are attached to proper names: Catherine the Great, the Scripture, Holy Writ, Honest Abe

16. To name specific academic classes when they refer to an entire class in a specific school: the Freshman class at Yale, the UCLA Senior class; but not when freshman, sophomore, junior, and senior are general designations or when they refer to an individual: a freshman, the sophomore year, senior studies; Knowles, the junior

17. For the foreign particles *le, la, de, du, di* when they do not follow a name or title: D'Artagnan, De Gaulle, La Rochefoucauld, "L'Allegro," Du Bartas. Do not capitalize these particles when they follow a first name or title: Charles de Gaulle, the Duc de la Rochefoucauld, Gabriele d'Annunzio. Foreign names fully naturalized in English are exceptions, although some families prefer to follow foreign usage: Thomas De Quincey, but Alfred I. du Pont

18. To begin scientific names of phyla, classes, orders, families, and genera: Chordata, Mammalia, Carnivora, Castoridae, Panthera. Not capitalized are the names of species or English derivatives from scientific names: leo, sapiens; chordate, mammal, carnivorous

19. To begin the salutation and the complimentary close of a letter: Dear Mr. Brown, Very truly yours. Do not capitalize adjectives in salutations or any word but the first in the close: My dear Sir, Yours sincerely

20. To distinguish letters used to indicate form or shape: T bar, I beam, U turn; or to differentiate phenomena: X ray, Vitamin B

card-stacking   Biased argument in which pertinent evidence for one's own view is emphasized and pertinent evidence against it is suppressed. The device also includes any biased interpretation of evidence, biased statistics, and biased choice of words. Card-stacking is also a fallacy in statistical induction. See INDUCTIVE REASONING 2.

caricature   An exaggerated representation of a person or action. Compare BAROQUE and THEOPHRASTAN CHARACTERS.

carol   1. A dance; also spelled *carole*. 2. A song sung at such a dance; e.g., the folk carol, "Here We Go Round the Mulberry Bush." 3. A literary song; e.g., Charles Wesley's Christmas carol, "Hark, the Herald Angels Sing."

REFERENCES: Percy Dearmer *et al.,* eds., *The Oxford Book of Carols;* Richard Greene, ed., *The Early English Carols;* E. K. Chambers and F. Sidgwick, eds., *Early English Lyrics;* David Cecil, ed., *The Oxford Book of Christian Verse;* Carleton Brown, *Religious Lyrics of the Fifteenth Century.*

Caroline   Pertaining to the reigns of the English Kings Charles I (1625–1649) and Charles II (1660–1685). See CAVALIER POETS.

carpe diem   Literally, "Seize the day"; or "Make hay while the sun shines" or "Make the most of your opportunities." In literature, especially poetry, a prevalent theme: e.g., Herrick's "Gather ye rosebuds while ye may" and Marvell's "But at my back I always hear / Time's winged chariot hurrying near," in which the poets urge the ladies addressed to become more active lovers before it is too late.

casuistry   1. In rhetoric, equivocation or deliberate ambiguity. 2. In literature and religion, cases of conscience in love relations. Solutions to such cases have varied radically in different times and cultures. In his *Confessions* (ca. 400), Saint Augustine argued that people are basically corrupt and helpless without the discipline of Church law. In the early 1100s Peter Abelard, confronting problems of reconciling erotic passion with responsibility (he was castrated by Fulbert for seducing the latter's young niece Heloise), argued that any human act must be judged by its intention. Abelard's concern with such casuistry was reexamined by Blaise Pascal in *Provincial Letters* (1656), in which he defended a friend against the strictures of the Church. Later, in his posthumously published *Pensees,* Pascal championed mystical over rational solutions to problems of conscience: "The heart has its own reasons." (Allusions to Pascal's casuistry lace Eric Rohmer's film *My Night at Maud's,* 1970). 3. In seventeenth-century literature, a devout Christian's code of conduct, also known as "case divinity." This ranged from "how to behave in church," as outlined in George Herbert's poem "The Church Porch," to a defense of divorce, as argued in John Milton's tract *Tetrachordon.* Other popular casuistry, like Joseph Hall's *Characters of Virtues and Vices* (1608) and Jeremy Taylor's *Holy Living* (1651), profoundly influenced the thought and lives of the Puritans.

REFERENCES: Peter Abelard, *Letters to Heloise;* Etienne Gilson, *Heloise and Abelard;* H. M. Beyle ["Stendhal"], "The Twelfth Century Code," *On Love;* Denis de Rougement, *Love in the Western World;* Wallace Fowlie, *Love in Literature;* G. A. Starr, *Defoe and Casuistry;* Kenneth Kirk, *Conscience and Its Problems;* Thomas Wood, *English Casuistical Divinity . . . 17th Century;* Elizabeth Hardwick, *Seduction and Betrayal.*

catachresis   The misuse of words, by carelessness rather than by design. It may include almost any verbal mistake, or SOLECISM, such as the use of *infer* for *imply, convince* for *persuade,* "nucular" for *nuclear, except* for *accept,* "homogenous" for *homogeneous,* "substantuation" for *substantiation.* Catachresis may also include MALAPROPISM and MIXED METAPHOR.

catalexis   In poetry, the deliberate omission of a syllable in an otherwise metrical line to avoid monotony. Such a line is called *catalectic* or *truncated.*

catastrophe   Literally, "downfall." In tragic drama, the final scene in which most of the characters die or are dying. (While dying, incidentally, they give long speeches; *Hamlet:* "O good Horatio ... / Absent thee from felicity awhile, / And in this harsh world draw thy breath in pain, / To tell my story"—this some dozen lines *after* he has said, for the second time, "Horatio, I am dead.") The term catastrophe is appropriate not only because it describes a theater stage strewn with the mighty fallen but also because it describes the culmination of the plot action, which has been "falling" since the CLIMAX. See DRAMATIC STRUCTURE.

categorical syllogism   See SYLLOGISM 1.

catharsis   The "purging" or cleansing of a spectator's or reader's emotions by means of emotional agitations. The term, used by Aristotle in *The Poetics* in the description of TRAGEDY, has been much debated and analyzed. It is generally taken to mean that the play-goer who hangs on every word and action of a drama and who is stirred to pity and terror may say, "I'd never want to get into *that* kind of mess!" Such a spectator has experienced *catharsis* and leaves the theater a better person (at least for a few hours). Catharsis, while usually a phenomenon experienced by the spectator, may also be experienced by one of the few characters who do not die in a tragic drama. Thus, Horatio in *Hamlet* will undoubtedly "absent" himself "from felicity [death] awhile."

REFERENCES: Aristotle, *The Poetics;* Lily Bess Campbell, *Shakespeare's Tragic Heroes;* "The Power of the Word," in Margot Astrov, ed., *American Indian Prose and Poetry;* D. M. Hill, "Catharsis," *Essays in Criticism;* Darwin Turner, *Katharsis.*

causal induction   See INDUCTIVE REASONING.

causal reasoning   Reasoning about causes and effects. *This need not be fallacious,* though it often is. The general fallacy in causal reasoning is that a supposed result ("effect") is mistakenly ascribed to one or another innocent "cause." This fallacy, in which the effect turns out on close examination not really to have followed from the alleged cause, is called a NON SEQUITUR. ("The fault [cause], dear Brutus, is not in our stars / But in ourselves.") More often, non sequiturs do not need elaborate examination—they are perfectly obvious: "Something the Lastradonians ate caused them to make war." Compare POST HOC.

cavalier   From the Italian and French, "knight," and ultimately the Latin, "horseman." Having the characteristics of libertinism, elegance, wit, and high spirits. Specifically, one of the followers of the Cavalier party of Charles I. See CAVALIER POETS.

Cavalier poets   A group of witty and clever young poets—chiefly Thomas Carew, Sir John Suckling, and Richard Lovelace—who served as courtier-soldiers at the court of Charles I (1625–49) and so were identified with the King's Cavalier (Royalist) party. Their lyrical verse, written for the entertainment of the court and marked by grace, elegance, high spirits, and wit, often sounded the note of CARPE DIEM. Their themes turned generally on love and chivalry. Though not courtiers, such other seventeenth-century poets as Robert Herrick and Edmund Waller are usually classed with the Cavalier poets because their verse is characterized by the same lyrical sensuousness. The oft-recited Cavalier lines "Gather ye rosebuds while ye may" are from Herrick's "To the Virgins to Make Much of Time." Perhaps the most famous cavalier poem of all is "On Julia's Clothes":

> Whenas in silks my Julia goes,
> Then, then, methinks, how sweetly flows
> That liquefaction of her clothes.
> Next, when I cast mine eyes and see
> That brave vibration each way free,
> Oh, how that glittering taketh me!

REFERENCES: Robin Skelton, *Cavalier Poets;* Earl Miner, *The Cavalier Mode ... ;* J. William Hebel and Hoyt H. Hudson, eds., *Poetry of the English Renaissance (1509-1660);* John F. Danby, *Poets on Fortune's Hill.*

censorship   The official act of disallowing publication or distribution of a part or the whole of material that the officials deem unsuitable. A censor is ordinarily a person or group other than the creator or intended publisher, so that the selection, emendation, or editing of material for publication is not censorship. However, an editor who deletes or emends any part of a previously published work because of its objectionable qualities may be termed a censor. (Compare BOWDLERIZED.) Censorship may be military, political, or moral. Military censorship is intended to keep an enemy from knowing anything that would help that enemy and harm the "home" cause. Political censorship is often intended to protect a party, government, or society from the effects of making public anything its leaders deem harmful to themselves or the whole. Moral censorship is often aimed at "protecting" innocent minds from the "harmful" effects of ideas that the censors, official or self-appointed, find objectionable. (Compare COMSTOCKERY.) Even when censorship has worthy aims, there is difficulty in defending it as policy, chiefly because of the problem of selecting the censor: Who deserves the power to determine what others should see or know? That problem is pointed up in John Milton's famed essay on freedom of the press, "Areopagitica" (1644). Another difficulty lies in the problem of defining OBSCENITY and deciding whether obscenity is harmful—and to whom.

REFERENCES: John McCormick and Mairi MacInnes, eds., *Versions of Censorship, an Anthology;* Robert Downs, ed., *The First Freedom;* NCTE Committee on Right to Read, *The Student's Right to Read* (pamphlet); Anne Haight, *Banned Books;* James A. Farrer, *Books Condemned to Be Burned;* Wayne Booth, "Censorship and the Values of Fiction," *The English Journal* (March, 1964); Ralph McCoy, *Freedom of the Press;* Olga and Edwin Hoyt, *Censorship in America;* Lee Burress and Edward Jenkinson, *The Students' Right to Know.*

central intelligence   See FOCUS OF NARRATION.

chapbook   A small penny-book or pamphlet sold by "chapmen" or peddlers, mostly in Elizabethan England. Even more so than BROADSIDE BALLADS, chapbooks were anonymous or pseudonymous, especially those that contained political attacks on people in high places. A celebrated exception, a *signed* chapbook, was Robert Greene's *Groatsworth of Wit Bought with a Million of Repentance* (1592), containing an envious slur on Shakespeare as "that Shakescene."

REFERENCES: *Harvard Catalogue of English and American Chapbooks;* W. Harvey, *Scottish Chapbook Literature.*

characters   See THEOPHRASTAN CHARACTERS, DRAMATIC STRUCTURE, SPEAKING VOICE.

chiaroscuro   "Light and shade." In painting, and by extension architecture, sculpture, music, poetry, and so on, representation by means of contrasts—light and dark, loud and quiet (*fortissimo* and *pianissimo*), fast and slow, and so on. Yeats said that in poetry he preferred "silences" between substantive words (including contrast words) in order that the latter might count for more.

REFERENCES: William Butler Yeats, "The Cutting of an Agate," *Essays and Introductions;* Paul Valéry, "On Literary Technique," *The Art of Poetry;* Eugene Delacroix, *The Journal;* Henry Adams, *Mont St. Michel and Chartres.*

chiasmus   **1.** A rhetorical device in which the two end-words and the two inner-words share respectively common parts of speech; for example, "handsome lads and maidens fair" (adjective noun and noun adjective). Chiasmus also produces a contrast of ideas by a sort of reverse parallelism. In "She would be *always true, false never,*" the contrasted elements appear in reverse order. Phrases or clauses may be reversed to produce chiasmus: "Vigor is the way of youth; the way of age is wisdom"; "We succeed if we persevere; if we falter, we fail." See also ANTITHESIS, BALANCE, and PARALLELISM. **2.** The crisscross effect in ironic plots of fiction and drama. For example, in Hardy's *Jude the Obscure* Jude and Sue exchange postures: Jude begins as proestablishment and ends as anti-, whereas Sue begins as anti- and ends as pro.

chivalric romance   A metrical or a prose narrative with a background of court, kings, knights, ladies, love, adventure, intrigue, and religious fervor. The term is a synonym for medieval romance. From the eleventh to the fifteenth century many French romances were translated into English. Two of the most celebrated were *Guy of Warwick* (ca. 1300) and Malory's *Morte d'Arthur* (fifteenth century). The exaggerated prowess attributed to the hero of romances in the 1300s was parodied in the portrait of Sir Thopas in *The Canterbury Tales* (1387–1400). See COURTLY LOVE and METRICAL ROMANCE.

choriamb   See METER.

chorus   **1.** In Greek drama, the group of actors who, while participating in the action to some extent, serve mainly as observers of the other characters. The Greek chorus spoke in unison, as one character, and usually moved in unison as well, in the slow stylized motions by which the tragedies were "danced." In Sophocles' *Oedipus Rex,* the Theban Elders, a collective body, participate by advising the king of the citizens' point of view, greeting newly entered characters, questioning the messenger, and so on. Their more important function, however, is to witness and comment upon Oedipus's curse on the unknown polluter of Thebes and his gradual discovery that the accursed person is himself. Traditionally, the chorus represents the Greek middle way—"nothing overmuch"—and mistrusts extremes of feeling or action on the part of the protagonist. In its role of witness it is able both to intensify the audience's reactions by giving them audible expression and to raise questions which the playwright wishes the audience to think about—for example, the forces behind Oedipus's downfall, the possible absence of a consistent and ordered rule of divine beings. With ancient Greek overtones, but with Christian ideology, Milton used a chorus in *Samson Agonistes;* T. S. Eliot in *Murder in the Cathedral.*

    2. In modern popular songs, the repeated verse or refrain between the "story" verses; usually the chorus is the more memorable part.

REFERENCES: H. D. F. Kitto, *Greek Tragedy;* Friederich Nietzsche, *The Birth of Tragedy;* F. L. Lucas, *Tragedy;* George Steiner, *The Death of Tragedy.*

chronicle   **1.** A history; for example, Alfred's *Anglo-Saxon Chronicles* or Holinshed's [Elizabethan] *Chronicles.* See HISTORY AS LITERATURE. **2.** A play that dramatizes history; for example, Shakespeare's plays about English kings from Richard II to Henry VIII.

REFERENCES: Felix Schelling, *The English Chronicle Play;* C. Leech, *Chronicles.*

chutzpah   Unmitigated gall (from the Hebrew). A classic example of a character with chutzpah is the son who, after murdering his parents, throws himself on the mercy of the court because he is an orphan.

cinquain   A one-sentence poem of five lines invented by Adelaide Crapsey (1878–1914). Line one contains two syllables; line two, four; line three, six; line four, eight; and line five, two. This cinquain was composed by a seventh grader: "Airship / Gay and carefree / Yielding, climbing, soaring / Fulfilling human ecstasy / Freedom." Compare HAIKU and TANKA.

circular reasoning   See BEGGING THE QUESTION 2.

circumlocution   Roundabout statement. See DEADWOOD 3.

classic   1. A work of art so universal in appeal that it has transcended the boundaries of time and place; it has survived the "tests of time." 2. One of the GREAT BOOKS.

classical   Pertaining (1) to things Greek and Latin or (2) to classicism.

classicism   The spirit of art characterized by traditional form, with greater emphasis on reason than on emotion. A good deal of balance, of bilateral symmetry, characterizes classical furniture, music, and rhetoric. Such taste especially characterized eighteenth-century France and England (the age of Voltaire, Pope, and Johnson). Eighteenth-century England was called the "Augustan" age because many statesmen and writers of the time imagined England to be a kind of re-creation of the age of the Roman emperor Augustus and the Roman poets Vergil and Horace. In literature and art, classicism reflects the standards and models of Greek and Roman antiquity and thus inclines toward order, repose, symmetry, and an intellectual, objective view of life. Classicism is often contrasted with ROMANTICISM, the two supposedly corresponding to contrary impulses in human nature. On the one hand, are the desire for solid traditional values and perhaps the need to control emotions and to have positive and clear thoughts. On the other hand, are love of individual expression, intoxication, and passion, and yearning for the faraway and the unobtainable. From age to age, the pendulum of fashion has swung between classicism and romanticism—most notably, toward classicism in the seventeenth and eighteenth centuries and toward romanticism in the nineteenth. But it is a misconception that any writer can be classed exclusively as a classicist or as a romanticist. Even the most "classical" of classical writers sometimes express profound emotion. Perhaps it can only be said that they tend to purify their emotions by subjecting them to the simplicity of universal designs.

The major principles of classicism may be summarized as follows:

1. *Imitation of the ideal.* Setting a high value on order and stability, the classical artist seeks to portray what is lasting and universal in life, to represent what is typical and essential in humanity or nature rather than what is individual, transitory, or accidental. The classical artist strives, in short, to present life in its essential purity or idealized form. The classic Greek hero, for example, whether in drama or in marble art, is simple in form and appears almost godlike, lifted above the level of everyday life to superhuman stateliness.

2. *Practical-mindedness.* Even in idealizing, however, the classical artist's chief concern is with life present and observable, with things essentially as they

are. Such a highly objective outlook does not allow the artist to proceed beyond the horizon to things exotic, faraway, ethereal, or mysterious. Even so great a flight of the imagination as Jonathan Swift's *Gulliver's Travels* has a rational, sobering air of truth in its acid criticism of contemporary human society.

3. *A taste for civilization.* The classicist tends to favor the town over the countryside, civilized society over primitive life—even in pastorals the shepherds and shepherdesses are likely to have an urbane air. And novels of country life usually focus on the cultivated gentry, with scant attention paid to the raw farmhand (except, perhaps, to ridicule). To the classicist the refined products of society are more interesting than are the effusions of wild nature— formal parks and forums are preferred to the irregularities of jagged mountains and untamed fields and forests. Madame de Staël's château on Lake Geneva, for example, faced landward onto formal, harmoniously proportioned gardens, as the antiromantic T. E. Hulme observes.

4. *Moderation.* Self-control, restraint, the "golden mean," "nothing to excess" all describe the classicist's handling of art. Such products of high seriousness are marked by repose, graceful symmetry, and harmony of parts, avoiding emotionalism, discordance, romantic embellishment, and individualism. In satire and comedy—modes in which the classicist is usually more successful than the romanticist—the critical targets are extremism, pretension, pettiness, bigotry, pedantry, and the other forms of excess.

5. *Adherence to traditional form.* A deep respect for tradition and a desire to communicate clearly within a framework familiar to everyone incline the classical artist toward the use of traditional literary and artistic forms. Innovations and complexities of design are rejected, for these might puzzle the audience. Thus, the eighteenth-century English poets wrote chiefly in HEROIC COUPLETS, a traditional English verse form that is sonorous, clear, and neatly rounded. (Greek and Roman EPIC POETS had used the DACTYLIC HEXAMETER; the French, the ALEXANDRINE.) In drama the classicist adheres to the traditional UNITIES. Compare ROMANTICISM.

REFERENCES: Gilbert Highet, *The Classical Tradition;* Walter Jackson Bate, *From Classic to Romantic;* Harold Nicolson, *The Age of Reason.*

clerihew   A witty quatrain about a well-known person, who is named in the first line. An example:

> Sir Humphrey Davy
> Detested gravy.
> He lived in the odium
> Of having invented sodium.

The clerihew was invented by E. Clerihew Bentley in collaboration with G. K. Chesterton. Twentieth-century clerihewists include W. H. Auden.

cliché   When FIGURATIVE LANGUAGE becomes widely repeated, it is on its way to becoming a cliché—an expression too worn to bear fresh meaning. Because it comes to mind too easily, the cliché ordinarily falls short of exactness; it lures the user into a rut when the topic demands exploration of the higher ridges. Gabriel Conroy, for example, in James Joyce's story "The Dead" delivers an after-dinner speech full of such clichés. However, repeated use alone does not make a cliché, for many phrases occur repeatedly in speech and writing and do not offend; *the only way, the same thing, if you please, more often than not* have not become clichés; they say what they mean. But *the shadow of a doubt* and *a bee in your bonnet* are often used when there is no thought of shadows or of apiary headgear. It is inexactness of expression, not repetition, that makes the cliché. See also BROMIDE, PLATITUDE, STEREOTYPE.

REFERENCES: Eric Partridge, *A Dictionary of Clichés;* William Sparke and Clark McKowen, *Montage;* Barnet Kottler and Martin Light, *The World of Words;* Jacques Barzun, tr., Flaubert's *Dictionary of Accepted Ideas.*

climax   The highest point; the culmination of a rising suspensive action within a scene or over-all plot of a novel or play. See DRAMATIC STRUCTURE.

clipped form   A word made by clipping off one of its parts; e.g., *intro* for introduction. The clipping of an initial sound is *apheresis;* the clipping of a final sound is *apocope;* the clipping of a middle sound is *syncope.* Examples of apheresis, syncope, and apocope: *specially,* for especially; *gen'ral* for general; *supposin'* for supposing.

cloak and dagger   A label for the fiction and drama of espionage and intrigue. British examples include John Buchan's *Thirty-Nine Steps* (1915); Graham Greene's *Stamboul Train* (1932) and *Our Man in Havana* (1958); Ian Fleming's "James Bond" series; and the spy stories of Len Deighton. Compare CLOAK AND SWORD.

cloak and sword   A label for the fiction and drama of swashbuckling romance and adventure, whether historical or pseudo-historical, usually revolving around aristocracy, athletic heroes, perspicacious ladies, and a chivalric code that leads to sword or pistol duels or both. The expression is a translation of the Spanish epithet *capa y espada,* the cloak and sword having been part of the attire of the nobility and upper middle class in the sixteenth and seventeenth centuries. The master playwrights of cloak-and-sword comedy in Spain were Lope de Vega (1562–1630) and Pedro Calderón (1600–81). In modern times some cloak-and-sword romances have been *The Three Musketeers* (1844) and *The Count of Monte Cristo* (1845) by the French novelist Alexandre Dumas; and *Cyrano de Bergerac* (1897) by the French playwright Edmond Rostand. British examples include Anthony Hope's *Prisoner of Zenda* (1894) and Daphne Du Maurier's *Jamaica Inn* (1936). American examples include Charles Major's *When Knighthood Was in Flower* (1898) and George Barr McCutcheon's "Graustark" series (1901–1928).

REFERENCE: A. L. Lazarus and Victor H. Jones, *Beyond Graustark.*

closed   1. "Complete in itself," as in reference to a line, a COUPLET, a verse, a QUATRAIN, or any other STANZA. Contrast ENJAMBEMENT. 2. Of a literary work, one that seems to have only one level of meaning.

closet drama   A play more often read than staged; for example, Milton's *Samson Agonistes,* Shelley's *The Cenci,* and Browning's *Pippa Passes.*

closure   1. The conclusion of any literary work. 2. A kind of ending, different from the conventional, that may generate interest not only in its content but also in its technique. In conventional endings of novels and plays few plot-strands are left hanging; the audience is told what happens even to very minor characters. On the other hand, a story like Frank Stockton's "The Lady or the Tiger?" deliberately leaves to the reader's imagination the final destinies of the two chief characters. (This closure has struck some as a TOUR DE FORCE.) During the Victorian era, authors of magazine serials (PART PUBLICATION) often received letters from readers begging that a certain character headed for destruction be spared. A case in point is Dickens's Little Emily in *David Copperfield*. In response to his readers, Dickens changed his originally intended demise for Emily and had her found prospering in Australia. Other novelists have provided their readers with a choice between two alternative endings—John Fowles, for example, in *The French Lieutenant's Woman*.

Some of the most memorable poems end by *suggesting* more than they say. Richard Cory "went home and put a bullet through his head." The reason is only suggested, although it is not terribly mysterious, given the poem's context. At the end of a more complex poem, "The Second Coming," Yeats, rather than *telling* us, *asks* "And what rough beast, its hour come round at last / Slouches toward Bethlehem to be born?" In short, many poets subscribe to anti-closure—shun "box-closing clicks," prosaic assertions, strong declarations, and exhortations. These poets prefer closing with images that may at first seem like irrelevancies ("throwaways") but that do relate however ambiguously—often tantalizingly—to the poem's context. Examples include Coleridge's "milk of Paradise" ("Kubla Khan"), Emily Dickinson's "opening of a door," ("Elysium"), Wallace Stevens's "pigeons ... downward to darkness on extended wings" ("Sunday Morning"), and Dylan Thomas's "Though I sang in my chains like the sea" ("Fern Hill"). Compare HAIKU and OBJECTIVE CORRELATIVE.

REFERENCES: Frank Kermode, *The Sense of an Ending;* Barbara Hernstein Smith, *Poetic Closure;* Walker Gibson, *Poems in the Making;* Robin Skelton, *The Practice of Poetry;* Norman O. Brown, *Closing Time.*

cognitive domain, affective domain   In the reading of literature, the first pertains to rational or referential experience; the second, to emotional and aesthetic experience—hence to audience responses to literature and the arts. Critical levels of responses in both the cognitive and the affective domains are codified in the well-known "Taxonomies" by Benjamin Bloom and David Krathwohl and are spelled out in J. N. Hook et al., *Representative Performance Objectives in English.* For in-depth studies of these phenomena see Norman Holland, *The Dynamics of Literary Response,* and Louise Rosenblatt, *The Transactional Theory of the Literary Work.*

coherence   The quality of effective relation among the elements of a discourse—the "sticking together" of those elements. Clear connection among the parts of an utterance (from the phrase up to the long literary work) depends upon the care given to (1) sequence of ideas—a proper arrangement in time, space, or logic; (2) consistency of subject—a constant focus upon the central element as the grammatical subject of most sentences; (3) repetition of key words; (4) clear reference of pronouns to key nouns; (5) parallelism—the use of similar structures for ideas of similar function; (6) careful transition—words and phrases that lead clearly from one idea to the next.

CEA College English Association   A non-profit organization of college instructors and university professors devoted to "effecting a substantial nexus between teaching and scholarship." In this enterprise, the CEA seeks to combine the goals of the MLA with those of the NCTE. The CEA was founded in 1939. In collaboration with regional affiliates, the CEA holds annual conferences in major cities of the United States. Its publications include *The CEA Critic* (devoted to scholarship) and *The CEA Forum* (devoted to pedagogy). The current Executive Director is Professor Elizabeth Cooper. Headquarters are at the University of Houston, Downtown Campus, Houston, Texas, 77002.

CEEE College Entrance Examination Board.   A non profit organization that composes and administers examinations for high-school students applying for admission to colleges. Dissatisfied with the chaotic contrariety of college admission requirements, Nicholas Murray Butler of Columbia University founded the CEEB in 1900. The CEEB board of directors later delegated to the ETS (Educational Testing Service) of New Jersey the responsibility of composing and administering tests in key academic subjects, including English language and literature. In preparing these tests, the ETS involved prominent scholars and teachers affiliated with the MLA and the NCTE. During the 1960s, the CEEB English Commission, in collaboration with several university English departments, elicited from the Carnegie Foundation and the United States Office of Education grants to improve the preparation of English-teachers. This enterprise became known as Project English, although each of the eighteen universities that won grants developed a project with an emphasis of its own.

REFERENCES: Albert Kitzhaber, *Themes, Theories, and Therapy;* Floyd Rinker, *Freedom and Discipline;* Michael Shugrue, "New Materials for the Teaching of English," *PMLA* (September, 1966); A. L. Lazarus *et al., The Purdue Project English Units;* J. N. Hook *et al., Representative Performance Objectives for High-School English.*

colon   A mark of punctuation (:) used chiefly as an introducer, an indication that an example, explanation, or division of what went before is about to follow. The colon is used:

1. To announce an example or list of examples:

What danced through her mind were pictures: last year's Christmas tree, the mud on Jamie's shoes, the grocer's frown as he weighed the turkey.

2. To announce a restatement in apposition to what has gone before:

Art is long: It comes only to him who persists.

3. To announce an explanation of what has gone before:

She could hardly invite him to dinner: There was nothing but ice in the refrigerator.

4. To announce the body of a statement after a conventional salutation or introduction:

Dear Sir: We hereby resolve:

5. To announce a list of parts or members of what has been generally named:

The whole family went: mother, father, son, daughter, and pet turtle.

In addition, the colon is used conventionally for miscellaneous technical problems.

6. To separate hours from minutes in writing the time of day, to separate chapter from verse in Biblical references, to separate volume number from page numbers in bibliographical references:

6:24 P.M.   Matthew 5:20   *Atlantic* 209:73–77

7. To separate place of publication from name of publisher in a formal bibliographical entry:

New York: Oxford University Press, 1982

8. To separate a cue line from the speech in a dramatic script:

ALGERNON: Oh! it is absurd to have a hard-and-fast rule about what one should read and what one shouldn't. More than half of modern culture depends on what one shouldn't read.

9. To separate the terms in a mathematical ratio:

$5 : 19 = 32 : x$

Should a capital letter follow a colon? Yes, if what follows the colon would ordinarily be capitalized or if what follows the colon is capitalized in an original that is being quoted. See CAPITALIZING.

When a colon is used with quotation marks, the colon always goes outside:

Two things can be said about "style": It is indefinable, and it is unmistakable.

Any colon that appears at the end of quoted matter is dropped, so the colon never appears just before a closing quotation mark.

comedy   1. One of the major MODES. 2. A play, not necessarily humorous, designed primarily to amuse, as distinguished from TRAGEDY, which is designed to evoke such emotions as pity and terror. The protagonist of a comedy almost always solves the major problem (instead of being overcome by it, as is the protagonist in tragedy). But such a solution may not necessarily be happy as far as society is concerned. (Compare, for example, some of the comedies of George Bernard Shaw.) Nevertheless, most comedies do engage both protagonist and audience in more laughter than tears, more satire than reportage, more thought than emotion.

The earliest Greek comedy consisted of loose episodes, choruses, and ritual dialogues in honor of Dionysus, the god of fertility. (*Comedy* is the Greek term for Dionysian revel.) It was not until the advent of Aristophanes (died ca. 388 B.C.) that Greek Old Comedy developed plot structure along with brilliant wit, repartee, and SATIRE. Celebrated plays by Aristophanes are *The Clouds* (a satire on sophists), *The Knights* (a satire on politicians), and *Lysistrata* (a comedy in which the Athenian women boycott their husbands to end a war). The Greek New Comedy, chiefly the plays of Menander (died ca. 291 B.C.), was characterized by much less wit and satire and by more clichés of plot and characterization, especially the character of humours. There now appeared such stereotypes as the braggart soldier, the libertine master, and the insolent slave. This kind of play, along with the stereotyped comedy-of-errors plot, was soon imitated by the Roman playwrights Plautus and Terence, who flourished in the second century B.C.

During the early Christian era, classical comedy practically disappeared, no doubt because the early Church fathers regarded the theater as frivolous and irreverent. Nevertheless, comedy managed to survive in certain folk plays and festivals, especially in the FARCES and MORALITY PLAYS of the Middle Ages. Nor was this comedy always as crude as is usually supposed, even if crudity and slapstick did characterize a few of the best-known CRAFT CYCLE PLAYS (the Wakefield *Noah* and the Chester *Deluge*) and later, in the sixteenth century, the Italian COMMEDIA DELL'ARTE.

During the English renaissance, comedy revived, and was developed in several forms. John Heywood wrote some of the best-known INTERLUDES, especially *The Playe of the Four P's* (ca. 1521). Nicholas Udall and John Lyly revived the classical New Comedy, as did Shakespeare in *The Comedy of Errors.* Ben Jonson developed the comedy of humours—creating characters, later to be stereotyped, like the parasite (in *Volpone*) and the woman-hater (in *Every Man in His Humour*). Shakespeare also created such humour-characters as the glutton-souse Falstaff and the egregious fool Malvolio. But both Jonson and Shakespeare raised their characters above classical stereotypes by adding a good many individualistic traits and bringing in much local London color. Shakespeare's genius prompted him to range even further, in a repertoire that included, as well, tragicomedy and such romantic comedies as *The Tempest, Twelfth Night,* and *As You Like It.* The last play represents typical Shakespearian virtuosity in realizing the double vision of romance and anti-romance, or comic realism.

The closing of the London theaters by the Puritans in 1642 produced an eighteen-year hiatus in comedy, but it resumed with éclat at the RESTORATION. Such comedies as George Etherege's *Man of Mode* (1674), William Wycherly's *Country Wife* (1675), and William Congreve's *Way of the World* (1700) were marked by wit, brilliant repartee, and much sexual innuendo. Because Restoration comedies satirized contemporary manners, mores, sports, and pastimes, they came to be called "comedies of manners." Because of their urbane wit, they also became known as "high comedy," to distinguish them from the "low comedy" and buffoonery of the interlude. The comedy of manners retained its popularity through most of the eighteenth century, especially with the often-produced plays mentioned above and with Oliver Goldsmith's *She Stoops to Conquer* (1773) and Richard Brinsley Sheridan's *School for Scandal* (1777).

Comedy suffered an eclipse at the beginning of the nineteenth century, especially during the early years of Queen Victoria's reign. But after the middle of the century it returned, at first somewhat cautiously, and then hilariously, in the operettas of W. S. Gilbert and A. S. Sullivan (*H. M. S. Pinafore,* 1878, and *The Pirates of Penzance,* 1880) and in the sophisticated plays of Oscar Wilde (*The Importance of Being Earnest,* 1895) and George Bernard Shaw (*Candida,* 1898, *Man and Superman,* 1905, and *Pygmalion,* 1913). At the same time there appeared the sentimental comedies of James M. Barrie (*Peter Pan* and *What Every Woman Knows*) and the Irish comedies of J. M. Synge (*The Playboy of the Western World*) and of Sean O'Casey (*Juno and the Paycock* and *The Plough and the Stars,* the latter surcharged with tragic IRONY).

Celebrated comedies, including musical comedies, of the first half of the twentieth century include *The College Widow* (1904) by George Ade; *Abie's Irish Rose* (1922) by Anne Nichols; *Showboat* (1927) by Edna Ferber, Jerome Kern, and Oscar Hammerstein; *See Naples and Die* (1929) by Elmer Rice; *Bittersweet* (1929) by Noel Coward; *The Green Pastures* (1930) by Marc Connelly; *Of Thee I Sing* (1932) by George Kaufman and George Gershwin; *The Time of Your Life* (1940) by William Saroyan; *South Pacific* (1948) by Richard Rodgers and Oscar Hammerstein II; *The Matchmaker* (1954) by Thornton Wilder, a revision of an earlier play and the basis of the musical *Hello, Dolly!* (1963).

Recent experimental comedy includes the BLACK HUMOR of playwrights like Samuel Beckett (*Waiting for Godot*) and Eugene Ionesco (*Rhinoceros*). Nevertheless, most plays and cinemas continue to be comedies; tragedy, with some few exceptions, seems to have been left to another time, another place. See DRAMATIC STRUCTURE.

REFERENCES: F. M. Cornford, *Origins of Attic Comedy;* Hazelton Spencer, ed., *Elizabethan Plays;* Dougald MacMillan and Howard Mumford Jones, eds., *Plays of the Restoration and Eighteenth Century;* Charles M. Gayley, ed., *Representative English Comedies;* M. C. Bradbrook, *Growth and Structure of English Comedy;* Joseph Wood Krutch, *Comedy and Conscience after the Restoration;* George Meredith, *The Idea of Comedy and the Uses of the Comic Spirit;* Northrop Frye, "Comic Fictional Modes," *The Anatomy of Criticism;* John J. Enck *et al.,* eds., *The Comic in Theory and Practice;* Henri Bergson, "Laughter," in Wylie Sypher, ed., *Comedy;* R. W. Corrigan, ed., *Comedy: Meaning and Forms;* Paul Lauter, ed., *Theories of Comedy;* C. L. Barber, *Shakespeare's Festive Comedy;* W. K. Wimsatt, ed., *The Idea of Comedy;* Louis Kronenberger, *The Thread of Laughter;* James Feibleman, *In Praise of Comedy;* Oscar Mandel, "... Nature of the Comic," *Antioch Rev.* (Spring, 1970); Edith Kern, *The Absolute Comic.*

comedy of humours   See HUMOURS.

comic relief   In drama and fiction, the humorous scenes or episodes presented between tragic or serious scenes in order to relieve the audience's tensions. A classic example is the scene in *Macbeth* in which the wry porter chatters his earthy speculations about the people knocking at the gate as he goes to answer them. His soliloquy delays the opening and aggravates the knocking, but the low comedy serves as a relief after the more intense episodes of murder.

REFERENCE: Thomas De Quincey, "On the Knocking at the Gate in Macbeth," in Philip Stern, ed., *Selected Writings of Thomas De Quincey.*

comma   A mark of punctuation (,) that aids understanding by separating elements in a written utterance. Rife as it is with ambiguity, the English language has great need of the comma to do in writing what intonation often does in speech: sort and separate, group and array the elements of thought. If the writer's ear is bad, the use of (or lack of) commas will reflect a failure to "hear" the sense-bearing intonations of the writer's own speech, and the writing will continually send the reader off on false leads. Today's written English tends toward fewer commas than were used a century ago. But to suppose that the trend proves commas are not needed, or to suppose that the trend is in every instance right, is wrong. The teacher who tells students of the comma, "When in doubt, leave it out," is after all offering only a rule of thumb on the stipulation that they have first of all seen no reason for putting the comma in. The rule for sense supersedes all other rules. Thus one cannot learn the effective use of the comma without also learning something of ideas and how they fit together. Fundamentally, the comma *(a)* separates elements that have equal form or status in an utterance, *(b)* sets off elements that are subordinate to the main idea, *(c)* sets off elements that, although worthy in themselves, could be removed without damage to the main idea, and *(d)* separates elements that, if not separated, might be misread. The comma is also used conventionally for certain technical matters, such as grouping figures (1,000, etc.). In accordance with the four functions mentioned, use the comma:

1. To separate independent clauses that are linked by *and, or, nor, but, so, for,* or *yet.*

Sister Mary rapped quietly on the desk, and her pupils aligned themselves like filings near a magnet.
Swans glided toward our crumbs, but the quicker ducks got most of the food.

The comma is sometimes omitted when the clauses are very short.

We rang twice and the door swung open.

2. To separate words, phrases, or clauses in a series.

Words, phrases, or *clauses* may form a series.
He has distinguished himself *in poetry, in drama,* and *in criticism.*
Theirs is the toil, theirs is the blood, and *theirs is the victory.*

Some writers, particularly journalists, omit the comma between the last two items in a series. To omit the comma, however, often leads to distortion of meaning: "In his oddly manful squeak, T. R. advised all boykind: 'Don't flinch, don't foul and hit the line hard!'" (*Time,* February 7, 1964, p. 49). Did T. R. mean "don't ... hit the line"? The comma before *and* in a series should be omitted only when the last two items are to be understood to form a unit: "Give me *eggs, toast, coffee and cream.*"

3. To separate consecutive modifiers that apply to a single element.

His *broad, heavy* hand pushed against the wall.
Our little Swedish visitor has such a *shy, appealing* smile.

(Since no one would say, "Our little *and* Swedish visitor ... ," there is no comma between *little* and *Swedish.*)

4. To set off an introductory adverb clause.

While you're up, get me another toothpick.
If trouble develops in the lab, the alarm will sound automatically.
Although the sky is dark, no rain is expected.
Once we gain the summit, the view will prove worth the climb.

5. To set off an introductory verbal modifier.

Smashing a fist into the bag, Kayo gave the workout all the energy he had.
Taken at its best, the work of the young artist shows remarkable promise.
To protect his lead, Marsh took every turn at full throttle.

Introductory verbal phrases are not set off when they are not used as modifiers.

To protect his lead was Marsh's only thought.

6. To set off appositive (renaming element) that is not needed to *identify* what it renames.

Karl Pippin, *the boy who won the contest,* said he would enter again next year.
His father, *Major Pippin,* just laughed.
It was an astounding performance, *a masterpiece.*

7. To set off an adjective clause that could, without damage to the main, be omitted. Such nonessential clauses are also called NONRESTRICTIVE.

Karl, *who plays as well as most professionals,* has never had a lesson.
His games, *which always thrill the spectators,* are classics of form.
In Minneapolis, *where he was born,* they are already calling him "The Champ."

Adjective clauses *that could not be omitted without damage to the sense* are not enclosed or set off by commas (the italics here marking an example). Such essential clauses are also called RESTRICTIVE.

8. To set off an adverb clause that could, without damage to the meaning of the sentence, be omitted.

Wertz was ineligible, *since he had gained too much weight.*
Joe may be interested, *although golf is not his game.*
The third question, *while it lasted,* held the audience in suspense.

Adverb clauses that are essential to the import of the sentence are not enclosed or set off by commas: "The game will be canceled *if the rain persists*" (in which omission of the *if* clause would leave the statement not necessarily true); "Harry didn't lose his job *because he was inefficient*" (in which we are led to infer that he lost his job for some *other* reason).

9. To set off absolutes that substitute for adverb clauses.

The hour being later than midnight, she skipped.
The slipper falling from her foot, she limped toward the pumpkin coach.
The prince caught by her beauty, romance was inevitable.

10. To set off such transitions as *however, therefore, on the other hand, of course.*

We cannot, *of course,* ignore the possibility of engine failure. *On the other hand,* we should not exaggerate its likelihood. Let us, *therefore,* be calm.

11. To set off interjections and such absolutes as *yes* and *no.*

"*Oh,* you saw him yesterday?"
"*Yes,* I did. *Gosh,* did he look good!"
"*Well,* then he is fully recovered?"

12. To set off nouns of direct address.

"*Mother,* where are you?"
"Come out, *Jim,* and quit that idiotic hiding."
"Your friend Oliver is here to see you, *Son.*"

13. To set off such elements in written dialogue as *he said, she replied,* and *Johnny shouted.*

"Please come out," *his mother pleaded.*
"I don't want to see Oliver," *snarled Jim* from under the bed.
"Listen," *said Oliver,* "I brought you a new frog."

14. To take the place of an omitted verb in certain elliptical structures.

In the ballad the first and third lines have four feet; the second and fourth lines, three feet.

15. To avoid awkward run-on reading of words when misunderstanding might result.

Whatever *is, is* right.
In the *morning, glory* seems most glorious.
All over the *ground, squirrels* had disturbed the leaves.

16. To set off the salutation and complimentary close in a friendly, informal letter, and the complimentary close even in a business letter.

Examples: Dear Harry,   Sincerely,

17. To separate the two clauses of an "echo" question.

"Frank didn't have a chance, did he?"
"Drop in to see Aunt Ellen, will you?"

18. To set off an introductory prepositional phrase that is very long or that deserves special emphasis.

On the morning after his first visit to the downtown section of the biggest city in Brazil, Parker sat down to write.
In view of the time, it will be wise to adjourn.

19. To separate the elements in dates, titles, and geographical names.

Thursday, November 24, 1966.
Francis T. Harriman, director, personnel division.
Omaha, Nebraska.

20. To separate groups of figures.

Congress appropriated $14,657,330 for a new water project.

When commas are used with quotation marks, the comma always goes inside the end quotation mark:

"Just now," he said, "I had a twinge."
She had read "Il Penseroso," but not "L'Allegro."

Faulty use of the comma grows from negligence in observing the practice of effective writers and editors. For discussion of ways in which the comma is frequently misused, see COMMA FAULT and COMMA SPLICE.

comma fault   The use of a comma in a misleading way. The salt-and-pepper punctuator, uncertain of the sense-making sound, or INTONATION, is as likely to use a comma in the wrong place as to omit one from the proper place. A *comma fault* occurs when a comma is used where a clear reading of the sentence demands none.

Perhaps the most notorious of comma faults is the COMMA SPLICE—the use of only a comma between independent clauses, where a semicolon or period would give the reader an easier clue to sense.

Other comma faults are:

1. A single comma between subject and verb in a clause or sentence: "Several heavy *trunks, sat* on the dock." "The *man* in the gray flannel suit, suddenly *raised* his hand." (But a *pair* of commas may enclose parenthetical

matter between subject and verb: "Several heavy trunks, *each with a brass lock,* sat on the dock.")

2. A single comma between a verb and its object or other complement: "Jim dragged from under the bed, *a green frog.*" "What I want to know *is, the answer* to that first question." (Again, a *pair* of commas may enclose parenthetical matter; but the single comma is misleading.)

3. A single comma between *two* words or phrases that are joined by *and, or,* or *nor:* "We enjoy *Beethoven, and Brahms.* We first heard their music when we were *young, and impressionable.* That's when you either *like it, or leave it.*" (But if *three or more* such items are used in a series, commas would be proper: "We enjoy *Beethoven, Brahms, and the Beatles.*")

4. A comma that sets off a modifying clause or phrase that is essential to the full sense of its sentence: "There goes the policeman, *who stopped us last week.*" (The comma implies that the modifying clause is not needed, as if "There goes the policeman" would be clear enough by itself; but the statement would leave the reader asking, "What policeman?") Other examples of this comma fault: "I didn't eat, *because I was hungry.* I ate, *because everyone else did.*" "The little fellow, *in the red jacket,* has a cold." (In each example the comma misleads the reader.)

5. A comma that sets off a short introductory prepositional phrase: "*In the morning,* we awoke early." "Between meals, he eats like a horse." (The comma tends to overemphasize the prepositional phrase; it may be proper when such emphasis is wanted, or when the phrase is long and could become unwieldy.)

6. A comma that sets off an introductory verbal noun: "*Staying on the horse,* is the idea of the event." (This comma fault is the same as (1), but the careless writer may commit it believing that a comma is required after an introductory verbal phrase.)

comma splice   The result of the omission of a conjunction from a compound sentence so that the clauses have only a comma to separate them: "The day was stifling, we suffered for want of the old swimming hole." Considered an illiteracy by most teachers of formal writing, the comma splice can be corrected either by supplying the conjunction (in this case *and*) or by using a semicolon rather than the comma. An apparent comma splice, however, may actually be a deliberate omission of *and*—a practice now in some vogue among even skilled writers (see ASYNDETON). The omitted *and* produces, for these writers, an emphasis upon the close connection—whether of sequence or of BALANCE—between the ideas in the two clauses. Some examples: "There is no such thing as general education, there are only specific individual educations" (Howard Mumford Jones); "You circle in what seems an endless regular dance, you provide for us not only a place to live but also a magnificent spectacle for our enjoyment" (Joseph Wood Krutch); "They know it's a movie, they know it must be fake, still, they are weeping" (William Saroyan).

commedia dell'arte   Literally, "comedy of the profession." A kind of theatrical entertainment performed by troupes of professional actors. It was popular in Italy from the sixteenth through the eighteenth centuries and was characterized by pantomime, stock situations, and such stock characters as Harlequin,

Columbine, and Pantaloon. Some of the conventions of this art form originated in Attelan Comedy (as reflected in the *Fabulae Attelanae* of early
Rome)—such conventions, for example, as the stock plots, the *concetti* (stock
responses for certain emotions), and the *lazzi* (stock stage business). The
character Harlequin (compare English "harlequinade") usually wore a black
mask and a costume spangled with diamond-shaped patches of red, blue, and
green; he also carried a wooden sword, forerunner of the SLAPSTICK. His
sweetheart was the servant Columbine. None of the female characters wore a
mask, nor did those males assigned to more speaking than pantomiming. The
character Pedrolino, forerunner of the clown Pagliaccio and of the French
Pierrot, acted the part of a dreamer with a sad, whitened face. The character
Pulcinella, a villainous girl-chaser, was the forerunner of Punch in the English
Punch-and-Judy shows. Aside from the influence that the *commedia dell'arte*
had on later mimes, it proved to be the source of many character types
subsequently appearing in the comedy of HUMOURS. The commedia with certain
adaptations, including improvisation, is still kept alive today in several cities of
Europe, notably in Copenhagen's outdoor theater at the Tivoli Gardens.

REFERENCES: K. M. Lea, *The Italian Popular Comedy;* Pierre L. Ducharte, *The Italian
Comedy;* Allardyce Nicoll, *Masks, Mimes, and Miracles;* Giacomo Oreglia, *Commedia
dell'Arte.*

complication   In any RISING ACTION, the tension in a scene arises from the
conflict or prospective conflict between a character and various obstacles.
Often, in a given scene or episode this conflict is only partially resolved. In
Macbeth, for example, there is a partial resolution when Macbeth overcomes
the first obstacle, Duncan, by murdering him. But this solution is temporary
and incomplete, since Duncan's two sons, Malcolm and Donalbain, who are
sure to seek revenge, escape. This development is called a complication. A
similar complication arises when Macbeth kills Banquo, only to learn that
Banquo's son and avenger, Fleance, has fled. Each complication thus tends to
be more suspensive than its predecessor since it contributes to a cumulative
force (in *Macbeth,* the Battle of Birnam Wood).

Another kind of complication in the plot, or STORY-LINE, of fiction and
drama is a suspensive incident or development that confronts characters with
crucial decisions; for example, the unexpected return of the husband, Ford, in
The Merry Wives of Windsor; in Henry James's *Ambassadors,* Strether's
realization that he prefers to stay in Paris rather than return to America with
young Chad, although Strether had originally undertaken the mission in order
to win the hand of Chad's widowed mother, Mrs. Newsome.

REFERENCE: Caroline Gordon, *How to Read a Novel.*

comstockery   Moralistic CENSORSHIP, after Anthony Comstock (1844–1915).
Sometimes, the attitude that favors such censorship, whether or not it is
carried out—as in the suggestion by the Moral Majority in the 1980s that
television programs offensive to traditional morals should be boycotted or
banned. Compare BOWDLERIZED; see OBSCENITY.

REFERENCE: Elmer Davis, "The Comstock Lode," *Show Case.*

conceit   **1.** In general contemporary usage, egotism or exaggerated self-importance. **2.** In sixteenth- and seventeenth-century poetry (especially that of Shakespeare, Donne, and the METAPHYSICAL POETS), a fanciful notion; something *conceived,* or created, or "dreamed up" out of the imagination (for example, Donne's imagination of his own autopsy, in which the face of his lady would be discovered in his heart). **3.** Strained or farfetched imagery, for example, in *Romeo and Juliet,* I, iv, where Mercutio says to Romeo, "O, then I see Queen Mab hath been with you. / She is the fairies' midwife, and she comes / In shape no bigger than an agate stone / On the forefinger of an alderman / Drawn with a team of little atomies / Over men's noses as they lie asleep." See METAPHYSICAL POETS.

REFERENCE: K. K. Ruthven, *The Conceit.*

conclusion   **1.** In a SYLLOGISM, the third and last statement. **2.** In a composition, a formal close, now outmoded and to be distinguished from *conclusions,* which constitute the formal close of a scientific paper, study, or experiment. **3.** The third section of an oversimplified outline (Introduction, Body, Conclusion). **4.** In an informal essay—to say nothing of poetry, drama, and fiction—no formal conclusion is nowadays expected, as it often was in the past, when classicists demanded "a beginning, a middle, and an end." The modern essayist more often than not allows readers to draw their own conclusions.

concrete poetry   **1.** Loosely, any poetry emphasizing imagery as opposed to philosophic (i.e., abstract) statement. **2.** More specifically, poems whose arrangement on the page re-creates such concrete graphics as a Christmas tree, a cornucopia, a comma, a question mark, a lightning bolt, a wine goblet, a crucifix, or any other concrete configuration. In 1968 concrete poetry occupied an entire issue of the *Beloit Poetry Journal.*

REFERENCES: Mary Ellen Solt, ed., *Concrete Poetry;* Eugene Wildman, ed., *Anthology of Concretism;* Emmett Williams, ed., *An Anthology of Concrete Poetry.*

concrete universal   See ARCHETYPE and OBJECTIVE CORRELATIVE.

conditional syllogism   See SYLLOGISM 2.

confessional   Pertaining to any literary work that consciously or subconsciously reveals the writer's deepest convictions. Echoing Freud, Virginia Woolf observed, "Every secret of a writer's soul, experiences of his life, every quality of his mind is written large in his works."

confessional verse   Verse in which the poet painfully publicizes private aspects and episodes of personal experience, the self-expression serving as a kind of confession, therapy, or exorcism. Anglo-Saxon (*The Wanderer*) and medieval poets (Chaucer and Jean de Meun) used the confession as a device to reveal the feelings and beliefs of a character; confession made directly to the audience, without the use of a PERSONA, is observable mainly in such poets as Sylvia Plath, Anne Sexton, W. D. Snodgrass, and Robert Lowell (especially in the latter's "At the Altar"). Compare EXPRESSION and PROJECTIVE VERSE.

conflict   In drama and fiction, the impact of the PROTAGONIST, or hero, on antagonists or obstacles. See DRAMATIC STRUCTURE.

connotation   Whatever is *suggested* beyond what is actually said. "A violet by a mossy stone" *denotes* a certain kind of flower next to a stone and the colors violet and moss green. But the same phrase in the context of Wordsworth's poem "She Dwelt Among the Untrodden Ways" *suggests* such images and ideas as death, a shy and unaffected girl, and so on. Even out of context *slithers* connotes more than does *goes*: *slithers* suggests a snake or a snakelike movement. Connotations arise from experience, both individual and general (or widely shared) acquaintance with things and words. Every person, because of unique experience, has private associations with words—personal feelings about what they name—and these become part of the meaning of the words. And every person shares with society some associations with words—some connotations beyond the literal meanings. Semanticist S. I. Hayakawa (in *Language in Thought and Action*) has distinguished two sorts of connotation— *informative* and *affective*. Informative connotations include socially agreed upon definitions and denotations; affective connotations are the partly private, partly shared suggestions of words. It is affective connotation that makes *politician* quite different from *statesman,* or *slender* more complimentary than *thin*. Speakers and writers must attend to the connotations of their words if they are to communicate effectively, for affective connotations often speak louder than dictionary meanings do. Contrast DENOTATION; see also DICTION and TONE.

REFERENCES: Richard Altick, *Preface to Critical Reading;* Judson Jerome, *Poetry: Premeditated Art;* X. J. Kennedy, "Connotation and Allusion," *An Introduction to Poetry;* J. M. Morse, *The Irrelevant English Teacher.*

consonance   **1.** A sound-effect arising from repetition or close occurrence of consonants within words; for example, "an e*dg*er for fu*dg*e"; "li*k*e the sound of the ony*ch*a / When the pho*c*a has the pi*c*a" (Edith Sitwell). **2.** The occurrence of identical consonant sounds in stressed syllables whose vowel sounds differ; for example, "a *f*rai*l* a*ll*iance of *l*aughing *l*i*l*ies," in which the *f* and *l* sounds in words are repeated in an irregular pattern of initial, internal, and final position. It is the irregularity of position that distinguishes consonance from ALLITERATION, which is usually of initial sounds and need not be in stressed syllables. Some poets use consonance as a subtle variation from RHYME, as *air / fire* or *rule / sail*. Contrast ASSONANCE.

context   An oral or written continuum that is more meaningful as a whole than is any single fragment thereof. Thus "apple" has different meanings in the context of "apple of the King's eye" and in the context of "Adam and Eve ate the apple of knowledge," and still different meanings when by itself. Quoting out of context must be guarded against by both the transmitter and the receiver of a communication.

REFERENCES: Richard Altick, *Preface to Critical Reading;* Mortimer Adler, *How to Read a Book;* I. A. Richards, *How to Read a Page;* Donald Sears, *The Sentence in Context.*

contraposition   See SYLLOGISM 2.

contrast   Comparison of opposites often helps dramatically to clarify the attributes of a thing or one's attitudes toward a thing. Thus, *contrast* is among the major methods of EXPOSITION. Contrasts may be presented in brief or at length: in the two-word phrase (see OXYMORON) or in the full essay of extended contrast. Rhetorical forms employing contrast include (in addition to OXYMORON) PARADOX, ANTITHESIS, and CHIASMUS. In school and college examinations the word *contrast* (used as a verb) means to compare the differences between two or more particulars.

controlling question   See THESIS QUESTION.

controlling statement   See THESIS STATEMENT.

convention   1. In literature, any accepted practice, style, or structure; for example, invoking the blessings of a deity or muse, as did the writers of EPICS; using ALLITERATION rather than RHYME for poetry, as did the Anglo-Saxons; or furnishing COMEDY with a pair of minor as well as major lovers, as do most playwrights. **2.** More broadly, a climate of taste, manners, and morals. Thus, as reflected in medieval romances, knights and ladies practiced a set of conventions known as COURTLY LOVE. **3.** STYLE, as, for example, the BAROQUE styles and influences characterizing the arts, including literature, during most of the seventeenth to nineteenth centuries; hence a set of conventions adding up to a *tradition,* as in the PASTORAL tradition, the METAPHYSICAL tradition, and the like. The opposite of convention is *invention* or individual talent. T. S. Eliot argues, in his essay "Tradition and the Individual Talent," that a writer cannot fully realize the latter until the former has been absorbed.

REFERENCES: John Livingston Lowes, *Convention and Revolt in Poetry;* F. R. Leavis, *The Great Tradition;* Frederick A. Pottle, *The Idiom of Poetry;* Robert Hapgood, "Dramatic Conventions in *All's Well," PMLA* (March, 1964); Helen Trimpi, "Conventions in *Moby Dick," Southern Rev.* (Jan., 1971); C. E. Nelson and H. F. Salerno, eds., *Drama and Tradition;* M. Yetman, "Emily Dickinson . . . Romantic Tradition," *TSLL* (Spring, 1973).

coordination   The proper tying together of language elements that have equal rank. The underlying principle is that two or more things that are equal in relation to other elements must have equal form of grammar and syntax. Within a sentence the coordination of these equal-rank elements usually calls for such conjunctions as *and, or, nor, but;* or such conjunctive adverbs as *however, therefore, nevertheless.* Careful writers give equal form to coordinated elements even to the extent of not mixing active and passive voices, abstract and concrete ideas, or ideas from different spheres of thought. Faulty coordination occurs in these sentences: (1) "Oscar is *a European,* but Larry is *a college graduate*"; (2) "The moon *rose,* and the stars *were seen*"; (3) "He acquired *a bride* and *much happiness.*" See also BALANCE, ANTITHESIS, PARALLELISM, SYLLEPSIS, and ZEUGMA.

copyright   The exclusive right of the creator or author of an original literary or artistic work to benefit from its creation, either by publishing the work personally or by licensing publication. Two kinds of copyright are recognized— common-law copyright, which resides in the author before publication, and statutory copyright, which *may* reside in the author after publication if specific actions are taken in accordance with law. The term of statutory copyright in the United States is now governed by the Copyright Revision Act of 1976. For works copyrighted (published with notice of copyright) before 1978, the term is twenty-eight years, with renewal term of forty-seven years if renewed prior to the end of the initial term. For works copyrighted since the end of 1977, the term is the life of the author plus fifty years—and to the end of that last calendar year. Though it is not necessary to publish a work to establish copyright by common law, publication and notice of copyright do provide many protections. At publication—the offering of the work for sale to the public—the work *must* bear a notice of copyright. Placement of such notice varies for different kinds of work; for most literary works it must appear on the verso of the title page. The notice is usually worded (for the broadest possible protection): "Copyright" [or " © "], year of publication, and the name of the copyright holder, followed by the words "All rights reserved." Immediately after publication, two copies of the work, accompanied by a completed application for registration and the registration fee, must be deposited with the Register of Copyrights in the Library of Congress, Washington, D.C. 20559.

After expiration of copyright, the work passes into the "public domain"; that is, anyone may publish the work.

The aspiring writer should note these points: (1) In the quoting of passages from copyrighted works, the use of more than five hundred words (and sometimes less) from a single source requires the consent, or permission, of the publisher or author who holds an unexpired copyright. Often the payment of a fee is required, determined usually by the extent of the quotation. (In the case of poetry, permission should be sought if more than two lines are used.) (2) The mechanical reproduction of a copyrighted work in any way without permission of the copyright holder is an infringement of copyright. (3) Certain works cannot be copyrighted, including, specifically, the official publications or documents or papers of the United States government and its officers. (4) An author who circulates a manuscript among friends or who mechanically reproduces it for submission to publishers retains common-law copyright—so long as copies of the manuscript are not offered for sale to the public. Such manuscripts need not bear the usual copyright notice, but should perhaps carry a legend like this: "For confidential use only—not for circulation, distribution, or publication. All rights in this work are the property of...."

REFERENCES: Ronald F. Johnston, *Copyright Handbook;* Barbara A. Ringer and Paul Gitlin, *Copyrights.*

Corpus Christi Day   See HOLIDAYS.

counter words   Vague and general words used when the speaker or writer is too lazy to search out the more precise words. In current English every level of usage has its counter words, ranging from the handy but unimaginative terms of approval or disapproval in conversation (*fine, awful, fabulous*) to the catchall usage of the young (*like, far out*) and the empty echoes of the intellectuals (*adjusted, area, aspect, factor,* and anything ending with *-wise*). Counter words, akin to jargon and slang, lack the precision of the most useful jargon and the color of the best slang. When vagueness does no harm, counter words are appropriate enough; they are best avoided in serious writing.

couplet   1. Two rhyming lines of verse. 2. HEROIC COUPLETS are in iambic pentameter: "Know then thyself; presume not God to scan; / The proper study of mankind is Man" (Alexander Pope). See METER.

courtesy books   Renaissance etiquette books like the ones imported from Italy—e.g., Castiglione's *The Courtier* (1528). Courtesy books suggest what the gentleman should wear and how he should behave around ladies, horses, and fencing companions. After Sir Thomas Hoby's translation of Castiglione in 1561, Italian fashions, manners, and pastimes were reflected not only in the "Italianate gentleman," but also in plays that at first aped and later lampooned these conventions.

courtly love   A set of conventions in manners, morals, and pastimes of knights and ladies in medieval England and on the Continent, especially in Provence. These sports and pastimes are described and reflected in the works of Chrétien de Troyes (twelfth century), in the thirteenth-century love allegory *Roman de la Rose,* and in CHIVALRIC ROMANCE such as Chaucer's *Troilus and Criseyde* (1385), Malory's *Morte d'Arthur* (1471), Spenser's *Faerie Queene* (1590), and Tennyson's *Idylls of the King* (1859). Among the doctrines of courtly love were humility, courtesy, adultery (for the lady was usually married), chivalry, and the religion of love. See CHIVALRIC ROMANCE, METRICAL ROMANCE, and CASUISTRY.

REFERENCES: C. S. Lewis, *The Allegory of Love;* Sidney Painter, *French Chivalry;* Jean Froissart, *Chronicles;* W. C. Miller, *A Knight's Life in the Days of Chivalry;* Andreas Capellanus, *The Art of Courtly Love;* F. X. Newman, *The Meaning of Courtly Love;* Wallace Fowlie, *Love in Literature;* N. R. Shapiro and J. B. Wadsworth, eds., *The Comedy of Eros.*

craft cycle plays   A series of plays presenting the story, or cycle, of Christian history from the Creation to the Last Judgment; also known as mystery plays because they dramatized events of Christian history that could not be explained but had to be taken on faith. These plays were enacted on Corpus Christi day during the fourteenth, fifteenth, and sixteenth centuries by members of local craft guilds in various English towns. The most complete surviving cycle, a series of forty-eight plays, is from the town of York. The Wakefield cycle (also called the Towneley plays because the scripts were kept at Towneley Hall) consists of thirty-two plays, five of which are variations of York plays. Other plays exist from the towns of Coventry and Chester. Each play was performed on its own pageant, or wagon-stage—an ark on wheels for the play of Noah, a garden of gilded trees perhaps for Paradise, a gaping gargoyle mouth issuing smoke and flame for the entrance to Hell. The use of very literal props and settings provided opportunities for the guilds producing the plays to show off their particular crafts. Thus, the armourers traditionally produced the expulsion of Adam and Eve from Paradise, which called for a two-edged sword; the chandlers were charged with the Shepherd's play with its dazzling star of Bethlehem; the bakers prepared quite an edible Last Supper. The plays are simply constructed, each composed of two or three scenes, with extraneous details either reported or remembered. As the audience surely knew the outcome of these scenes, having heard the stories many times in church, their enjoyment consisted partly in the DRAMATIC IRONY of knowing what was going to happen.

The authors of the English cycle plays are unknown to us, but the evidence in the plays shows these authors to have been well-read, witty, sensitive to what would make "good theatre" and that at least one of them was a master of versification. There are twenty-two different stanzaic forms in the forty-eight plays comprising the York cycle, all employing the same northern dialect. Many of these stanza forms are French, handled with skill and sophistication. Some are in the English tradition of ACCENTUAL VERSE, and are heavily alliterative. Other plays are in metrical verse, but still somewhat alliterative. Here is an example of this sort of stanza from Play No. VII, on the sacrifice of Cain and Abel:

> *Angel*   Thowe cursyd Cayme, where is Abell?
> Where hais thowe done thy broder dere?
> *Cayme*   What askes thowe me that taill to tell?
> For yit his keper was I nere.
> *Angel*   God hais sent thee his curse downe,
> Fro hevyn to hell, *maldictio dei.*
> *Cayme*   (hitting the angel) Take that thyself, evyn on thy crowne,
> *Quia non sum custos fratris mei,* To tyne.
> *Angel*   God hais sent thee his malyson.
> And inwardly I geve thee myne.

REFERENCES: (For more general references regarding medieval religious drama, see MIRACLE PLAYS.) H. F. Westlake, *The Parish Guilds of Medieval England;* Martial Rose, ed., *The Wakefield Mystery Plays;* Lucy T. Smith, ed., *York Mystery Plays;* E. K. Chambers, *The Medieval Stage.*

cretic   See METER.

crisis   In fiction and drama a crucial moment in a scene or in the entire work in which the PROTAGONIST faces a dilemma and must make a decision. In Ibsen's *A Doll's House* the crisis of one scene is Torvald's reading of the letter incriminating his wife, Nora; in the play the chief crisis (the CLIMAX) comes just at the moment before Nora decides to leave Torvald, to walk out of the doll's house forever.

critic   A writer who evaluates literature and other works of art. The German playwright Gotthold Lessing observed that "Critics create rules, and artists create literature." While it is true that artists create literature, most critics do not create rules, but rather try to discover in masterworks the rules by which artists have been consciously or unconsciously guided. Critics thus serve not only as evaluators, but also—and perhaps primarily—as interpreters. They also enrich our understanding of a difficult work, or jog us into re-examining our own notions about it. The fact that a critic spends time (sometimes a lifetime) studying, interpreting, and writing about certain works implies immediately that these works must be valuable. See NEW CRITICS.

Among the world's great critics and their masterpieces of criticism have been Plato (ca. 427–347 B.C.), *The Republic;* Aristotle (384–322 B.C.), *The Poetics;* Horace (65–8 B.C.), *The Art of Poetry;* Longinus (ca. 213–272), *On the Sublime;* Dante (1265–1321), *The Banquet;* Sidney (1554–86), *An Apology for Poetry;* Corneille (1606–84), *On the Three Unities;* Dryden (1631–1700), *An Essay of Dramatic Poesy;* Pope (1688–1744), *An Essay on Criticism;* Johnson (1709–84), *Preface to Shakespeare;* Buffon (1707–88), *Discourse on Style;* Lessing (1729–81), *Laocoön;* Goethe (1749–1832), *Conversations with Eckermann;* Coleridge (1772–1834), *Biographia Literaria;* Shelley (1792–1822), *A Defence of Poetry;* Sainte-Beuve (1804–69), *What Is a Classic?;* Poe (1809–49), *The Poetic Principle;* Flaubert (1821–80), *The Correspondence;* Arnold (1822–88), *The Function of Criticism;* Henry James (1843–1916), *The Art of Fiction;* Croce (1866–1952), *Aesthetics;* Eliot (1888–1964), *Essays;* and Edmund Wilson (1895–1972), *Axel's Castle.*

criticism   The interpretation, comparison, and evaluation of literary works. *Theoretical criticism* discovers and establishes principles and standards of excellence. *Practical criticism,* applying those principles, interprets ("explicates") a particular work, or judges it, or does both. *Impressionistic criticism* is concerned with how a critic feels about or responds to a given work. *Schools of criticism* include the *New Criticism* (see NEW CRITICS); *Freudian criticism,* devoted to psychoanalytic problems of interpretation; and *Marxian criticism,* devoted to socioeconomic problems of interpretation. For an entertaining comparison of these and other schools of literary criticism, read F. C. Crews, *The Pooh Perplex.* See STRUCTURALISM.

REFERENCES: I. A. Richards, *Practical Criticism;* David Daiches, *Critical Approaches to Literature;* J. H. Smith and E. W. Parks, eds., *The Great Critics;* Lawrence Hall, *A Grammar of Literary Criticism;* Northrop Frye, *Anatomy of Criticism;* Stanley Edgar Hyman, ed., *Burke's Terms for Order;* Walter Sutton and Richard Foster, eds., *Modern Criticism.*

cumulative sentence   A sentence whose introductory clause has been enriched ("rendered") by the addition ("cumulation") of concrete details, usually in the form of absolute and participial phrases. An example: "The fall came early that year, the trees turning bare overnight, their yellow leaves scattered by the winds." The last two phrases, grammatically absolute, the second riding piggyback on the first, spell out rhetorically what the initial clause introduces only skeletally. Such cumulative spelling out is also known as RENDERING, and if the concrete details succeed in re-creating in the reader the emotion felt or intended by the writer, they are called OBJECTIVE CORRELATIVES. In the specimen sentence above, the intended emotion is no doubt depression as contrasted with the exhilaration that might have been evoked with some such add-on phrase as "the leaves turning flame red." Like the LOOSE SENTENCE, which can be terminated after its initial clause, the cumulative sentence is the opposite of the PERIODIC SENTENCE. Yet to terminate an intended cumulative sentence prematurely is to diminish the writer's power of re-creating personal emotions in the reader.

REFERENCE: Francis Christensen, *Notes toward a New Rhetoric.*

cycle plays   See CRAFT CYCLE PLAYS.

D

dactyl In verse, a word or word-group consisting of one heavily stressed syllable followed by two lightly stressed syllables; e.g., *murmuring*. See METER.

Dadaism An aesthetic movement characterized by antirational, nonsensical, and often outrageous improvisations in literature, music, and artifacts (for example, utilizing balloons and bedpans) in protest against war and other insane behavior. The movement was started in Zurich in 1916 by the Romanian expatriate Tristan Tzara and the Alsatian Hans Arp. A few years later Tzara took it to Paris, where it captivated rebellious young poets and artists from several other cities in Europe. The Dadaists published handbills, manifestos, and little magazines—among them *Dada,* the title connoting "nonsense" or "nothing" (compare NIHILISM). The chief contributors, besides Tzara, included André Breton, Louis Aragon (inventor of the "Glass Syringe"), and Phillipe Soupalt (inventor of the "Musical Urinal"). They gave concerts, exhibits, and lectures, which elicited the ridicule of establishment critics. During the 1920s, with the ascendancy of André Breton, who had published his own *Manifesto* (1924), the movement merged with SURREALISM. Compare CAMP and IMMEDIATE THEATER.

REFERENCES: Tristan Tzara, "Memoirs of Dadism," in Edmund Wilson, *Axel's Castle;* Malcolm Cowley, *Exile's Return;* Manuel Grossman, *Dada;* Robert Motherwell, ed., *Dada Painters and Poets: An Anthology;* Mary Ann Caws, *The Poetry of Dada and Surrealism;* Joseph Slate, "Kora in Opacity: Williams' Improvisations," *Journal of Modern Literature* (May, 1971); Roger Shattuck, "The D-S Expedition," *New York Review* (May 18, 1972).

dangler In a sentence, a modifier lacking its intended substantive. No fault of sentence structure is more notorious. The chief types:

1. *Dangling participle:* "*Sitting up in the stands,* our team looked pretty flashy." (Was the team sitting in the stands?) "*Aroused* from my slumber, my day was ruined." (Was my day aroused from slumber?)

2. *Dangling gerund:* "After *taking* the exam, our grade average improved." (Did the grade average take the exam?)

3. *Dangling infinitive phrase:* "*To lose weight,* starches should be avoided." (Are the starches expected to lose weight?)

4. *Dangling prepositional phrase:* "*At the age of nine* my father took me on an African safari." (A nine-year-old father?)

5. *Dangling elliptical clause:* "*Although wealthy,* nobody would honor his check." (Who was wealthy? Nobody?) The construction is called an elliptical clause because subject and verb have been elided: "Although [he was]

wealthy...." (When the subject and verb are supplied, there is no dangler.) See also ELISION.

Repairing a dangler is not difficult. Usually the repair can be accomplished in either of two ways: *(a)* by making a full clause of the dangling phrase: "*From where we were sitting in the stands,* our team looked pretty flashy"; "*After we took the exam,* our grade average improved"; "*When I was nine years old,* my father took me on an African safari"; or *(b)* by supplying for the main clause a subject that is properly modified by the phrase in question: "To lose weight, *you* should avoid starches"; "Although wealthy, *he* could find no one to honor his check."

Dartmouth Conference   Also known as the Anglo-American Seminar, a meeting of British and American teachers and professors of English at Dartmouth College, New Hampshire, in 1966 for an exchange of experience and opinion on improving the language arts curriculum in the schools and colleges. Thanks to the Dartmouth Conference the idea and practice of "creative writing" and ROLE PLAYING have come to be increasingly re-examined.

REFERENCES: Herbert Muller, *The Uses of English;* John Dixon, *Growth through English;* Lois Josephs, "A Disciplined Approach to Creative Writing," *English Journal* (October, 1962); Geoffrey Summerfield, ed., *Creativity in English;* Gary Tate and E. P. J. Corbett, eds., *Teaching High School Composition;* J. N. Hook, *Writing Creatively;* Walker Gibson, *Persona.*

Darwinism, social Darwinism   **1.** The processes of "natural selection" and "survival of the fittest" (Herbert Spencer's phrase). **2.** The dog-eat-dog behavior dramatized in novels and plays that reflect the vision of life known as NATURALISM—the novels of Zola, for example, and the plays of O'Neill.

REFERENCES: Richard Hofstadter, *Social Darwinism in American Thought;* Philip Appleman, ed., *Darwin: Texts, Backgrounds ... Critical Essays;* Irving Stone, *The Origin.*

dash   Like other marks of punctuation, the dash (—) is not to be sprinkled upon the page—though many untutored writers use it slapdash, letting it fall wherever they are not quite sure what punctuation is needed. Properly used, the dash helps to organize thoughts and display them effectively; it separates, it emphasizes, it lends suspense or irony, it lends informality, it lends—dash.

Properly, the dash is used:

1. To set off an appositive when commas would not do enough and parentheses would do too much: "Brucie growled back at all the animals—lions, leopards, llamas, and lynxes."

2. To mark a suspension of thought, whether the thought simply stops unfinished, takes off on a new tack, or continues with some repetition or twist: "Ah, I see you've—."

"Arrived early? Yes, I wanted to be sure—well, you know how it is."

"Of course, I've done it myself often--more often than you'd guess."

3. To enclose parenthetical matter when commas would lack the desired emphasis or would cause difficulty in reading: "Men—not children—are what this work requires." "Those piercing eyes—hard, sharp, unrelenting—were unforgettable."

4. To set off a summarizing clause that follows a listing of things in apposition: "Clarity, economy, variety—these are marks of style." "He had dawdled, he had delayed, he had put off, he had procrastinated—in short, he hadn't done the assignment."

5. To create a feeling of suspense before a sudden revelation or afterthought: "The choice at last was—Mozart!" "Drop that revolver—or else!"

6. After a quotation, to set off the title or the name of the author: "If music be the food of love, play on!"—*Twelfth Night*.

Dashes do not usually appear next to commas, semicolons, colons, or periods. When the dash is used, other marks—even those that might otherwise be expected—are ordinarily omitted. Sometimes even a terminal period is omitted when a dash shows a suspended thought: "Please, Uncle Sam, I'd rather—" (What follows then begins a new paragraph.)

dead metaphor   See FADED METAPHOR.

deadwood   Whatever can be removed from a statement without altering its meaning or reducing the effectiveness of style; it is sometimes called *redundancy*. Deadwood repeats ideas in different words (as in *pleonasm* and *tautology*), or it labors the obvious (as in the several forms of *verbosity*: *circumlocution, periphrasis, prolixity, verbiage*).

1. *Pleonasm* repeats what is implicit by adding a word or phrase that could be cut away:

as of yet	later *on*
both alike	*make a* study *of*
chairman *in charge*	*make a* survey *of*
continue *on*	near*by* the lake
defeated *by a score of 2-1*	*new* beginner
equally as	*old* adage
fall *down*	oldest *one of them all*
first *of all*	*only* just arrived
Ford *car*	*past* experience
have *got*	*past* history
his *or her*	plan *on*
inside *of*	raise *up*
invited guests	rarely *ever*
invited *to attend*	*take a* look at
	in *the area of*

2. *Tautology* repeats what is explicit, as if the writer were unaware of the import of the words:

adequate *enough*	*needed* prerequisites
and etc.	now *at this time*
bibliography *of books*	petite *little* girl
combines *together*	red *in color*
consecutive times *in a row*	*round* circle
consensus *of opinion*	short *in length*
I nodded *my head*	I waved *my hand*
different varieties	square *shape*
few *in number*	*still* persists
gathered *together*	vocabulary *words*
heavy *in weight*	*wild* savage
modern times of today	*youthful* teen-ager
necessary requirements	

3. *Circumlocution* is "talking around" a topic. Words dilute the thought by *overphrasing* (expanding a word into a phrase):

was		acted as
many		a number of
now		at the present time
when		at which time
named		by the name of
meet	BECOMES	come in contact with
because		due to the fact that
stated		made a statement
by		on the part of
visited		paid a visit to
appear		put in an appearance

or by *overpredication* (expanding words and phrases into clauses):

library books	books *that are* in the library
classes in session	classes *that are* in session
teacher in charge	teacher *who is* in charge
broken window	window *that is* broken

4. *Periphrasis* is a form of circumlocution, but more thoughtfully used and often allowable. It uses indirect forms of expression, often wordier than the direct. As a device of EUPHEMISM, periphrasis may be defended on grounds of courtesy ("members of the Jury" instead of "Jurors") or on grounds of effectiveness of rhythm ("the house of Mr. Pennington" instead of "Mr. Pennington's house"—and other such PERIPHRASTIC GENITIVES). Unfortunately, periphrasis has recently become one mark of OFFICIALESE and GOBBLEDYGOOK.

5. *Prolixity* is the tedious proliferation of detail. Not content with getting to the point, the prolix writer or speaker must make the point abundantly clear—and often wanders into the irrelevant. Someone who can't tell about a vacation without supplying the exact dates and times of arrival and the names of the bellhops is prolix.

6. *Verbiage* is words that say nothing—a sort of meaningless prattle.

Deadwood is not the same as REPETITION, though some forms of deadwood are indeed repetitive. While repetition often reinforces utterance, deadwood weakens. By violating the principle of ECONOMY, deadwood taxes a reader's patience—and often so dilutes a thought that it precludes communication. An occasional bit of deadwood will not offend; but a pervasive wordiness does. Speech will bear more deadwood than writing, since the ear is less attentive than the eye and less readily absorbs lean sentences.

decadence   1. In literary criticism, a relaxing of critical standards—especially the standards upheld by the critics in fashion. 2. The moral and economic deterioration of once socially prominent families, as depicted in the fiction of Faulkner and Steinbeck and in the plays of Tennessee Williams. 3. The literary movement of the DECADENTS.

Decadents, the   A late nineteenth- and early twentieth-century group of French and English writers who revolted against many a CONVENTION, regarded art as its own reward, and developed a cult of necro-aesthetics—of finding beauty in death, decay, and evil. (Baudelaire's *Flowers of Evil* is a representative work by one of its devotees.) In France the group included Verlaine, Rimbaud, and Baudelaire. In England four of the Decadents were Oscar Wilde, Ernest Dowson, Aubrey Beardsley, and Frank Harris. See FIN DE SIÈCLE.

REFERENCES: Frank Harris, *Oscar Wilde;* G. L. Roosbroeck, *Legend of the Decadents;* H. Jackson, *The 1890s;* Yvor Winters, *Primitivism and Decadence;* Oscar Cargill, "The Decadents," *Intellectual America;* Graham Hough, *The Last Romantics;* Enid Starkie, *Baudelaire;* P. Jullian, *Dreamers of Decadence;* Richard Gilman, *Decadence: The Strange Life of an Epithet;* Karl Beckson, ed., *Aesthetics and Decadents of the 1890s.*

decorum   Appropriateness or consistency. See UNITIES.

deductive reasoning   Reasoning from the general to the specific; a form of logical argument beginning with a generalization and leading to an assertion of its application to special or particular cases. Deduction follows rigid forms and rules prescribed to ensure the validity of the conclusion. The formal deductive argument is the SYLLOGISM, which has four chief forms: the *categorical,* the *conditional,* the *alternative,* and the *disjunctive.* Each of these forms, in turn, has its own rules for validity. Each, when valid, produces a conclusion that is absolute and certain—not just a probability. Contrast INDUCTIVE REASONING.

REFERENCES: Jeremy Pitt and Russell E. Leavenworth, *Logic for Argument;* John Sherwood, *Handbook of Logic and Semantics.*

deep image   Just as contemporary grammarians (especially transformationists) speak of "deep structure" beneath the surface features of an utterance, so certain contemporary poets and critics (among them May Swenson and Robert Bly) speak of images that come from the poet's subconscious and from SURREALISM. These images, even when translated into recognizable levels of meaning, retain a mysterious, universal, archetypal quality. Such images may be found in the surrealist poems of May Swenson, as, for example, in "Sightseeing in Provincetown": "If your elbow were an eagle's head / and your loins / the mouth of a cat / its tongue / many ripped tongues of flame...." See SURREALISM and PROJECTIVE VERSE.

defining   Explaining the meanings of words or the nature of concepts or processes. Defining is a refined logical process at least on the formal level. The student who hopes to understand the dictionary or to make terms clear needs to be aware of several kinds of defining—and of some of the pitfalls. Definitions are essentially *ad hoc;* that is, they define for a given purpose or situation. Thus one cannot assume that a definition can apply always and everywhere. We define in several ways: (1) by *showing* or *pointing* (ostensive definition): "*This* is a horse"; (2) by citing *examples:* "The *moon* and *Sputnik* are satellites"; (3) by listing *properties:* "A paddle is a *small, rounded, flat* piece of wood *with a handle*"; (4) by telling what something *does* (operational definition): "The heart *pumps* blood to the arteries"; (5) by citing *purpose:* "Compass: an instrument *for ascertaining direction*"; (6) by citing *process from origin:* "Coffee is a beverage made from the roasted and ground seeds of beans found in the fruit of a tropical evergreen shrub...."; (7) by citing *cause:* "Steam is the gas or vapor into which *water is changed by boiling.*" And occasionally we define (8) by *stipulation,* usually only for the purposes of a given discourse: "By *recall* we shall mean *restoration.*" In stipulative definition both writer and reader agree that the term defined probably means something else in another context.

The following are major guidelines in defining:

A definition should be clearer than the term being defined: its terms must be better known than the term in question, and without obscurity or AMBIGUITY; a definition should thus avoid repeating the term being defined. "Truth is the quality of being true" is not a useful definition. Compare BEGGING THE QUESTION 3.

A definition should be positive, saying what a word *means* or a thing *is,* not what it does *not mean* or *is not,* although such a dimension may be a useful *additive,* as Richard Ohmann has observed.

A definition should be properly limited: it should include all that lies within the limits of what is defined, but nothing outside those limits.

deism   The conviction of those who, while believing in a Creator, reject the possibility of direct communication between Him and His creatures. As opposed to revealed religion, deism is also called "natural religion" and RATIONALISM. It flourished during the Enlightenment. It was the belief of Voltaire and of several eighteenth-century British writers, notably Edward Gibbon, and of such Americans as Thomas Paine, Benjamin Franklin, Thomas Jefferson, George Washington, and Abraham Lincoln.

REFERENCE: Ernst Cassirer, *Philosophy of the Enlightenment.*

denotation   The specific meaning of a word, or the object (the referent) that the word names, is the *denotation* of that word. The denotation of a word, of course, depends always upon context; in one context *dog* may refer to Fido; in another, *dog* may refer to a despicable person. Concrete nouns are thought of as having denotations. In this sense denotation is one kind of extensional meaning. Compare CONNOTATION.

REFERENCE: Richard Altick, *Preface to Critical Reading.*

dénouement   Literally, "unraveling" or resolution; the end of a comedy or story, in which every character, even the most minor, and every complication, even in a subplot, is accounted for. Thus, by the end of Act V in *The Tempest,* not only are the major conspirators against Prospero exposed, with their conflicts resolved, and the lovers Ferdinand and Miranda engaged, but also the problems of such comparatively minor characters as Stephano, Trinculo, Caliban, and Ariel are disposed of or set right.

dependence   See INFLUENCE.

depth psychology   See PSYCHOANALYSIS.

depth reading   **1.** In expository prose, reading for meaning beyond what is said in so many words; "reading between the lines"; understanding most of the total context of a literary work as well as just parts or details; identifying the writer's ASSUMPTIONS and implications. (See Mortimer Adler, *How to Read a Book,* and I. A. Richards, *How to Read a Page.*) **2.** In BELLES LETTRES, a kind of intellectual skindiving beneath the surface (the manifest STORY-LINE) for an examination of secondary, tertiary, and other currents of meaning, based strictly, however, on actual images and symbols floating in the diver's view; understanding the place that the work has in the artist's vision of life. In Emily Dickinson's poem "Bring Me the Sunset in a Cup," for example, the first-stanza line, "Tell me how far the morning leaps," can be read superficially to mean the speaker's request for a report from the reader. A depth reading reveals that "tell" is a challenge (almost impossible to fulfill) that has been used in the bank-teller sense of "counting"; that the speaker, the banker, may be God, or Zeus, or even the poet herself as a trustee on the board of the Nature Savings and Loan Association; that the person addressed may be Ganymede or a kind of sexton in the halls of heaven. In this context the imperatives ("Bring me ..." "Tell me ..." "Reckon ...") turn out to be not only "dares" but also arguments that one cannot measure Nature's aesthetic riches. See EXPLICATION DE TEXTE.

REFERENCES: I. A. Richards, *Practical Criticism;* Ezra Pound, *ABC of Reading;* Stanley R. Hopper and David L. Miller, eds., *Interpretation: The Poetry of Meaning;* Edgar Roberts, *Writing Themes about Literature.*

description   One of the four forms of discourse, description sets out to make a reader or listener see, hear, feel, taste, and smell something—at least in the imagination. At its best it does not talk about, but rather re-creates, sensory experience. Compare RENDERING.

Seldom appearing as an end in itself, or in its pure form, description usually serves to orient a NARRATIVE or realize its characters, to lend detail to an EXPOSITION, to support some bit of ARGUMENTATION. In contemporary writing description is usually unobtrusive; it is not presented in long, concentrated passages, but unfolded bit by bit.

Good description is never random. It is always guided by a purpose, controlled by some clear order; it is rarely without specific sensory detail and freshness of diction. Lack of purpose, order, detail, and style will make a description both useless and dull—the "part most likely to be skipped." More than any of the other forms of discourse, description concerns itself with what exists physically, concretely—with people, places, objects. Good description takes pains "to distinguish a particular cab-driver from the cabbies around him," as Flaubert observed.

Differing methods and purposes lead writers to take several approaches to description: scientific, literary, and journalistic.

Scientific description is objective, thorough, precise. It measures, analyzes, and classifies accurately, deliberately avoiding attitude or bias. It uses literal (and therefore often abstract) words, but never vague words. Compare operational DEFINING.

Literary description is guided by a special purpose: the mood, the theme, or the thesis of the work in which it appears. It is subjective, attempting to re-create not merely what is to be seen, but also the attitudes through which the writer wishes it seen. It seeks to emphasize an impression and leave the reader with that impression unmistakably. Thus, literary description is highly selective: the writer selects those details of a subject that will enhance that impression, and omits or subordinates other details. Literary description is often as much figurative as literal in its choice of words: it draws upon SIMILE and METAPHOR, and deploys words for their connotative values.

Journalistic description combines some of the methods of both other kinds. Like scientific description, its purpose is to inform, to be accurate, to be unbiased. Yet, like literary description, it selects details that point toward a dominant impression, interprets through attitude (though a general and unbiased one), and employs much FIGURATIVE LANGUAGE to bring the subject into the reader's experience.

REFERENCES: Walker Gibson, *Seeing and Writing;* Hart Leavitt and David Sohn, *Stop, Look, and Write!*; John Nist, *Speaking into Writing.*

detective story   A short story or novel in which the detective, given certain clues, solves a baffling murder case in suspensive steps that reverse the actual sequence of events. Almost always eccentric and usually male, the detective is likeable either because of or in spite of his snobbishness, astuteness, or naiveté, and his exploits are usually demonstrated in sequel after sequel. He is usually portrayed as a virtuoso not only in his main profession of sleuthing but also as a hobbyist (e.g., as violinist or chef). Standard minor characters include an assistant or secretary and a police inspector. (In some detective stories an inspector is the hero.) Among other conventions of this genre is the climactic assembly of suspects, including the inevitable butler, wherein the detective explains how the crime was committed, and the motives for it, and finally reveals the identity of the murderer. (When one or another of the features described above is missing—especially if the crime is not murder—the work is regarded less a detective story than a "mystery.") Often laced with wit and exotic settings, detective stories have attracted many an intellectual reader, although Edmund Wilson, the intellectual's intellectual, has derogated the genre.

The most celebrated detectives include Edgar Allan Poe's Auguste Dupin, Arthur Conan Doyle's Sherlock Holmes, G. K. Chesterton's Father Brown, Agatha Christie's Hercule Poirot and Miss Marple, Frederic Dannay and Manfred Lee's Ellery Queen, Dorothy Sayers' Lord Peter Wimsey, E. D. Biggers' Charlie Chan, Rex Stout's Nero Wolfe, Leslie Charteris's The Saint, Dashiell Hammet's Sam Spade, S. S. Van Dine's Philo Vance.

Writers of mystery and espionage fiction include Graham Greene, Ian Fleming, Lee Deighton, John Le Carré, and Georges Simenon.

REFERENCES: Jacques Barzun and W. H. Taylor, *A Catalogue of Crime;* Howard Haycraft, ed., *Murder for Pleasure;* J. D. Carr, *Life of Sir Arthur Conan Doyle;* John McAleer, *Rex Stout;* Anthony Boucher, *Ellery Queen: A Double Portrait.*

determinism   The philosophic and literary position that every event is the inevitable result of (unalterable) antecedents and that human choice is predetermined by heredity and environment; the opposite of "free will." (Compare FATALISM and CALVINISM.) Thomas Hardy's novels are said to be deterministic or fatalistic in this sense. Compare NATURALISM.

REFERENCE: Jacques Loeb, *The Mechanistic Conception of Life.*

deus ex machina   Literally, "god out of a machine." In Greek drama, a device by which a mythological god descends to rescue the hero, as happens in Euripides' *Orestes,* when "the god Apollo suddenly appears *ex machina* above the palace" and commands Orestes *to marry* Hermione instead of *killing* her. This is such an unconvincing solution that the device has since been avoided by most writers, except those of MELODRAMA. Critics use the term to derogate shoddy plot construction.

dialectic   **1.** Broadly, the art of argumentation or debate. **2.** In classical literature, especially in Plato's *Dialogues,* the tradition of the perennial debate or "continuing conversation"; that is, of forever open, unsettled issues and polarities such as "good vs. evil," "the individual vs. society," and so on.

REFERENCES: Robert Hutchins, *The Great Conversation;* Mortimer Adler, *Great Ideas from the Great Books;* Steve Allen, *Meeting of Minds.*

3. In philosophy, especially Hegel's, a systematic analysis of an idea or problem in the order of *(a) thesis, (b) antithesis,* and *(c) synthesis,* on the assumption that life's contradictions can be resolved. Thus, for example, if "capitalism" were the *thesis,* and "socialism" the *antithesis,* then "cooperative ownership" might be a *synthesis.*

REFERENCES: G. W. F. Hegel, *The Science of Logic;* Norman O. Brown, "Instinctual Dialectics," *Life Against Death;* William Bache, *Measure for Measure as Dialectical Art;* W. D. Shaw, *The Dialectical Temper* [in Browning].

4. In RHETORIC, an adaptation of **(3)** in which the writer starts with a thesis statement, then qualifies it with an opposing (if minor) objection or two, then arrives at a compromise, which is nevertheless close to the original thesis.

REFERENCES: Sheridan Baker, *The Practical Stylist;* Leslie Fiedler and Jacob Vinocur, eds., *The Continuing Debate;* Robert Knoll, ed., *Contrasts.*

dialogue   **1.** A synonym of DIALECTIC or discussion; some reconciliation between antagonistic views may or may not emerge. ("Progress in civilization sometimes emerges out of intelligent dialogue between opposing powers.") **2.** In fiction and narrative verse, the speeches of the characters. **3.** In drama, the same as in (2), but also the chief means by which the development of plot is communicated. (See MONOLOGUE and SOLILOQUY.) Unlike real-life conversation, literary dialogue is organized toward a purpose and thus usually presents a controlled conflict of ideas in a directed sequence. Effective dialogue develops plot or characterization or both. Except by design (for example, in the plays of Pinter, who deliberately uses small-talk and simulated silences), dialogue is generally free of the deadwood of real-life conversation and comes in brief give-and-take installments, in a kind of ping-pong effect (STICHOMYTHY). In the dialogue of fiction, good writers tend to use the simple "he said" and "she said" forms in preference to more elaborate forms like "asserted," "exclaimed," "expostulated," "gasped," and the like. **4.** A specific genre, as in *The Dialogues of Plato* and certain interviews called "Conversations," in which literary celebrities talk informally with editors and other literary persons.

REFERENCES: *The Dialogues of Archibald MacLeish and Mark Van Doren; Writers at Work,* The Paris Review Series; Rozanne Knudson, "Conversation with May Swenson," *Quartet* (Winter, 1969); W. C. Knott, "Dialogue," *The Craft of Fiction;* Ruby Cohn, *Dialog in American Drama.*

diary   A JOURNAL or day-by-day record of the writer's experiences. Most diaries are kept for personal satisfaction, and are not intended to be published. Among the diaries that did get published whether or not in accordance with the authors' intentions, perhaps the most famous are those of John Evelyn (the 1600s), Samuel Pepys (from 1659), William Byrd (from 1700), Sarah Knight (from 1704), Eugene Delacroix (from 1822), Robert Kilvert (1870–79), and Anne Frank (1942–44).

dicho   An expression that lends itself to its *vice versa* with little loss of general truth. For example, "Creativity is the enemy of old age." "Old age is the enemy of creativity." Ernest Hemingway is said to have been fond of inventing *dichos.* Compare PALINDROME.

REFERENCES: A. E. Hotchner, *Papa Hemingway;* Carlos Baker, *Hemingway, The Writer as Artist.*

diction   Choice and arrangement of words. The diction of speech or writing contributes importantly to TONE and STYLE. The chief mark of "good diction" is appropriateness to the author's purpose. Good diction is also consistent, avoiding mixtures of JARGON with standard vocabulary or of informal with formal expressions, unless deliberately.

REFERENCES: Thomas Quayle, *Poetic Diction;* Barnet Kottler and Martin Light, *The World of Words;* Hans Guth, *Words and Ideas.*

dictionaries   Word-books that furnish such information as definitions, spellings, pronunciations, derivations, usage statuses (formal, colloquial, slang, dialectal, regional), synonyms, grammatical and inflectional forms (plurals of nouns, principal parts of verbs, comparative and superlative forms of adjectives and adverbs). The types and amounts of information vary, of course, with the size of the dictionary: from the largest unabridged, to the desk-size, to the pocket size. But the quality of a dictionary depends less on its size than on the scholarship of its editors. Both size and quality criteria apply to single-language (e.g., English) and to bilingual (e.g., English-Spanish) dictionaries. Most dictionaries today tend to be descriptive rather than prescriptive; i.e., they report the language as it is used. Users, however, tend to regard even the least reputable dictionaries as (prescriptive) authorities.

Lexicography (dictionary-making) was an ancient science in Chinese, Islamic, and Grecian cultures, but English dictionaries remain comparatively recent phenomena. Shakespeare and his contemporaries used varying spellings for one and the same word since no uniform codifications were available to them. The first English dictionary worthy of the name appeared in 1721: Nathan Bailey's "Universal Etymological." This was superseded in scholarship, judgment, and wit by Samuel Johnson's *A Dictionary of the English Language* (1755). Johnson denied that it was a labor of love; he quipped to Boswell, his biographer, "No man but a blockhead ever wrote except for money." Still, Johnson's dictionary remained the standard for over a century. Reflecting the blind homage it commanded, Thackeray has his Miss Pinkerton of Cheswick Hall Academy (in *Vanity Fair*) present each of her graduating students with a copy of Dr. Johnson's "dixionary."

In 1783 the celebrated American lexicographer Noah Webster published his *Grammatical Institute of the English Language.* The first section of this work, devoted to spelling, was reprinted in many editions and became known as the "blue-back speller." It sold millions of copies a year for many years. In 1806 Webster published his *Compendious Dictionary of the English Language,* proclaiming his faithfulness to "what the English language is, and not how it might have been made." He thus opposed Dr. Johnson's wish that the "purity" of the language "be preserved." In 1828 there appeared Webster's *An American Dictionary of the English Language,* one of the capstones of his career. Publication rights to all of his dictionaries were ultimately purchased by the G. and C. Merriam Company. From that company's board of scholars there emerged several revised "Websters," both desk-sized and the encyclopedic "Unabridged."

In England, in 1857, the Philological Society began collecting specimen excerpts of usage from literary works. This research led to the publication, over the years, of the *New English Dictionary on Historical Principles* (in 1928, twelve volumes; later with supplements) better known as the *Oxford English Dictionary* or the "O. E. D." Since the 1930s at least one revised and abridged version of the OED has appeared in every decade. Here is an example of how the OED works. Suppose that you wish to trace historically the meanings of the word *nice.* You find in the OED that the present meanings (*pleasant; refined; in good taste*) did not come into wide use until 1830; that John Milton (1600s) used *nice* in the sense of *scant* ("Ere the n. Morn ... from her cabin'd loophole peep"); that Shakespeare used *nice* in the sense of *foolish* (Jul. C., IV, iii, 8); that *nice* has been used in the sense of *particular* since 1661 ("The Parliament is very nice ... on this point"); that Jane Austen wrote a "nice long letter"; that a character in a Thomas Hardy novel says "How nice it must be to be able to get about in omnibuses ... again!"

REFERENCES: J. B. Hulbert, *Dictionaries British and American;* R. L. Collison, *Dictionaries of English and Foreign Languages;* Alexander McQueen, "Dictionary," *Encyclopaedia Britannica, 14th Edition;* Wilson Follett, "Sabotage in Springfield," *Atlantic* (January, 1962); Elisabeth Murray, *Caught in the Web of Words.*

didactic novel   1. In general, any novel more intent on teaching a lesson than on telling a story, more devoted to character development in the moral sense than to characterization with psychological introspection; for example, Horatio Alger's *Struggling Upward.* 2. In particular, one or another of the eighteenth-century fictionalized works embodying an ideal education for the young gentleman. Influenced in some few instances by the Elizabethan COURTESY BOOKS, but in most instances by Rousseau's *Emile* (1762), a fictionalized plan to make young people morally and intellectually self-reliant, the didactic novel enjoyed immense popularity in England during the late 1700s. The most popular included Henry Brooke's *Fool of Quality* (1766–70), which emphasized the advantages of physical as well as moral training; Thomas Day's *Sanford and Merton* (1783–89), which urged young people not only to practice the cardinal virtues but also to study astronomy, botany, ethnography (especially the black man and the American Indian), geography, political economy, and zoology; Elizabeth Inchbold's *Simple Story* (1791), which advised against boarding schools; the first part of William Godwin's *Caleb Williams* (1794), which was on the whole more sentimental than didactic; Maria Edgeworth's *Parents' Assistant,* which was issued in a series in the 1790s; and parts of Thomas Holcroft's *Hugh Trevor* (1794), although the latter was essentially a BILDUNGSROMAN. (In the latter kind of novel—loosely called "pedagogical"— didactic elements appear more or less incidentally.)

The didactic novel was the forerunner of the modern pedagogical novel, which, even when it propagandizes or argues a thematic issue—for example, the exploitation of children, as in Dickens's *Nicholas Nickleby* (1839) and John Hersey's *Child Buyer* (1960)—attends much more to characterization and narrative development than did the early prototypes. The best-known nineteenth-century pedagogical novel, after Dickens, was Edward Eggleston's *Hoosier Schoolmaster* (1871), which set the pattern for the frontier method of handling young bullies, a stereotype situation in scores of later novels, among them Faulkner's *Hamlet* (1940).

In the 1900s the best-known pedagogical novels have been: F. Scott Fitzgerald, *This Side of Paradise* (1920); Thomas Wolfe, *Look Homeward, Angel* (1929); James Farrell, *Young Lonigan* (1932); George Santayana, *The Last Puritan* (1936); John Marquand, *Wickford Point* (1939); William Maxwell, *The Folded Leaf* (1945); J. D. Salinger, *The Catcher in the Rye* (1945); Ivy Compton-Burnett, *Two Worlds and Their Ways* (1949); Mary McCarthy, *The Groves of Academe* (1952); Jessamyn West, *Cress Delahanty* (1953); C. P. Snow, *The Masters* (1953); Frances Patton, *Good Morning, Miss Dove* (1954); Evan Hunter, *The Blackboard Jungle* (1954); Kingsley Amis, *Lucky Jim* (1954); Herman Wouk, *Marjorie Morningstar* (1955); Howard Nemerov, *Homecoming Game* (1957); Vladimir Nabokov, *Pnin* (1957); John Knowles, *A Separate Peace* (1959); John Updike, *The Centaur* (1962); and Bel Kaufman, *Up the Down Staircase* (1964).

REFERENCES: Wilbur Cross, *Development of the English Novel;* Ian Watt, *Rise of the Novel;* Arnold Lazarus, "Educational Thought in Modern Fiction," in G. F. Kneller, ed., *Foundations of Education,* Second Edition.

didacticism   From the Greek verb "to teach." The tendency to emphasize instruction or moralizing; in contemporary literary criticism a derogation, since the assumption is that literary works are essentially descriptive (Aristotelian) rather than prescriptive (Platonic). (The DIDACTIC NOVEL is treated in a separate article.) Examples of didactic poetry are Ella Wheeler Wilcox's "Laugh and the world laughs with you; / Weep and you weep alone"; Kipling's "If" and "Ballad of East and West"; and Longfellow's "Psalm of Life." (Ironically, lines from the last two poems are frequently quoted out of context so that the lesson intended in each poem as a whole is reversed.) Examples of didactic drama include MELODRAMA in general and, in particular, such eighteenth-century sentimental plays as Richard Steele's *Conscious Lovers* (1772); George Lillo's *London Merchant* (1731) and *The Christian Hero* (1735); and Hugh Kelley's *False Delicacy* (1768). All of these are clear-cut examples of didacticism, reflecting intentions that few critics today would disagree over. But these criteria that distinguish a didactic from a nondidactic work remain all too simplistic; the problem is actually more complex. When, for example, is the theme of a poem, novel, or play a *descriptive* philosophic observation and when is it a *prescriptive* "moral"? Whether or not a theme is stated in the grammatical imperative (for example, "Don't go near the water") is after all a trivial distinction. Although such critics as Matthew Arnold and T. S. Eliot must have cringed at overt didacticism, they did insist respectively on moral "high seriousness" and on the social and moral function of literature. And to hear George Bernard Shaw, one would think that even intentional didacticism on the part of an author is no literary crime. In the Preface to *Pygmalion*, for example, he says

It [Pygmalion] is so intensely and deliberately didactic ... that I delight in throwing it at the heads of the wiseacres who repeat the parrot cry that art should never be didactic. It goes to prove my contention that art should never be anything else.— *Complete Plays*, Vol. I, p. 194.

But Shaw was a notorious iconoclast, and *Pygmalion* remains less memorable for its didacticism than for its wit, its entertaining situations, and its charming characterizations. See ALLEGORY, APHORISM, GNOMIC, MORAL, PHILOSOPHIC STATEMENT, and THEME 2.

REFERENCES: Matthew Arnold, *Culture and Anarchy;* T. S. Eliot, *The Use of Poetry and the Use of Criticism;* George Bernard Shaw, Preface to *Pygmalion;* W. K. Wimsatt, "Poetry and Morals," in Eliseo Vivas and Murray Krieger, eds., *The Problems of Aesthetics.*

dieresis   A mark (¨) placed over the second of two successive vowels to indicate that it is to be sounded separately. The mark has fallen from favor in American orthography, its function having been assumed by the hyphen or not at all. In such a word as *naïve,* it serves a valuable purpose, indicating two syllables are to be pronounced; but *coöperate* has given way to *co-operate* or *cooperate, preëmpt* to *pre-empt* or *preempt.* In poetry the dieresis is still sometimes used to mark a sounded syllable that in normal speech would not be sounded:

A huge horse made, high raisëd like a hill

dilemma   A form of DEDUCTIVE REASONING that presents a pair of alternatives, one of which must be faced and both of which are usually, though not necessarily, unpleasant. For example, "Here we are at a crucial fork in the road. One route leads through a treacherous swamp; the other skirts dangerously close to a precipice. Which route shall we take? We must take one or the other, because everything behind us is burned out." Notice that dilemma poses a real and legitimate pair of alternatives ("horns") and is thus to be distinguished from FALSE DILEMMA or DISJUNCTIVE DILEMMA.

dimeter   In verse, a line with two major stresses; for example, *Láughing wăters.* See METER.

Dionysian   Pertaining to Dionysus, Greek god of revelry, and to ROMANTIC ardor as opposed to Apollonian restraint or CLASSICAL moderation.

dirge, threnody   In poetry, a lament, or "keening" (Irish) for a dead person. Unlike an ELEGY, a dirge has no prescribed forms.

discovery   1. In literature, an unfolding in which a character proceeds from ignorance and innocence to knowledge and experience. Thus, in Sophocles' *Oedipus* the protagonist is initially ignorant of his real parentage and gradually becomes informed. Such "unfoldings" are also basic to the short stories called *epiphanies*. Many of the stories in James Joyce's *Dubliners* are superb examples. 2. When a protagonist discovers something that the reader or audience already knows—and especially when the audience knows what the protagonist has yet to discover—the situation is called DRAMATIC IRONY. 3. In logic, exposition, and learning, discovery is an inductive process in which the reader makes general inferences from given data. Such discovery is the opposite of *deductive instruction,* in which the general principle is given, and the reader or student then seeks specimen data to support the generalization. 4. Often, the discipline of the *form* or technique helps a writer "discover" what to write. Compare INVENTIO.

REFERENCES: Mark Schorer, "Technique as Discovery," in James Miller, Jr., ed., *Myth and Method;* Morris Beja, *Epiphany in the Modern Novel.*

disjunctive dilemma   A specious argument that asserts that two possible things cannot both pertain at the same time, as in "It can*not* be *both* raining *and* snowing." Such a statement is of course false—and if used in a disjunctive syllogism (see SYLLOGISM 4) would constitute a false premise. Compare FALSE DILEMMA.

disjunctive syllogism   See SYLLOGISM 4.

dissociation of sensibility   See SENSIBILITY 2.

dissonance   A clashing combination of sounds. The dissonance may be deliberate and purposeful, or it may be the result of the author's "tin ear." Compare CACOPHONY.

distich   Literally, "two-lined." A COUPLET; any two-line stanza; a pair of rhyming lines written in the same METER. For example, "Anthologies and lecture tours and grants / Create a solvency which disenchants" (Donald Hall).

distributed term   See SYLLOGISM 1 G.

dithyramb   1. Originally, in Greek verse, an extravagant paean to, or song in praise of, Dionysus, the god of creative intoxication. 2. Now a more general label, usually derogatory, for any extravagantly emotional passage of prose or verse. Thus, in Thomas Wolfe's novel *Look Homeward, Angel* the final paragraph of Chapter 30 may be called a dithyramb: "O lost and by the wind grieved, ghost come back again, as first I knew you in the timeless valley...."

REFERENCE: Jane Harrison, *Themis.*

ditrochee   See METER.

ditto marks   The paired marks (") used to indicate that material printed directly above is to be repeated. Ditto marks are used in classroom notes, but not in formal writing.

division of words   See SYLLABICATION.

documentation   In research work, the set of conventions the writer follows when citing authorities and acknowledging indebtedness to sources. Documentation is achieved through *bibliography* and *footnotes.*

Bibliography is a formally arranged list of books and articles pertinent to a given topic. A researcher's *working bibliography* is a compilation of cards, each citing a work *to be* consulted as the researcher seeks information; the *final bibliography* is a list of works that *have been* consulted. If the final bibliography lists all works consulted for the project, it is a *full* bibliography; if it lists only the works actually referred to in the text and cited in the footnotes, it is a *selected* bibliography.

The working bibliography. After the researcher has tentatively defined the topic and knows what subjects (or topic headings) to consult in reference works, compilation of the working bibliography begins. Each discovered reference to a possible source of pertinent information is noted on a 3″ x 5″ card. Such cards facilitate later arrangement of the materials as the project requires them, and they provide for final arrangement into alphabetical order.

Using the most complete available reference library, the researcher first consults the standard reference works—dictionaries and encyclopedias—and pertinent specialized reference works. But such works are not usually considered useful sources for a term paper or thesis, for in a sense they *are* term papers (though on topics not sufficiently limited). The researcher's attempt is to bring together materials that have not already appeared in reference works.

The researcher next attempts a systematic search for books and articles that may contain information on the topic. A search under several subject headings in the library's card catalogue may lead to useful books. For each, the researcher transcribes onto a 3″ x 5″ card the needed information: author's name, title of book, city of publication, publisher's name, and date of publication. It is advisable at this step that the researcher use the precise form that must appear in the final bibliography, to avoid later waste of time and to diminish the chance of error.

Most widely used among scholarly forms for bibliography is the *MLA Style Sheet,* published by the Modern Language Association. Other style guides are available and are sometimes required by a school or a teacher; but mastery of the MLA style will help establish habits of accuracy, and the researcher-student can easily adapt those habits to some other style if called upon to do so.

The *MLA Style Sheet* sets a tone for documentation: "Prose is more pleasant to read if it does not require one to jump constantly to the foot of the page or to the back of the book. Every effort should be made to make the text self-sufficient, to make the annotation unobtrusive, and to consolidate footnote references." The aim of the MLA style is to provide "a uniform system of annotation whose conventions make possible compression without loss of comprehension."

Following the *MLA Style Sheet*, the researcher will use these forms for bibliography, indenting the second and subsequent lines of each entry:

Book with one author

Mills, Gordon H. *Hamlet's Castle: The Study of Literature as a Social Experience.* Austin: Univ. of Tex. Press, 1976.

Book with two authors

Nilsen, Don L., and Alleen Nilsen. *Language Play: An Introduction to Linguistics.* Rowley, Mass.: Newbury, 1978.

Book with three or more authors

Bloom, Edward A., and others. *The Order of Poetry: An Introduction.* New York: New York Univ. Press, 1962.

Book (anthology) with editor(s)

Michaels, Leonard, and Christopher Ricks, eds. *The State of the Language.* Berkeley: Univ. of Calif. Press, 1980.

Book in several volumes

Anderson, George K., et al. *Literature of England.* 2 vols. 3rd ed. Glenview, Ill.: Scott, 1979.

Book (edited)

Pope, Alexander. *Literary Criticism of Alexander Pope.* Ed. Bertrand A. Goldgar. Lincoln: Univ. of Neb. Press, 1965.

As the examples show, the *MLA Style Sheet* recommends abbreviated forms for names of states and months and for the word "University." Dates of periodicals are in day-month-year order: 14 Feb. 1982.

If the researcher uses pamphlets, the sponsoring agency or corporation should be shown in author position, then, in order: the pamphlet's title (underlined for italics), the name of the author (if known), the series and number of the pamphlet (if pertinent), the edition number, the place of publication, the date, the number of pages in the pamphlet. A sample:

Congressional Quarterly, Inc.
Editorial Research Reports, Vol. I, No. 10.
Suzanne de Lesseps.
"News Media Ownership."
Washington, D.C., 11 Mar. 1977, 20 pp.

When using the library's card catalogue, the researcher will be wise to note on each card the *call number* of the book referred to. This will facilitate finding the book on the shelves and checking it out for use, and will preclude a wasteful return trip to the catalogue.

Since much of the most recent as well as the most valuable material on many topics appears not in books but in periodicals, the researcher must next turn to magazines and newspapers. There are several indexes, regularly published, that catalogue by topic (and often by author) many of the thousands of articles published in periodicals, both general and specialized. A good research library will have available at least some of these indexes:

Readers' Guide to Periodical Literature (indexes articles in a selected group of American magazines—from 1900 to the present)

Poole's Index to Periodical Literature (indexes general interest articles in magazines—from 1802 to 1906)

International Index to Periodicals (indexes American and some foreign articles, especially in scholarly journals—from 1907 to the present)

Specialized indexes:

Agricultural Index (from 1916 to present)
Art Index (from 1929 to present)
Dramatic Index (from 1909 to 1950)
Education Index (from 1929 to present)
Engineering Index (from 1892 to 1906) and *Engineering Index Annual* (from 1906 to present)
Index Medicus (from 1879 to present, indexing medical periodicals, books and pamphlets)
Index to Legal Periodicals (1908 to present)
Industrial Arts Index (from 1913 to present)
National Geographic Index (limited to articles in a single publication)
New York Times Index (from 1913 to date, indexing only articles that appeared in *The New York Times,* but often useful for locating national interest stories in other newspapers by date)
PMLA [Publications of the Modern Language Association] (an annual listing of books and articles dealing with the literature of all modern languages)
Public Affairs Information Service Bulletin (from 1915 to present, indexing periodicals, books, documents, and pamphlets in economics, political science, and sociology)

In most of these indexes the researcher will find entries in this form:

(a) Subject entry	Sabotage in Springfield: Webster's third edition. W. Follett. Atlan 209:73–7 Ja'62
(b) Author entry	FOLLETT, Wilson Sabotage in Springfield. Atlan 209:73–7 Ja'62

The form used in *Readers' Guide* (and most other periodical indexes) is much abbreviated, and the researcher must "translate" the information into the proper bibliographic form. Under the subject entry, where the researcher initially finds the information, the author is listed as "W. Follett"; but because the single initial is improper for bibliography, the researcher must look under "Follett," the author entry in *Readers' Guide,* to find the full name. The title of the magazine is abbreviated, and the researcher who does not recognize the title must turn to the list of "Abbreviations of Periodicals Indexed" (just inside the front cover of *Readers' Guide*). The researcher must also translate the numbers: the number before a colon is a volume number; those after a colon are page numbers. Dates are abbreviated: Ja, F, Mr, Ap, My, Je, Jl, Ag, S, O, N, D. Years are abbreviated with apostrophe to replace the century: '82. Thus for the *Readers' Guide* entry: Follett, W. Sabotage in Springfield, Atlan 209: 73–77 Ja '62, the researcher must fill out the bibliography card thus:

Follett, Wilson.
"Sabotage in Springfield."
Atlantic, Jan. 1962, pp. 73–77.

Some variant forms of periodical entries:

Two authors

Foster, Garrett R., and G. L. Richardson.
"Micropolitics of Innovation—Revisited."
Phi Delta Kappan, Nov. 1980, pp. 172–73.

Magazine without volume number, unsigned article

"Are the Optimists Premature?" *Business Week,*
4 Feb. 1980, pp. 24–5.

Newspaper article (with byline)

Kerr, Walter.
"Surrounded by Creatures of Habit."
New York Times, 11 Apr. 1982, Sec. 2, pp. 3, 17.

Newspaper article (unsigned)

"Expert Says Find Disputes History of Pompeii."
New York Times, 14 Feb. 1982, Sec. 1, p. 21.

After compiling the bibliography cards for all needed (or potentially needed) references, the researcher is ready to consult the books and articles themselves, using the cards as a directory to locations in the library. The "notetaking" begins. See RESEARCH PAPER.

The final bibliography. When the paper is finished, the researcher appends a list of works used in its preparation. It will be either a *full bibliography* (listing *all* the works consulted) or a *selected bibliography* (listing only those actually referred to in the text and footnotes). The researcher alphabetizes the pertinent bibliography cards and transcribes from them all their information, using a hanging indention format—authors' surnames flush to the left margin of the sheet. The final bibliography may look something like this:

BIBLIOGRAPHY

Anderson, George K., et al. *Literature of England.* 2 vols. 3rd ed. Glenview, Ill.: Scott, 1979.
"Are the Optimists Premature?" *Business Week,* 4 Feb. 1980, pp. 24–5.
Bloom, Edward A., and others. *The Order of Poetry: An Introduction.* New York: New York Univ. Press, 1962.
Congressional Quarterly, Inc. *Editorial Research Reports,* Vol. I, No. 10. Suzanne de Lesseps. "News Media Ownership." Washington, D.C., 11 Mar. 1977, 20pp.
"Expert Says Find Disputes History of Pompeii." *New York Times,* 14 Feb. 1982, Sec. 1, p. 21.
Follett, Wilson. "Sabotage in Springfield." *Atlantic,* Jan. 1962, pp. 73–7.
Foster, Garrett R., and G. L. Richardson. "Micropolitics of Innovation—Revisited. *Phi Delta Kappan,* Nov. 1980, pp. 172–3.
Kerr, Walter. "Surrounded by Creatures of Habit." *New York Times,* 11 Apr. 1982, Sec. 2, pp. 3, 17.
Michaels, Leonard, and Christopher Ricks, eds. *The State of the Language.* Berkeley: Univ. of Calif. Press, 1980.
Mills, Gordon H. *Hamlet's Castle: The Study of Literature as a Social Experience.* Austin: Univ. of Tex. Press, 1976.
Nilsen, Don L., and Alleen Nilsen. *Language Play: An Introduction to Linguistics.* Rowley, Mass.: Newbury, 1978.
Pope, Alexander. *Literary Criticism of Alexander Pope.* Ed. Bertrand A. Goldgar. Lincoln: Univ. of Neb. Press, 1965.

Note that the final bibliography is a single alphabetical list: books are not separated from articles. Every item is listed in its alphabetical place according to the first letter of the entry, whether that be an author's name or a title.

Footnotes are immediate citations of sources. Everything taken from a printed source must be credited to that source. The footnotes provide the necessary credit and the authentication.

The following should be footnoted: (1) all statements of opinion (it is usually assumed that researchers do not report their own opinions, though they may draw *conclusions* from cited evidence); (2) all facts not well known to the intended readers of the paper; (3) all facts (even if well known) upon which any part of the paper's thesis may depend.

As the term implies, footnotes usually appear at the *foot* of the page on which the cited material appears, although some publishers and teachers ask that footnotes be compiled in a list at the end of the paper.

Footnotes in a research paper follow a single sequence, every footnote with its own number. A new numbering sequence is not begun on every page, but a new sequence is begun for each chapter in a thesis, dissertation, or book.

Footnote form differs from bibliography form in several ways: (1) footnotes are not alphabetized; therefore, the authors' names are not reversed; (2) footnotes are assumed to be abbreviated sentences; therefore, commas are used in some instances in which bibliography notes use periods—after authors' names and titles; (3) footnotes do not include names of publishers; (4) footnotes do include page numbers, since they refer to specific points within a book or article, rather than to the entire book or article.

Footnotes are not properly used for "asides" to the reader. They are, in most scholarly work, strictly citations of sources.

The use of such Latin terms and abbreviations as *ibid., op. cit., loc. cit.,* and *et al.* is now discouraged by the *MLA Style Sheet,* since an author's name and page number will usually be clearer, and the English term *and others* seems less pompous than *et al.* The student-researcher may need to be familiar with the Latin terms to interpret other scholarly, documented works.

Here is a sample sequence of footnotes and (following) an explanation of the devices properly used:

[1]Don L. Nilsen and Alleen Nilsen, *Language Play* (Rowley, Mass.: Newbury, 1978), p. 67.

[2]Nilsen, p. 69.

[3]Wilson Follett, "Sabotage in Springfield," *Atlantic,* Jan. 1962, p. 74.

[4]Walter Kerr, "Surrounded by Creatures of Habit," *New York Times,* 11 Apr. 1982, Sec. 2, p. 3.

[5]Nilsen, p. 69.

[6]Kerr, p. 17.

[7]"Are the Optimists Premature?" *Business Week,* 4 Feb. 1980, p. 25.

[8]Follett, p. 73.

[9]"Are the Optimists Premature?" p. 24.

Explanation of footnote sequence: (1) First reference to a book; note that the footnotes are numbered in sequence throughout a paper or chapter; the numbers are "superior"—that is, raised slightly above the typing line. (2) Repeat of the immediately preceding reference, with change of page number. (3 and 4) First reference to a magazine article. (5) Reference to previously cited book. (6) Reference to previously cited magazine article, with change of page number. (7) First reference to magazine article without by-line. (8 and 9) Reference to previously cited magazine article, with change of page number. Note that second or subsequent references to a work use shortened forms: the surname of author or a title shortened as much as possible with full clarity. If two or more works by a single author are cited, the surname of author must be followed by a short title for clear reference.

Some students complain that, when typing the final draft, they cannot plan ahead for the space that footnotes will require. They will find this method helpful: In writing the first draft of a research paper, stop immediately when a footnote number has been written in the text; type the footnote at that point, rather than at the foot; after typing the footnote, go ahead with the text until another footnote number is reached, type it in; when typing the final draft, simply skip the footnotes, and when the last line of text has been typed, there will be just enough space left for the footnotes on that page.

REFERENCES: *MLA Style Sheet;* D. F. Bond, *A Reference Guide to English Studies;* James Thorpe, *Literary Scholarship;* Milton Byrd and Arnold Goldsmith, *Publication Guide for Literary and Linguistic Scholars;* Donald Sears, *Harbrace Guide to the Library and Research Paper;* W. E. Colburn, *A Concise Bibliography for Students of English.*

doggerel   1. Trivial, singsong verse; e.g., "Jack and Jill go down the hill to get their bread at Baker's Mill." 2. Doggerel is also a derogatory epithet applied to unintentionally bad verse. (See Wyndham Lewis and Charles Lee, eds., *The Stuffed Owl: An Anthology of Bad Verse.*)

donnée   The "given"—such factual elements of a literary work as setting, manifest story-line (or plot), and at least the names and apparent attributes of the characters. The term, introduced by the novelist Henry James, is based on the analogy of a geometry problem, in which certain elements are "given"; the reader then takes it from there, trying to solve the puzzle, to get at meaning. The donnée may include THEME, if by that is meant something general like "alienation," "retribution," and so on. But such a factual element is to be distinguished from any PHILOSOPHIC STATEMENT implicit in the deeper structure of a literary work. Compare VISION OF LIFE. More often than not, the donnée consists mainly of the cast of characters (*dramatis personae*) with their most overt identifications (names, ages, sexes, outward appearances, and so on), the setting (time, place, socio-economic condition, and so on), and the manifest story-line. See LEVELS OF MEANING.

REFERENCES: Henry James, "The Art of Fiction," in James Miller, Jr., ed., *Myth and Method;* C. S. Brown, "Difficulty and Surface Value," in Peter Demetz, ed., *The Disciplines of Criticism.*

Doppelgänger   See ALTER EGO.

double dactyls   Also known as JIGGERY-POKERY. Light verse consisting of two four-line stanzas in which the last line of the first stanza rhymes with the last line of the second stanza and in which each line consists of two DACTYLS, for example, "Higgledy, piggledy." Although the METER is ancient, the verse form is a modern invention of the poets Anthony Hecht and John Hollander, authors of the collection *Jiggery-Pokery.*

double entendre   An utterance with two intended meanings, the less obvious of which suggests something indelicate or risqué. When Hamlet tells Ophelia, "Get thee to a nunnery ... Or if thou wilt needs marry, marry a fool; for wise men know well enough what monsters you make of them," his "monster" suggests not only a fierce creature but also the pitiable creature with horns, a cuckold. PUNS are double entendres, though not all double entendres are puns. An AMBIGUITY arising from a verbal—e.g., "She enjoys exciting dates"—is also often a double entendre. "Exciting," understood as a transitive gerund rather than as a participle or adjectival, suggests a rather aggressive subject-agent.

Careful speakers and writers do not confuse double entendre with double-entente, which idiomatically takes an adjectival position: "He's always making double-entente remarks."

double negative   The use of two negative words ("There wasn't nothing we could do") when only one negation is intended. The double negative is not used in standard English, but its absence is a matter of fashion rather than of logic, since two negatives in an utterance do not, after all, make an affirmative. Certainly, no one hearing a child say, "I've *never* had *no* black shoes," will honestly believe that the child *has* had black shoes. If two negatives really made an affirmative, would *three* negatives restore the appropriate logic? Probably not, for "I have*n't never* had *no* black shoes" remains negative and nonstandard.

A troublesome double negative often occurs in nonstandard usage with "scarcely" or "hardly": "I *can't hardly* do that." Standard usage calls for "I *can hardly* do that," meaning "I cannot easily do that" or "I cannot do that at all." When two negations are intended, then two or more negative words are used properly: "We could *not* understand why he did *not* speak up," or even "I was *not* sure that the letter had *not* been sent for *no* good purpose." But when multiple negations are used, the style becomes involved and the message unintelligible. Revision to the clearer affirmative may well be the wiser alternative.

drama   See DRAMATIC STRUCTURE.

dramatic irony   See IRONY 3.

dramatic monologue   A poem in which one character, frequently revealing a particular personality, speaks for all the other characters; that is, one character constantly reports what the other characters say and do. The result is a purposely limited FOCUS OF NARRATION. An example is Browning's "My Last Duchess," in which the Duke speaks for the entire cast of characters. This kind of speaker is manifestly a member of the cast, of the *"dramatis personae."* Compare PERSONA.

dramatic structure   A combination of the following: (1) rising suspensive action or conflict between the PROTAGONIST and any obstacle(s), the latter being another character or one of the protagonist's traits; (2) the protagonist's success or failure in overcoming these obstacles, each one larger and more complicated than its predecessor; (3) the protagonist's confronting the most crucial obstacle (in the CLIMAX) and either overcoming it (in COMEDY) or being overcome by it (in TRAGEDY). In *Macbeth,* the protagonist's goal is to gain clear, uncontested title to the Throne of Scotland. His first obstacle is King Duncan. By killing Duncan, Macbeth gets this obstacle out of the way, but creates a larger, three-headed obstacle in the persons of the suspicious General Banquo and Duncan's sons, Malcolm and Donalbain, who get away. Macbeth cannot do anything about Duncan's sons for the moment; but he has Banquo murdered. Overcoming this obstacle is not wholly successful either, since Banquo's son, Fleance, gets away. Meanwhile, Duncan's sons have been able to muster the help of Lord Macduff. Macbeth's brutal slaughter of Macduff's wife and children only motivates the climactic action: the victims' relatives and other enemies of Macbeth combine against him in the Birnam Wood battle, which he fails to overcome, and which in fact overcomes him. Thus in dramatic structure each obstacle (or scene built on an obstacle) is tied to its predecessor or successor in a cause-and-effect chain.

Contrasted with dramatic structure is *episodic structure,* in which one scene is tied to another only loosely, usually because what happens, happens to the main character (as in a PICARESQUE NOVEL like *Anthony Adverse*) or to the main personage (as in a BIOGRAPHY like *Always the Young Strangers*). Any suspense or excitement in episodic structure is limited to, and bounded by, a given episode or scene, with little or no reference to other episodes or scenes.

In dramatic structure, on the other hand, the suspense (rising suspensive action) grows cumulatively up to the most crucial scene or climax. If the protagonist overcomes the climactic obstacle, the play turns out to be a comedy, and the *falling action* (the action from the climax to the end) is called the DÉNOUEMENT. If the protagonist is overcome by the climactic obstacle, the play is a tragedy, and the falling action is, or culminates in, the CATASTROPHE.

Because of long speeches and even COMIC RELIEF, the falling action of tragedy tends to be longer than that of comedy. Most comedies are built around a very hectic climax, followed by a brief DÉNOUEMENT.

In fiction and drama most of the basic plots include the following: (1) *Boy meets girl*—boy falls in love with girl, boy temporarily loses girl, boy ultimately wins girl. The variation: *Girl meets boy.* (2) *The triangle*—two men love one woman, or two women love one man, situations that often involve two of the lovers in adultery. (3) *The quest*—struggling against formidable obstacles, the protagonist succeeds (or fails) to gain an ambitious goal. The goal may be religious (e.g., "the holy grail"), secular (e.g., climbing the highest mountain or discovering a cure for a dreaded disease), or psychological (search for self-understanding, self-discovery). See DISCOVERY.

REFERENCES: Norman Friedman, "Forms of the Plot," *Journal of General Education* (July, 1955); Arnold Lazarus, "Plot Graph," *Adventures in Modern Literature,* Fifth Edition; Alan Downer, *The Art of the Play;* Georges Polti, *The Thirty-six Dramatic Situations;* Robin Farquhar, "Dramatic Structure in the Novels of Ernest Hemingway," *Modern Fiction Studies* (Autumn, 1968); D. M. Church, "Structure and Dramatic Technique in Gide's *Saul,*" *PMLA* (October, 1969); Frederick Litto, "Introduction," *Plays from Black Africa;* Jackson Barry, *Dramatic Structure;* John Taylor, *Rise and Fall of the Well-Made Play;* Toby Cole, ed., *Playwrights on Playwriting;* Seymour Chatman, "The Structure of Fiction," *University Rev.* (March, 1971); J. W. Rathbun, "Structure, *Red Badge of Courage,*" *Ball State Forum* (Winter, 1969); David Goldknopf, "What Plot Means in the Novel," *Antioch Rev.* (Winter, 1970); J. P. Pusack, trans., *Narrative Situations in the Novel;* Elizabeth Dipple, *Plot;* R. M. Henkels, *The Novel as Quest;* David Holbrook, *Quest for Love.*

dramatism   One of Kenneth Burke's systems for the analysis of literature and human motivation. It is based on the premise that literature, language, and thought are primarily modes of action. ("Somebody is always doing something to somebody else.") Burke's theoretic model is so close to the basic sentence patterns of Western languages, especially English, that he calls his two chief books dealing with dramatism, among other matters, "a grammar" and "a rhetoric." The notion that "someone is doing something" is the "S-V-O" (subject-verb-object) sentence pattern, while the observation that there may be a recipient of this action calls to mind the "S-V-iO-O" (subject-verb-indirect object-direct object) pattern.

Some such dramatistic model is also common to most plays, short stories, novels, epics, and narrative poems. Burke subsumes under his "S-V-O" model the notion that "something is this or that"—what some structural linguists call the "S-LV-C" (subject-linking verb-complement) pattern. Within this frame one can order metaphors and main themes or thematic motifs or philosophic implications, not only of the literary genres just mentioned, but also of such genres as lyric poems, familiar essays, and essays in literary criticism.

The five key terms ("pentad") in Burke's dramatism are *act, scene, agent, agency,* and *purpose. Act* seeks to answer "What happened?" (in thought as well as in deed). *Scene* answers "Where did it happen?" *Agent* seeks to answer "Who did it?" Answers to "Who did it?" may range from a solution in an ephemeral "Whodunit" to the most complex unmasking of a PERSONA. *Agency* answers "How was it done?" The answers would include not only the instruments used, but also the author's tone and attitude toward the material. *Purpose* seeks to answer "Why?" It is in answer(s) to this last question that Burke as virtuoso orchestrates the contributions of anthropology, sociology, linguistics, SEMANTICS, psychology, and PSYCHOANALYSIS.

REFERENCES: Kenneth Burke, *A Grammar of Motives* and *A Rhetoric of Motives;* Stanley Edgar Hyman, ed., *Terms for Order;* David W. Thompson and Virginia Fredericks, *Oral Interpretation of Literature: A Dramatistic Approach;* James Mullican, *Kenneth Burke's Rhetorical Theory.*

dramatis personae   The cast; a list of characters. To be distinguished from PERSONA.

dream vision   **1.** A character's dream or fantasy, often of an ideal world or situation; for example, Nausicaa's dream in *The Odyssey,* Book VI. **2.** A literary form, also known as dream allegory, in which the narrator's dream serves as a frame for unifying the vision of various persons, places, and experiences. Well-known examples include Dante's *Divine Comedy,* Chaucer's *Book of the Duchess,* Bunyan's *Pilgrim's Progress,* and Tennyson's "Dream of Fair Women." Compare FRAME STORY.

REFERENCES: C. S. Lewis, *Allegory of Love;* C. W. Dunn, ed., *The Romance of the Rose;* Sigmund Freud, *The Interpretation of Dreams.*

dumb show   See COMMEDIA DELL'ARTE.

E

eclogue   Literally, "choice selection," "morsel," or "tidbit." Originally, a short poem or section of a poem dealing with pastoral themes. From earliest times the eclogue was associated with pastoral poetry; that is, with poetry of the countryside, of shepherds, flocks, peacefulness. Classic examples are the *Idylls* of the Greek Theocritus (third century B.C.) and the *Eclogues* of the Roman Vergil (first century B.C.). The most celebrated eclogues in English literature are Edmund Spenser's *Shepheards Calendar* (1579), with one poem for each month. Eclogues are characterized by *(a)* singing contests, *(b)* playful dialogue, with boasting about one's flocks or sweethearts, *(c)* formal courtship, and *(d)* laments for the dead. According to Barriss Mills, in the introduction to his verse translation of *The Idylls of Theokritos,* eclogues "invite us to forget for a while man's destiny ... and to indulge ourselves in a daydream of rustic simplicity and romantic love."

REFERENCES: Patrick Cullen, "Imitation and Metamorphosis: The Golden Age Eclogue in Spenser, Milton, and Marvell," *PMLA* (October, 1969); Walter W. Greg, *Pastoral Poetry and Drama.*

economy in writing   Brevity is courtesy—and self-defense. A writer cannot grasp a reader by the lapels to force an audience, and none will stay to be bored; so a writer who has much to say must be brief. But economy in expression is an achievement, not a gift. It comes to those who study the language, refine their thoughts, and respect the reader's quickness of mind. To gain economy the writer must sharpen and extend vocabulary, to know how much or how little a word will do, for weak or watery vocabulary leads to wordiness; the writer who knows, for example, what the prefix *re-* imports will not burden "return" with a REDUNDANCY ("Return the book *back* to the library"). A writer must analyze a thought and trim from it all the fat, for only such tough RENDERING will rescue the work from flabbiness. A writer must trust the reader's quick intelligence while not overrating such information, for the reader may be confused by the omission of some unknown key fact. See DEADWOOD, GOBBLEDYGOOK, PARSIMONY, NOUNIFICATION, AGENT, WHICH/THAT.

REFERENCE: Ken Macrorie, "Tightening," *Telling Writing.*

eiron   **1.** A dissembler—one who says less than what he or she thinks or means. **2.** In the comedies of the Greek playwrights Aristophanes and Menander (also in the comedies of the Roman playwrights Plautus and Terence), the eiron often deflates braggarts. See IRONY 2.

either/or fallacy   See FALSE DILEMMA.

elegant variation   The use of pretentious synonyms in the mistaken belief that repetition must always be avoided. See VARIETY.

elegy   A poem in an elevated style, written in praise of, and mourning for, a specific dead person. An elegy sometimes contains general reflections on death, often with a rural or pastoral setting—in which case it is called a pastoral elegy. The elegy is to be distinguished from the general poem on death, which speaks primarily about the typicality of death. Among the most celebrated elegies are Chaucer's *Book of the Duchess,* Milton's *Lycidas,* Gray's "Elegy in a Country Churchyard," Shelley's *Adonais,* Tennyson's *In Memoriam,* Arnold's "Thyrsis," Whitman's "When Lilacs Last in the Dooryard Bloomed," and Rilke's *Duino Elegies.* More restrained, less dithyrambic than a DIRGE, an elegy dispenses as quickly as possible with its lament and gets on with an idea, observation, or meditation. Three of the most moving modern elegies, which do just that, are Dylan Thomas's "A Refusal to Mourn the Death, by Fire, of a Child in London," John Crowe Ransom's "Bells for John Whiteside's Daughter," and W. H. Auden's "In Memory of W. B. Yeats."

REFERENCES: Thomas P. Harrison, *The Pastoral Elegy;* L. A. Muinzer, *The Elegy.*

elision   In poetry, the omission of an unstressed vowel or syllable from a word to preserve the meter; for example, "is't" for "is it"; "i'th'earth" for "in the earth"; "th'expense" for "the expense"; " 'twas" for "it was." In modern poetry, such elisions are shunned as "poeticisms." Other elisions, such as "t'other" for "the other," are peculiar to backwoods DIALECTS.

Elizabethan   Pertaining to the era and reign of Elizabeth I (1558–1603). The Elizabethan Age, noted for religious controversy, world exploration, expansion of trade and sea power, was accompanied by a flowering of literature—especially lyric poetry and drama. During this RENAISSANCE, which reached England much later than it reached the countries of the Continent, flourished such poets and playwrights as William Shakespeare, Sir Philip Sidney, Samuel Daniel, Thomas Campion, Ben Jonson, John Donne, Christopher Marlowe, John Lyly, Robert Greene, Thomas Kyd, George Chapman, John Marston, Thomas Heywood, and Thomas Dekker.

REFERENCES: John E. Neal, *Queen Elizabeth I;* Robert Kimbrough, *Sir Philip Sidney;* Hazelton Spencer, ed., *Elizabethan Plays;* J. William Hebel and Hoyt H. Hudson, eds., *Poetry of the English Renaissance (1509–1660);* A. L. Rowse, *The England of Elizabeth;* E. M. W. Tillyard, *The Elizabethan World Picture;* Paul J. Alpers, ed., *Elizabethan Poetry: Modern Essays in Criticism;* Norman Kotker and L. B. Smith, eds., *The Horizon Book of the Elizabethan World;* E. K. Chambers, *The Elizabethan Stage;* G. Gregory Smith, ed., *Elizabethan Critical Essays;* David Bevington, *Tudor Drama and Politics;* Louis B. Wright, *Middle Class ... Elizabethan England.*

ellipsis   1. The omission of any element from a sentence so that the grammatical structure is incomplete although the sense is clear. Conversational English is especially elliptical: "Hi!" "Morning!" "Got troubles?" "Sure have." "Lost a friend?" "No, just tired." "Up late last night?" "Yeah. Big party." (The conversation communicates even though no full sentence appears.) Even formal English uses ellipsis and the MINOR SENTENCE, which, however, must be distinguished from the FRAGMENT, in which the sense is unclear and the unfinished structure awkward. Ellipsis is a characteristic of the LACONIC style; it appears often in EPIGRAM, APHORISM, proverb, and MAXIM. One special sort of ellipsis is the purposeful omission of *and* (see ASYNDETON). **2.** The omission of elements from quoted material—usually in formal writing—may be indicated by the use of three "dots" (...); the mark is called an ellipsis. The use of ellipsis calls for a careful and honest study of the quoted material so that nothing essential to sense or intent is omitted. The ellipsis mark may also be used to indicate a suspension of a remark ("The fellow was ... oh, I don't know what") or an implied continuation of a sequence ("So it went, day and night, day and night ... "). See APOSIOPESIS.

emblem book   Shortly after the introduction of the art of engraving, a popular RENAISSANCE publication built upon, or introduced by, an emblem. An emblem consisted of a symbolic picture (e.g., an archer shooting an arrow) over a motto (e.g., "Speak little and come to the point") and a short poem (e.g., "Parler Peu") amplifying both picture and motto. Spenser's *The Shepheards Calendar* (1579) reflects the influence of emblem books. Francis Quarles's *Emblems* (1635) remained popular for almost a century.

emotional appeals   Most of these are treated in separate articles in this handbook under the following entries: AD CAPTANDUM (bandwagon); AD HOMINEM (appeal to personal prejudices); AD IGNORANTIAM (appeal to ignorance); AD MISERICORDIAM (appeal to pity); AD POPULUM (appeal to popular prejudices); AD VERECUNDIAM (snob appeal); FRIEND OF THE ENEMY (guilt by association); RED HERRING (smokescreen; smoked herring); TU QUOQUE ("You did it, too!"). See also PROPAGANDA DEVICES and FALLACIES OF REASONING.

empathy   A reader's or spectator's feeling of identification ("That could be me") with a character. Empathy is involuntary, and should be distinguished from *sympathy,* which is voluntary.

REFERENCES: Louise Rosenblatt, *Literature as Exploration;* Norman Holland, *Dynamics of Literary Response;* Walter Slatoff, *With Respect to Readers.*

emphasis   A principle of organization by which the elements of an utterance or a composition are clearly placed as to their importance. Elements may be emphasized by (1) pointing at them with tags: ("Most important is ... ," "Foremost is ..."); (2) placing them at beginning or end (in a sentence, a paragraph, or a full discourse); (3) giving them fullness of treatment (more space than is given to less important elements); (4) repeating them; (5) setting them apart (as in a very short paragraph that draws attention by contrast with longer ones); (6) couching them in terse independent clauses or sentences; (7) inserting a "do"-verb (do, does, did, etc.) before the predicate verb (e.g., "These women do speak with authority."); (8) buffering key words with such signals as "admittedly," "fortunately," "unfortunately," and the like.

Proper emphasis cannot be achieved by such hackneyed devices as false exaggeration, underlining, italicizing, or exclamation-marking.

end-stopped   A synonym for "closed line." Contrast ENJAMBEMENT.

enjambement   In poetry, the continuation of a sentence from one line into the next, or of two lines or more into the next; respectable "run-on lines." In Edwin Arlington Robinson's "Richard Cory": "In fine, we thought that he was everything / To make us wish that we were in his place." In Stephen Vincent Benét's *John Brown's Body*: "And bleak New England farms, so winter-white / Even their roofs look lonely, and the deep / The middle grainland where the wind of night / Is like all blind earth sighing in her sleep."

Enlightenment   See DEISM and RATIONALISM.

enthymeme   An elliptical argument in which one or more elements of a SYLLOGISM are implicit. For example, "Nice girls don't go there" implies (1) "there" is not respectable, (2) you are a nice girl, and (3) therefore you won't go there. In argumentation, the enthymeme is often used to make the audience draw its own conclusions.

REFERENCE: Lawrence Green, "Enthymemic Invention," *College English* (February, 1980).

envoy (envoi)   See BALLADE.

epanadiplosis   See ANAPHORA.

epanalepsis   The device of ending a sentence with the same word or phrase used at its beginning: "Nothing will come of nothing." (*King Lear*, I, i).

ephebe   A self-appointed protégé of, or apprentice to, an established master; literally, young trainee. Compare EPIGONE.

epic   A long narrative poem unified by a hero who reflects the customs, mores, and aspirations of a nation or race and who undertakes legendary and historic exploits, usually over a long period of time. The celebrated epics of world literature include the *Shah Namah* (Persia), *The Mahabharata* (India), *The Kalevala* (Finland), the *Niebelungenlied* (Germany), *The Cid* (Spain), and Camoëns' *Lusiads* (Portugal). Perhaps the best-known epics in Western literature are Vergil's (Latin) *Aeneid* and his ancient Greek models: the *Iliad* and the *Odyssey*. The latter two are usually attributed to Homer, but they are also called folk epics because of possible group authorship and because of their oral transmission over many generations. The *Iliad*, the *Odyssey*, and the *Aeneid* use dactylic hexameter.

The best-known epic poems in English are the Anglo-Saxon folk epic *Beowulf*, written in ALLITERATIVE VERSE, and Milton's *Paradise Lost*, written in BLANK VERSE. The American poet Longfellow attempted, in *Hiawatha*, an epic poem of the American Indian. And the modern American poet Stephen Vincent Benét attempted, in *John Brown's Body*, an epic poem of the War between the States.

An epic poem will exhibit most of the following CONVENTIONS: the invocation of a MUSE appropriate to the theme; the appearance of supernatural forces; the use of the IN-MEDIAS-RES narrative technique; the cataloging of genealogies and battle equipment; the delivery of formal, often pretentious, speeches; and the elaboration of long, drawn-out similes. See EPIC SIMILE.

REFERENCES: E. M. W. Tillyard, *The English Epic and Its Background;* Jan Devries, *Heroic Song and Heroic Legend;* Charles M. Gayley and Benjamin P. Kurtz, *Lyric, Epic, and Allied Forms of Poetry;* Gilbert Highet, *The Classical Tradition;* Gilbert Murray, *The Rise of the Greek Epic;* W. P. Ker, *Epic and Romance;* James Justus, "Epic Design of *Absalom, Absalom,*" *Texas Studies in Literature and Language* (Summer, 1962).

epic simile   An extended and elaborate simile conventional in EPIC poetry. An example from John Milton's *Paradise Lost* (Book II, lines 284–290):

> He scarce had finished, when such murmurs filled
> Th'Assembly, as when hollow Rocks retain
> The sound of blustring winds, which all night long
> Had roused the Sea, now with hoarse cadence lull
> Sea-faring men orewatcht, whose Bark by chance
> Or Pinnace anchors in a craggy Bay
> After the Tempest....

Long before the Bark has anchored in the Bay we smile (perhaps *with* Milton) at the "blustring winds," for it is to these sounds that he compares the applause of the fallen angels for their comrade Mammon. Epic simile is not always humorous, but it is vulnerable to PARODY.

epicene   Having both male and female traits.

epicurean   **1.** The term originally pertained to the cult of the Greek philosopher Epicurus (342–270 B.C.), who taught that the goal of humanity is lasting rather than fleeting pleasure; that we can find this only in temperance and in cultivating the intellect, morality, and serenity. **2.** More loosely, pertaining to a taste for things exotic, especially luxurious food, beverages, and other indulgences of the senses.

epigone   Imitator; weak impersonator.

epigram   A brief, witty saying, often in verse. In classical literature, one of the most prolific writers of epigrams was the Roman, Martial. One of Martial's celebrated epigrams in an eighteenth-century English translation goes like this: "I do not love you, Dr. Fell. / The reason why I cannot tell. / But this I know, and know full well: / I do not love you, Dr. Fell."

The epigram incarnates the soul of wit: brevity. Though to the Greeks the epigram was but an "inscription" or a short, solemn poem, the Romans took the solemnity out of it and added a barb, employing the epigram usually as LAMPOON or SATIRE. Today the epigram is more often prose than verse, and it may be either satire or philosophical observation, but it remains brief, clever, pointed. Its favorite device is ANTITHESIS. Some examples: "The trouble with living it up is that it's so hard to live down"; "You can take the boy out of the country, but you can't take the country out of the boy." A writer whose work is larded with epigrams may be said to have an *epigrammatic style*. Among such writers: Alexander Pope, Ralph Waldo Emerson, George Eliot, Mark Twain, Ambrose Bierce, H. L. Mencken, J. V. Cunningham, and many columnists and reviewers.

REFERENCES: Barriss Mills, trans., *The Epigrams of Martial;* J. V. Cunningham, *The Exclusions of a Rhyme;* G. R. Hamilton, *English Verse Epigrams.*

epigraph   A brief quotation or motto prefixed to a written work and used to suggest its theme. For example, Ernest Hemingway uses as an epigraph to *For Whom the Bell Tolls* the passage from John Donne beginning "No man is an island," which contains the title of the novel. An epigraph that suggests particularly well the theme of Roger Shattuck's *Banquet Years* is from Plato's *Symposium*, in which Socrates suggests that "the genius of comedy is the same as that of tragedy" and that "the writer of tragedy ought to be a writer of comedy also."

epilogue   A short conclusion to a work; formerly, to a play. In the epilogue to *The Tempest* Prospero makes a poetic bid for applause: "Now my charms are all o'erthrown / ... so release me from my bands [bonds] / With the help of your good hands!"

epiphany   See DISCOVERY.

episode   See DRAMATIC STRUCTURE.

epistolary novel   Prose fiction narrated through personal letters exchanged by the characters. This device allows the author to remain in the background while re-creating each character-narrator's thoughts and feelings with a sense of immediacy. See FOCUS OF NARRATION. The device also affords the author the opportunity for some keen play of IRONY and DRAMATIC IRONY, inasmuch as one character's letter can reflect a frame of reference utterly opposed to that of another character. Among the best-known examples are Aphra Behn's *Love Letters Between a Nobleman and His Sister* (1683), Samuel Richardson's *Pamela* (1740) and *Clarissa Harlowe* (1748), Tobias Smollett's *Humphrey Clinker* (1771), and Fanny Burney's *Evelina* (1778).

REFERENCES: Natascha Wurtzbach, ed., *The Novel in Letters;* R. H. Costa, "The Epistolary Monitor in *Pamela," Modern Language Quarterly* (March, 1970); D. L. Ball, *Samuel Richardson's Theory of Fiction.*

epitaph   1. Any brief inscription in prose or verse on a tombstone. 2. A short formal poem of commemoration, often a credo written by the person whose tombstone it will grace. Perhaps the most celebrated epitaph is Shakespeare's: "Good friend, for Jesu's sake forbear / To dig the dust enclosed here. / Blest be the man that spares these stones. / Cursed be he that moves my bones." Well known also is Robert Louis Stevenson's "Here he lies where he longed to be; / Home is the sailor, home from the sea / And the hunter home from the hill." Compare ELEGY. 3. The epitaph as a conventional form is sometimes used for ironic and humorous verse, as it is, for example, by David McCord in "Epitaph on a Waiter": "By and by / God caught his eye."

epithalamion   A formal poem in honor of a marriage, one of the loftiest and best known being Spenser's *Epithalamion* (1595), commemorating his own marriage. Spenser succeeds in re-creating the tension between patience and impatience by means of such lofty Platonic lines as these:

> Behold whiles she before the altar stands
> Hearing the holy priest that to her speakes
> And blesses her with his two happy hands....

and the impatient lines:

> Ah! when will this long weary day have end,
> And lende me leave to come unto my love?

epithet   **1.** An adjunctive or descriptive phrase attached to a person's name with either complimentary or disparaging effect: *Honest Abe, William the Conqueror, Alfred the Great, Philip the Bold, Stonewall Jackson, broad-shouldered Bunyan, rare Ben Jonson, Leo the Lip, the incomparable Max* [Beerbohm], *Scarface Al.* Compare *robin redbreast* and Milton's *resplendent Eve.*

2. *Homeric epithet* is used repeatedly in the *Iliad* and the *Odyssey*: *rosy-fingered dawn, cloud-gathering Zeus, Poseidon the Earth-shaker.* The Homeric epithet is akin to the Anglo-Saxon KENNING.

3. Epithets are sometimes also METONYMS, especially the formal circumlocutions for simple, less formal nouns: *finny tribe* for *fish,* and *briny deep* for *ocean.* Such phrases used repeatedly are called *stock epithets.* Sometimes the pompousness of these circumlocutions is somewhat softened by intended humor. Dr. Samuel Johnson probably kept tongue in cheek when he called chickens "gallinaceous fowl." At other times a stock epithet like *long, last sleep* for death is intended as a EUPHEMISM.

4. *Transferred epithet* is a poetic device in which an adjective is transferred from the noun it would ordinarily precede to another noun, thus giving a pleasant shock-effect. In "Fern Hill," for example, instead of a "lilting boy about the house," Dylan Thomas sings the praises of a boy about the "lilting house"; instead of "whinnying horses," "whinnying ... stable." This transfer enables the poet to suggest that the building is practically shaking with sound.

5. *Ironic epithet* is *(a)* an obvious twisting of facts or meaning (compare OXYMORON) or *(b)* a satire on a common, well-known epithet. To suggest "audio-visual aids," Patrick D. Hazard has used for the word *books* the ironic epithet "printed aids." Similarly, "to hurl epithets at [someone or something]" —"fellow traveler," "pinko," "fascist," "beatnik"—is the same as NAME-CALLING.

epitrite   See METER.

epode   See ODE.

eponym   A historical, legendary, or fictive person whose name has come to be associated with a certain function or attribute—Caesar, for example, with dictatorship; Circe, with seduction; Helen, with beauty; Mata Hari, with spying; Sherlock Holmes, with detective work; Benedict Arnold, with betrayal. Compare METONYMY.

equivocation   Hedging or misleading by giving "equal voice" to two meanings so that the utterance can be taken either of two ways. Compare AMBIGUITY. In logic, equivocation also arises when a term within an argument has more than one meaning and its established meaning changes in the course of the argument. For example:

Someone loves me.
Mary is someone.
Therefore Mary loves me.

The conclusion is invalid, for the meaning of *someone* (a person) in the major premise has shifted to *Mary* (a specific person) in the minor premise.

essay   From the French *essai,* literally "attempt." Brief nonfiction reflections in prose; developed, though not originated, by Michel de Montaigne (1533–92) and Francis Bacon (1561–1626); popularized by Joseph Addison (1672–1719) and Richard Steele (1672–1729). In *The Spectator* and *The Tatler* Addison and Steele did not try to conceal their editorializing under the guise of reporting (or the other way around). They indulged a tongue-in-cheek humor and exploited the leisurely mood of their times—as did many of their successors, in this genre, during the eighteenth and nineteenth centuries: Samuel Johnson, Charles Lamb, William Hazlitt, Thomas De Quincey, Oliver Wendell Holmes, Ralph Waldo Emerson, Henry David Thoreau, Walter Pater, Matthew Arnold, Andrew Lang, Robert Louis Stevenson, G. K. Chesterton, and Max Beerbohm. Most essays written before the 1940s reflected the tranquillity of clouds on a summer's day or the fireside easy chair of a winter's evening. When essays were not poking fun at contemporary manners and mores (as in the humorous, sometimes satirical essays of Stephen Leacock, H. L. Mencken, Robert Benchley, James Thurber, E. B. White), they were extolling the pleasures and inspirations of Nature with a capital N (as in the essays of E. V. Lucas, Walter Pritchett, Christopher Morley, Donald Culross Peattie, Rachel Carson, Joseph Wood Krutch, Loren Eiseley).

As distinguished from the ARTICLE or *feature story,* both of which, however informal, are devoted mostly to informing, the essay (also known as *familiar essay* and *personal essay*) is devoted to entertaining, or reflecting, or inspiring. It tends to be relaxed and philosophic, or witty, or poetic, or all of these at once. And it is comparatively brief—approximately five hundred words but rarely longer than a thousand. It takes such a commonplace ("familiar") subject as "pigs," for example, and treats it in an original manner; for example, "Pigs as Pets." The style of an essay is both informal and urbane—the voice of a civilized speaker in conversation with a civilized audience, an audience well-read enough to recognize and appreciate ALLUSIONS.

In writing an essay, no matter how commonplace the topic, the writer strives for unusual treatment. An anecdote or a personal experience ("narrative hook") or an appropriate quotation may introduce feelings and opinions that are further illuminated and supported with appropriate examples. Above all, the reader is led to discover the main drift, attitude, theme. To qualify as an essay, in fact, the piece of writing must make a point expressly or by implication.

REFERENCES: Robert Scholes and Carl Klaus, *Elements of the Essay;* William T. Moynihan, ed., *Essays Today;* Alton C. Morris *et al.,* eds., *The Modern Essay;* Alfred Kazin, ed., *The Open Form;* Paul Jorgensen and Frederick Shroyer, eds., *The Informal Essay;* David Daiches, ed., *A Century of the Essay;* Houston Peterson, ed., *Great Essays;* Mordecai Marcus and Henry F. Salerno, eds., *Cross Section: Essays on Contemporary America;* W. O. S. Sutherland and Robert L. Montgomery, eds., *The Reader: A Study of Form and Content;* Arthur Mullin, ed., *The Questing Mind;* Leslie Fiedler, ed., *The Art of the Essay;* Brock Brower, "The Article," in Paul Engle, ed., *On Creative Writing;* Ernece Kelly, ed., *Points of Departure;* H. Wendell Smith, *Elements of the Essay.*

euphemism   The substitution of a mild or inoffensive expression for one that might shock or offend; e.g., "You almost passed" instead of "You failed the course." George Orwell, in "Politics and the English Language," deplores politicians' irresponsible use of such euphemisms as "clean bomb" and "relocation center" (for concentration camp).

In the climb up the socio-economic ladder many trades and professions have sought to promote themselves, often with unconsciously ridiculous euphemisms. Cases in point are *sanitary engineer* for *garbage collector, mortician* for *undertaker,* and *hospital* for *repair shop.*

Obviously useful in everyday conversation, where it helps us avoid giving offense, euphemism in its less commendable forms may disguise error or deception. Fowler calls euphemism "slurring over badness by giving it a good name." It is one of the prime characterisitcs of GOBBLEDYGOOK, a style that generally obscures thought and hides purpose (as the charlatan may hide his purpose from the crowd). Especially useful in achieving euphemism are UNDERSTATEMENT and LITOTES, which tone down expression by choosing words with mild connotations. The "Newspeak" of Orwell's *1984* never used the word *bad,* but always *ungood.*

Some representative euphemisms: a *slender* girl (skinny), a *conservative* man (stingy), a *liberal* spender (wasteful), *man of leisure* (bum), an *untruth* (lie), *people's democracy* (communist dictatorship), *went to his reward* (died).

Euphemism became a mark of the verbal delicacy of the nineteenth century, when legs were *limbs,* undergarments were *unmentionables,* and even the breast of a chicken was *white meat.* Modern usage generally calls for a simple, natural, direct recognition of facts. But euphemism will probably never go out of popular style, nor will politicians fail to exploit its infinite possibilities.

REFERENCES: H. L. Mencken and Raven McDavid, *The American Language;* George Orwell, "Politics and the English Language," *A Collection of Essays;* R. J. Voorhees, *The Paradox of George Orwell.*

euphony   The pleasing combination of the sounds of language. Euphony is a quality that resists precise analysis, since it is essentially in the ear of the listener. Yet certain contributory principles may be identified.

Vowel sounds are generally considered to be more pleasing to the ear than consonants, and the "long" vowel sounds (and diphthongs) more so than the "short." Among consonants, the *resonants* (*m, n, ng, l, r, w, y*) are the most euphonious, as Poe observed. Runners-up, perhaps, are the *fricatives* (*f, v, th, s, sh, z*). Usually the least agreeable to the ear are the *stops* (*p, t, k, b, d, g*); but even the stops contribute generously to euphony when they are combined with resonant long vowels or diphthongs.

Repetition of sounds, as well as a harmonious variety of them, contributes to euphony. The echoing devices of ONOMATOPOEIA, ALLITERATION, ASSONANCE, and CONSONANCE are usually observable in euphonious prose, and RHYME often enhances the sound of verse; but these must be used with discretion lest they produce a sauce to drown in.

It is by no means certain that sound alone makes for euphony. Rhythm—or INTONATION (pitch, stress, and pause)—may also contribute; and of nearly equal importance is the choice of words with pleasing referents—since a harsh name for a revered object may seem more euphonious than a melodious name for something hated.

Since euphony, like all pleasure, is more felt than defined, most writers do not strive consciously to produce it. Rather, it is often achieved by negative means—the avoidance, or careful excision of, the harsh and clumsy. The careful writer avoids sound-effects that bend the sense to the sound. He heeds Alexander Pope's advice: "The sound should seem an echo to the sense." Contrast CACOPHONY.

euphuism   A kind of rhetoric characterized by excessive ANTITHESIS, ALLITER-ATION, ALLUSION, and DIDACTICISM. The label derives from the prose romance *Euphues* by John Lyly (1554–1606). An example: "Be merry but with modesty; be sober but not too sullen; be valiant but not too venturesome; let your attire be comely but not too costly." Although some of Lyly's contemporaries (among them John Lodge and Robert Greene) admired and imitated this style, Shakespeare must have regarded it as egregious, as reflected in his putting euphuisms into the mouth of one of his most egregious characters, Polonius. Compare Polonius's exhortations to his son, Laertes: "Be thou familiar but by no means vulgar ..." (*Hamlet*, I, iii). A more satirical slap at euphuism appears in Walter Scott's character Sir Piercie Shafton in *The Monastery* (1820).

evading the issue   See RED HERRING, AD HOMINEM, and ARGUMENT AGAINST THE MAN.

"every and all" fallacy   The mistaken assumption that "every" implies "all"; that is, the assumption that since every member of the family eats one slice of bread, the whole family eats one slice of bread. Ambiguity also mars a statement like "Our club collects ten dollars from all the members." How much does each member pay?

evidence   **1.** Facts and statistics interpreted as reasonably as possible; the testimony of unbiased, reputable experts (not just *any* "authority"). **2.** In literary scholarship, primary texts and original documents. The careful citer does not offer mere assertion or ANALOGY as evidence.

REFERENCE: W. W. Little et al., "Evaluation of Evidence," *Applied Logic.*

exclamation mark   An abrupt outcry is indicated in writing by an exclamation mark (!). Journalists call the mark the "screamer," a nickname that reveals why it should be used rarely and with discretion. Competent writers never use the mark when adequate force of utterance can be conveyed without it.

1. Use the exclamation mark after an emphatic exclamatory utterance or an emphatic command:

Wow! Has Charlie got a sunburn! Charlie, you darned fool!
Hit the dirt!
Get 'em, Casey!
Hurry!

2. An ironic or sarcastic statement may also be pointed up by an exclamation mark:

A fine friend you are!
And for this malarky he received one thousand dollars!

Rarely, and in parentheses, an exclamation mark may be used to make an ironic comment:

Phil got out of bed on time (!) to drag himself to breakfast.

When it appears next to a closing quotation mark, the exclamation mark goes inside if what is quoted is an exclamation; otherwise it goes outside: The sergeant yelled, "Get in line!" Then everybody "fell in"! See QUOTATION MARKS.

exemplum   A very didactic PARABLE.

existentialism   A comparatively modern philosophic movement (not a philosophic system) in revolt against traditional philosophies. Nor is this movement organized; in fact, there are several different kinds of revolt—some religious, some secular—and most writers either repudiate or resist the label "existentialist." Certainly Karl Jaspers (d. 1973), Martin Heidegger (d. 1976), and Jean-Paul Sartre (d. 1980), who appear on most lists of existentialists, are far apart on several of their convictions. Perhaps the one emphasis they share is a fierce individualism. In the view of an existentialist, Hamlet's dilemma—"To be or not to be?"—becomes "To overcome the forces of depersonalization or to be overcome?" This is, in fact, the central question of *Either/Or* by Søren Kierkegaard (d. 1855). Existentialist writers also stress the need for *(a)* the individual's self-actualization through self-expression, *(b)* coping rationally and realistically with human dilemmas, although Kierkegaard would add the need for passion as well as reason, *(c)* finding ways toward morality that have their foundation in the human condition rather than in theological dogma, and *(d)* becoming committed to, and involved in, whatever is good in society without doing violence to the individual's integrity. Kierkegaard, who was originally church-affiliated, developed in several books (especially in *Fear and Trembling*) his conviction that each individual needs to find Christ within the self rather than in organized religion and the forces of depersonalization. Other celebrated religious existentialists include Martin Buber (d. 1965)–Jewish; Jacques Maritain (d. 1965)–Catholic; and Paul Tillich (d. 1973)–Protestant.

The leading secular existentialist (and one who did not deny the label) was Jean-Paul Sartre. His best-known work, *Being and Nothingness,* exposes the meaninglessness of one's existence unless one actively assumes moral responsibility. In fiction, drama, and essay—and in his autobiography, *The Words*—Sartre developed the conviction that moral codes are man-made, not divine, and that man must be responsible to man. This tenet is shared by HUMANISM (among other philosophic movements); and several authors usually called existentialists have preferred to be called humanists, among them Sartre's companion Simone de Beauvoir and the Nobel Prize winner Albert Camus (d. 1960). (One of Sartre's essays is titled *Existentialism Is a Humanism.*) Existentialist approaches to the problems of good and evil are reflected in the works of such writers as Nietzsche, Dostoevsky, Melville, Rilke, Kafka, Brecht, and Arthur Miller.

REFERENCES: Walter Kaufmann, *Existentialism from Dostoevsky to Sartre;* Maurice Friedman, *The Worlds of Existentialism, a Critical Reader;* Frederick J. Hoffman, *The Mortal No;* Erich Heller, *The Disinherited Mind;* George F. Kneller, *Existentialism and Education;* George W. Morgan, *The Human Predicament;* William Barrett, *What Is Existentialism?;* W. J. Palmer, "History [and Existentialism] in *Our Mutual Friend,*" *PMLA* (Oct., 1973).

expatriates   Writers, artists, and patrons of the arts who leave home for various reasons to live in other countries. Byron, Shelley, and Keats come to mind, as does Robert Louis Stevenson. Among the best-known modern expatriates are Henry James, who left New York for Paris and London; James Joyce, who left Dublin, Ireland, for the continent (chiefly Italy, Switzerland, and France); D. H. Lawrence, who left England for Italy, Australia, and America; T. S. Eliot, who was born in St Louis but gave up American citizenship and became a British subject; Ezra Pound, who left the United States to live in London and in Rapallo, Italy, where he sympathized with Fascism; Henry Miller, who lived in France and Greece before settling in Big Sur, California; and Katherine Anne Porter, who lived in Mexico for a number of years. But perhaps the most celebrated group of expatriates is "the lost generation," which included Ernest Hemingway, F. Scott Fitzgerald, and Malcolm Cowley, who frequented the salon of Gertrude Stein. Miss Stein, who was born in San Francisco, had set up her salon on the Left Bank of the Seine.

REFERENCES: Ernest Earnest, *Expatriates and Patriots: American Artists, Scholars, and Writers in Europe;* Leon Edel, *Henry James;* James Joyce, *Exiles;* Ezra Pound, *Patria Mia* and *Letters, 1907–1941;* Ford Madox Ford, *Memories and Impressions* and *Thus to Revisit;* Richard Ellmann, *James Joyce;* Gertrude Stein, *The Autobiography of Alice B. Toklas;* Ernest Hemingway, *A Moveable Feast* and *The Sun Also Rises;* Harold Loeb, *The Way It Was;* Malcolm Cowley, *Exile's Return;* Arthur Mizener, *The Far Side of Paradise;* Henry Miller, *The Colossus of Maroussi;* Mary McCarthy, "A Guide to Exiles, Expatriates, and Internal Emigrés," *New York Review* (March 9, 1972); Ishbel Ross, *The Expatriates.*

explication de texte   A systematic study of a literary work; a close analysis of its words and images and its LEVELS OF MEANING and AMBIGUITY. This kind of literary study was popularized in France at the end of the 1800s and in the early 1900s, especially by the symbolists and by the poet-critic Paul Valéry (1871–1945). It was carried forward by Ezra Pound, T. S. Eliot, and the NEW CRITICS. The chief tenets of this approach to literary study are that (1) the meaning or meanings of a literary work reside mostly inside, not outside, the work, the primary text; (2) each literary work has a logic or integrity of its own; its form and content are right for each other, and each is inextricable from the other; (3) as Dante pointed out, a masterwork has several levels of meaning operating simultaneously. In this country the New Critics, who adopted these tenets, adapted them to what they called close reading. Because they resisted direct evaluation of a work, the New Critics regarded themselves less as critics, more as interpreters. See DEPTH READING, AMBIGUITY, AESTHETIC DISTANCE, BIOGRAPHICAL FALLACY, INTENTIONAL FALLACY, LEVELS OF MEANING.

REFERENCES: Cleanth Brooks and Robert Penn Warren, eds., *An Approach to Literature;* Ezra Pound, *ABC of Reading; The Explicator* Magazine; Monroe Beardsley, "The Logic of Explication," *Aesthetics;* I. A. Richards, *Practical Criticism;* Stanley R. Hopper and David L. Miller, *Interpretation: The Poetry of Meaning;* C. S. Singleton, ed., *Interpretation Theory and Practice;* Alan Purves *et al., Elements of Writing about Literature;* Seymour Chatman and Morse Peckham, *Word, Meaning, Poem;* George Arms and J. M. Kuntz, eds., *Poetry Explication: A Checklist.*

exposition   **1.** That form of discourse that presents and explains facts and ideas. *Investigative exposition* deals with facts and ideas in relatively straightforward prose, unadorned with FIGURATIVE LANGUAGE. It appeals more to the understanding than to the imagination. Such exposition (for example, an article on how something works) identifies, defines, classifies, illustrates, compares, and contrasts. Well-known examples are T. H. Huxley's "On a Piece of Chalk" and Rachel Carson's *The Sea Around Us.* **2.** *Interpretive exposition,* or EXPLICATION, is concerned with interpreting a difficult piece of literature. Examples are Allen Tate's essay on his own "Ode for the Confederate Dead"; Cleanth Brooks's "Case of Miss Arabella Fermor" explicating Pope's *Rape of the Lock;* Robert Heilman's explication of Henry James's "Turn of the Screw"; F. M. Bolderoff's *Reading Finnegans Wake.* **3.** In fiction and drama *exposition* is that part of the story-line which introduces facts that the audience must know to appreciate what happens next. The conventional method of sharing this information with the audience is via a messenger, a talkative servant, or an old friend of the family. In plays of the early 1900s the chief instrument for communicating exposition was a telephone in the hands of a maid or a butler; contemporary playwrights convey exposition more subtly, without delaying the action of the play.

REFERENCES: Harold Martin and Richard Ohmann, *The Logic and Rhetoric of Exposition;* Susan Sontag, "Against Interpretation," *Partisan Review Reader;* Israel J. Kapstein, *Expository Prose;* William G. Leary *et al., Thought and Statement;* William F. Smith and Raymond D. Liedlich, *From Thought to Theme;* Gerald Levin, *Prose Models;* Jerome W. Archer, *Exposition;* Morris H. Needleman, *Handbook for Practical Compositions;* J. N. Hook, *Guide to Good Writing;* Richard Dodge and G. S. Wykoff, *The Harper Handbook.*

expression, self-expression   **1.** In general, the free, uninhibited flow of one's thoughts and feelings in prose or verse. **2.** In Aristotelian rhetoric, disciplined delivery. **3.** In contemporary RHETORIC, *(a)* a derogatory term contrasting with *communication* and connoting a lack of discipline ("Easy writing makes devilish hard reading"); *(b)* a therapy for writers of CONFESSIONAL VERSE; *(c)* as necessary as "breathing" for writers of PROJECTIVIST VERSE; *(d)* pedagogy endorsed by most of the leaders of the DARTMOUTH CONFERENCE.

expressionism   An artistic movement of the 1920s, in which painters, dramatists, novelists, and poets went a step further than did impressionists of the previous decades in "expressing" their most subjective, often private, impressions of experience. Thus Kafka, in "The Metamorphosis," turns his protagonist into an actual cockroach rather than just suggesting, as an impressionist would have done, that the young man feels like a cockroach in his father's house. The expressionists also reflected Marxian revolt against the mechanization of labor and life, as in Elmer Rice's play *The Adding Machine,* in which the protagonist is Mr. Zero. Studies in Freudian and Jungian psychology also influenced the expressionists. Thus in Eugene O'Neill's play *The Emperor Jones,* the black protagonist relives—now consciously, now subconsciously— the history of his race. Most of the psychological, social, and cultural influences on the expressionists unite in James Joyce's novel *Finnegans Wake.*

REFERENCES: B. S. Myers, *Expressionism;* Max Brod, *Franz Kafka;* E. A. Engel, *The Haunted Heroes of Eugene O'Neill;* Eric Bentley, *The Playwright as Thinker;* Ronald Gray, *Bertolt Brecht;* Frances Boldereff, "The Poet Speaks," *Reading Finnegans Wake;* Mardi Valgemae, *Accelerated Grimace;* Travis Bogard, *Contour in Time;* R. S. Furness, *Expressionism.*

eye dialect   A literary approximation of what the speech of a character sounds like. To quote Mr. Dooley (the creation of Finley Peter Dunne): "As th' pote says, Opporchunity knocks at ivry man's dure wanst." Compare EYE RHYME.

eye rhyme   A pair of words that rhyme in spelling but not in pronunciation: seat, great; [hot] wind, kind. Some rhymes that are eye rhymes today (love, prove) were once actual rhymes; similarly, "historical rhymes" like Pope's "sign / join" reveal the way certain words were once pronounced. (Much evidence can be adduced that in Pope's day "join" was pronounced "jine.")

REFERENCE: H. C. Wyld, *Studies in English Rhymes from Surrey to Pope.*

F

fable   A brief narrative, more often in prose than in verse, usually about animals with human attributes and concluding with a memorable moral; e.g., "Nothing ventured, nothing gained." In world literature one of the earliest collections of fables, *The Panchatantra,* came from India. The best-known collection in Western literature, though no doubt with borrowings from the East, is that of the Greek slave Aesop (620–560 B.C.). Aesop's sources were largely FOLKLORE.

During the Middle Ages the wily fox became the subject of many fables and tales, including two "animal epics" of which he was the central character, the German *Reineke Fuchs* and the French *Roman de Reynard.* Fox stories appear in all the fable collections of that time, perhaps the best-known collections being those of Walter of England (based on the work of the Latin fabulist Romulus) and of Marie de France. The story of Chaunticleer, which Chaucer borrowed for *The Nun's Priest's Tale,* is a product of this tradition, as are later reworkings of Reynard material by Goethe and Lessing. Jean de la Fontaine (1621–95), a friend of Racine and Molière, collected and rewrote what remains the most celebrated collection of fables in verse, *The Fables of La Fontaine.* (An especially delightful translation is that of the American poet Marianne Moore.)

In the tradition of Aesop and La Fontaine, who enhanced their fables with wit and humor, the American writer Joel Chandler Harris (1848-1909) created his Uncle Remus fables, celebrating the exploits of "Br'er Rabbit." Two other American humorists, George Ade (1866-1944) and James Thurber (1894-1962), wrote, respectively, *Fables in Slang* and *Fables for Our Times.*

REFERENCES: Jean Shepherd, ed., *The America of George Ade;* Philip Robinson, *The Poets' Birds;* Willy Ley, *The Lungfish, the Dodo, and the Unicorn;* Daniel Hoffman, *Form and Fable in American Fiction;* Donald Sands, ed., *The History of Reynard the Fox;* J. B. Friedman, *The Monstrous Races in Medieval Art and Thought.*

fabliaux   Short bawdy stories in octosyllabic couplets, popular in France during the late Middle Ages. Fabliaux usually concerned intrigue, adulterous husbands and wives caught out and punished, the trickster tricked, and so on. These verses also satirized clerics, doctors, and lawyers and seemed to appeal to the rising mercantile class of the day. They served Chaucer as a model for some of *The Canterbury Tales,* notably the tales of the Reeve and the Miller, sometimes called fabliaux. More strictly, there is only one fabliau in English—"Dame Sirith." Balzac used the fabliau frame of reference in *Droll Stories.*

REFERENCES: E. K. Chambers, *English Literature at the Close of the Middle Ages;* Robert Hellman and Richard O'Gorman, trans., *Fabliaux: Ribald Tales from the Old French;* J. A. Bennett and G. V. Smithers, eds., *Early Middle English Verse and Prose;* Robert Harrison, *Gallic Salt.*

faded metaphor   A comparison, implied or express, the meaning of which is now taken for granted, its original novelty or freshness having faded; e.g., "running brook." Slang metaphor often fades in this way. "Square shooter," for example, has lost its association with actual "shooting irons," as have "table-leg" and "bottleneck" with the human body. Any word whose origin lies in metaphor but has come to be used literally with no awareness of the metaphor is a faded metaphor. The forgotten comparison that led to the word's first use is now known mainly to those interested in word origins. An example in everyday usage is the word *magazine,* used by most to mean a periodical publication. The word's original meaning (from Arabic), a *storehouse,* is seldom thought of; yet it is clear enough upon reflection, especially when another use of the word, *powder magazine,* is compared. Faded metaphors are also referred to as *dead* metaphors.

fallacies of reasoning   Most of the logical fallacies are treated in this handbook under the following entries:
AD CAPTANDUM, AD HOMINEM, AD IGNORANTIAM, AD MISERICORDIAM, AD POPULUM, AD VERECUNDIAM, ARGUMENT AGAINST THE MAN, ARGUMENT FROM AUTHORITY, ASSERTION, ASSUMPTIONS (mistaken), BEGGING THE QUESTION, CARD STACKING, CAUSAL REASONING, DISJUNCTIVE DILEMMA, EQUIVOCATION, "EVERY AND ALL" FALLACY, FALLACY OF COMPOSITION, FALLACY OF DIVISION, FALSE ANALOGY, FALSE DILEMMA, FALSE PREMISE, FRIEND OF THE ENEMY, GENETIC FALLACY, GLITTERING GENERALITY, HALF-TRUTH, HASTY GENERALIZATION, INDUCTIVE REASONING, IPSE DIXIT, NON SEQUITUR, POST HOC, RED HERRING, SWEEPING GENERALIZATION, SYLLOGISM, TU QUOQUE, UNDISTRIBUTED MIDDLE. See also EMOTIONAL APPEALS and PROPAGANDA DEVICES.

fallacy of composition   In logic, the confusion of collective with distributive and individual characteristics. Given the premise that every member of a class has a certain characteristic, it does not necessarily follow that the class collectively has that characteristic. Consider:
> Every member of the church owns property.
> Therefore the church owns property.

The conclusion may not hold up. We have attributed to the *whole* a characteristic of *each* of its members. The fallacy of composition is also known as "garbled syllogism." Contrast FALLACY OF DIVISION.

fallacy of division   In logic, the confusion of distributive with collective characteristics. Given the premise that a class as a whole has a certain characteristic, it does not necessarily follow that every member of that class has that characteristic. Consider:
> The school board is rich.
> Johnson is a member of the school board.
> Therefore Johnson is rich.

Obviously the conclusion may not hold up. We have confused a *collective* characteristic with a *distributive* characteristic. We have attributed to *each* the characteristics of *all.* Contrast FALLACY OF COMPOSITION.

falling action   See DRAMATIC STRUCTURE.

false analogy   In ARGUMENTATION, a comparison of two things or situations that purports to establish a belief that because the two things are alike in some ways, they are also alike in other ways. The reasoning is fallacious because it ignores some very clear differences in favor or some superficial likenesses.

false dilemma   In ARGUMENTATION, the "either/ or" premise; the presentation of a choice between two alternatives while assuming (or hoping that the audience will assume) that these two alternatives are the only ones available, and neglecting to note that it might not be necessary to accept either. For example: "Are we going to teach our children spelling, or are we going to teach them basket-weaving?"

false premise   In DEDUCTIVE REASONING, a nonfactual or not necessarily acceptable statement from which a conclusion is drawn. If a premise in a SYLLOGISM is false, then the conclusion is necessarily false, even though the conclusion may nevertheless be valid in itself. For example, a conclusion like "Grissom was a brave astronaut," though quite valid in itself, is fallaciously drawn from a premise like "All brave astronauts die in the line of duty."

familiar essay   See ESSAY.

fancy   1. In Elizabethan literature, especially Shakespeare's plays, a synonym for FANTASY or ILLUSION, also for a spookish supernatural phantasm. Compare, for example, the Duke's speech at the opening of *Twelfth Night,* "... so full of shapes is fancy / That it alone is high fantastical" with the physician's speech in *Macbeth,* "... she [Lady Macbeth] is troubled with thick-coming fancies / That keep her from her rest." 2. In modern usage, a synonym for taste or judgment; for example, in the utterance "That kind of movie is not to my fancy" or "I don't fancy that." 3. In modern literature, an ingenious image, invention, or idea (compare CONCEIT) or quality of mind, often whimsical or extravagant or both. When Milton used the term in "L'Allegro" ("sweetest Shakespeare, Fancy's child"), he intended a compliment. From the 1900s on, however, the term became somewhat *déclassé.* Compare IMAGINATION.

fantasy   1. In psychology, the imagining of an object or event in concrete images whether or not the object or event is actually there. 2. In literature, a character's experience of an object or event, usually supernatural, which may or may not be there and which the author usually leaves more or less open as an AMBIGUITY. Less open, for example, are Hamlet's experience of the ghost in *Hamlet* and Scrooge's experience of the ghosts in Dickens's *Christmas Carol.* More open, perhaps, is the governess's experience of Mr. Quint and Miss Jessel, the "apparitions," in James's *Turn of the Screw.* 3. In Shakespeare's diction and that of his contemporaries "fantasy" is often a synonym for FANCY. 4. A kind of fiction in which the author creates a special wild, whimsical, and folkloristic world, as does J. R. R. Tolkien in *The Hobbit* and *The Lord of the Rings;* hence, a literary MODE.

REFERENCE: Mark Hillegas, ed., *Shadows of Imagination.*

farce   1. Broad humor, often satirical. 2. A play, or elements in a play, using humor along with SLAPSTICK and STICHOMYTHIA. Examples range from Aristophanes' *The Frogs* to Kaufman and Hart's *Of Thee I Sing* (1931). In the latter, for example, the candidate for Vice-President of the United States is given the job of licking stamps, to exaggerate the trivial and ridiculous functions fulfilled by Vice-Presidents of that era.

REFERENCES: Eric Bentley, *The Life of Drama;* Leo Hughes, *A Century of English Farce.*

fatalism   The pessimistic belief that people have no control over their destinies; that everything is predetermined or predestined. Compare CALVINISM, DETERMINISM, EXISTENTIALISM, and NATURALISM.

Fates, the   In classical mythology the three sister goddesses who determined human destiny: Clotho (spinner of the threads of life), Lachesis (caster of lots), and Atropos (cutter of life threads); also called the Weird Sisters. Compare THE GRACES.

REFERENCES AND READINGS, see under MYTH.

faulty reference   The use of pronouns that, in context, do not clearly stand for nouns—that is, whose reference is uncertain. In current usage the personal pronouns (*he, she, it, they*), the relative pronouns (*which, that*), and the demonstratives (*this, that, these, those*) are the most carelessly used without clear reference. "I don't like music, which my friends cannot understand." (Does *which* stand for *music*—or for *I don't like music?*)

Ambiguous reference occurs when a context introduces two or more possible nouns for the pronoun to refer to: "His grandfather took him to Europe when *he* was on vacation." (Is *he* the grandfather or the grandson?) *Broad reference* occurs when a pronoun refers to an idea that is not actually expressed. For example, "She had little ambition; *this* made her seem lazy." *This* refers rather loosely to the whole idea, *she had little ambition.*

Faulty reference causes little difficulty in conversation, since the proper antecedent can usually be inferred from intonation or clarified by question and restatement. In writing, however, the fault is more troublesome, since the writer is not present to offer the clarification.

feminism   See WOMEN'S LIBERATION.

festschrift   Literally, "festival writing." A term borrowed from the German to denote a collection of scholarly articles, critical essays, or biographical testimonials in honor of an esteemed scholar-teacher. The writers are usually the scholar's colleagues and former students, and the occasion is usually the retirement or death of the person honored. Some examples: Vittorio Gabrieli, ed., *Friendship's Garland: Essays Presented to Mario Praz on His Seventieth Birthday;* Paul Sweezey et al., *F. O. Matthiessen;* Ray Browne and Donald Pizer, eds., *Themes and Directions in American Literature: Essays in Honor of Leon Howard.*

ficelle In fiction, a minor character or a non-participating observer whose chief function is to help the reader understand what is going on. An example of this device, as Henry James admits in his *Notebooks,* is Maria Gostrey in *The Ambassadors.* See UNRELIABLE NARRATOR.

REFERENCE: Wayne Booth, *The Rhetoric of Fiction.*

fiction See NOVEL, NOVELLA, NOVELETTE, SHORT STORY.

fictive audience 1. An audience (as distinguished from the reader) that a writer creates for a specific occasion or effect. In Emerson's "Concord Hymn," for example, the fictive audience addressed by the speaker is the "spirit that made those heroes [the embattled farmers] dare." 2. In another sense, the writer's audience is always a fiction, as Walter Ong has observed—always a kind of "mock reader," as Henry James put it. For even as a narrator may assume a fictive role or PERSONA, so too that narrator expects the reader to assume a correspondingly responsive role. Compare APOSTROPHE.

REFERENCES: Walter Ong, "The Writer's Audience Is Always a Fiction," *PMLA* (Jan., 1975); Wayne Booth, *The Rhetoric of Fiction;* Norman Holland, *The Dynamics of Literary Response.*

fictive character Legendary character; in legend and fiction, a character whose traits reflect somewhat romantically the real person supposedly being represented or with whom the character is usually associated. Natty Bumppo, for example, is a fictive character of the early American wilderness pioneer; similarly, Chingachgook represents certain of the noble traits of the American Indian. "George Catlin in paint and James Fenimore Cooper in the novel had fixed for the American imagination," writes Leslie Fiedler, "the *fictive* Indian and the legend of the ennobling wilderness ... where the Noble Savage confronted Original Sin." (Emphasis added.) Whatever or whoever is represented in a fictive character, the faithfulness to history, biography, and reality is on a high, usually romanticized, level of abstraction. Though all fictive characters have fictional characteristics, not all fictional characters are fictive; many fictional characters are individualistic. Compare STOCK CHARACTER and see BIOGRAPHICAL FALLACY.

REFERENCES: Leslie Fiedler, "Montana: or The End of Jean-Jacques Rousseau," *An End to Innocence;* Lowry Nelson, "The Fictive Reader," in Peter Demetz *et al.,* ed., *The Disciplines of Criticism;* W. G. Kay, "The Observer and the Voyeur," *Southern Quarterly* (Oct., 1970); W. H. Gass, *Fiction and the Figures of Life;* Maxwell Geismar, *Mark Twain: An American Prophet;* James Beard, *James Fenimore Cooper;* Nicholas Karolides, *The Pioneer in The American Novel.*

figurative language Apt and imaginative language intended to mean something other than what it says (as opposed to LITERAL LANGUAGE). Figurative language arises when the mind associates one thing with another—another that is somehow *(a) related* in common experience, *(b) opposite* in one or more respects, or *(c) similar* in one or more respects. Figures of relationship include ALLUSION, EPITHET, PUN, METONYMY, and SYNECDOCHE. Figures of opposition include IRONY, PARADOX, OXYMORON, and (in the sense of expressing an extreme) HYPERBOLE, UNDERSTATEMENT, and LITOTES. Figures of similarity —the most widely prevalent figurative language—include SIMILE, METAPHOR, and PERSONIFICATION.

In all figurative language (as, indeed, in all language in general) appropriateness counts; inappropriate use of any of the mentioned figures of speech wearies the reader. An example illustrating inappropriate and unimaginative figures: "His television contract calls for more coin of the realm than any other artist has ever nailed down." The expression "coin of the realm" is a CLICHÉ; the expression "nailed down" is a FADED METAPHOR and in relation to "coin" and "artist" contributes to MIXED METAPHOR. Such artless language is almost always inappropriate. But appropriateness of figures also depends upon one's purpose, audience, and PERSONA or speaking voice. For example, such a comparison as "The road curves like an S" or "The road is S-shaped," however unimaginative, is perfectly appropriate (perfectly clear and useful) in exposition, in an engineer's instructions intended to inform, let us say, a demolition crew. For an imaginative piece like a poem, however, a more appropriate comparison might be something like Alfred Noyes's "The road was a ribbon of moonlight" or a figure in which the two things compared are as far as possible from being alike in actuality; for example, "The road was a ribbon-snake."

figure of speech   See FIGURATIVE LANGUAGE.

fin de siècle   Literally, "end of the century." The 1890s, characterized by the "new woman" seeking political and social emancipation, by the iconoclastic plays of George Bernard Shaw, and by such DECADENTS as Oscar Wilde and Frank Harris. (In France the artist Toulouse-Lautrec, who painted an unflattering portrait of Wilde, was also a prominent figure associated with *"fin de siècle."*)

REFERENCES: Mario Praz, *The Romantic Agony;* Thomas Beer, *The Mauve Decade;* R. V. Johnson, *Aestheticism;* Holbrook Jackson, *The 1890s;* Raymond Rudorff, *Belle Epoque.*

First Folio   The first authentic collection of Shakespeare's plays. It was published in 1623 by his friends Heming and Condell.

REFERENCES: Charlton Hinman, *The Printing and Proofreading of the First Folio;* Walter W. Greg, *A Bibliography of the English Printed Drama to the Restoration;* Helge Kokeritz and C. T. Prouty, eds., *The Yale Facsimile Edition of the First Folio.*

flashback   A narrative technique in which the writer orders EXPOSITION and even dramatic scenes in a sequence other than strict chronology. Given a chronology of scenes 1, 2, 3, 4, 5, and 6, for example, the writer may start with scene 3, then flashback to scenes 1 and 2, then resume with scenes 4, 5, and 6. Or the writer may start with the final scene, or with a middle scene, then flashback to strategic portions of the preceding scenes, revealing only what is necessary for an unfolding of the story. Flashbacks are used by Dickens in *A Tale of Two Cities,* by Ford Madox Ford in *The Good Soldier,* by Arthur Miller in *Death of A Salesman,* and by Hemingway in "The Snows of Kilimanjaro." Compare IN MEDIAS RES.

REFERENCES: Caroline Gordon, *How To Read a Novel;* Jean B. Mosley, "Triple-Threat Flashback," in A. S. Burack, ed., *The Writer's Handbook;* Hans Meyerhoff, *Time in Literature.*

flatting   See UNDERSTATEMENT.

Fleshly School   A Victorian critic's (Robert Buchanan's) derogatory EPITHET for Swinburne, Rossetti, Morris, and other poets whose works, in revolt against restraints of the era, emphasize the beauties of the body. Swinburne lashed back in *Under the Microscope* (1872).

focus of narration   A synonym for "point of view" in the sense peculiar to fiction and other narrative forms. Regardless of who is telling the story (an all-knowing behind-the-scenes author or one of the major or minor characters), it is almost always told from the point of view of only one person or "central intelligence." This technique is among the chief ways in which a masterwork achieves its unity. In some few exceptions—e.g., Browning's *Ring and the Book* and Lawrence Durrell's *Alexandria Quartet*—a story is deliberately told from several different points of view. But most novels, stories, and plays use a single focus of narration, so that audience and readers soon know (in fact, often identify with) the chief character, through whose eyes, thoughts, and feelings, the action unfolds. This chief character is called the PROTAGONIST, or hero, though the character may not always be heroic in the traditional sense.

In order to have the reader re-create experience through the eyes, thoughts, and feelings of one major character, the author may tell the story in the third person, focusing upon one character, one central intelligence, as the chief "he" or "she." This focus is said to be *omniscient* or, more strictly, *limited omniscient,* since very rarely does an author use "pure" or unlimited omniscience; to do so would be to focus on no one character in particular and thus eliminate a truly "chief" character. An alternative is to have one character, acting as "narrator," tell the story—a focus called the *participating point of view.* In participating focuses the narrator (the "I" speaking) may be either the chief character or an observer. As an observer the narrator may be a major or a minor character, may be impartial ("objective") or emotionally involved ("subjective").

As Brooks and Warren have suggested (in *Understanding Fiction*), the traditional dichotomy between the "omniscient" and the "participating" narrator is oversimplified. Actually, the narrator may be located on a *participation continuum,* which, though anchored to the extremes of omniscient nonparticipation on one end and autobiographical participation on the other, allows for degrees of participation (involvement) in between. Some examples should make these degrees of participation clear.

Defoe's *Robinson Crusoe* ("I was born in the year 1632 ...") is obviously at the autobiographical extreme of the continuum. And aside from the autobiographical "first person grammar," the whole story is told from the point of view of the narrator and hero, Robinson Crusoe. Not at this extreme but close to it, Hemingway's *Farewell to Arms* is told from the point of view of the protagonist, Frederic Henry ("In the late summer of that year we lived in a house in the village that looked across the river ..."); notice the narrator's "we."

At the other extreme of the continuum, or close to it, is Dickens's *Tale of Two Cities,* in which the narrator is the author himself. And though he is not purely objective and omniscient, he is sufficiently all-knowing to describe what is happening concurrently in London and in Paris. (This omniscience is sometimes called *panoramic*.) Except in quoted conversation, he uses "third person grammar" ("She looked so beautiful in the purity of her faith") and focuses mainly on Lucie Manette. Similarly, in Eliot's *Silas Marner* the author-narrator is omniscient, and she actually intrudes occasionally (as does Dickens) with some philosophic comment. Nevertheless, the story is told through the central intelligence of Silas. It is *his* story, just as *A Tale of Two Cities* is Lucie Manette Darnay's story.

Between these extremes or near-extremes on the continuum, and regardless of whether the story is told in the third person or the first, *the narrator may participate as a character in various degrees of involvement*—as an *objective observer* (as does Poe's Visitor in "The Fall of the House of Usher"), as a more *subjectively involved* but still minor character (as does Conrad's Marlowe in *Lord Jim*), or as one of the *major characters, though still not the protagonist* (as does Ford Madox Ford's Dowell in *The Good Soldier*).

REFERENCES: Cleanth Brooks and Robert Penn Warren, *Understanding Fiction;* Percy Lubbock, *The Craft of Fiction;* Henry James, "The Art of Fiction," *Critical Essays and Prefaces;* David Lodge, "Uses and Abuses of Omniscience," *Critical Q.* (Autumn, 1970); P. L. Irvine, "The Witness Point of View . . ." *So. Atlantic Q.* (Spring, 1970).

foil   In drama and fiction, a character whose traits are contrasted with those of another character; e.g., Falstaff and young Hal (Shakespeare's *Henry IV,* Part I), Godfrey and Dunstan (Eliot's *Silas Marner*), Mr. Leggatt and the Captain (Conrad's "Secret Sharer"), Demian and Emil (Hesse's *Demian*), Gene and Phineas (Knowles's *Separate Peace*).

folklore   LEGEND, FABLE, PROVERB, riddle, joke, APHORISM, BALLAD, CAROL, MYTH, fairy tale, tall tale, charm, hex, and the like that have been orally transmitted for many generations before being recorded; hence of cumulative authorship and multiple versions. The term *folklore* was introduced in 1846 by William John Thoms in an issue of *The Atheneum* magazine. In the nineteenth century a revival of interest in collecting folklore occurred in England under the stimulus of (Thoms's) Camden Society and later the London Folklore Society. Folklore societies seek to collect, identify, and compare the survivals of ancient beliefs, customs, and tradition. See also BESTIARY, FOLK SONG, FOLKTALE.

REFERENCES: Funk and Wagnalls, *Standard Dictionary of Folklore;* Stith Thompson, ed., *Motif Index to Folk Literature;* B. A. Botkin, ed., *A Treasury of American Folklore;* Richard Dorson, ed., *American Folklore;* R. D. Abrahams, *Jump-Rope Rhymes: A Dictionary;* Iona and Peter Opie, *Children's Games;* Susan Stewart, *Nonsense* [*Aspects of Folklore and Literature*]; Ray Browne, ed., *The Celtic Cross.*

folk song   A poem of unknown original authorship, transmitted orally for many years in several different versions and ultimately recorded in one or more of its versions. Often the words or music or both migrate from one country to another; for example, "Foggy Foggy Dew" migrated to the United States from England via Australia and New Zealand. The folk song is characterized by brevity, simplicity, and the repetition of certain lines or phrases, especially the incremental repetition in such "rounds" as "Three Blind Mice" and "Row, Row, Row Your Boat." Unlike literary songs and poems, which are more or less "frozen," folk songs continually undergo changes, each generation adding its version, each interpreter varying the nuance, as reflected in the alternative versions in printed collections like Thomas Percy's *Reliques of Ancient English Poetry* (1765) and John and Alan Lomax's *Folk Song U.S.A.* (1948). This characteristic of *cumulative* authorship (as in "Green Grow the Rushes") is no doubt a more accurate description than the "communal authorship" often ascribed to folk songs and other folk genres. For "communal authorship" implies an original collaboration, which, though not impossible, is in most instances unlikely. It was no doubt the phenomenon of cumulative authorship that prompted the celebrated folklorist and philologist Jacob Grimm (1785–1863) to say that "a folk song composes itself."

The best-known English folk songs include "Scarborough Fair," "Greensleeves," "Pop Goes the Weasel," "London Bridge Is Broken [Falling] Down," "Once I Loved a Maiden Fair," "The British Grenadiers," "The Twelve Days of Christmas," "Good King Wenceslas," and even "God Save the King." Best-known Scottish folk songs include "Auld Lang Syne" [not originally composed by Robert Burns], "Blue Bells of Scotland," "Weel May the Keel Row," and "Leezie Lindsay." Best-known Irish folk songs include "Londonderry Air," "The Rose of Tralee," "Cockles and Mussels," and "Green Grow the Lilacs."

In the United States the best-known Negro folk songs (often called "spirituals") include "Swing Low, Sweet Chariot," "Nobody Knows De Trouble I've Seen," "Go Down, Moses," and "Joshua Fit De Battle of Jericho." The best-known songs of cowboys, sailors, railroad and steel workers include "The Old Chisholm Trail," "Home on the Range," "Git Along, Little Dogies," "Bury Me Not on the Lone Prairie," "The Erie Canal," "Yo, Heave Ho!" "John Henry" [aside from several ballad versions], "I Been Wukkin on de Railroad," "Casey Jones," and "Big Rock Candy Mountain." Other American folk songs include "Yankee Doodle," "Blue Tail Fly," "Turkey in the Straw," "Skip to My Lou," "Lil Liza Jane," "Old Smoky," "Clementine," "There Is a Tavern in the Town," "Down in the Valley," "Red River Valley," "Blow the Man Down," "She'll Be Comin' Round the Mountain," "John Brown's Body," and "The Man on the Flying Trapeze." See BALLAD, CAROL, FOLKLORE.

REFERENCES: Margaret Boni, ed., *The Fireside Book of Folk Songs;* Leonard Deutsch, ed., *Treasury of the World's Finest Folk Songs;* R. M. Lawless, *Folksingers and Folksongs in America;* Bruno Nettl, *An Introduction to Folk Music in the United States;* Carl Sandburg, *The American Songbag.*

folktale   A narrative originally handed down by word of mouth with each narrator usually contributing some variation; hence a story of cumulative authorship. Different versions of a basic story (for example, the abused orphan who ultimately marries a prince) migrate in different versions from country to country. From earliest times folktales have survived first in the oral, then in the literary tradition of practically every nation and culture. Such ancient Greek epics as the *Iliad* and the *Odyssey* (ca. 800 B.C.), for example, include many a folktale from an earlier Greece and Persia. And although the writing of these EPICS is attributed to one author, Homer, their authorship in pre-written (oral) stages of transmission must have been multiple and cumulative.

Similarly, *The Thousand and One Nights, or Arabian Nights' Entertainments,* translated into English first by Edward Lane in 1839–41 and by Sir Richard Burton in 1855–88, derive from Persian and Egyptian prototypes of the fourteenth and sixteenth centuries. And the Arabian stories of "Sinbad the Sailor" and "Ali Baba and the Forty Thieves" have counterparts in the folktales of ancient India, especially those collected in the *Panchatantra* (A.D. fifth century).

Except for some of Chaucer's retelling of tall tales and fables as incidental parts of his original works (for example, Chaunticleer the cock and Reynard [or "Russel"] the fox in "The Nun's Priest's Tale"), medieval English writers were given less to retelling secular folktales, more to Biblical stories. Of course, the Judaeo-Christian Bible—like the sacred book of every other religion—is full of folktales, as Sir James Frazer showed in *Totemism* (1887) and in his monumental twelve-volume study, *The Golden Bough* (1890–1915). One hastens to add that the folk origin of these tales need not make them unbelievable; even when they cannot be "scientifically true," they contain much truth on a higher level of abstraction. "Humble folk tale," observes Harold Watts, "is but myth that has lost its mooring in rite."

Perhaps the first influential collector of secular folktales in modern times was the Frenchman Charles Perrault (1628–1703). In 1697 he surreptitiously published his *Contes de ma mere l'Oye,* addressed to children and containing such folktales as "Cinderella," "Bluebeard," "Sleeping Beauty," and "Little Red Riding Hood." Whether it was Charles Perrault himself or his son Pierre who wrote (that is, retold) these traditional tales is a purely academic matter, since all of them have since been traced to ancient sources (for example, by Elizabeth Mure, as early as 1831, in an unpublished manuscript in the Toronto, Canada, Public Library).

During the late eighteenth and early nineteenth centuries, concomitant with the new interest in philology, there developed a revival of interest in collecting and recording folktales. To collect their famous *Märchen* (1812) Jacob Grimm (1785–1863) and his brother Wilhelm (1786–1859) interviewed peasants who had been retelling stories that had been told in their families for several generations.

The dividing line between genuine folktales and literary tales based on a folk tradition is often tenuous. Little folklore is reflected in such essentially original tales as "The Emperor's New Clothes," "The Ugly Duckling," "The Red Shoes," and "The Little Mermaid" by Denmark's Hans Christian Andersen (1805–75). But because of his enchanting creations (reflected in much of the statuary in Copenhagen) and because of his visits to other Scandinavian countries and to England from 1840 to 1857, he inspired many folk collectors and collections—among them Anthony Montalba, *Fairy Tales of All Nations* (1849); Anne and Eliza Keary, *The [Norse] Heroes of Asgard* (1857); Mary Frere, *Old Deccan [Hindu] Days* (1868); and, above all, the celebrated *Blue Fairy Book* (1889) by Andrew Lang (1844–1912). Lang, a writer and scholar of amazing versatility, was one of the leading members of the London Folklore Society and in 1888 had translated and edited *Perrault's Popular Tales.* Two of Lang's best-known reconstructions were "Tom Thumb" and "Jack the Giant Killer."

In the United States, meanwhile, aside from such highly original treatments of folk stories as Longfellow's *Hiawatha* and Washington Irving's "Legend of Sleepy Hollow" and "Rip Van Winkle," many Negro folktales were retold by Joel Chandler Harris in *Tales of Uncle Remus* (1880). But perhaps the best-known American folktales came from the frontier, the "tall" tales about Paul Bunyan, Tony Beaver, Johnny Appleseed, Mike Fink, John Henry, and Pecos Bill. These were first collected by Thomas Thorpe, in *The Mysteries of the Backwoods* (1846), and by W. B. Laughead, in *Paul Bunyan and His Big Blue Ox* (1914). See also LEGENDS, MYTH, FOLKLORE, BALLAD, FOLK SONG.

REFERENCES: Milton Rugoff, ed., *A Harvest of World Folk Tales;* Stith Thompson, ed., *Tales of the North American Indians* and *One Hundred Favorite Folk Tales;* Walter Blair, *Tall Tale America;* Richard Dorson, ed., *American Folklore;* Martha Pappas, ed., *Heroes of the American West;* Peter Poulatis, ed., *American Folklore;* Mentor Williams, ed., *Schoolcraft's Indian Legends;* Harold Watts, *The Modern Reader's Guide to Religions;* Donald M. Winkelman, "Three American Authors as Semi-Folk Artists," *Journal of American Folklore* (April-June, 1965).

footnotes   See DOCUMENTATION.

foreshadowing   In fiction and drama, a device to prepare the reader for the outcome of the action; "planting" to make the outcome convincing, though not to give it away. In *Macbeth,* for example, Shakespeare uses the various witch scenes in part to foreshadow Macbeth's doom: "Thou shalt get kings, though thou be none."

foreword   PREFACE; a statement by the author or another person preceding the text of a book. Compare INTRODUCTION.

REFERENCE: Jacques Barzun, *The Modern Researcher.*

four-term fallacy   See SYLLOGISM 1*h.*

fragment   An utterance that lacks subject or verb or both; still generally considered unsatisfactory unless the missing element is clearly implied or is supplied by context. The unsatisfactory incomplete utterance is called a fragment, and it is among the most common weaknesses of inept writing.

When a fragment appears, the fault may usually be repaired by attaching the loose limb to the preceding full sentence, so that the offender no longer offends. Fragments usually occur in one or another of these patterns:

1. *Subordinate clause*: "Harvey was still at the table. *While all the other guests had retired to the drawing room.*" ("Harvey was still at the table, while....")

2. *Prepositional phrase*: "She said she would meet him in the library. *After the exam.*" ("She said she would meet him in the library after the exam.")

3. *Verbal phrase*: "All the players jumped from the bench. *Shouting their disapproval.*" ("All the players jumped from the bench, shouting their disapproval.")

4. *Appositive*: "We had to memorize the Gettysburg Address. *One of the world's great speeches.*" ("... the Gettysburg Address, one of the world's great speeches.")

5. *Absolute element:* "The little party decided to make camp. *It being nearly sundown.*" ("It being nearly sundown, the little party decided to make camp.")

Not every incomplete utterance is an offending fragment, however. Acceptable incomplete sentences abound in conversation (and dialogue), in highly informal writing, and in modern prose in which the attempt is to suggest the tentative workings of the mind (as in STREAM OF CONSCIOUSNESS). For discussion of acceptable incomplete sentences, see MINOR SENTENCE and ELLIPSIS.

REFERENCES: Alan Casty, *The Art of Writing and Reading;* Richard Dodge and George Wykoff, *Handbook of College Composition;* H. Wendell Smith, *On Paper.*

frame story   A group of stories that would be unconnected if they were not tied to some central framework or situation, such as a pilgrimage (*The Canterbury Tales*), a plague (*The Decameron*), or the threat of execution (*The Arabian Nights*). In each of these the element in which the author establishes the setting and situation is called the frame. The stories within this frame are the frame stories. It is in this sense that a frame story is sometimes defined as "a story within a story."

free verse   A form of poetry free from RHYME and traditional METER but not usually from patterns unique to each poem. The verses may adhere to a set number of lines or even syllables in each STANZA (where there is more than one stanza) or to a certain configuration as in CONCRETE POETRY. Free verse often uses key repetitions of words or key placements of words, for example at beginnings or ends of lines, or a combination of these devices and their variations. In short, as John Ciardi has observed, so-called free verse is not really undisciplined. Robert Frost's quip "Free verse is like playing tennis with the net down" remains a minority view. Among the most memorable free verse is Walt Whitman's *Leaves of Grass.* Here is an excerpt from his poem "Grass":

> Tenderly will I use you, curling grass.
> It may be you transpire from the breasts of young men,
> It may be if I had known them I would have loved them,
> It may be you are from old people; or offspring taken too soon
> out of their mothers' laps.

Note that despite the absence of rhyme and traditional meter (though not of cadence) Whitman reiterates his "It may be" clause in a parallel pattern (see PARALLELISM). Among contemporary poets one of the most ingenious is May Swenson. In her well-known poem "The Key to Everything," which begins "Is there anything I can do?" she sings a brilliant aria of *do's* counterpointed with *don'ts* and *its.*

Other writers who have used free verse include Matthew Arnold, Stephen Crane, Edgar Lee Masters, Amy Lowell, Ezra Pound, T. S. Eliot, Archibald MacLeish, Conrad Aiken, William Carlos Williams, W. S. Merwin, Allen Ginsburg, William Stafford, Maxine Kumin, Nancy Willard, and Colette Inez.

REFERENCES: John Ciardi, "How Free Is Free Verse?" in A. S. Burack, ed., *The Writer's Handbook;* A. C. Partridge, "Free Verse," *The Language of Modern Poetry;* Karl Shapiro, *A Prosody Handbook;* Linda Wagner, "And the Farming of Our Ancestors," *Windsor Review* (Fall, 1969); Donald Stanford, "Robert Bridges and the Free Verse Rebellion," *Journal of Modern Literature* (Sept., 1971); Stephen Berg and Robert Mezey, eds., *Naked Poetry;* Justin Kaplan, "Illuminations" in *Walt Whitman, A Life.*

Freudian slip   Any inadvertency of speech or writing, any "slip of the tongue," that can be taken as revealing a state of mind or "hidden motive." Sigmund Freud (1856–1939), the originator of psychoanalysis, held that every such "mistake" is caused, whether or not the speaker is aware of the cause. An example: "Would you care for an olive, branch—I mean Blanche!"
REFERENCE: Sigmund Freud, *Psychopathology of Everyday Life.*

friend of the enemy   In ARGUMENTATION, an emotional appeal in which the speaker, to avoid a rational analysis of the issue, says, in effect, "But the *bad guys* are in favor of your proposal!" thus implying "You are a friend of our enemies!" and, by extension, "You, too, are an enemy." This appeal is familiarly known as "guilt by association." In a different context a writer may strengthen an argument by quoting the opposition's friends: "Even my opponent's *friends* agree with me!"
REFERENCE: Harry H. Crosby and George Estey, *The Rhetorical Imperative.*

Fugitive Poets, the   John Crowe Ransom, Allen Tate, Robert Penn Warren, Donald Davidson, and other American poets and critics associated with the *Fugitive* magazine (1922–25) at Vanderbilt University. Both the poetry and the criticism of the Fugitives reflect their commitment to Southern agrarianism (see ROMANTICISM and SENSIBILITY) and to the concretist aesthetics of the NEW CRITICISM, which they themselves helped to establish.

fundamental figure, central image   The metaphor or image that unifies, or contributes to the unity of, a literary work. A classic example is the cat image that unifies Carl Sandburg's poem "Fog." A dominant image often recurs in fiction—blackness, for example in Conrad's "The Lagoon"; rain, in Hemingway's *Farewell to Arms;* bloodstains, in Yukio Mishima's "Swaddling Clothes"; flowers, in D. H. Lawrence's *Sons and Lovers.*

futurism   1. An aesthetic movement that started in Italy and Russia in the early 1900s and that foreshadowed Mussolini's fascism. The poet F. T. Marinetti, in his MANIFESTOES of 1908 and 1912, attacked things academic (including museums) and espoused speed, violence, and war—"the dynamics of movement and the glories of danger." Like Walt Whitman (at least in aesthetics) Marinetti believed that poetry should spring from a sense of rebellion and should abandon traditional rhetoric and syntax. Among his devotees were the American e. e. cummings (1894–1962) and the Russian Vladimir Mayakovsky (1893–1930). Mayakovsky, in disillusionment with futurism and the socialist New Left, committed suicide. Futurism influenced the fine arts more than it influenced literature, and was the forerunner of cubism, DADAISM, EXPRESSIONISM, and SURREALISM.
    2. A contemporary consciousness, if not a cult, concerned with problems and possibilities of life in the near future. Whether through science-fiction or nonfiction, writers speculating about the quality of life in the future tend to divide into utopians and alarmists. Some of the utopians—B. F. Skinner, in *Walden Two,* and Arthur Clarke, in *Childhood's End*—envision pragmatically ideal societies. But these visions alarm the HUMANISTS. Humane alarmists Ray

Bradbury in *Fahrenheit 451* and Ivan Illich in *Deschooling Society* decry the Orwellian *1984* world, in which the individual, like Auden's "Unknown Citizen," is diminished to a computer number. Contemporary futurists are perhaps too cavalierly dismissed for "bankruptcy in their knowledge of the past" (Edmund Wilson's charge). Wilson would no doubt prefer that futurists expose themselves to less future-shock and more shock of recognition.

REFERENCES: R. W. Flint, trans., *Manifesto of Futurism;* Felix Stefanile, trans., *Some Italian Futurist Poets;* E. J. Brown, *Mayakovsky and His Circle;* Barry Marks, *E. E. Cummings;* Norman Friedman, *E. E. Cummings;* Alvin Toffler, *Future Shock;* Arthur Clarke, *Reach for Tomorrow;* Isaac Asimov, *Fact and Fancy;* Sallie Sears and G. W. Lord, eds., *The Discontinuous Universe;* Robert Theobold, *Futures Conditional;* Edmund J. Farrell, *Deciding the Future;* Edmund Wilson, ed., *The Shock of Recognition;* Ann and Samuel Charters, *I Love* (a biography of Vladimir Mayakovsky).

G

Gallicism　1. An IDIOM or expression peculiar to the French language but used in another language. Many French words and expressions have been transplanted into English and are thoroughly at home in it; others are resisted or rejected. The worst of Gallicisms is the use of French in English to affect superior knowledge. 2. An English expression fractured to sound like French idiom; e.g., "It is to laugh, Baby!" (English is also sometimes fractured to sound like German: "We are already gepooped!") Compare the Anglicized treatment of borrowings from other languages; e.g., "Don Kwixit" for *Don Quixote.*

REFERENCE: H. L. Mencken and Raven McDavid, "Loan Words and Non-English Influences," *The American Language.*

game playing　See ROLE PLAYING.

genetic fallacy　The mistaken assumption that an idea is false or a discovery worthless because it was originated by someone we do not like. Compare ARGUMENT AGAINST THE MAN.

genre　A literary form, as, for example, NOVEL, SHORT STORY, PLAY, POEM, ESSAY, and the like. In each of these major genres there are subgenres; for example, subgenres of the poem include the BALLAD, the SONNET, the MADRIGAL, these three being lyrical as distinguished from dramatic poems. PLAYS and EPICS were the most prestigious genres in antiquity; in modern times, novels and lyric poems. The genre or form of any literary work signals part of its meaning, just as the structure of a sentence signals part of its meaning aside from its lexical content. Compare MODE.

REFERENCES: Kenneth Burke, *The Philosophy of Literary Form* and *Terms for Order;* Northrop Frye, "Theory of Genres," *Anatomy of Criticism;* Mark Schorer, ed., *Galaxy: Literary Modes and Genres;* Alton C. Morris *et al.,* eds., *College English, The First Year;* W. O. S. Sutherland and Robert L. Montgomery, eds., *The Reader: A Study of Form and Content;* E. D. Hirsch, "Concept of Genre," *Validity of Interpretation;* Heather Dubrow, *Genre.*

gestes　From the Latin for "[heroic] deeds." A literary form, popular in the Middle Ages, in which heroic deeds or tales of these exploits are recounted. Three representative examples are the *Chanson de Roland* (eleventh century), *The Pilgrimage of Charlemagne* (twelfth century), and *The Gest Historiale of the Destruction of Troy* (ca. 1350). These works were also known as *chansons de gestes* and are to be distinguished from *jestes,* the Elizabethan word for *jokes. Note:* Despite what the title suggests, the *Gesta Romanorum* (ca. 1300) is a collection of moralized tales used by medieval preachers.

REFERENCE: E. K. Chambers, *English Literature at the Close of the Middle Ages.*

Gilded Age   The decade after the War between the States, an era marked by depression and corruption. Mark Twain and Charles Dudley Warner's novel *The Gilded Age* (1873) is a ROMAN A CLEF of that period—i.e., its fictive portraits only thinly veil the portraits of real-life persons, including the corrupt Boss Tweed.

glittering generality   When arguing in favor of a point, the arguer (or propagandist) may, whether consciously or not, attach complimentary terms, or EUPHEMISMS, to that point and thus make it seem attractive. In doing so the troublesome task of presenting supporting argument is avoided and, in each such attachment of "good" words to the propagandist's side of the matter, a *glittering generality* is produced. The technique is the reverse of NAME-CALLING, which attaches unfavorable words to an opponent or a particular side of the matter. The complimentary terms are usually vague or otherwise too slippery to pin down; they seem to glitter but may not be gold, after all. "My plan for this city's *welfare* is *honest* and *scientifically trustworthy,* and would bring a *fair* and *democratic order* to a citizenry that deserves the *best.*" See SWEEPING GENERALIZATION.

gnomic   1. In early Greek literature (sixth century B.C.) the "Gnomic Poets" wrote a kind of verse full of APHORISMS or MAXIMS. Since then, the term "gnomic verse" (meaning moralistic or DIDACTIC) has become a derogation. 2. In FOLKLORE, pertaining to *gnomes,* a race of hunchbacked or otherwise misshapen dwarfs who were supposed to live deep in the earth, guarding its treasures. Their literary identification, along with their relationship to such similar spirits as sylphs, nymphs, and salamanders, is variously credited to the medieval Rosicrucians and to Dr. Theophrastus Paracelsus (1493–1541), a Faustlike person about whom Robert Browning wrote his narrative poem *Paracelsus* (1835). Gnomes and "little people" appear in various shapes under various names in the folklore and folkloristic literature of several nations. Compare the Norse trolls and troll-imps in Ibsen's *Peer Gynt,* the leprechauns in *Finian's Rainbow,* and the gnomelike creatures in Tolkien's *The Hobbit.*

gobbledygook   Stuffy, pretentious, wordy, roundabout language. Senator Maury Maverick of Texas coined the word *gobbledygook* (also spelled *gobbledegook*) to name, and in a sense describe, the prose style so often found in government documents and in other official communications. Reflective of the twentieth-century rise of technology and breakdown of individualism, gobbledygook results from a paradoxical approach to subject matter and audience: the writer or speaker is at once timid (fearing to say anything too bold) and pompous (striving for a scientific-sounding tone of rightness). Characteristics of gobbledygook are (1) prolixity—much DEADWOOD, especially redundancy; (2) pedantry—obscure terms, jargon, and makeshift words like *actualize, regulationed, societality, personalwise;* (3) hedging—the protective covering of EQUIVOCATION, which provides an "out" for the writer in case of a challenge ("Some experiments might seem to indicate ... ," "One could possibly say ... ," "It is not impossible to assume that ...."); (4) abstractness—big and obscure words where short and direct words would do; (5) EUPHEMISM—the glossing over of whatever may offend; the softer, roundabout expression in place of the harsh or straight-on; (6) fuzzy thought; (7) stale expression—many CLICHÉS and ready-cut phrases; (8) impersonality—the deliberate avoidance of reference to the first person (*I* or *We*) in favor of a neutralized and unemotional third person (usually *one,* or *a person,* or *an individual*) or in favor of an even more impersonal passive voice.

Gobbledygook may arise from several motives. The self-suspicious student, uncertain of facts or ideas, may adopt gobbledygook to hide weakness of thought and make the work "sound more important." The politician may adopt it, hiding unpopular ideas behind verbiage and doubletalk. The writer of office bulletins or official announcements may adopt it to make the work seem more dignified, impressive, or objective (and this prose is often called *officialese*).

REFERENCES: William Safire, *An Anecdotal Dictionary of Catchwords, Slogans, and Political Usage;* J. R. Masterson and W. B. Phillips, *Federal Prose: How to Write in and/or for Washington.*

Goliardic verse   Satirical Latin verse of a kind popularized by an irreverent "Bishop" Golias in the twelfth century. The chief theme was CARPE DIEM: Eat, drink and be merry today, for who knows what tomorrow will bring? During the Middle Ages university students and clerics (among them the popular Walter Map) wandered through Germany, France, and England composing and singing Goliardic verses very much in the manner of contemporary "protest" singers. The *Carmina Burana,* a collection of Goliardic poems, has become well known through the choral setting of the composer Carl Orff. Compare TROUBADOUR.

REFERENCES: Helen Waddell, *The Wandering Scholars;* George F. Whicher, trans., *The Goliardic Poets.*

Gothic   1. The East Germanic language used by Bishop Ulfilas (fourth century) to translate the Bible. 2. The kind of medieval church architecture characterized by verticality; tall, pointed windows; steeply arched, vaulted roofs; flying buttresses; gargoyles side by side with saints; and so on. 3. In literature, the GOTHIC NOVEL or SOUTHERN GOTHIC.

gothic novel   A kind of mystery novel intended to shock or titillate and dependent for its psychological effects on Gothic architecture, bleak old castles with secret passageways, medieval armor, ghosts or rumors of ghosts, and decadent lone survivors of once proud families that are desperate for fresh young blood to stave off further decay. The writers of this genre assumed, perhaps justifiably, that their readers would accord it a willing suspension of disbelief. The gothic novel was developed in eighteenth-century England by Horace Walpole, with *The Castle of Otranto* (1764). Other popular "gothics" were *Vathek* (William Beckford, 1786), *The Monk* (M. G. Lewis, 1795), *Mysteries of Udolpho* (Ann Radcliffe, 1795), and *Frankenstein* (Mary Shelley, 1818). In America this genre had its representative in *Wieland* (Charles Brockden Brown, 1798). Aside from the impact that the gothic novel has made as an art form in its own right, it influenced the poetry of Keats (in "The Eve of St. Agnes"), Shelley (in *The Cenci*), and Byron (in *Manfred*); and the fiction of many a subsequent author. Gothic elements abound in the short stories of Poe (especially "The Fall of the House of Usher"), Hawthorne's *Marble Faun,*

Charlotte Brontë's *Jane Eyre*, Emily Brontë's *Wuthering Heights*, and Henry James's *Turn of the Screw*. The gothic novel refurbished with subtler mysteries and revelations—the tunnels and cellars of the psyche—has been revived by the contemporary British writer Iris Murdoch. In *A Severed Head*, for example, the incestuous Honor Klein hovers like a black cloud over all the extramarital intrigues. Miss Murdoch's fiction is also a PARODY of the gothic novel. For aside from re-introducing standard gothic trappings, she re-examines some of them as hitherto repressed sexual symbols. She has her characters act out gothic sexual episodes, which in the eighteenth-century prototypes remained half-conscious stirrings or fantasies.

REFERENCES: Wilbur Cross, *Development of the English Novel;* Lowry Nelson, "Night Thoughts on the Gothic Novel," in Eleanor T. Lincoln, ed., *Pastoral and Romance;* H. P. Lovecraft, *Supernatural Horror in Literature;* Patricia Spacks, *Insistence of Horror;* Ann Tracy, *The Gothic Novel . . . Plot Summaries and Index to Motifs.*

Grace   See CALVINISM.

Graces, the   In classical mythology, the three sister goddesses who bestowed charm, beauty, and joy on nature and humanity: Thalia (abundance), Euphrosyne (mirth), and Aglaia (elevation). Compare the FATES.

graffiti   Literally, "inscriptions," especially those scratched into rocks and walls. For the most part graffiti are anonymous, satirical (often pornographic and scatological) comments in prose and verse scribbled on walls of public and institutional rooms. The comments range from the childish to the bitter remarks of social protest.

REFERENCES: Albert Kalson, "The Theatre of Graffiti," *Journal of Popular Culture* (Summer, 1967); Robert Reisner, *Graffiti.*

grand tour   A tour through two or more countries of Europe ("the Continent") usually by walking (or, in modern times, cycling) for the purpose of "finishing" one's formal education. Since the Elizabethan era, Oxford and Cambridge graduates have traditionally taken such a tour, and in modern times American graduates and undergraduates have emulated this practice. In these tours, which usually take several weeks or longer (sometimes months), the traveler tests a knowledge of the "target" language(s); studies art, architecture, and historical monuments; and observes, at first hand, people, places, customs, mores, and pastimes. Such experiences John Stuart Mill categorizes as "The End of Education and the Beginning of Self-Education" in his celebrated *Autobiography*. The grand tour is more elaborately described in other biographies and is reflected in much modern fiction. In *Abroad* Paul Fussell observes that one travels "to experience the past."

REFERENCES: John Addington Symonds, "Foreign Travel," *Sir Philip Sidney;* John Milton, "Italian Tour, 1638–1639," *Second Defence of the English People;* Laurence Sterne, *A Sentimental Journey through France and Italy;* Chauncey B. Tinker, *Young Boswell;* Frederick A. Pottle, ed., *Boswell's Journals;* William Wordsworth, *Descriptive Sketches* [of a Walking Tour through France and Switzerland]; Jacques Barzun, ed., "Traveler and Poet: Aetat. 21–26," *Selected Letters of Lord Byron;* André Maurois, "A Six Weeks' Tour," *Ariel: The Life of Shelley;* Aileen Ward, *John Keats: The Making of a Poet;* Henry Adams, *The Education of Henry Adams;* Lincoln Steffens, *Autobiography;* Harrison Smith, ed., "Travel on Two Continents," *From Main Street to Stockholm;* Richard Haliburton, *The Royal Road to Romance;* Paul and Elizabeth Elek, eds., *The Age of the Grand Tour;* Janet Mandelstam, "The Grinds on the Grand Tour," *Saturday Review* (February 21, 1970).

Graveyard school   A group of eighteenth-century poets—among them, Thomas Gray, Robert Blair, Thomas Parnell, and Edward Young—who wrote on funereal subjects.

Great Books, the   **1.** Certain classics of literature selected by such educators as Charles W. Eliot, for the "Harvard Classics" or "Five-Foot Shelf"; John Erskine, for the Columbia Great Books Course; Stringfellow Barr, for St. John's College, Maryland; and Robert Hutchins and Mortimer Adler, for the University of Chicago program in General Education. **2.** An adult-education society organized by Hutchins and Adler in many communities across the country, with leaders who meet small groups every other week to discuss an assigned classic. For a list of these classics, see the Appendix to Adler's *How to Read a Book*. (See also Adler, *The Great Ideas* and *The Syntopicon,* an index to the ideas and issues in the Great Books.) **3.** The chief instructional materials of an educational philosophy known as "perennialism," the major tenet of which is that education is essentially a continuing dialectic.

REFERENCES: Robert Hutchins, *The Great Conversation;* Mortimer Adler, *The Syntopicon;* Quentin Anderson and Joseph Mazzeo, eds., *The Proper Study;* Vincent Milosevich, ed., *Toward Excellence.*

great chain of being   The idea that all the components of the universe are arranged in a chain, or hierarchy, with each thing or creature occupying a God-given place. At the bottom of the chain is inanimate matter; farther up, things that grow but do not reason; then rational man, "a creature in a middle state," as Pope described him; above man, the angels; finally, at the top, God. The idea of the chain is said to have come from Milton—"hanging in a golden chain / This pendent world"—while the concept of orderly links derives from Plato's theories of the relations between mind and matter in the *Timaeus* and his "idea of the good" in *The Republic.* Plato's concepts were elaborated in the *Enneads* of Plotinus (A.D. 204–269), who more directly inspired the Neo-Platonists of both the Italian and the English RENAISSANCE. Most of these writers—among them Edmund Spenser, in his *Hymns in Honour of Love and Beauty* (1596), and Henry More, in his *Platonical Song of the Soul* (1642)—emphasized the beauty of the universe and the aesthetic character of the relations between man and God. Such ideas were easily accommodated to the Judaeo-Christian belief in God's love for man as a binding-principle or covenant. To this principle in its Neo-Platonic version Shakespeare made frequent reference, especially in *Troilus and Cressida* (1609). Certain seventeenth-century poets who could find no unity in the physical world turned inward in an attempt to unify themselves, their own sensibilities. Given to fanciful CONCEITS and the invention of God-man links that seemed to the man of "New Science" to be too far removed from scientific reality, they were ridiculed as METAPHYSICAL (literally, "beyond nature") by John Dryden and by Samuel Johnson. But all seventeenth- and eighteenth-century writers were very much concerned with man's place in the world of nature. And next to the word *nature,* according to A. O. Lovejoy, the phrase "great chain of being" was the most sacred utterance of the eighteenth century. For as astronomers continued to discover a much more immense universe than had previously been realized, making Milton's "pendent world" look like a child's bauble, poets responded to the deeply felt human need of spiritualizing what might otherwise seem harshly impersonal and irrational. And poets like Pope and Thomson sought for rational rather than just aesthetic or mystical bonds between the earthly and the heavenly. In the long poem *Essay on Man* (1732–34) Pope reverently addressed himself to the "Vast chain of being":

> Vast chain of being! which from God began,
> Nature's ethereal, human, angel, man,
> Beast, bird, fish, insect, what no eye can see,
> No glass can reach; from Infinite to thee,
> From thee to nothing.—On superior pow'rs
> Were we to press, inferior might on ours;
> Or in full creation leave a void,
> Where, one step broken, the great scale's destroyed:
> From Nature's chain whatever link you strike,
> Tenth, or ten thousandth, breaks the chain alike.

Unlike the metaphysical poet George Herbert, who in his poem "The Pulley" (1633) had been concerned with a more personal and direct bond between himself and his God, the Neo-Platonist James Thomson in the long poem *The Seasons* (1726–30) re-created—in stones, plants, beasts, men, and angels—a more rational chain to the All-Perfect. The great chain of being assumed, finally, the following three tenets: *(a)* plenitude, or infinite supply, *(b)* continuity and linked or shared attributes, and *(c)* hierarchy, or orderly arrangement of the links.

REFERENCES: A. O. Lovejoy, *The Great Chain of Being;* Frederick A. Pottle, "Dogma, Science, and Poetry," *The Idiom of Poetry;* Louis Martz, *The Poetry of Meditation;* E. M. W. Tillyard, *Elizabethan World Picture;* Sheridan Blau, "Pope's 'Chain of Being' and the Modern Ecological Vision," CEA *Critic* (Jan., 1971); Peter Viereck, *The Unadjusted Man;* T. G. Bergin and M. H. Fisch, trans., "Poetic Cosmography," in *The New Science of Giambattista Vico.*

H

hackneyed usage   See TRITENESS.

haiku (Hokku)   A classic Japanese verse form in three unrhymed lines of, respectively, five, seven, and five syllables. An example:

> In all the May rains
> there is one thing not hidden—
> Bridge at Zeta Bay.

Almost always a haiku establishes the season, usually in the first line. Like the TANKA, haiku are characterized by compression, restraint, and suggestion rather than explicit statement or description. The images are OBJECTIVE COR-RELATIVES, which contribute to a tight unity of mood and tone. Occasionally, haiku are written in pairs or in related series ("*garlands*"). An example of a pair:

> *Decorations on a Japanese Fan*
>
> *Side 1*
>
> Wearing autumn reds
> and golds of maple driftings
> ladies live in leaves
>
> *Side 2*
>
> Limbs turn lovelier
> when leaves attach themselves to
> trees and dress the woods

REFERENCES: Harold Henderson, ed., *Haiku: An Anthology from Basho to Shiki;* Glenn Swetman, "The Haiku, the Sonnet, and the English Language," *Quartet* (Summer, 1964).

half-truth   A kind of misrepresentation that gives the audience the truth in part but not the whole truth, or that withholds saying anything about aspects that may be damaging to the persuader's case. Compare CARDSTACKING.

REFERENCES: Vance Packard, *The Hidden Persuaders;* John Kenneth Galbraith, *The Affluent Society;* C. Northcote Parkinson, *The Law and the Profits.*

hamartia   Tragic flaw. See TRAGEDY.

hanging indention   See DOCUMENTATION.

Harlem Renaissance   A flowering of literature, especially poetry, by black writers during the 1920s and 1930s in the Harlem district of New York. James Weldon Johnson (d. 1938), Countee Cullen (d. 1946), Claude McKay (d. 1948), Langston Hughes (d. 1967), and Arna Bontemps (d. 1973) formed the nucleus of this group. Their sponsors included W. E. B. Du Bois (d. 1963), editor of the NAACP journal *The Crisis;* Witter Bynner (d. 1968), co-author of *Spectra,* a controversial PARODY; Ernestine Rose, a librarian; and A'Leila Robinson, whose literary salon, "The Dark Tower," was named after one of Cullen's poems. Although Harlem poetry of that period was criticized by the unsympathetic as derivative, such anthology favorites as Cullen's "Ballad of the Brown Girl" and Hughes's "The Negro Speaks of Rivers" still ring with authenticity. See BLACK LITERATURE.

REFERENCES: Arna Bontemps, "Harlem Renaissance," *Saturday Review* (March 22, 1947); Langston Hughes and Arna Bontemps, eds., *Poetry of the Negro;* James Weldon Johnson, *The Book of American Negro Poetry;* Blanche Ferguson, *Countee Cullen and the Negro Renaissance;* Richard Barksdale and K. Kinnamon, eds., *Black Writers of America;* Nick Aaron Ford, ed., *Black Insights;* Addison Gayle, ed., *Black Expression;* Nathan Higgins, *Harlem Renaissance.*

hasty generalization   A fallacious conclusion resulting from a failure to compile sufficient data (especially in statistical INDUCTIVE REASONING) or from a failure to examine the available data.

head rime   See ALLITERATION.

Hebraism and Hellenism   As codified by Matthew Arnold, the spirit of Hellenism is "life as it is"; of Hebraism, "life as it ought to be." Thus the Hebraic emphasis is essentially moral; the Hellenic, aesthetic. In *Culture and Anarchy* and other essays Arnold argued that his self-righteous Victorian contemporaries needed less Hebraism, more Hellenism.

REFERENCES: Matthew Arnold, "Culture and Anarchy" in Lionel Trilling, ed., *The Portable Matthew Arnold;* essays by Eliot, Trilling, Burke, Farrell *et al.* in Bernard Oldsey and Arthur Lewis, Jr., eds., *Visions and Revisions ... ;* David DeLaura, *Hebrew and Hellene in Victorian England.*

hemistich   A half line of poetry, two of which make up a metrically complete line, as in Anglo-Saxon ALLITERATIVE VERSE. The poet W. H. Auden uses the hemistich in his poem "Always in Trouble."

hendiadys   An idea normally expressed in a phrase (*try to win, very ready, far away*) and presented instead with *and* (*try and win, good and ready, far and away*). This rhetorical device was much used in Greek and Latin poetry as a refinement.

hermeneutics   A science of interpretation, especially of the Bible; to be distinguished from *exegesis,* the more subjective art of interpretation. Derivation of the term is controversial. Hermes was the Greek god of science; Hermes Trismegistus was an Egyptian alchemist and astrologer.

heroic couplet   Also called **riding rhyme.** Rhymed pairs of iambic pentameter lines. Chaucer introduced this verse form into English, having developed it in 17,000 lines of *The Canterbury Tales* (ca. 1387). The heroic couplet, along with the Chaucerian style of dramatic narrative, was used by Spenser in the satirical "Mother Hubberd's Tale" (1590) and by Marlowe in the erotic poem "Hero and Leander" (1598). Marlowe preferred blank verse for his plays (as did Shakespeare and many other Elizabethan playwrights) and used heroic couplets in them only sporadically. The heroic couplet was developed to perfection, however, by Dryden and Pope. In Dryden's satirical *Absalom and Achitophel* (1682) the heroic couplets, while retaining Chaucer's narrative flow, also demonstrated the sophistication of EPIGRAM. Compare, for example, these couplets from Chaucer's "Wife of Bath's Prologue"

> I know that Abr'am was a holy man
> And Jacob too, as far as is my ken;
> And each of them had spouses more than two
> (As many another holy man did, too).
> When did you ever see in any age
> Our God on high forbidding marriage
> By express word? Please do enlighten me;
> Or where did he demand virginity?

with these couplets from *Absalom and Achitophel,* Part One

> In pious times, ere priestcraft did begin,
> Before polygamy was made a sin;
> When man on many multiplied his kind,
> Ere one to one was cursedly confined;
> When nature prompted, and no law denied
> Promiscuous use of concubine and bride....

Chaucer's influence on Pope is reflected in the latter's "Paraphrases from Chaucer" (ca. 1709). But Pope's brilliance shines with its own light in such epigrammatic couplets as these from his *Essay on Criticism* (1701):

> True ease in writing comes from art, not chance,
> As those move easiest who have learned to dance.
>
> Men must be taught as if you taught them not,
> And things unknown proposed as things forgot.
>
> A little learning is a dangerous thing;
> Drink deep, or taste not the Pierian spring.

The above excerpts also illustrate Pope's art of the *closed* heroic couplet; that is, the couplet containing one complete sentence. But Pope was also a master of the *open* heroic couplet; that is, verse in which a sentence flows from one couplet into another, as, for example, these lines from his *Essay on Man* (1733–34):

> Let us, since life can little more supply
> Than just to look about us, and to die,
> Expatiate free o'er all this scene of man;

in which the main exhortation is "Let us ... expatiate." Those same lines illustrate Pope's virtuosity with varying the CAESURA, a device that serves to prevent sing-song effects.

Another virtuoso of the varying caesura and the open couplet was Robert Browning, whose poem "My Last Duchess" (1842) begins,

> That's my last duchess painted on the wall,
> Looking as if she were alive. I call
> That piece a wonder, now; Fra Pandolfo's hands
> Worked busily a day, and there she stands.

Heroic couplets were used by such poets as Byron, Keats, Shelley, Swinburne, and William Morris, but gradually waned in fashion toward the end of the nineteenth century.

REFERENCES: John A. Jones, *Pope's Couplet Art;* W. B. Piper, *The Heroic Couplet;* W. K. Wimsatt, "On Relationship of Rhyme to Reason," *The Verbal Ikon;* Jacob Adler, *The Reach of Art.*

heterography   Spelling in which the same letter represents several sounds. Only a strictly phonetic alphabet could avoid it. In English, heterography plagues the student, who is both annoyed and amused that *c* should sound different in *call* and *cell,* that *g* should sound different in *gum* and *gem,* and that the combination *gh* should be so erratic in a *rough fight.* See SPELLING.

hexameter   See METER.

hiatus   In writing or speech, a break in continuity, such as a missing part of a manuscript or a brief vocal pause in midword, as between the successive vowels in *preempt.* Compare CAESURA.

historical novel   A novel based on historical events and on one or more historical personages, but shaped otherwise by the novelist's imagination. Some of the most celebrated historical novels are *War and Peace* (Tolstoy), *Ivanhoe* (Scott), *Vanity Fair* (Thackeray), *A Tale of Two Cities* (Dickens), *The Last Days of Pompeii* (Bulwer-Lytton), *The Cloister and the Hearth* (Reade), *Northwest Passage* (Roberts), and *Gone with the Wind* (Mitchell).

Critics have argued about whether an historical novel is really fiction. Perhaps the tenet most widely accepted by authors and critics is that liberties may be taken with comparatively obscure or unverified historical events, but that violence must not be done to major historical events and personages; this tenet was developed by, among others, Lessing in his *Hamburgische Dramaturgie* (1767). Thus, whether a minor character like Dr. Manette (in *A Tale of Two Cities*) was imprisoned or actually existed is comparatively unimportant; it is perfectly plausible that a person like him could have been imprisoned. What Dickens could not have afforded to take liberties with, however, is the major circumstances of the French Revolution, the Reign of Terror, the tumbrils, and the guillotine. He might well have slipped into a tumbril a fictional character or two, but he could not very well have tampered with the recorded executions of well-known historical personages. The critic Georg Lukacs believes that historical novels should deal responsibly, not just romantically, with social and political events.

REFERENCES: Georg Lukács, *The Historical Novel;* for a bibliography of historical novels arranged according to events and periods (as well as by authors and titles), see Ernest Baker, *A Guide to Historical Fiction;* for another select list of historical novels and short stories and for the view of historians on the value of such works, see Oscar Handlin *et al., Harvard Guide to American History.*

history as literature   In a broad sense history may be taken to comprehend any record purporting to give facts about events and actions and to draw conclusions from those facts. Thus, articles, reports, memoranda, diaries, and the like may be construed as history; but most often they are not literature, though they may be the materials of either history or literature. (In this sense, a scientist's report on an experiment may be taken as a micro-history of a micro-event.) In a narrower sense, history as literature comprehends those writings—annals, chronicles, memoirs, journals, diaries, narratives, and the like—that are presented with imaginative style. The writer of history, unlike the writer of an historical novel, may take few liberties with the facts, but may combine all the skills of the novelist in the dramatic presentation of the materials. The writing of history as a discipline or profession is a development of comparatively recent times; but over the centuries many distinguished histories meriting attention by the student of literature have been written.

In classical antiquity the celebrated examples include the *History* [of Greece and Persia], by Herodotus, "the Father of History"; *The History of the Jews,* by Josephus; *The History of the Peloponnesian Wars,* by Thucydides; *The Anabasis,* by Xenophon; and the *Histories* and *Annals* [of Rome], by Tacitus.

In medieval times the most famous history was Jean Froissart's *Chronicles* [of France, Spain, Portugal, and England].

During the English Renaissance the two most famous histories were *The History of the World,* by Sir Walter Raleigh, and the *Chronicles* [of England, Scotland, and Ireland], by Raphael Holinshed, the latter being the source for several of Shakespeare's plays.

In modern times histories celebrated for their literary style include *The Decline and Fall of the Roman Empire* (Edward Gibbon), *The History of Charles XII* [of Sweden] (Voltaire), *The French Revolution* (Thomas Carlyle), *The Rise of the Dutch Republic* (J. L. Motley), *The History of England* (Thomas Macaulay), *The Civilization of the Renaissance in Italy* (Jacob Burckhardt), *The Renaissance* (John Addington Symonds), *The Conquest of Mexico* and *The Conquest of Peru* (both by William Prescott), *The Epic of America* (James Truslow Adams), *The Tragic Era* (Claude Bowers), *The Rise of American Civilization* (Charles and Mary Beard).

Recent notable histories include *The Story of Civilization* (Will and Ariel Durant), *The History of the English-Speaking Peoples* (Winston Churchill), *The Rise and Fall of the Third Reich* (William Shirer), *Red Star over China* (Edgar Snow), *History of the Russian Revolution* (Leon Trotsky), *Ten Days That Shook the World* (John Reed), *The Guns of August* (Barbara Tuchman), *Black Lamb and Grey Falcon* (Rebecca West), *Hiroshima* (John Hersey), and *The Armies of the Night* (Norman Mailer). Compare HISTORICAL NOVEL and BIOGRAPHY.

REFERENCES: Edmund Wilson, *To the Finland Station: A Study of the Writing and the Acting of History;* Arnold Toynbee, *A Study of History;* H. G. Wells, *An Outline of History;* Oscar Handlin *et al., The Harvard Guide to American History;* Orville Prescott, ed., *History as Literature;* Donald Pizer, "Documentary Narrative as Art," *Journal of Modern Literature* (Sept., 1971).

holidays mentioned in literature

Advent, season beginning four Sundays before Christmas.

All Hallows.   See *Hallowe'en.*

All Saints' Day, November 1, commemorates martyrs and Pope Boniface IV's converting the heathen in A.D. 834.

All Souls' Day, November 2, is a day of prayers and alms-giving to alleviate the suffering of souls in Purgatory.

Arbor Day, date varies, has been since 1872 a day devoted to the planting of trees, usually by schoolchildren.

Armistice Day, November 11, commemorates the day World War I ended officially (the eleventh hour of the eleventh day of the eleventh month). Now called *Veterans Day.*

Ascension Day, the fortieth day after Easter, commemorates Christ's ascension to Heaven on the fortieth day after His resurrection.

Ash Wednesday, the first Wednesday in Lent, signifies the beginning of Lent and Christian humility. The custom of sprinkling ashes on the forehead was popularized by Pope Gregory the Great, who had adapted it from an old Roman and Jewish custom.

Candlemas, February 2, Feast of the Purification of the Virgin.

Christmas, December 25, commemorates the birth of Christ. The French word for Christmas, *Noël,* and the Scandinavian *Jul* (Yule) are also used in English. The burning of the yule log, the decoration of the tree, the hanging of stockings, the placing of shoes and other receptacles for gifts—these customs had their origins in pre-Christian societies. The Angles of Britain, for example, celebrated December 25 as a combination New Year's Day and Mother's Day. As with many other holidays, several of the pre-Christian rites and customs of this day were merged with the Christian rites. In 1644 the English Puritans abolished most of the "pagan" aspects of Christmas, but these were restored by Charles II. The Christmas feast, celebrated sometimes on Christmas Day and sometimes on Christmas Eve, traditionally included a roast goose, as in Dickens's *Christmas Carol.* Groups of young people going from house to house to sing carols on Christmas Eve is also an adaptation of a pre-Christian custom.

Columbus Day, October 12, commemorates Columbus's discovery, in 1492, of the "West Indies."

Corpus Christi Day, the Thursday after Trinity Sunday, which is the Sunday after Pentecost, commemorates the Eucharist (the Lord's Supper of Holy Communion, which uses bread wafer and wine symbolically for the body and blood of Christ). It was on this day that the medieval English trade guilds of York, Coventry, and Chester produced their mystery and MIRACLE PLAYS.

Decoration Day, May 30, commemorates all American soldiers killed in all past wars; also called *Memorial Day.*

Easter, the first Sunday after the first full moon of the spring (March 21 or any of the twenty-eight days thereafter; hence not earlier than March 21 nor later than April 25), was originally a pagan Teutonic festival celebrating the spring equinox, in honor of the dawn goddess. (The Germanic *oestre* is a linguistic relative of several comparable words meaning *dawn.*) When the Church Fathers converted the Angles and Saxons, along with other Teutonic and Celtic peoples, they amalgamated into the Christian holiday many pre-Christian rites and customs.

Election Day, in the United States the first Tuesday after the first Monday in November of even-numbered years; also called *General Election Day.*

Empire Day, May 24, in the British Commonwealth honors Queen Victoria; also called *Victoria Day.*

Epiphany, January 6, commemorates the appearance (*epiphane* is Greek for *appearance*) of the Star of Bethlehem to the Three Wise Men.

Father's Day, the third Sunday in June. See also *Mother's Day.*

Flag Day, June 14, commemorates the adoption in 1777 of the American flag; it is not a legal holiday.

Good Friday, the Friday preceding Easter Sunday, commemorates Jesus' crucifixion by the Romans. "Good" is a transliteration of the Anglo-Saxon word for "holy"; in folklore anyone born on Good Friday (or on Christmas) has the power to see spirits and to give them orders.

Hallowe'en, October 31, among the Old Celts was the last day of the year, when witches and warlocks were supposed to celebrate their rites; when the pagans were Christianized, this holiday was converted to the Eve of All Hallows' or All Saints'.

Hannukkah, the end of the third or the beginning of the fourth Jewish month, commemorates the victorious revolution, under the Maccabbee patriots, against Antiochus IV of Syria, and the dedication of the Temple in Jerusalem in 165 B.C. It is also called the *Feast of Lights.* Hannukkah usually comes around Christmastime, and since it, too, is a time when gifts are exchanged, it is sometimes, all too loosely, called "the Jewish Christmas."

Holy Thursday, the day before *Good Friday.*

Independence Day, July 4, commemorates the signing in 1776 of the Declaration of Independence.

Labor Day, the first Monday in September, celebrates American labor and gives a day of rest to wage-earners.

Lady Day, March 25, commemorates the Feast of the Annunciation.

Lent, the forty weekdays from Ash Wednesday to Easter, commemorates Jesus' fasting in the wilderness. Devout Christians, in self-abnegation, give up some personal indulgence, especially some food like meat, which they enjoy during the rest of the year. The night, or the few nights, before Lent is usually celebrated as a kind of "feast before the famine" with a Mardi Gras (as in New Orleans) or a Carnival (as in Europe). A *mardi gras* is, literally, "fat Tuesday"; *carnival* derives from *vale* and *carne*—"farewell to meat."

Mardi Gras.   See *Lent.*

May Day, May 1, is an ancient holiday rooted in spring fertility rites, especially in India and Egypt. In medieval England, and later in the United States, it was the custom on May Day to decorate a Maypole and then to dance around it (as, for example, in Hawthorne's "May-Pole of Merry Mount"). Freudian critics regard the Maypole as a phallic symbol. In the U.S.S.R., May Day is a legal holiday devoted to political speeches and to demonstrations of military might.

Memorial Day.   See *Decoration Day.*

Michaelmas, September 29, is the Festival of St. Michael, who fought dragons and now weighs the souls of the risen dead. In England the day is noted for *(a)* roast goose feasts, *(b)* election of magistrates, and *(c)* collection of rents. (Dickens refers to Michaelmas in the opening passage of *Bleak House.*)

Mother's Day, the second Sunday in May, honors all mothers. The pre-Christian Angles and Saxons celebrated a mothers' day of sorts on December 25. The medieval Europeans, who thought of "mother" as the Virgin Mary, had numerous days in her honor—not only as an intercessor ("paraclete") on their behalf but also and more generally, according to Henry Adams (see "The Dynamo and the Virgin," in *The Education of Henry Adams*), as a deeply respected and loved exemplar of matronly fertility and strength.

New Year's Day, January 1 in Western cultures; various other dates in other cultures, such as the Jewish Rosh Hashana, the Chinese New Year's and so on. For fascinating information on various New Year celebrations, see James Frazer, *The Golden Bough.*

New Year's Eve, December 31.

Noel.   See *Christmas.*

Palm Sunday, the Sunday before Easter, commemorates Jesus' entry into Jerusalem, when palm branches were strewn in his path.

Paschal time, the Easter season. *Paschal* pertains to the lamb that was ritually killed and eaten at Passover; in Christian symbolism, the Paschal Lamb is Jesus (*Agnus Dei,* the Lamb of God).

Passover, beginning at sundown on the fourteenth of Nisan, the Jewish seventh month, is observed for eight days. It commemorates the Exodus from Egypt, the story of which is recounted at the Seder (Passover Supper) as it is read from the *Haggada.* Eating only unleavened bread (Matzoth) and refraining from any other leavened food products is a requirement for the observance of the holiday. It commemorates not only the Exodus but also the Angel of Death's "passing over" the Jewish homes the night before. Having marked their door posts with lamb's blood, the Jews were spared death by plague—the Tenth Plague—which killed the Egyptian first-born.

Pentecost, the sixth and seventh days of Sivan, the Jewish ninth month, is the Jewish Festival of Shavuoth, which commemorates Moses' receiving on Mount Sinai the tablets inscribed with the Ten Commandments. The Christian holiday, the seventh Sunday after Easter, commemorates the descent of the Holy Spirit over the Apostles; also called *Whitsunday.*

Purim, the fourteenth day of Adar, the Jewish sixth month, is the Jewish Feast of Lots, which commemorates the day on which the Jews of Persia were to be annihilated, the order to be determined by the drawing of lots. Queen Esther, the Jewish wife of King Ahasuerus, managed to save the Jews with the help of her uncle Mordecai. Haman, the mastermind of the anti-Jewish plot, was hanged. Celebration of the holiday involves hearing a reading of the "Megilla" (*Scroll of Esther,* recording the events of the holiday), the sending of gifts of food to friends and the poor, and merrymaking.

Rosh Hashana, the first of Tishri, is the Jewish New Year, which is reckoned from 3761 B.C., the traditional date of the Biblical Creation.

St. Agnes' Eve, January 20, is the holiday on which a girl, on performing certain rites, was supposed to have a vision of her future husband. See Keats's "Eve of St. Agnes."

St. Nicholas' Day, St. Nicholas is the patron saint of Russia, of scholars, of sailors, of pawnbrokers, and of little boys. He was the original Santa Claus. Many Eastern Orthodox people still celebrate St. Nicholas' Day; the Dutch people also celebrate this day, but they have tended to merge it with Christmas Eve.

St. Patrick's Day, March 17, commemorates the saint who, though not Irish himself, converted the pre-Christian Irish and rid Ireland of snakes and vermin. In explaining the Holy Trinity, St. Patrick used a shamrock.

St. Swithin's Day, July 15, celebrates the saint vaguely associated with rain: "If it rains on St. Swithin's Day, it will rain for forty days."

St. Valentine's Day, February 14, commemorates the Roman priest who gave aid and comfort to the persecuted Christians. This is "lovers' day," when even the birds choose their mates for the year, as Chaucer observes in *The Parliament of Fowls.* In England on this day young people draw lots and exchange gifts, a modification and extension of an ancient pagan rite honoring Juno or Venus.

Shrovetide, the three days preceding Ash Wednesday.

Thanksgiving, the fourth Thursday in November in the United States, was originally any day of thanks-giving, but is now traced to the day of thanksgiving when the Pilgrims commemorated their survival during the first harsh winter in New England, thanks in part to gifts of food from the native Indians. The turkey feast is traditional, and the thanks offering has developed into a more general reverence for all blessings. Canadians celebrate a similar day of thanksgiving, the second Monday in October.

Trinity Sunday, the Sunday after Pentecost.

Veterans Day.   See *Armistice Day.*

Whitsunday.   See *Pentecost.*

Yom Kippur, the tenth day of Tishri, the Jewish first month, is the Jewish Day of Atonement. Since the Jewish day is always reckoned from sundown to sundown, the holiday actually begins the evening before. Fasting and praying for forgiveness of sins mark the observance of this day.

Yuletide, Christmas.

REFERENCES: *Oxbridge Omnibus of Holiday Observances;* Mary Haseltine, *Anniversaries and Holidays;* George W. Douglas, *The American Book of Days;* Sir James Frazer, *The Golden Bough;* Robert Chambers, *The Book of Days;* E. O. James, *Seasonal Feasts and Festivals;* A. J. Nevins, ed., *The Maryknoll Catholic Dictionary.*

homeric epithet   See EPITHET 2.

homily   1. Originally, a sermon or moral story, such as the Anglo-Saxon *Blickling Homilies.* 2. Generally, a derogatory term for a sermon or sermonlike lecture.

homographs   Words with the same spelling but different origins, meanings, and pronunciations: "He *wound* a bandage about the *wound.*" Since pronunciation and meaning tend to change more rapidly than spelling, words that were once HOMONYMS may become only homographs (as did *wind,* which once rhymed with *behind* whether it meant "an air current" or "to coil").

homonym   Two words spelled alike and pronounced alike which have far different meanings and derivations; each is the other's homonym. *Pitch* black and wild *pitch,* for example, have no connection in meaning, though they look and sound alike. The word *homonym* is often used loosely to mean the same thing as *homophone.* Compare HOMOPHONE and HOMOGRAPH.

homophone   Two words that sound alike but have different spellings, origins, and meanings, e.g., a *piece* of music and a lasting *peace.*

horn book   **1.** In seventeenth-century New England, a child's primer consisting of a single sheet of paper protected by a transparent piece of horn and mounted on a small board. From horn "books" children learned the alphabet, numbers, the Lord's Prayer, and much of their earliest catechism ("In Adam's fall / We sinned all."). **2.** Thomas Dekker's *Gull's Horn Book* (1609) was a satirical primer for the young fop or Italianate gentleman, who was beginning to be smiled at in Elizabethan comedies and who was to be lampooned in JACOBEAN comedies.

Hudibrastic   See BURLESQUE.

hubris   Excessive pride; one of the tragic flaws. See TRAGEDY.

REFERENCE: Virginia Floyd, *Toward a Definition of Hubris.*

humanism   **1.** A generality often used too loosely, as Howard Mumford Jones has observed for "humaneness" and for "the humanities"; that is, for studies in literature and the arts. **2.** A movement of enlightenment championed by Desiderius Erasmus (1466–1536) and others in reaction to medieval scholasticism. Although both the humanists and the scholastics were interested in Greek and Roman studies, the humanists emphasized matters of human, as distinguished from ecclesiastical, interest. See RENAISSANCE 2. **3.** A modern religious movement that, like Unitarianism, emphasizes rational, as opposed to mystical, beliefs. Its official publication is *The Humanist.* **4.** In contemporary literature and thought, a kind of secular existentialism. See EXISTENTIALISM; compare NEW HUMANISM.

REFERENCES: Howard Mumford Jones, *One Great Society;* Ernst Cassirer, *An Essay on Man;* Erwin Panofsky, *Meaning in the Visual Arts;* Georges Simenon, *The Novel of Man;* A. R. Evans, ed., *Four Modern Humanists;* Lawrence Lipking, *Idea of the Humanities.*

humor   **1.** A "pleasant disappointment of expectation"—Max Eastman. **2.** Loosely, a synonym for pleasantry or WIT, though the latter is generally more conscious and sophisticated while humor is broader and unconsciously rooted in idiosyncrasy of personality. Thus the amusing behavior (speech as well as actions) of Bottom the Weaver, in Shakespeare's *Midsummer Night's Dream* is humorous, whereas the amusing utterances of Professor Higgins, in Shaw's *Pygmalion,* are witty.

REFERENCES: Max Eastman, *The Sense of Humor;* Walter Blair, *Native American Humor;* Luigi Pirandello, *Humor;* Henri Bergson, *Laughter;* Sigmund Freud, *Jokes and Their Relation to the Unconscious;* Louis Rubin, ed., *The Comic Imagination in American Literature.*

humours   **1.** The four body fluids assumed by most medieval and some RENAISSANCE writers to govern people's dispositions—*(a)* blood, *(b)* choler, *(c)* black bile, and *(d)* phlegm. In a healthy person the humours were thought to be in balance, with no one fluid predominating. If a person's metabolism went out of balance, it was thought that one of the humours was "stirring up an ascendancy." Thus a person suffering from an imbalance of one of the humours could be diagnosed as *(a)* sanguine or overly cheerful, *(b)* choleric or grumpy, *(c)* melancholy or lovesick, or *(d)* phlegmatic or stolid. **2.** The humours were not only the four standard psychosomatic symptoms mentioned in (1) but also more individualistic psychological traits motivating certain characters in comedy, especially the comedy of humours. Thus, aside from the stock melancholy of a Jaques, in *As You Like It,* or the sanguine conceitedness of a Malvolio, in *Twelfth Night,* humours were also such individualistic human foibles as possessiveness, self-righteousness, affectation, misogyny, and the like. Some classic examples occur in Ben Jonson's play *Every Man in His Humour* (1598). In this comedy the choleric old merchant Kitely's individualistic humour is possessive jealousy of his pretty young wife, who he suspects is having an affair with the young Edward Knowell. Edward's father, phlegmatic and stolid, is obsessed with the individualistic humour of excessive concern for his son's morals. After a series of farcical intrigues involving such St. Paul's Church bench-warmers as the stock braggart Captain Bobadill and the young Knowell's cronies, the chief obsessed characters are somewhat disabused of their humours by the compassionate Justice Clement. *Every Man in His Humour* is celebrated not only because Shakespeare acted in it, but also because its Prologue ends with Jonson's theory of what good comedy should consist of:

> ... deeds and language such as men do use
> And persons such as ...
> ... would show an image of the times.
> It should sport with follies, not with crimes;
> Except we make 'em such, by loving still
> Our popular errors, when we know they're ill.
> I mean such errors as you'll all confess,
> By laughing at them, they deserve no less;
> Which when you heartily do, there's hope left, then,
> You, that have so graced monsters
> May like men.

Humours or human foibles, then, and the therapy of laughing at them are the obverse analogues of TRAGIC FAULTS and the therapy of CATHARSIS.

REFERENCES: C. H. Talbot, *Medicine in Medieval England;* J. B. Priestly, *The English Comic Characters;* John Palmer, *Comic Characters of Shakespeare;* James Parton, *Caricature and Other Comic Art;* William F. Fry, *Sweet Madness;* Francis Fergusson, *The Idea of a Theater.*

hymn   Religious (chiefly Judaeo-Christian) songs of praise, thanksgiving, supplication, and certitude. Aside from Christmas carols and Biblical Psalms, the best-known examples include Frederic Root's "Rock of Ages," Sarah Adam's "Nearer, My God, to Thee," Sabine Baring-Gould's "Onward, Christian Soldiers," Martin Luther's "A Mighty Fortress Is Our God," Richard Heber's "Holy, Holy, Holy," Isaac Watts's "Joy to the World," John Henry Newman's "Lead, Kindly Light," Charles Wesley's "Glory Be to God on High," William Cowper's "Sometimes a Light Surprises," John Greenleaf Whittier's "O Love Divine," Josiah Conder's "Day by Day the Manna Fell," Katherine Hankey's "I Love to Tell the Story," Mary Baker Eddy's "Feed My Sheep."

REFERENCES: W. J. Reynolds, *A Survey of Christian Hymnody;* H. W. Foote, *Three Centuries of American Hymnody;* Albert Christ-Janer et al., ed., *American Hymns Old and New.*

hyperbole   (hy–per–bo–le). Gross exaggeration for rhetorical effect—e.g., "I'm dead." We find it natural to say, "I've been waiting for *hours*" (though it has really been ten minutes), "His face fell *a mile*" (he showed mild disappointment), or "Your jokes really *kill* me" (they bring a smile), or "She was *hysterical* over that new dress!" (she said she liked it). American speech abounds in hyperbole, inherited perhaps from the early settlers, who found the mountains, rivers, and plains bigger than could be described in restrained words. Such national heroes as Davy Crockett, Daniel Webster, and the legendary Paul Bunyan were celebrated for their size, shrewdness, skills, and zest for life—they were big "as all outdoors." Exaggeration became a prime device of the frontier language. These famed "tall tales" have become an American art form, still cherished. The national Liars' Club each year awards a prize for the most astounding "whopper." So common is hyperbole in American speech that even our least exciting ideas may be described as *great, stupendous, terrific*. Advertising, now a fixture that creates as well as expresses the American way of life, uses hyperbole as a standard means of luring attention. Every product is the *best* of its kind, of course, the biggest, the longest-lasting, the "most." But hyperbole has its dangers. The constant user of hyperbole soon finds such remarks taken lightly, or nearly ignored, and may find need for hyperbole's opposites, UNDERSTATEMENT and LITOTES.

hyphen   Though often thought of as a mark of punctuation, the hyphen serves chiefly as a device of spelling. It is a means of linking or of separating words or word parts to reduce the likelihood of misreading. The mark (-) is an appreciable help in adapting English speech to the printed page: It often does in writing what intonation does in speech. For example, *high-school grades* may mean something quite different from *high school-grades*. The difference is signaled in speech by intonation, in writing by the hyphen. The hyphen is generally used:

1. To link words that form a compound adjective:

red-hot stove	*fast-moving* train
blue-green water	*sit-down* strike
leveling-off period	*come-as-you-are* party
Watson-Prager Bill	*twenty-two*
three-eighths	

2. To indicate the breaking of a word from one line of print to the next. See SYLLABICATION.

3. To separate prefixes from roots whenever

   (a) a meaning other than the usual is intended:

   Please *re-form* the line.
   They *re-sent* the gift.

   (b) the root word begins with a capital letter:

   pro-British   non-Catholic   pre-Neanderthal   anti-Semitic

   (c) the prefix *semi-* is used with a word that begins with i:

   semi-independent   semi-infinite

   (d) the prefix is *ex-, cross-, half-, self-, vice-*:

   ex-sailor   cross-country   half-awake   self-confidence   vice-consul

4. To stand for the word "to" in certain phrases:

the Chicago-Philadelphia jet   pp.44-46

5. To indicate prefixes, infixes, suffixes, or syllables written alone:

Of course, *un-* is not the same as *dis-*, so one cannot be dissatisfied if one is unsatisfied.

6. In typing, to indicate a dash (--); in this instance, two hyphens are necessary.

hysteron proteron   The rhetorical device (sometimes, the error) of putting the last thing first, as the effect before the cause, or the end of a story before the beginning. For example, "It was easy getting down after we got up." Now and then a striking freshness can be brought to a stale expression by reversing the order of its elements: "Man is forever chasing *tide and time*"; "Don't *chew* more than you can *bite off*." In telling a story, the writer may start with the ending and then relate the events that led to it. In logic one may, in the *conditional* SYLLOGISM, commit the fallacy of hysteron proteron by asserting a consequent and then inferring an antecedent: "If the water is cold, Phil won't swim; Phil will swim—therefore the water isn't cold." See *affirming the consequent* under SYLLOGISM 2.

I

iamb   See METER.

iconology, iconography   In literature and art history the study of secular and religious pictures and illustrations. These often symbolize MOTIF, THEME, or MYTH and hence serve to reconstruct thought and culture. For example, the medieval painting *Skull, Candle, and Hourglass* symbolizes the transitory nature of things, and a knowledge of the medieval *Fortuna* (wheel of fortune) clarifies one's reading of "The Monk's Tale" in Chaucer's *The Canterbury Tales.*

REFERENCES: Irwin Panofsky, *Studies in Iconology;* Marshall McLuhan and Harley Parker, *Through the Vanishing Point;* Gertrude Schiller, *Iconography of Christian Art;* J. Apteker, *Iconography ... in the Fairie Queene;* J. B. Friedman, *The Monstrous Races in Medieval Art and Thought.*

idealism   **1.** A philosophy rooted in the conviction that ideas and ideals are more genuine than the world of the senses—that reality centers not in material things but in spiritual values, which may have inspired them; for example, not in a painting but in the idea of beauty. Two of the best-known idealists of ancient Greece were Socrates and Plato. Plato re-created much of Socrates's idealism in *The Apology* and other "dialogues." (4th century B.C.)

2. The value systems that, through the ages, have undergirded much literature, both AGRARIAN and urbane. The agrarian, nature-loving writers, especially those who flourished in the era of ROMANTICISM, were influenced by Jean Jacques Rousseau (1712–1778). (Compare SENSIBILITY.) The urbane idealists—among them Immanuel Kant (1724–1804), Matthew Arnold, and Ralph Waldo Emerson—while not dismissing nature (in fact, one of Emerson's famous essays is "On Nature,") gravitated to the ideal values of the civilized city, the lecture-hall ("lyceum"), the theater, and the concert-hall.

REFERENCES: A. C. Ewing, ed., *The Idealist Tradition;* Lucien Goldmann, *Immanuel Kant;* A. O. Lovejoy, *Essays in the History of Ideas;* L. M. Trawick, ed., *Backgrounds of Romanticism;* Irving Babbitt, *Rousseau and Romanticism* [an attack]; M. H. Abrams, *The Mirror and the Lamp;* Harold Bloom, *The Visionary Company.*

idiom   **1.** An expression peculiar to a language; this expression may or may not make sense literally, but it is common and quite respectable. An example: "What are you up to?" **2.** In literature and the other arts, a style of expression peculiar to an artist: "In the *idiom* of Faulkner—mankind will survive, endure, prevail."

if/then reasoning   See SYLLOGISM 2.

illusion of reality   That which *seems* real even though it may not be; the results of SELECTIVE REPRESENTATION as distinguished from random or candid representation; that is, a portrait as opposed to a photograph; one aspect of Aristotle's MIMESIS.

In the theater, for example, if the audience seems to be more aware of Hamlet than of the Richard Burton or John Gielgud performing the role, then the actor (as well as the playwright) can be said to have successfully created an illusion of reality, the audience response a "willing suspension of disbelief" (Coleridge's phrase).

Similarly, if the reader of *War and Peace* finds that in the Napoleonic sack of Moscow "he is there," then Tolstoy may be said to have successfully created an illusion of reality. Illusion of reality is almost always "a transaction between author and audience" (as Louise Rosenblatt has put it). As such, it is a possibility subject to retesting by ever-new readers. Compare SELECTIVE REPRESENTATION.

REFERENCES: Eric Auerbach, *Mimesis;* Hazard Adams, "Imitation and Creation," *The Interests of Criticism;* Allen Tate, "Techniques of Fiction," in B. S. Oldsey and A. O. Lewis, Jr., eds., *Visions and Revisions;* T. J. Reiss, *Toward Dramatic Illusion;* Stanley Poss, "The Facts of Fiction," *Northwest Review* (Fall, 1970).

imagery   **1.** Traditionally, a verbal representation of objects appealing primarily to the sense of vision. **2.** More broadly today, language that appeals to any or all of the senses. In Frost's poem "Out, Out ... ," for example,

> The buzz saw *snarled and rattled* in the yard
> And made *dust* and dropped *stove-length sticks of wood,*
> *Sweet-scented stuff* when the *breeze* drew across it. [Emphasis added.]

Snarled and *rattled* are auditory images; *dust* is at once visual, tactile, and olfactory; *stove-length sticks of wood* appeal visually until Frost turns them to *sweet-scented stuff;* then *breeze* adds its tactile impression.

Thus, every concrete noun, along with many verbs, adjectives, or adverbs related to concrete nouns, is an image. When images and sensuous appeals are deliberately mixed, as in "a land, sour green," the resulting device is SYNESTHESIA.

In poetry, which usually contains more imagery than does prose, the image is a basic building block in a kind of image-metaphor-symbol complex. Thus, Frost's imagery "And miles to go before I sleep" is also a FADED METAPHOR for "much to accomplish," as is "before I sleep" for "before I lie down on the job"; and the whole context may be symbolic of the "journey toward death."

REFERENCES: "Image, Metaphor, Symbol, Myth," in René Wellek and Austin Warren, *Theory of Literature;* Philip Rahv, *Image and Idea;* Caroline Spurgeon, *Shakespeare's Imagery;* Rosemond Tuve, *Elizabethan and Metaphysical Imagery;* John Ciardi, "Single and Multiple Imagery," *How Does a Poem Mean?;* Martha Cox, ed., *Image and Value;* Robert Gessner, *The Moving Image;* X. J. Kennedy, "Imagery," *An Introduction to Poetry.*

imagination   **1.** In general, the talent for making original interpretations of facts, original syntheses of raw data. By no means a talent exclusively displayed by writers, imagination is attributed to scientists as well, Helmholtz and Einstein, for example, having been praised for their "imaginative leaps." *Lack* of imagination in this sense, conversely, is what second-raters suffer from, according to *The Dialogues of Archibald MacLeish and Mark Van Doren* (pp.116–18).

2. In literary criticism imagination can be a term of judgment, as in (1), but more often has another, special sense—"the ability to make an image in one's mind," according to poet May Swenson. This is also the NEO-CLASSICAL sense expounded by Joseph Addison in "The Pleasures of the Imagination," a more acceptable notion today than that of the RENAISSANCE writers, who only distinguished imagination from reason. Francis Bacon, for example, observed that "imagination is to poetry what reason is to philosophy." A more discriminating distinction, which was to prove provocative for over a hundred years, was that of Samuel Taylor Coleridge (and of other ROMANTIC poets)—the distinction between imagination and fancy. While FANCY is merely an "associative power" or "mode of memory," imagination is a "shaping and modifying," a "re-creating power." In "The Marriage of Heaven and Hell" and elsewhere William Blake regards imagination as the essential medium through which God is revealed in human beings. The Victorian critic Sir Leslie Stephen, along with George Santayana, also assigns a higher niche in the poetic hierarchy to imagination than to fancy. Stephen, after slapping Coleridge's wrist for not living up to Victorian "morals," concedes to him the best touchstone for imagination in any literary work—"total dynamic effect [on the reader]." Santayana's view is that "imagination rediscovers deep ARCHETYPES and meanings beneath fanciful re-creations" as distinguished from fancy, which "only superficially reassembles images." An example of contemporary literature that comes very close to meeting all the above-mentioned criteria for imagination is J. R. R. Tolkien's *Lord of the Rings*.

3. Technically, "imaginative literature" is understood to consist of such genres as poetry, drama, and fiction, although this does not rule out the possibility that such expository genres as article, essay, and biography can be written with imagination.

REFERENCES: I. A. Richards, *Coleridge on Imagination;* M. H. Abrams, "Coleridge's Mechanical Fancy and Organic Imagination," *The Mirror and the Lamp;* R. L. Brett, *Fancy and Imagination;* Rozanne Knudson, "Conversation with May Swenson," *Quartet* (Winter, 1969); Samuel Taylor Coleridge, "Imagination and Fancy," *Biographia Literaria;* Leslie Stephen, "Coleridge," *Hours in a Library;* George Santayana, "Imagination," in Arthur Eastman *et al.,* eds., *The Norton Reader;* Alton C. Morris *et al.,* eds., *Imaginative Literature;* James Heffernan, *Wordsworth's Theory of Poetry: The Transforming Imagination;* Benjamin De Mott, *Supergrow;* J. P. Houston, *The Daemonic Imagination;* Arthur Koestler, *The Act of Creation.*

imagism   See IMAGISTS.

imagists, the   A group of poets, notably T. E. Hulme, HD (Hilda Doolittle), Richard Aldington, and Ezra Pound, who decided around 1912 to write a new kind of poetry, chiefly free verse characterized by concrete, jewel-like imagery, direct treatment of subject matter, little or no authorial comment on the thing being treated, and the use of no word that did not contribute to the effect or meaning of the poem. Many of these ideas were characteristic of Chinese and Japanese poetry, of the lyrics of the ancient Greek poet Sappho, and of the work of certain nineteenth-century French poets, particularly Gautier and Laforgue. The particular kind of poetry the imagists wrote was referred to as *imagism.* Here is a representative imagist poem by Ezra Pound, titled "In a Station of the Metro":

> The apparition of these faces in the crowd;
> Petals on a wet, black bough.

Among the best known of the poets whose work exhibits the characteristics of imagism are, besides Pound, T. S. Eliot and William Carlos Williams. The term was adopted by or applied to other poets as well, whose work was often far from the original conceptions of the movement. Among those poets the most notable is Amy Lowell, especially in her collection *A Dome of Many-Colored Glass.*

REFERENCES: Wallace Martin, "The Sources of the Imagist Aesthete," *PMLA* (March, 1970); Hugh Kenner, *Ezra Pound.*

Immediate Theater   A mode of dramatic presentation featuring much improvisation and audience participation. Similar to the THEATER OF THE ABSURD, with which it shares a dislike for plot, the Immediate Theater (also called Living Theater) has given a home to the most experimental kinds of plays, especially those with a minimum of "script." The improvisation is not restricted to minor stage business (as is allowed the insane inmates, for example, in Peter Weiss's *Marat/Sade*) but extends (as in Jack Gelber's *Connection* and *The Apple*) to the audience. The rationale for audience participation is that play-acting is or properly should be role playing; that the role of the audience has all too long remained passive, when it should have been active; that the roles of actors and spectators need to be switched as in psycho-drama.

As early as 1958 directors Judith Malina and Julian Beck began to follow in their Living Theater the poet Antonin Artaud's advice to throw away the script. In the 1960s the Immediate Theater achieved serious development under the Polish playwright and director Jerzy Grotowski, the British director Joan Littlewood, and the American director Peter Brook. Off-Broadway productions included such plays as *Paradise Now; Dionysus in 69; Massachusetts Trust; Claudius; Philadelphia, Here I Come;* and Paul Foster's *Tom Paine.* According to the drama critic Walter Kerr, the Immediate Theater often alienates rather than integrates audience and actors. Compare THEATER OF THE ABSURD.

REFERENCES: Peter Brook, "The Immediate Theater," *Atlantic* (November, 1968); Walter Kerr, "The Theater of Say It! Show It! What Is It?" *New York Times Magazine* (September 1, 1968); Jan Kott, *Theatre Notebook: 1947–1967;* Robert Brustein, *The Third Theater;* Elenore Lester, "The Final Decline and Total Collapse of the American Avant-garde," *Esquire* (May, 1969); *The Drama Review.*

implication   See ASSUMPTIONS and INFERENCE.

impressionism   1. An aesthetic movement which developed in France at the end of the 1800s and flourished in the early 1900s. The impressionists strove to paint, not objects, but light reflected from objects. This is why their paintings, however imprecise in outlines of things, are light and airy and full of ethereal colors. Since light is constantly changing, any object reflects different colors at different times. Thus Monet painted series of one object (a cathedral, a river bank, a haystack) at different times of the day, capturing changing qualities of light as these qualities appeared to him. In fact, such impressionists as Degas and Renoir strove to objectify their personal experiences of light and color. In his paintings of ballet dancers, for example, Degas avoided stock photographic details in favor of his impressions of certain effects the dancers made on him. Unlike the EXPRESSIONISTS of later decades, who carried impressionism deep into their private SYMBOLISM (sometimes into distortion), the impressionists demonstrated a respect for communication with spectators.

2. In literature, the rendering of details as they appear immediately to the senses. Imagination developed among the IMAGISTS and among such novelists as Virginia Woolf and John Dos Passos. In the trilogy *U.S.A.*, for example, Dos Passos used the impressionistic device of "the camera eye," which paradoxically enough was not photographic but rather a kind of quick brush stroke—the novelist's subjective impression of one element of experience, one point in space and time, followed by his impression of another point—very much as an impressionist painter offers dots and strokes to be blended by the eye of the beholder.

REFERENCES: John Rewald, *The History of Impressionism;* Bernard Berenson, "Introduction," *Aesthetics and History;* Monroe Beardsley, "The Object and Its Presentations," *Aesthetics.*

incunabula   Books printed before 1500 (in the "cradlehood" of printing). Classed as incunabula are the Gutenberg Bibles and about thirty thousand editions of books from the early presses of such other printers as William Caxton, Nicolas Jenson, and Aldus Manutius. Notable collections can be seen in the British Museum, The Hague, the Oxford (Bodleian) Library, the Library of Congress, and the Huntington Library (San Marino, California).

REFERENCE: Margaret B. Stillwell, *Incunabula and Americana 1400–1800.*

indefinite reference of pronoun   The careless use of a pronoun whose antecedent might be any of several nouns in a given context. See FAULTY REFERENCE.

indention   The leaving of space between the margin and the first letter of a line of print or handwriting. Usually indented are (1) first lines of paragraphs (in typing, usually five spaces), (2) certain lines of poetry (ordinarily the rhyming lines being equally indented), (3) all lines of a blocked quotation inserted in a discourse (*Note:* in such quoted blocks, quotation marks are dropped from the beginnings and ends), (4) the subordinate items in an outline (the items of equal rank being equally indented), and (5) the lines following the first line of a bibliographical entry. See DOCUMENTATION.

index   An alphabetical list of the topics (whether discussed or merely mentioned) in a written work; each item is shown with a list of the pages on which the topic is referred to. A *bibliographical index* is a guide (arranged by topic and sometimes by author) to published works; for example, the *Readers' Guide to Periodical Literature* and the card catalog of any library. See DOCUMENTATION.

indirect discourse   Speech reported second-hand as distinguished from speech quoted exactly as uttered. Examples should clarify the distinction. *Direct discourse*: "I'm on my way to the library," said Sue. *Indirect discourse*: Sue said that she was on her way to the library. One form of discourse may be preferable to the other, depending on whether the writer wishes to emphasize dramatic immediacy (direct discourse) or interpretive exposition (indirect discourse). Hemingway, along with other twentieth-century novelists except Faulkner, characteristically uses much direct discourse and thus depends upon the reader to infer much of the portraits of characters from what they actually say. On the other hand, such novelists as Dickens, Thackeray, and Henry James use more indirect discourse or a mix of the two types. Here, for example, is an excerpt from Henry James's *The American* (1877):

He [Christopher Newman] stood looking at it [copy of a painting from the Louvre] complacently . . . and M. Nioche hovered near, smiling and rubbing his hands.
"It has wonderful *finesse*," Nioche murmured caressingly. "And here and there are marvelous touches . . ."
The language spoken by M. Nioche was a singular compound, which I shrink from the attempt to reproduce in its integrity. . . . His vocabulary was defective and capricious. He had repaired it with large patches of French, with words anglicized by a process of his own . . . The result would be scarcely comprehensible to the reader, so that I have ventured to trim and sift it.

Rather than trim and sift, Henry James should probably have quoted some of M. Nioche's anglicized patches of French—should have shown them, not just told about them. Indeed, James was afterwards aware of his need to use more direct discourse, to dramatize more; and in his later novels he did so. Compare SCENE and SUMMARY.

REFERENCES: Leon Edel, *Henry James;* Mark Lambert, *Dickens and the Suspended Quotation.*

induction   **1.** Reasoning that draws inferences from given data or specimens. **2.** In literature, the characteristic method of most fiction, in which the specific incidents that unfold lead the reader to a (general) conclusion, PHILOSOPHIC STATEMENT, or THEME. **3.** A RENAISSANCE equivalent of the modern word *introduction,* as, for example, the Induction in Shakespeare's *Taming of the Shrew* and the philosophic Induction (Preface) to Sackville's *Mirror for Magistrates.*

REFERENCE: Thelma Greenfield, *The Elizabethan Induction.*

inductive leap   In INDUCTIVE REASONING, the necessary act of arriving at a conclusion without having at hand all the pertinent facts or evidence, the latter often latent at subconscious levels.

inductive reasoning   Reasoning from the specific to the general; the examination of particular facts and the attempt to account for them in a generalization. If a veterinary doctor observes a white Persian cat and finds it is deaf, then observes another white Persian cat and finds it also deaf, then observes another white Persian cat, then another and another—he may infer that *all* white Persian cats are deaf. He has reasoned from a series of particular facts to a general INFERENCE, or conclusion. But this conclusion is not absolute truth; it is only *probable*—and more or less probable, depending upon how accurate the observations and how adequate their number.

1. *Perfect induction.* If we observe all possible cases, the conclusion is a perfect induction. This is possible only when the number of cases is limited and all have been observed. These are some examples of perfect induction:

All puppies in this litter have brown eyes.
All members of the math class are present today.
All of Mrs. Oliver's children are girls.
You have always been late to our appointments.

These perfect inductions are of limited usefulness. They do not go beyond the observed facts; thus, they are often tautological, seldom significant.

2. *Statistical induction.* The number of possible cases is often limited, but too large to make convenient an examination of every one. On the morning after a frost, we may discover that all the oranges on a certain tree have been frozen and spoiled. Because we know that the cause (the frost) obtained with all the other trees in the grove, we may justifiably conclude that *all* the oranges in the grove also suffered the effect—all have been frozen and spoiled. This extension of the perfect inductive method is reliable enough to justify our drawing the conclusion as if *all* cases had been observed.

Statistical induction in general produces valid inferences only if care is taken to ensure that the statistics are of sufficient number and are truly representative. The fallacies that often appear are those of *(a)* insufficient data or statistics (sometimes called HASTY GENERALIZATION) and *(b)* biased statistics (sometimes called CARD-STACKING). For example, we may see one elderly driver ignore a red light; we then conclude that all elderly drivers are careless breakers of traffic regulations (a *hasty generalization*); and at the same time we ignore the fact that we have seen dozens of elderly drivers properly obeying red lights (*card-stacking;* ignoring pertinent evidence).

The statistical syllogism arrives at a conclusion with a probability of less than 100 per cent. If investigation has shown us that 80 per cent of the voters in a certain town are Republicans, and we learn that Mr. G. is a voter in that town, we may conclude that Mr. G. is a Republican—and our conclusion has a *probability* of 80 per cent. This sort of statistical reasoning underlies much of what is today used as basis for life insurance rates, gamblers' odds, and opinion-poll predictions of election results.

A special form of the statistical syllogism is *argument from authority,* in which we assert that A is true because a certain person says A is true. Obviously, the reliability of such a conclusion depends upon to what degree that person is a reliable authority concerning A. If we know that most of the statements on that general topic are reliable, then we know that the statement about A is probably true. We reason thus:

> Most of this person's statements are true.
> "A is true" is one of this person's statements.
> Therefore, A is true—probably.

The validity of the conclusion depends upon our avoiding certain fallacies: *unreliable authority* (we must be certain that the person actually is an authority on the topic and that the statements in the past actually have been true); *misquotation* (we must be sure that the person is accurately quoted and the remarks properly interpreted).

A reverse of the argument from authority is ARGUMENT AGAINST THE MAN, in which we assert that A is false because a certain person says A is true. This time the validity of our conclusion depends upon the person's being a "reliable *anti-authority*"—which is not the same thing as being an "unreliable authority." We must know that the person is almost always wrong in such statements on the general topic; if we know the person is usually wrong, we may reason:

> Most of this person's statements are false.
> "A is true" is one of this person's statements.
> Therefore, A is false—probably.

Again fallacies must be avoided: the person must actually be a habitual non-authority on the topic, and must not have been misquoted or misinterpreted. Similarly to be avoided is the GENETIC FALLACY.

3. *Causal induction.* Much scientific and everyday knowledge is concerned with causes and their effects. We observe footprints on wet sand and infer that someone has recently walked there; that is, we observe the effect and infer the cause—*we reason from effect to cause.* We can do this validly, of course, only about things whose causes are generally known. When causes are not known, we must follow a careful procedure of observing effects, putting forth an assertion of possible cause (a *hypothesis*), then testing experimentally by producing that cause—carefully eliminating other possible causes—to see whether that cause does indeed produce those effects. Such inductive reasoning is a part of the "*scientific method.*"

In ARGUMENTATION, a speaker or writer may use causal induction as the basis of an order of presentation, asserting the existence of one thing (a cause) and then attempting to demonstrate that certain other things (effects) must follow. This method is called *a priori*—reasoning from cause to effect. On the other hand, if the existence of certain effects is asserted, followed by the demonstration that certain things must be their cause, then this method is called *a posteriori*—reasoning from effect to cause.

Both kinds of argument are subject to difficulties. In reasoning *a priori*, we must be certain that the known cause is sufficient to produce the supposed effect and that nothing has intervened (or can intervene) to prevent its producing that effect. In reasoning *a posteriori*, we must be certain that the known effect is always the result of the supposed cause and that no other cause could produce that effect. These certainties are, of course, difficult to achieve.

One possible error in reasoning either *a priori* or *a posteriori* is that of assuming that because one thing seems always to occur before another, the first must be a cause of the second. This is the *post hoc* fallacy—more fully, *post hoc, ergo propter hoc,* or "after this, therefore because of this." The rooster always crows before the dawn, but it is certainly fallacious to assume that the rooster's crowing causes the sun to rise.

4. *Reasoning by analogy.* Much scientific induction as well as everyday argument proceeds by drawing comparisons between things of different types. That is, it asserts that two things are alike in certain ways and therefore are probably alike in certain other ways too. This *reasoning by analogy* follows this pattern:

Both A and B have the properties *p, q,* and *r.*
A has the property *s.*
Therefore, B also has the property *s*—probably.

It is this sort of reasoning that underlies the scientist's use of rats or other animals to test the effects of certain drugs. Rats are like humans in certain significant ways: if the drug cures disease X in rats, it will *probably* also cure disease X in humans.

Obviously, reasoning by analogy has its pitfalls. The reliability of an analogy depends heavily upon the relevancy of the ways in which the things compared are similar, and upon the number of similarities as compared to the number of dissimilarities. If the things compared in the analogy are more unlike than they are alike, or if they are alike in ways that have no bearing upon the matter at hand, the argument is weak because it relies on FALSE ANALOGY.

REFERENCES: Jeremy Pitt and Russell E. Leavenworth, *Logic for Argument;* John Sherwood, *Handbook of Logic and Semantics;* Randall Decker, *Patterns of Exposition.*

inference   1. Unaccepted as a synonym for "implication." 2. Strictly, what the reader (or listener) draws from a written or spoken communication by reading (listening) beneath the lines, beneath what is said in so many words. Thus, in a statement like "Fifty thousand buyers can't be wrong," the speaker *implies* "You wouldn't be wrong to follow suit." And some such implication decoded by the reader (listener) is an inference. Notice the need not only for making inferences but also for examining their validity. 3. In logic, the drawing of conclusions from real or tentative evidence. Compare ASSUMPTIONS.

REFERENCES: Edgar Dale, *How to Read a Newspaper;* Mortimer Adler, *How to Read a Book;* J. N. Hook, "Inferring," *Handbook of Performance Objectives . . . .*

influence   In literary criticism, the general effect that writer A seems to have exerted on writer B; the unintended borrowing by writer B from writer A. "The good poet steals [outright]," said T. S. Eliot, "while the poor poet betrays an influence." Writers who quote from, or deliberately allude to, a predecessor's work have not necessarily been "influenced." For example, an author who writes that "Johnny with shining morning face creeps unwillingly to school" (an allusion to *As You Like It,* II, vii, 139) cannot be said to have been influenced by Shakespeare. Similarly, Shakespeare was not influenced by, but borrowed outright from, Plutarch. (Compare PLAGIARISM.) Only writers who unintentionally echo the VOICE or STYLE of a predecessor—and then only in certain works—are said to have been influenced. Oscar Wilde, in his "Ballad of Reading Gaol," was influenced by Coleridge's *Rime of the Ancient Mariner,* but Wilde was much more original in other works. Vergil's *Aeneid* was influenced by Homer's *Odyssey;* Milton's *Paradise Lost* was influenced by Spenser's *Faerie Queene;* Wordsworth was in general influenced by Milton. In *The Waste Land* T. S. Eliot did much deliberate alluding, but he also borrowed somewhat unconsciously from the SYBOLISTE poet Laforgue. A great writer can unconsciously borrow bits and pieces from numerous sources yet make them so personal that no signs of influence appear. A case in point is Coleridge, whose miniscule borrowings for "Kubla Khan" have been traced in a brilliant detective study by John Livingston Lowes.

Indeed, influence is not always to be decried. Poetic influence since the RENAISSANCE has been traced by Harold Bloom, who argues that without influence or "wilful revisionism," modern poetry could not exist. He adds that poetic influence involving two strong poets "always proceeds by a misprision [misreading] of the prior poet."

The tracing of influence is hazardous; it can result in far-fetched claims. To prevent these, Gilbert Highet offers some litmus tests: First it must be proved that writer B has actually read writer A's work. Then a close similarity of thought or imagery must be demonstrated; then a clear structural similarity.

REFERENCES: Gilbert Highet, *The Classical Tradition;* Samuel Johnson, "On Imitation," *Prose Works;* "Epilogue," *The Concise Cambridge History of English Literature;* John Livingston Lowes, *The Road to Xanadu;* J. L. Capp, *Emily Dickinson's Reading;* A. A. De Vito and W. J. Palmer, "A Pair of Blue Eyes Flash at *The French Lieutenant's Woman,*" *Contemporary Literature* (Spring, 1974); Daniel Hoffman, "Misinterpretations," *American Scholar* (Autumn, 1974); Harold Bloom, *The Anxiety of Influence;* Michael Yetman, "Exorcising Shelley Out of Browning," *Victorian Poetry* (Summer, 1975).

in medias res   Literally, "into the midst of things." A narrative technique, used in the Homeric epics and in Vergil's *Aeneid,* by which an author, bypassing a chronological beginning, introduces readers to a sensational moment or scene. To catch the reader's attention, many a novelist uses this technique in the opening chapter, then reserves for the second chapter or for subsequent FLASHBACKS such narration and exposition as the reader needs for the complete picture. James Baldwin's *Another Country* is an example. Some writers (e.g., Joyce and D. H. Lawrence) prefer to have revelations unfold gradually.

inns-of-court plays   Plays produced (and sometimes written) by members of one or another of the four legal societies of London—Lincoln's Inn, Gray's Inn, the Middle Temple, and the Inner Temple—which could admit candidates to the practice of law ("the bar"). From the Middle Ages to the nineteenth century these inns of court served as universities or cultural centers. (Today they are mainly clubs.) In the sixteenth and seventeenth centuries, when they were quasi-universities, they fostered all sorts of literary and theatrical ("Thespian") interests. It was the "fellows" of the Inner Temple, for example, who produced *Gorboduc* (ca. 1561), the first English tragedy, before Queen Elizabeth at Whitehall. And in 1594 the fellows of Gray's Inn produced Shakespeare's *Comedy of Errors*. Inns-of-court productions are to be distinguished from productions in inn courtyards; the latter were performed by professional companies for the entertainment of travelers and other guests at the inn.

REFERENCES: E. K. Chambers, *The Elizabethan Theater;* Lily Bess Campbell, *Scenes and Machines on the English Stage.*

innuendo   A subtle implication of something derogatory. An innuendo may arise from the tone of an utterance, though nothing derogatory appears in the literal meaning; or an innuendo may arise from a subtle IRONY, an utterance whose words can be taken to mean their opposite. Much ironic innuendo occurs in Jonathan Swift's *Modest Proposal* and in Mark Twain's *Mysterious Stranger.*

intention   The general intentions or purposes of writers are (1) to inform or instruct, (2) to explain or interpret, (3) to convince, (4) to persuade or move to action, (5) to entertain or delight, (6) to inspire or elevate, (7) to express or relieve oneself.

Although communicating for the sake of communicating is a worthy human activity needing no apology, communicating in an expository paper (as in a formal speech) more often than not achieves success when the sender decides initially what the chief purpose is—to inform, to delight, etc. Of course, the paper may have more than one purpose. If so, chances of contact with the audience will be improved if the primary purpose is stated clearly. See AUDIENCE.

Whereas articles, academic papers, and other forms of EXPOSITION characteristically state the specific intentions ("It is the intention of this paper to show that ..."), a work of literature—POETRY, DRAMA, FICTION, imaginative PROSE—like any other work of art more often *implies* its intention. Occasionally authors, spurred by critics who have misconstrued their intentions, may state them in a formal reply. George Bernard Shaw did this in his defense of *Major Barbara,* where the *general* purposes are to entertain (shock, perhaps) and convince. But in the preface to a late edition Shaw says that his *specific* intention is to show through Undershaft, the play's hero, that one of the worst of crimes is poverty. (Compare Samuel Butler's *Erewhon.*)

A specific statement of intention may also be ironic. Consider Swift's *Modest Proposal*: "For preventing the Children of Poor People from being a Burden to their Parents and Country, and for making them beneficial to the Public." (In which one way to achieve this end is to butcher the children for food and hides.)

Just as any writer heightens the effectiveness of a work by deciding on how to limit the subject (what the emphasis shall be, who the audience is, what tone or attitude will be taken toward the material, and the like), so may the writer heighten its effectiveness by writing down—if only for personal clarification—the specific purposes or intentions. Whatever the writer's intention, however, the acid test for successful communication is the actual *effect* of the written piece on the reader, as Morris Finder observes.

REFERENCES: Monroe Beardsley, "The Artist's Intention," *Aesthetics;* James McCrimmon, *Writing with a Purpose;* Thomas S. Kane and Leonard J. Peters, *Writing Prose: Techniques and Purposes;* William Riley Parker, "The Question of Audience," *MLA Style Sheet;* Morris Finder, "Comprehension: An Analysis of the Task," *Journal of Reading* (December, 1969).

intentional fallacy   In literary criticism, the theory that it is a mistake to assume that *(a)* the author has only one intention; *(b)* a literary work always says what the author intends it to say; *(c)* a literary work succeeds or fails according to whether it fulfills or does not fulfill the author's intention; *(d)* the author of a work is the best authority on its meaning and value.

Thus readers are likely to be betrayed if they take at face value the intentions stated in the prefatory "Notice" to *The Adventures of Huckleberry Finn*: "Persons attempting to find a motive in this narrative will be prosecuted; persons attempting to find a moral in it will be banished; persons attempting to find a plot in it will be shot." That celebrated critics have disagreed over Twain's real intentions in this masterpiece is on record in such a contrariety of speculations as those by William Dean Howells (*My Mark Twain,* 1910); Bernard de Voto (*Mark Twain's America,* 1932); T. S. Eliot (Introduction to the Cresset edition of *Huckleberry Finn,* 1950); Van Wyck Brooks (*The Ordeal of Mark Twain,* 1920); Lionel Trilling (essay in *The Liberal Imagination,* 1950); and Leslie Fiedler (*Love and Death in the American Novel*).

An intention generally accepted in one era or place or milieu may be rejected in another. One of the best-known cases in point is John Milton's intention in *Paradise Lost*. Even though Milton was regarded as something of a heretic in his own milieu (as Cleanth Brooks has observed), it was generally understood by Puritan and non-Puritan alike in the seventeenth century and for two centuries thereafter that Milton's intention in *Paradise Lost* was "to justify the ways of God to man." Over the years the scholars and critics who re-examined this EPIC to see whether it really did, for them, reflect this intention delivered negative verdicts. Along with such critics the contemporary reader does not generally accept the notions that Adam and Eve's sexual knowledge is shameful, that children and hard work are a curse, or that a vindictive God deliberately creates floods, tornadoes, and earthquakes. Cleanth Brooks believes Milton intended rather to show that self-knowledge is part of man's destiny and his "predicament in which he experiences alienation and yet must strive for wholeness." Brooks adds that the modern reader may do better to think of Milton as a great poet, who, "whatever his beliefs as a man, is committed to a dramatic presentation of them ... who does his reader the honor of letting him infer the meaning from the drama rather than preaching down to him" (from the Introduction to the Modern Library edition of Milton).

"A poet's primary concern," says Northrop Frye, "is to produce a work of art, and hence his intention can only be expressed by some kind of tautology" (*Anatomy of Criticism,* p. 86). See also "The Intentional Fallacy," in W. K. Wimsatt, *The Verbal Ikon.*

interior monologue   See STREAM OF CONSCIOUSNESS and ASIDE.

interlocking rhyme   A design in which an unrhymed line in one stanza signals the rhyme in the following stanza. See TERZA RIMA.

interlude   **1.** A comic skit, a form popular in late medieval and early Renaissance England. It was addressed, in simple plot and coarse language, to the uneducated. Representative is John Heywood's *Four P's* (ca. 1520), in which a pedlar, a palmer, a pardoner, and a 'pothecary vie with one another in a contest of tasteless slander against women. **2.** The court interlude, designed for more genteel and sophisticated audiences, was a short comic play, topical, mundane, and aristocratic. It was usually presented at court, in schools, or at the homes of nobles between the banquet and the nightcap of spiced wine. The court interlude approached, at least in language and tone, the MASQUE. The earliest of these plays, first acted at Lambeth Palace in 1497, is *Fulgens and Lucrece* by the Tudor dramatist Henry Medwall. The Tudor interludes characteristically embodied elements of ALLEGORY, SLAPSTICK humor and low comedy, songs, witty dialogue, and even debates. Two well-known and still stageable interludes are Nicholas Udall's *Ralph Roister Doister* (ca. 1553), written for students at Eton, and John Still's *Gammer Gurton's Needle* (ca. 1566), written for students at Christ's College, Cambridge.

REFERENCES: Joseph Quincy Adams, ed., *Chief Pre-Shakespearian Dramas;* Tucker Brooke, *The Tudor Drama;* Frederick S. Boas, *An Introduction to Tudor Drama;* A. W. Reed, *Early Tudor Drama;* Charles M. Gayley, "Historical View of the Beginnings of English Comedy," *Representative English Comedies;* Ian Lancashire, ed., *Two Tudor Interludes.*

internal rhyme   See RHYME.

ISGS   International Society for General Semantics, a non-profit association of persons interested in learning, using, and advancing general SEMANTICS. Founded in 1943 with headquarters in San Francisco, the Society has members in seventy-two countries. It promotes the teaching of general semantics in schools, colleges, universities, and other institutions, basing its principles chiefly upon the work of Alfred Korzybski, author of *Science and Sanity* (1933).

introducing quotations   See QUOTATIONS, INTRODUCING.

introduction   A statement, usually a chapter, that precedes and leads into a long written work. An introduction serves to provide the essentials of the subject under discussion and often delimits the scope of the work. Shorter works tend to dispense with formal introductions.

inventio   Literally, "invention" or "discovery." In classical rhetoric, one of the three major powers requisite to an accomplished speaker or writer (the other two being *dispositio,* or effective arrangement of one's material, and *elocutio,* or effective presentation). Today *inventio* is still invoked much as it was in ancient Greece—as the power of finding one's subject, of finding something to say that is worth saying because one knows it well as a part of one's own experience.

REFERENCES: Aristotle, *Rhetoric;* Plato, *Phaedrus;* Scott Elledge, "Inventio," The CEEB Commission on English: Film Series on Writing.

inversion   The transposing of a sentence part from its normal order, especially in verse, to achieve emphasis (and sometimes just to accommodate a rhyme). Thus, instead of saying, "The gunner went down," the song-writer said, "Down went the gunner!" And instead of "The wrinkled sea crawls beneath him," Tennyson wrote, in "The Eagle," "The wrinkled sea beneath him crawls." He inverted the natural word order, no doubt, to get a rhyming word for "walls" and "falls."

inverted pyramid   The structural device in journalistic reporting that places essentials first, nonessentials last, in an order of descending importance. The device came into newspaper reporting because of the need to cut a story's length arbitrarily to fit space: The last paragraphs could be cut away without loss of any essential details. The inverted pyramid has lost much of its usefulness and appeal; modern reporters turn to more dramatic order of details and often delay some essentials in building to a climax.

investigative paper   See RESEARCH PAPER.

invocation   In EPIC poetry, the convention of calling upon a muse for inspiration and guidance. In the *Aeneid,* Vergil, after announcing his theme—"Of arms and the man ... I sing"—calls upon Calliope, the muse of epic poetry, to tell him "Why ... did the Queen of Heaven urge on such a good man ... to circle through all these afflictions?"

In *John Brown's Body,* Stephen Vincent Benét begins, "American muse, whose strong and diverse heart / So many men have tried to understand / But only made it smaller with their art / ... Where the great huntsmen failed, I set my sorry / And mortal snare for your immortal quarry." Invocations reflect the tastes of their times.

ipse dixit   Literally, "He himself said [so]." An assertion made without any evidence—in fact, in lieu of evidence—of its truth or validity.

Irish Renaissance   The flowering of Irish literature, especially drama, during the early 1900s. W. B. Yeats, leader of the revival of interest in Celtic culture, besides writing plays and poems, inspired John Synge, Lady Gregory, Lord Dunsany, James Stephens, and Sean O'Casey, whose plays were produced at the Abbey Theatre, Dublin.

REFERENCES: U. M. Ellis-Fermor, *The Irish Dramatic Movement;* Ray Browne, *The Celtic Cross;* A. R. Eager, *Guide to Irish Bibliographical Material;* George B. Saul, *The Age of Yeats;* Barton Friedman, "Returning to Ireland's Fountain," *Arizona Q.* (Fall, 1966); Vivian Mercier and David Greene, eds., *1000 Years of Irish Prose.*

irony   **1.** *Verbal irony.* Saying the opposite of what is meant—e.g., "Tiny" as a nickname for a gigantic person; also Mark Antony's "and Brutus is an honorable man," when he meant the opposite. Irony as a manner of expression has not usually been admired. Since the early Greeks, the term has connoted slyness, foxlike cleverness, sometimes hypocrisy. In the comic theater of the Greeks the *eiron* was the quiet deadpan whose ironic remarks seemed to mean much more than they said—comments that tended to deflate the *alazon,* or braggart, and show him up as an impostor. This kind of irony is close to UNDERSTATEMENT. Verbal irony lends itself to humor. Washington Irving describes the Old Dutch burgomaster Wouter Van Twiller as "a model of lordly grandeur"—and follows with a dimensional picture to prove it: "He was exactly five feet, six inches in height and exactly six feet, five in circumference." Verbal irony is often, but not always, tinged with SARCASM. But irony may also be gentle and subtle.

2. *Socratic irony.* Socrates always understated his own knowledge and wisdom; indeed, he often pretended complete ignorance. He taught his young students, not by telling them *his* thoughts, but by asking and goading them for *theirs,* so that they seemed to be teaching themselves. Socrates was, in a sense, a real-life *eiron,* teaching by leading real-life *alazons* to reveal their own pretentiousness and thus to discover their own logic and illogic. Socratic irony thus received its name, with Aristotle describing it as Socrates' dialectic.

3. *Dramatic irony.* A device by which the audience is made aware of things that certain characters do not know. The characters' lines thus seem to mean far more to the audience than they do to those who speak them. When Oedipus vows revenge on the murderer of his father, the audience is horrified, because it knows, as Oedipus does not, that he himself is the murderer. Outside the theater, dramatic irony often occurs in everyday situations. We see dramatic irony in the words of friends whenever their remarks bear upon things about which we know facts, or secrets, that the friends do not know. Dramatic irony may be classified into three subcategories: *irony of speech* (words contrast with the facts); *irony of character* (outward appearance and behavior contrast with real nature); and *irony of events* (expectations contrast with fulfillment).

4. *Irony of fate.* Close kin to dramatic irony, it is a matter of event rather than of language. Like all irony, it depends upon the unexpected, a twist of events that produces what is contrary to the foreseen, or shockingly opposed to beliefs or desires. The astronaut survives the hazards of space only to break an elbow when he slips in the bathtub at home. The young soldier survives many months of front-line battle without a scratch; on leave at home he is permanently disabled in an auto accident. The famed swimming champion drowns in his own backyard pool. Because they know the fascination of the unexpected, news reporters seek these ironies—and the newspapers almost daily record examples of the irony of fate.

5. Broadly, any ANTITHESIS, especially as depicted on the large canvases of such writers as Thomas Hardy, Henry James, and Katherine Anne Porter.

REFERENCES: Robert Penn Warren, "Katherine Anne Porter, Irony with a Center," *Kenyon Review* (Winter, 1942); Richard Poirier, *The Comic Sense of Henry James;* Anthony E. Dyson, *The Crazy Fabric: Essays in Irony;* D. C. Muecke, *The Compass of Irony;* R. B. Sharp, *Irony in the Drama;* Robert Scholes, "The Anti-Metaphorical Language of Irony," *Elements of Poetry;* Lee Capel, trans., Søren Kierkegâard's *The Concept of [Socratic] Irony.*

Italianate gentleman   See COURTESY BOOKS.

italics   Inspired by the cursive, slanted lettering of tenth-century Italian monks, Aldus Manutius (1450–1515), a Venetian scholar and printer, created the printing type now called italic. Today italics are used chiefly to mark some brief matter that deserves special distinction—certain titles; foreign phrases, words, or abbreviations; emphasized words or phrases; and words used as words. In the preparation of a manuscript for printing, the writer indicates italics by underlining, and the compositor sets the underlined matter in italics. See EMPHASIS and UNDERLINING.

J

Jacobean   Pertaining to the era of "Jacobus" (the Latin name for James), in this instance James I of England (reigned 1603–25), who sponsored the first "authorized" English translation of the Bible; hence, King James Version. The Jacobean period marked the climax of the English RENAISSANCE, when there appeared the greatest plays of Shakespeare, Jonson, Chapman, Webster, Middleton, and Beaumont and Fletcher. It was during the Jacobean period that John Donne published much of his poetry, Francis Bacon his major works, and Robert Burton *The Anatomy of Melancholy*. METAPHYSICAL POETRY appeared at this time, and a kind of prose fiction in the character sketches by Joseph Hall and Sir Thomas Overbury.

REFERENCES: Basil Willey, *The Seventeenth Century Background;* Douglas Bush, *English Literature of the Early Seventeenth Century;* Marjorie Nicolson, *The Breaking of the Circle ... Seventeenth Century Poetry;* John R. Brown and Bernard Harris, eds., *Jacobean Theatre;* Joan Webber, *The Eloquent "I": Style and Self in Seventeenth Century Prose;* F. P. Wilson, *Elizabethan and Jacobean;* G. E. Bentley, *The Jacobean and Caroline Stage;* Brian Gibbons, *Jacobean City Comedy;* L. S. Champion, *Tragic Patterns in Jacobean and Caroline Drama.*

jargon   The specialized vocabulary or language of a restricted group, as of a trade, a profession, a sect, or a class. When used among members of the group, jargon is appropriate; but when used in general discourse, it may defeat unity of tone and purpose of communication. Jargon is one characteristic of GOBBLEDYGOOK.

REFERENCES: Katherine Anne Porter, "Against Jargon," *Paris Review Interviews,* Second Series; Arthur Quiller-Couch, "Interlude: On Jargon," *The Art of Writing.*

jest books   Late medieval and early Renaissance joke books containing ribald and often coarse slurs on women, friars, foreigners, doctors, students, courtiers, and tradesmen. The earliest of English jest books was *A Hundred Merry Tales* (1526). Certain jest books were devoted to shady stories about one person—John Skelton, for instance, or Ben Jonson. (See P. M. Zall, ed., *A Nest of Ninnies.*)

jeu d'esprit   Literally, "play of the spirit or wit." A witty remark, a quip, or a *bon mot.*

jiggery-pokery   See DOUBLE DACTYLS.

journal 1. A DIARY; a daily record of a writer's experiences, especially reactions to them in impromptu prose and verse; reactions to persons, places, events, books, and other works of art; and designs-in-embryo of literary pieces for future development. Among the most celebrated journals are those of Da Vinci, Goethe, Samuel Pepys, James Boswell, Eugène Delacroix, John Woolman, Feodor Dostoevsky, Henri Amiel, Herman Melville, Charles Darwin, Joseph Conrad, Henry James, the Goncourts, André Gide, Arnold Bennett, Sherwood Anderson, Katherine Mansfield, Virginia Woolf, Juan Jiminez, F. Scott Fitzgerald, W. Somerset Maugham, and Anne Frank. 2. A periodical publication. See REVIEW.

REFERENCES: Robert Freier *et al.*, "Writers' Notebooks," *Adventures in Modern Literature*, Fifth Edition; Arthur Eastman, ed., "Journals," *The Norton Reader*; William Sparke and Clarke McKowen, *Montage*.

journey 1. A basic story-line for many works of mythology and folklore, as represented in the journeys of Jason, Hercules, Ulysses, and Aeneas. 2. The basic structure (*framework*) for such masterpieces as *The Divine Comedy, The Canterbury Tales, The Pilgrim's Progress,* and *Gulliver's Travels.* 3. An allegory of the human condition; that is, the human fate to journey through life, through "hell and high water," as dramatized by Ulysses, Aeneas, and Christian. Some critics interpret this journey symbolically in the context of Carl Jung's "racial unconscious," the theory that all of us vaguely remember our evolutionary journeys and those of the archetypal characters with whom we identify. See ARCHETYPE and MYTHOPOETICS.

REFERENCES: Northrop Frye, "The Archetypes of Literature," *Fables of Identity;* Carl Jung, *Archetypes of the Collective Unconscious;* Norman O. Brown, *Life Against Death;* Albert Guerard *et al.*, "The Journey Within," *The Personal Voice;* Harold Pagliaro, *Henry Fielding's Journal of a Voyage to Lisbon;* Stanley Weintraub, *Journey to Heartbreak* [*George Bernard Shaw*]; Morse Peckham, *Beyond the Tragic Vision.*

K

katharsis   See CATHARSIS.

kenning   An Anglo-Saxon metaphorical compound used instead of a single noun; e.g., "whale-road" instead of "ocean." Compare EPITHET.

REFERENCES: Margaret Williams, ed., *Word-Hoard, a Treasury of Old English Literature;* Roger Fowler, ed., *Old English Prose and Verse;* Robert Burlin, *The Old English Advent.*

kinetic imagery   Any image or images appealing to the sense of motion—riding, flying, climbing, falling, etc.

kitsch   **1.** Bric-a-brac, whether junk or junque. **2.** Trivial would-be literature; in this sense, a term used by Gilbert Highet in *A Clerk of Oxenford.*

REFERENCES: "Kitsch," in Irving and Harriet Deer, eds., *The Popular Arts;* Clement Greenberg, "Avant Garde and Kitsch," *Art and Culture;* Gillo Dorfles, *Kitsch: The World of Bad Taste.*

L

laconic style   Habitual brevity and terseness. Laconism was typical of the speech of ancient Laconia, whose capital was Sparta. It was the Spartans who, when warned that if their city were captured it would be burned to the ground, responded: "If." Laconism is typical of the EPIGRAM and the APHORISM.

lay (lai)   **1.** Short narrative verse made popular by Marie de France (twelfth century) and the Breton minstrels. The content was mostly Arthurian legend. **2.** More broadly, any short narrative song or BALLAD. See, for example, Macaulay's *Lays of Ancient Rome*.
REFERENCE: Mortimer Donovan, *The Breton Lay*.

lampoon   A satirical attack, in prose or in verse, against a person; for example, Pope's portrait of Colley Cibber in *The Dunciad*. Compare BURLESQUE and CARICATURE.

laureate   See POET LAUREATE and NOBEL PRIZE.

lead   The beginning, usually a first paragraph but occasionally more, of a brief prose writing. The term originated in journalism, especially newspaper reporting, where the lead was traditionally expected to report the five W's and contain the most important facts of the story. See INVERTED PYRAMID and W'S.

leaders   A series of dots (periods) used in printing to lead the eye from one place to another. Leaders were once much used in tables, but the trend is to avoid using them except in dense, small-type statistical tabulations.

legend   **1.** Loosely, a caption or an explanatory comment under a map or picture. The legend, in this sense, was formerly distinguished from the caption, which appeared *above* the picture; now caption is used in both senses. In cartography, legend retains the original sense. **2.** A narrative transmitted orally and rooted more in the historical than in the supernatural, although it may be distorted history. Legends reflect a national spirit. Washington Irving's "Legend of Sleepy Hollow" reflects Dutch lore of the kind transplanted to the New Netherlands. Compare MYTH and FOLKLORE.

letters   **1.** A synonym for *literature*, as in the expression "She won an honorary degree in humane letters." **2.** *Letters to editors* of periodicals remain a popular form of citizen expression. Editors look for letters informed by UNITY (i.e., emphasizing one idea), COHERENCE, and brevity. **3.** Such social and utilitarian messages as *thank you ("bread and butter") notes* and *applications for jobs* require the virtues mentioned in (2), to say nothing of literate-looking SPELLING. More important, all letters should reflect the writer's sincerity. Except, perhaps, in *love letters,* eloquence and lengthiness remain virtues of bygone eras, although even today lengthy love letters elicit "close reading of the text" and reading between the lines.

4. *Pamphleteer letters* are a kind of politico-economic, cultural, or religious propaganda. They profess to come from objective reporters or from travelers (outsiders looking in) writing home. Under their own names or under PSEUDO-NYMS these letter-writers criticize (sometimes praise) certain life styles. As a rule, they criticize domestic and praise foreign models. Examples of pamphleteer letters include Montesquieu's *Lettres Persanes,* Voltaire's *Letters on the English,* Swift's *Drapier's Letters,* Savile's *Letter to a Dissenter,* Crève-coeur's *Letters from an American Farmer,* William Wirt's *The Letters of a British Spy,* Ann Hulton's *Letters of a Loyalist Lady,* John Dickinson's *Letters of Fabius,* Edmund Burke's *Letter to the Sheriffs of Bristol,* Washington Irving's *Letters of Jonathan Oldstyle, Gent.,* Charles Kingsley's "Parson Lot" letters to *Fraser's Magazine,* Sydney Smith's *Letters to Archdeacon Singleton,* C. S. Lewis's *Screwtape Letters,* and Brian Grant's *Conciliation and Divorce: A Father's Letters to His Daughter.*

5. *Correspondence between eminent persons* adds an enriching dimension to biographies. Such letters reveal milestone experiences or provide insights into personalities. Said Samuel Johnson, "In a man's letters, madam, his soul lies naked." In biographies and in books of "collected letters" notable letter-writers through the ages include Alexander and Darius III, Cicero and Horace, St. Paul, Heloise and Abelard, Leonardo and Michelangelo, the Pastons (fifteenth-century England), Erasmus and Luther, Spinoza (to Albert Burgh), Goethe and Schiller, Lord Chesterfield (to his son), Samuel Johnson (to Chesterfield), Johnson and Boswell, Ben Franklin (to Miss Hubbard), Washington (to the Continental Congress), John and Abigail Adams, Jefferson (to William Fielding), Napoleon and Josephine, Lord Byron (to the Countess Guiccioli), Shelley and Mary Godwin, Keats (to Fanny Brawne), Carlyle and Disraeli, Lincoln (to Mrs. Bixby), Robert Browning and Elizabeth Barrett, Emily Dickinson and Colonel Higginson, Emerson and Thoreau, Emerson to Whitman, Mark Twain and President Grant, Nietzsche and Wagner, Zola (to the President of France), Darwin and Wallace, Marie and Pierre Curie, Captain Scott (from the South Pole), George Bernard Shaw and Ellen Terry, Maxwell Perkins (to Fitzgerald, Hemingway, and Thomas Wolfe), Sacco and Vanzetti, Thomas Mann (to a University of Bonn dean), Martin Luther King (from a Birmingham jail).

6. *Memorable letters in drama and fiction* (other than EPISTOLARY NOVELS, which consist entirely of letters) include those of Maria to Malvolio (Shakespeare's *Twelfth Night*), Cyrano to Roxane (Rostand's *Cyrano de Bergerac*), Krogstad to Nora (Ibsen's *A Doll's House*), Rodolphe to Emma (Flaubert's *Madame Bovary*), Mrs. Micawber to David (Dickens's *David Copperfield*), Clym to Eustacia (Hardy's *The Return of the Native*), and Red Chief's father to the kidnappers (O'Henry's "Ransom of Red Chief").

REFERENCES: M. L. Schuster, ed., *The World's Great Letters;* A. C. Ward, ed., *A Miscellany of Tracts and Pamphlets;* V. W. Crane, ed., *Benjamin Franklin's Letters to the Press;* Charles Neider, ed., *Mark Twain's Letters to the Press;* Dixon Wecter, ed., *The Love Letters of Mark Twain;* Alan McKenzie, "Two Letters . . . to Samuel Johnson," *PMLA* 86 (1971). *Note:* A tool for locating, in libraries and museums, correspondence between eminent authors is John Robbins *et al., American Literary Manuscripts* ("ALM").

levels of meaning   As the Italian poet Dante, author of *The Divine Comedy,* pointed out in 1304 in *The Banquet* (I, 1), a masterwork of literature contains simultaneously four or more *levels of significance* (layers of meaning): (1) the literal, (2) the allegorical, (3) the moral, and (4) the anagogical. By *literal level* he meant, as is ordinarily meant today, the manifest story-line. By *allegorical level* he meant the one-for-one representations observable in medieval and early renaissance MORALITY PLAYS, in which such virtues and vices as Kindness and Greed are personified. By *moral level* he meant an author's vision of life or at least the moral values stated or implied in a given work. By *anagogical level* he meant the deepest, most "mystical" (Dante's term) possibilities of interpretation, especially those inherent in Christian symbols.

For centuries Dante's multiple-levels theory was subscribed to by major writers and critics as basic to intelligent reading. But most readers, then as now, read superficially; and even if they sometimes dug beneath to ALLEGORY and symbolic mystery, they erroneously assumed that a work could have only one interpretation. See INTENTIONAL FALLACY.

In modern times one of the first artists and critics to call attention to levels of meaning was the novelist Henry James. In *The Art of Fiction* he decries the notion that there can be only one "correct" interpretation and urges the reader not to stop after apprehending the mere DONNÉE or "given." As in any other problem, puzzle, or game, what is given—important as it is—is only a base. The fun begins where the donnée ends.

The NEW CRITICS, among them Allen Tate, posit three major levels of meaning: (1) the literal, (2) the allegorical, and (3) the symbolic. Along with most other contemporary readers, they concede that a writer leads us inductively to a main theme, which in turn reflects a particular vision of life in that work, but they categorize this contribution to CONTEXT as one of the writer's "thematic values," rather than as a "level" or "layer of meaning." The New Critics also assign a broader role to allegorical meaning. While they concede Dante's definition of allegory to be the first and most easily recognizable kind of SYMBOLISM, they regard ALLEGORY as a metaphor capable of extending beyond the STEREOTYPE of The Good Guy and The Bad Guy, as it extends, for example, in Archibald MacLeish's play *J.B.*

It is perhaps the symbolic levels that contemporary critics—thanks to such depth psychologies as those of Freud and Jung—have explored most. Thus any object or experience suggesting the sex drive is called a Freudian symbol. And any object, experience, or character echoing the history, MYTHOLOGY, or rituals of humanity is called a Jungian ARCHETYPE. The emphasis, incidentally, is on the *individual* in Freudian symbolism; on the group, race, or culture, in Jungian symbolism. See Carl Jung, *Archetypes and the Collective Unconscious,* and Northrop Frye, *Fables of Identity.*

How these three major levels of meaning (the literal, the allegorical, and the symbolic) interact in a given work can be illustrated by a brief analysis of Edward Albee's play *Who's Afraid of Virginia Woolf?* (1962). On the surface the two major characters, Martha and George, are on such destructive terms with each other and with themselves as to make Virginia Woolf's suicide look tame by comparison. In most of their talk during the three acts (respectively entitled "Fun and Games," "Walpurgisnacht," and "The Exorcism") these characters mercilessly flay each other and their vapid guests Honey and Nick, who serve as FOILS. On this literal level we thus see a murderous power-play between George and Martha.

Extended to the allegorical level, this feud also represents the vying for power by Man and Woman, although the man in this particular case is impotent. But the play contains more complex allegory and symbolism than this. As a son, George has killed his parents; later, as a parent, he has killed an imaginary son. This counterpoint, along with references to Jesus both at the beginning and at the end, gives meaning to the play as a Christian allegory, in which the Son represents the son killed during "The Exorcism."

When these clues go deeper than a one-to-one representation of the Son as the son (the allegorical formula), into the more mystical (if not mysterious) possibilities of meaning, the reader is confronted with complex symbolism. Aside from the Freudian symbolism in George's patricide and in the impotence of George with Honey, all the characters echo the torments of humanity burdened with guilt, seeking redemption (integrity) either in Christian terms, through the Son of God or, in terms of secular EXISTENTIALISM, through rejection of supernatural responsibility for human behavior.

Because symbolism is so complex a ramification of Freudian and Jungian possibilities of interpretation, most contemporary EXPLICATION is concerned almost entirely with this third level. Readers may thus assume that the first and second levels (the literal and the allegorical) are readily understood. This assumption seems to undergird hundreds of interpretive essays on such works as *Moby Dick, The Catcher in the Rye,* and *Lord of the Flies.* Although several different interpretations may well be tenable, each within certain limits, a contrariety of critical approaches can be applied *ad absurdum* by the over-zealous, as Frederick Crews demonstrates in *The Pooh Perplex.*

In addition to these three major levels of meaning, the last of which, the symbolic, subsumes multiple sublayers, other elements of a literary work control and contribute to its meaning: the structure of the GENRE itself, its MODE, TONE, and FOCUS OF NARRATION.

Most contemporary critics assume that the meaning of a literary work emanates from what is *in* that work much more than from what is outside the work. They therefore de-emphasize the author's biographical background as an element in the interpretation of a work's meaning. See BIOGRAPHICAL FALLACY and AESTHETIC DISTANCE.

One group of contemporary critics and teachers, among them Louise Rosenblatt, author of *Literature as Exploration,* maintains that a so-called literary work is only a "text," that it does not become "a poem" ("a play," "a novel") until it is "experienced by the reader." (See "The Poem as Event," *College English,* November, 1964). Most critics discourage such subjectivity. While allowing leeway for a contrariety of interpretations, most critics limit the validity ("viability") of any interpretation to a test against "what is there" in the work or text. Despite their diametric emphases, however, these critics cannot escape sharing a certain amount of both subjective and objective process in wresting meaning from literature.

REFERENCES: William Empson, *Seven Types of Ambiguity;* Stanley R. Hopper and David L. Miller, eds., *Interpretation: The Poetry of Meaning;* Cleanth Brooks and Robert Penn Warren, *Understanding Fiction* and *Understanding Poetry;* A. Edelstein, "Levels of Meaning in *The Spoils of Poynton," Hartford Studies in Literature* (#2, 1970); Lynne Cheney, "Conrad's *Secret Agent* and Greene's *It's a Battlefield," Modern Fiction Studies* (Summer, 1970); Thomas Adler, "Albee's *Who's Afraid of Virginia Woolf?" Educational Theatre Journal* (March, 1973).

library classification systems   The numbers and letters on the spines of books (also the same notations on catalog cards that locate and identify books) according to the *Dewey Decimal System* or the *Library of Congress System.*

The Dewey Decimal System, used by most public libraries in this country and by many school and college libraries, was developed in 1876 by Melvil Dewey, a New York librarian and one of the founders of the modern public library movement in the United States. The system consists of ten major categories of books as follows:

000–099	General Works (including bibliography and library science)
100–199	Philosophy
200–299	Religion
300–399	Social Sciences (including education)
400–499	Philology (including languages)
500–599	Pure Sciences
600–699	Useful Arts (including medicine and engineering)
700–799	Fine Arts
800–899	Literature (including poetry, drama, and literary criticism, but not fiction, which is catalogued and shelved according to authors' last names, without numbers)
900–999	Biography (though many libraries now use "B" instead of the "920's"), history, geography, travel.

Each of these ten major categories is broken down into subcategories—e.g., the 900s into the 910s (geography and travel), the 920s (biography), the 930s (ancient history), the 940s (Europe), the 950s (Asia), the 960s (Africa), the 970s (North America), the 980s (South America), the 990s (Pacific Ocean Islands). A third digit identifies a more specialized category. Thus, under the subcategory of the 370s (education) the 371s are assigned to the special category "teaching." The system is called "decimal" because—aside from its ten main categories—a decimal point and an expandable number of digits to the right of this point allow for identifying individual titles within categories. Thus an individual title, *The Advancement of Teaching,* has the Dewey Decimal identification of "371.3."

Library of Congress Classification. The Library of Congress (established in 1800 in Washington, D.C.) and many large university libraries catalogue and identify titles by a combination of letters and numbers according to the following system:

A	General Works
B	Philosophy and Religion
C	Auxiliary Sciences of History
D	Universal History and Topography
E, F	American History
G	Geography and Anthropology
H	Social Sciences
J	Political Science
K	Law
L	Education
M	Music
N	Fine Arts
P	Language and Literature
Q	Science
R	Medicine
S	Agriculture
T	Technology
U	Military Science
V	Naval Science
Z	Library Science

Following each of these initial letters is a second letter that represents a subcategory. Under General Works (A) come encyclopedias (AE) and general reference works (AG). Under Philosophy and Religion (B) come metaphysics (BD), esthetics (BH), ethics (BJ), etc. Under Language and Literature (P) come Classical (PA), Romance (PC), Germanic (PD), Slavic (PG), Oriental (PJ), English (PR), and American (PS) language and literature. Psychology, reflecting its ancient origin, remains a subcategory (BF) under Philosophy and Religion (B). Judaism (BM) is accorded a subheading parallel with that for Religions (BL). But Christianity shares, along with Mohammedanism [*sic*], Bahaism, and Theosophy, the one berth, BP. Biography appears as a subcategory (CT) under the Auxiliary Sciences of History (C), following such auxiliaries as Numismatics (CJ), Heraldry (CR), and Genealogy (CS).

After the second, subcategorical letter there occur numbers for which the following, under Biography (CT), seem to be representative: 210–3150, National biographies; 3200–3910, Biographies of women; and 9960–9998, Miscellaneous, including biographies of imposters and cripples. See *Outline of the Library of Congress Classification,* Washington, D.C.: The Library of Congress, 1955.

Special Systems. Important, if less common, classification systems for organizing library materials include the following: (1) *the Universal Decimal Classification,* (2) *the Bliss Classification,* (3) *the Colon Classification,* (4) *the Classification of the Harvard Graduate School of Business Administration,* (5) *the Lamont Library Classification of Harvard College,* (6) *the Union Theological Seminary Classification,* and (7) *the Glidden Classification.*

library paper   See RESEARCH PAPER.

light verse   Verse designed or intended to amuse or question rather than to transport; verse that appeals more to urbanity and the intellect than to one's sense of beauty. Whether witty enough to evoke laughter, ingenious enough to win a smile, or satirical enough to sting (though not to wound), light verse almost always succeeds through its social relevance. (Much light verse is in fact *vers de société*.) This social and contemporary quality, however, tends to make it more perishable than serious poetry. Indeed, for certain dictionaries of poetry, light verse seems beneath notice, even if poets like Horace, Chaucer, Shakespeare, Marvell, Herrick, Pope, Byron, Browning, Oliver Wendell Holmes, T. S. Eliot, e. e. cummings, and W. H. Auden have written light verse that has as yet not perished. Among their "entertainments" have been EPIGRAMS, SATIRES, PARODIES, PUNS, RIDDLES, LIMERICKS, and even ACROSTICS. Auden and cummings saw no really basic difference between serious poetry and the best light verse. The most widely published contemporary light versifiers include Ogden Nash, Richard Armour, and Phyllis McGinley.

REFERENCES: W. H. Auden, ed., *The Oxford Book of Light Verse;* David McCord, ed., *What Cheer;* Oscar Williams, ed., *The Silver Treasury;* William Cole, ed., *The Fireside Book of Humorous Poetry;* Louis Untermeyer, *Play in Poetry;* Richard Armour, *Writing Light Verse;* J. V. Cunningham, *The Exclusions of a Rhyme.*

limerick   A five-lined nonsense verse in ANAPESTS rhyming *aabba;* with the first, second, and fifth lines having three stresses, the third and fourth lines two; and with an unexpected twist in the last line:

> There was an old man who said, "Hush!
> I perceive a young bird in the bush."
> When they joked, "Is it small?"
> He replied, "Not at all.
> It is five times as big as the bush!"

That limerick is one of hundreds attributed to Edward Lear (1812–88), the English bird watcher and painter. Other masters of this form are Lewis Carroll, Robert Louis Stevenson, Gilbert and Sullivan, Oliver Wendell Holmes, Rudyard Kipling, Eugene Field, and Gelett Burgess. There is no evidence for the notion that limericks originated in County Limerick, Ireland, though Irish and English devotees have transmitted limericks orally along with other folk literature. The limerick is frequently devoted to humorous treatment of erotic subjects.

REFERENCES: Bennett Cerf, ed., *Out on a Limerick;* Louis Untermeyer, ed., *Lots of Limericks;* G. Legman, ed., *The Limerick.*

lingua franca   **1.** A Frankish (Romance) language, with admixtures of Greek and Arabic, spoken chiefly in Mediterranean ports. **2.** Loosely, a hodgepodge or a hybrid language comparable to pidgin English. **3.** In criticism, the phrase is often used to describe certain current CONVENTIONS: "'Boy-meets-girl' is the *lingua franca* of Hollywood." "Strategy-wise, the *lingua franca* of Madison Avenue is now the 'soft-sell.'"

literal language   Words used in their commonly accepted meanings, as *house* is used when it means "a dwelling place" or *knife* when it means "a tool for cutting." These same words are nonliteral, or FIGURATIVE, when used to mean something other than the most common denotation, as *house* is sometimes used to mean "the audience in a theater" or *knife* to mean "go through sharply" (e.g., "to *knife* through the Alabama line"). Words often originate figuratively, through imitation of natural sounds, comparison of the new to the old, or association of the unknown with the known; but they tend to become literal by long use: their picturesque qualities wear away until the figurative basis is forgotten. (See FADED METAPHOR.) For example, *comet* began as a Greek word meaning "long-haired," the name thus picturing the appearance of the astronomical body. But today *comet* is used in English with no thought of hair, and thus no figurative sense: the word has become literal. Heavily literal language tends toward ABSTRACTION, since the abstract word least arouses the imagination; it tends to narrow meaning to the DENOTATION rather than the CONNOTATIONS. Contrast FIGURATIVE LANGUAGE and SYMBOLIC LANGUAGE.

literary prizes and grants   Among the hundreds offered *annually* (unless otherwise stated) the following represent opportunities of interest, in most instances, to college students. Applications and particulars can be obtained from the address following each entry.

American Book Awards ($1,000 each). For the year's most distinguished books of fiction, poetry, translation, history and biography, etc. Association of American Publishers, One Park Ave., New York, N.Y. 10016.

Atlantic Firsts (publication). For a first published story between 2,000 and 8,000 words. *Atlantic Monthly,* 8 Arlington St., Boston, Mass. 02116.

Balch Poetry Prizes ($500 each). *Virginia Quarterly Review,* 1 West Range, Charlottesville, Va. 22902.

Brandeis Creative Arts Awards (four at $2500). For promise in literature, music, theater arts, fine arts. Brandeis University, Waltham, Mass. 02154.

Dutton Animal Book Awards ($15,000 advance). For adult books and children's books about animals, fiction or nonfiction. E. P. Dutton & Co., 201 Park Ave., New York, N.Y. 10003.

Gauss Award ($2,500). For an outstanding book of literary scholarship or criticism. Phi Beta Kappa, 1811 Q St., N.W., Washington, D.C. 20009.

Grolier Award ($1,000). To a school or community librarian who has stimulated and guided reading by young people. Grolier, Inc., 575 Lexington Ave., New York, N.Y. 10022.

Guggenheim Fellowships (several in various amounts). For artists, writers, and scholars of high ability regardless of sex, race, color, creed, or marital status. Guggenheim Foundation, 90 Park Ave., New York, N.Y. 10016.

Guideposts Magazine "Youth Writing Contest" for high school juniors and seniors. *Guideposts* Magazine, 747 Third Ave., New York, N.Y. 10017.

Hillman Award ($750). For fiction or nonfiction on race relations, civil liberties, and world understanding. Hillman Foundation, 15 Union Sq., New York, N.Y. 10003.

Houghton Mifflin Literary Fellowships ($10,000). For fiction or nonfiction by promising writers needing financial assistance to complete their works. Houghton Mifflin Co., 2 Park St., Boston, Mass. 02107.

Mademoiselle Awards. For fiction ($750 and $300) by college students. Also Mademoiselle College Board Competitions (ten cash prizes along with salaried guest editorships) for college undergraduates in writing, arts, fashions, etc. *Mademoiselle* Magazine, 420 Lexington Ave., New York, N.Y. 10017.

O. Henry Awards ($300, $200, $100). For best short stories published in American magazines. Doubleday & Co., 277 Park Ave., New York, N.Y. 10017.

P. E. N. Translation Prize ($1,000). For the best translation into English from any foreign language published in the U.S. P.E.N. American Center, 156 Fifth Ave., New York, N.Y. 10010.

Poetry Magazine Awards (several). *Poetry* Magazine, 1018 N. State St., Chicago, Ill. 60610.

Poetry Society of America Awards (several from $300 to $3,500). For various kinds of poems—single, groups, and book-length collections. Poetry Society of America, 15 Grammercy Park, New York, N.Y. 10003.

Pulitzer Prizes ($1,000 each). To American authors for a distinguished novel, play, biography, book of verse, etc. Trustees of Columbia University, Morningside Heights, New York, N.Y. 10027.

Seventeen Magazine Prizes (several from $50 to $300). For short stories by students under age twenty. *Seventeen* Magazine, 320 Park Ave., New York, N.Y. 10022.

Yale Series of Younger Poets (book publication with usual royalties). For a 46- to 64-page collection of poems previously unpublished as a collection. Open to writers under age forty. Yale University Press, 149 York St., New Haven, Conn. 06511. (See also NOBEL PRIZE.)

REFERENCES: "Literary Prizes and Awards," *Literary Market Place* (New York: R. R. Bowker Co., annually); "Fellowships and Grants," *Midwest MLA* (annually); *Grants & Awards Available to American Writers,* P.E.N., 156 Fifth Ave., New York, N.Y. 10010.

litotes   A kind of understatement, the method of which is to deny the opposite of what is intended. We use litotes (a three-syllable word: lí-to-tēs) when we say that the shrewd young man is *no fool* or when we describe Mount Everest as *not exactly a foothill.* If one means that something is memorable, one may instead say that it is *unforgettable.* What is extremely urgent may become a matter *not unworthy of our attention.* Sir Winston Churchill, like many British speakers, made litotes a common mark of his speech. Addressing the Congress of the United States, he once referred to his own remarkable career as "My life, which has been long and *not entirely uneventful.*" Though litotes may produce an ironic tone, it is not to be confused with irony; for irony *states* the opposite of what is meant, while litotes *denies* the opposite of what is meant.

little magazines   When W. H. Auden in his poem "Under Which Lyre" speaks of "Our intellectual marines / Landing in the Little Magazines," he pays homage to one of the most vital movements in contemporary literature. Little magazines, even if individually short-lived, continue as a group to carry the torch for the new, the fresh, the experimental in poetry and fiction. In England, F. R. Leavis' *Scrutiny* (1932–1953), Wyndham Lewis's *Blast* (1914–1915), Ezra Pound and others' *The Egoist* (1914–1919), and Margaret Anderson's *Little Review* (1914–1929) provided the pages in which many celebrities-to-be (among them, Joyce, Eliot, and Hemingway) were first published. In the United States the new voices found hearings in Harriet Munro's *Poetry, a Magazine of Verse*, and in the late 1920s in Marianne Moore's *Dial.* In fact, a poet like William Carlos Williams had to "prove himself" in the early *Kenyon* before being recognized and accepted by such Establishment magazines as *The Atlantic, Harper's, The New Yorker, The Saturday Review,* etc. Most "little mags," as they are called by the up-and-coming young writer, who relies on them for a first public hearing, are short-lived because *(a)* they are under-financed by their patron-subscribers or by their sponsoring colleges and universities; and *(b)* the editors edit by avocation, most of them having other commitments. Nevertheless, most of these editors are dedicated men and women who encourage the experimental and sometimes share critical suggestions with young writers that show promise. At the time this handbook went to press, the following little magazines were being published and distributed to major American college and university libraries: *American Poetry Review, Antioch Review, Apalachee Quarterly, Approach, Archer, Arion, Ark River Review, Aspen, Beloit Poetry Journal, Bird, Bitterroot, Black American Literature Forum, Black Warrior Review, Bluestone, Burning Deck, California Quarterly, Canadian Forum, Caravel, Centering, Chelsea, Chicago Review, Cimarron Review, Collage, Cream City Review, Creative Pittsburgh, Cresset, Crosscurrents, Dalhousie Review, Dark Horse, December, Denver Quarterly, Descant, Discourse, Dust, Elizabeth, Epoch, Essence, Event, Faux Pas, Fiction (NYC College), Fiddlehead, Field, Firelands Review, Forms, Four Quarters, Galley Sail, Gamut, Generation, Genesis West, goodly co, The Goliards, Gothic, Great Lakes Review, Greensboro Review, Grist, Gusto, Haiku, Hanging Loose, Hearse, Hiram Poetry Review, Hudson Review, Hungry Years, Images, Inprint, Interstate, Iowa Review, Jump River, Kansas Quarterly, Karamu, Kayak, Kumquat, Lacuna, Literary Review, Loonfeather, Lyric, Mad River Review, Maelstrom, Markham Review, Massachusetts Quarterly, Michigan Quarterly Review, Midwest Quarterly, Minnesota Review, Mississippi Review, Modus Operandi, Mountain Review, Moving Out, Mundus Artium, Natchez Trace, Nebula, New Orleans Review, New Virginia Review, New York Quarterly, Nightshade, Nimrod, North American Review, Northwest Review, Ohio Review, Opus, Orbit, Oyez, Paintbrush, Parabola, Paris Review, Partisan Review, Pebble, Perspective, Pierian Spring, Ploughshares, Poetry, Poetry Today, Poetry Northwest, Prairie Schooner, Primavera, Prism,*

Quagga, Quarterly Review of Literature, Quartet, Radar, Rock Bottom, Sage-trieb, Salmagundi, Salt Lick, Satire, Samisdat, Second Coming, Sequoia, Sewanee Review, Shenandoah, Signs, Small Pond, The Smith, Snowy Egret, South & West, South Atlantic, South Carolina Review, South Dakota Review, Southern Review, Southwest Review, Sou'wester, Sparrow, Sun and Moon, Symptom, Synapse, Tamarack Review, Threepenny Review, Tri-Quarterly, Unicorn, University Review, University of Toronto Quarterly, Unmuzzled Ox, Villager, Virginia Quarterly Review, Waves, Western Humanities Review, Windsor Review, Wisconsin Review, Wormwood Review, Yale Review.

REFERENCES: "Little Magazines," *Encyclopaedia Britannica;* Leonard Fulton, ed., *Directory of Little Magazines* [annual]; Frederick Hoffman, et al., *The Little Magazine, A History and a Bibliography;* Lionel Trilling, "The Future of the Little Magazine," *The Liberal Imagination;* C. E. Olson, "The Furnace Where American Literature Is Being Forged," *St. Louis Post-Dispatch* (November 28, 1972); Felix Stefanile, "The Little Magazine Today," *Tri-Quarterly* (Winter, 1978); Reed Whittemore, *The Little Magazine and Contemporary Literature;* Norman Nathan, *Judging Poetry;* S. H. Goode, *Index to Little Magazines.*

Living Theater   See IMMEDIATE THEATER.

local color   The artifacts, clothing, dialects, manners, mores, and pastimes of a region or subculture. In Mark Twain's *The Adventures of Huckleberry Finn,* for example, the local color depicted along the Missouri shore of the Mississippi, especially in the environment of the Widow Douglas and Judge Thatcher, is distinctly different from that of the feuding Grangerfords and Shepherdsons farther south.

REFERENCES: G. H. Orians, *American Local Color Stories;* J. R. May, "Local Color in *The Awakening,*" *So. Rev.* (Oct., 1970); Arlin Turner, "Interpreting 19th Century Literature," *American Studies* (May, 1973); Henig Cohen *et al., Humor of the Old Southwest.*

locating information   In any library the four basic and first places to look for information are (1) encyclopedias; (2) the card catalog under the subject if you do not know authors or titles; (3) *The Readers' Guide to Periodical Literature* (for magazine articles), again under subject if you do not know authors or titles; and (4) the metal ("vertical") file cabinets that contain pamphlets, leaflets, and similar unbound materials usually kept up to date. Obituaries and back issues of newspapers (e.g., *The New York Times*) are generally available on library microfilms. To locate letters written by and to eminent persons, consult "ALM" (*American Literary Manuscripts*). This compendium identifies the libraries holding such letters, which are often available in photostats for a nominal fee. See RESEARCH PAPER.

REFERENCES: Donald F. Bond, *A Reference Guide to English Studies;* Ronald B. McKerrow, *An Introduction to Bibliography for Literary Students;* Charles Alexander and A. J. Burke, *How to Locate Educational Information; Information, Please, Almanac; Encyclopedia Americana; Encyclopaedia Britannica;* Richard D. Altick, *The Scholar Adventurers;* Louis B. Wright, *Of Books and Men.*

logic   A system of reasoning with *validity,* not necessarily with abstract *truth.* INFERENCE, the drawing of conclusions from real or supposed evidence, plays a large role in human discourse; thus logic, with its formulation of principles of valid inference, has certain connections with language and is indispensable to most GENRES of speaking and writing. Reference to the principles of logical inference gives writer and speaker, reader and listener, a check upon the validity of what is said—at least when what is said depends upon reason.

Methods of reasoning. Ordered reasoning (that is, logic) follows one of two methods, depending upon the nature of the material or the concepts to be reasoned about and upon the nature of the inferences to be drawn. These methods are (1) induction and (2) deduction.

1. INDUCTIVE REASONING begins with the observation of particular facts, then works toward assertion of a general inference that accounts for, or at least *probably* accounts for, those facts.

2. DEDUCTIVE REASONING begins with the assertion of a general law, or acceptable "truth," and works toward the explicit assertion of a particular fact that is implicit in that generalization.

These methods of reasoning are complementary, not antithetical. The chief distinction between induction and deduction lies in this: The conclusion reached by induction is limited by *probability,* but the conclusion reached by deduction is *absolute.* It is by inductive reasoning that much of experimental science proceeds. By observing past and present phenomena, the scientist is able to draw inferences to predict future phenomena with high probability; this conclusion adds to human knowledge. On the other hand, deductive reasoning does not add to knowledge; rather, its usefulness lies in allowing us to make proper applications of knowledge already possessed but never before applied to a specific instance.

For the speaker or writer and audience no thorough grounding in SCIENTIFIC METHOD may be necessary. But valid ARGUMENTATION, like valid science, depends in large measure upon the care and honesty with which facts are observed, the adequacy of those facts as grounds for inference, and the avoidance of FALLACIES—errors in reasoning. See INDUCTIVE REASONING, DEDUCTIVE REASONING, SYLLOGISMS, and FALLACIES OF REASONING.

REFERENCES: John Sherwood, *Discourse of Reason: Brief Handbook of Logic and Semantics;* Monroe Beardsley, *Thinking Straight;* Irving M. Copi, *Introduction to Logic;* Jeremy Pitt and Russell E. Leavenworth, *Logic for Argument;* Morris R. Cohen and Ernest Nagel, *An Introduction to Logic.*

Lollards   The intellectual ancestors of the Puritans; followers of John Wycliffe (1320–84); members of a popular religious movement in England during the late fourteenth century. The Lollards, most of whom were low in the socioeconomic and ecclesiastical scale, opposed the materialism of the Church rulers. The Lollards contributed portions of the Wycliffe Bible and, in 1395 presented to Parliament an unsuccessful petition for Church reform. This petition anticipated many of the tenets of the sixteenth-century Protestant Reformation. One of the tenets, no doubt the one for which many a Lollard was burned at the stake, was that war should be declared unchristian. Lollardism is mentioned or reflected in medieval literature, notably in Chaucer's *Canterbury Tales* (in the "Prologue" the host accuses the Country Parson of being a "Loller") and in Piers Plowman's "Creed."

REFERENCE: James Gairdner and William Hunt, *Lollardy and the Reformation in England.*

loose sentence   A sentence in which the main idea comes early, the subordinate ideas or modifiers following usually in a string, as ducklings tag after their mother. The loose sentence may, in the hands of a careless writer, lack discipline; for it keeps a loose leash upon ideas. But to suppose that there is no control at all is a great mistake. The loose sentence, after all, is the normal English sentence. It has the flow of conversation, a quieter subtlety than has its rhetorical opposite, the PERIODIC SENTENCE. When carefully made, the loose sentence ranges but does not wander; the ducklings do not get lost, and no ugly one appears.

The loose sentence was first cultivated as the basis of a literary style during the seventeenth century, when Ciceronian and anti-Ciceronian writers vied to create a memorable prose by following classical models. The Ciceronians, whose model was the ornate and formal style of the Roman orator Cicero, tried to construct their sentences so that the main idea always came near the end. (See PERIODIC SENTENCE.) The anti-Ciceronians, who felt that a prose style should at least appear natural, even if carefully constructed, modeled their work on Seneca's moral essays and Tacitus's histories, some preferring a curt manner with brief sentences and no connections, others building long leisurely sentences and paragraphs out of short clauses, informally connected, and with little symmetry. The English masters of this loose style were Sir Thomas Browne and Robert Burton. They employed both compound and complex sentences, often using prepositions and conjunctions without strict attention to their formal properties, or separating by a mere comma what we would probably set off by a semicolon, if not a period. (See COMMA SPLICE.) The effect of such a style upon the reader is one of intimacy, of being present in the writer's mind as an idea and its associations are considered for the first time. Here, for example, is Sir Thomas Browne:

Light that makes things seen makes some things invisible; were it not for darkness and the shadow of the earth, the noblest part of the creation had remained unseen and the stars in heaven as invisible as on the fourth day when they were created above the horizon with the sun, or there was not an eye to behold them.
—*The Garden of Cyrus,* Chapter IV.

Compound sentences are usually classed as loose, since one independent clause might have ended the sentence, yet another has been attached. Simple sentences may also be loose, having modifying phrases added after the essential subject and verb, and possible object or other complement (this sentence itself being an example). Complex sentences may be loose if their subordinate (and nonrestrictive) clauses follow the main clause. The loose sentences consisting of a main generalization (e.g., *Odysseus crossed the seas*) followed by one or more amplifying and RENDERING phrases (e.g., *his men working the oars, the water dripping from the wood*) is called a cumulative sentence, and it enriches the TEXTURE of an utterance.

The loose sentence reflects a mind *at* work; the periodic sentence, a mind that *has* worked. But despite its being abusively named, the loose sentence can reflect a civilized informality. The following is an example by the Victorian writer Walter Pater:

One of the most beautiful passages of Rousseau is that in the sixth book of the *Confessions,* where he describes the awakening in him of the literary sense. An undefinable taint of death had clung always about him, and now in early manhood he believed himself smitten by mortal disease. He asked himself how he might make as much as possible of the interval that remained; and he was not biased by anything in his previous life when he decided that it must be by intellectual excitement, which he found just then in the clear fresh writings of Voltaire: "Well! we are all *condamnés* as Victor Hugo says: we are all under sentence of death but with a sort of indefinite reprieve."—*Studies in the History of the Renaissance.* Compare CUMULATIVE SENTENCE.

Lost Generation   See EXPATRIATES.

love casuistry   See CASUISTRY.

lowercase   Small letters as opposed to capitals. See CAPITALIZING.

lyric   **1.** According to Elder Olson, a poem in which "a single perception or feeling is overtly expressed." More broadly, any song or short subjective poem with songlike qualities; hence, such forms as the AUBADE, BALLAD, BALLADE, hymn, MADRIGAL, ODE, RONDEL, serenade, SONNET, and VILANELLE. **2.** In contemporary popular songs, the words as distinguished from the music. **3.** In contemporary musical comedy, the songs as distinguished from the book or story.

REFERENCES: Elder Olson, "The Lyric," *Papers of the Midwest Modern Language Association* (No. 1, 1969); C. Day Lewis, *The Lyric Impulse;* G. L. Brook, ed., *The Harley Lyrics;* Katherine Ing, *Elizabethan Lyrics;* Herbert Grierson, ed., *Metaphysical Lyrics and Poems;* F. T. Palgrave, ed., *The Golden Treasury of the Best Songs and Lyrical Poems;* Richard Crowder, "Poetry: 1900 to the 1930s," *American Literary Scholarship Annual* (1970); Stephen Dunning and Edward Lueders, eds., *Reflections on a Gift of Watermelon Pickle;* Elizabeth Hampsten, "A Woman's Map of Lyric Poetry," *College English* (May, 1973); Barbara Graves and D. J. McBain, eds., *Lyric Voices ...;* John Schmittroth and John Mahoney, eds., *New Poets, New Music;* Laura Chester and Sharon Barba, eds., *Rising Tides.*

M

macaronic   Pertaining to a kind of light verse, often DOGGEREL, that mixes languages (for example, Latin and English). A classic example, attributed to William Drummond of Hawthornden (1585–1649), begins "Cane carmen Sixpence, pera plena rye," obviously a mixed Latin and English version of the Mother Goose rhyme "Sing a song of sixpence, a pocket full of rye."

madrigal   A short LYRIC intended to be sung by several voices, usually four. Early Italian experiments with the form ("motets") appeared in Petrarch's *Rime* (ca. 1350). The more consistently developed forms that appeared in Pietro Bembo's *Rime* (1530) consisted of six to thirteen lines with no more than three rhymes, although he himself practiced and expressly invited variation. Luca Marenzio (1553–99) wrote twenty-three books of madrigals, which circulated all over Europe, several in English translation. The native English adaptations varied widely but had in common, as did their Italian models, planned repetition of words and phrases, affording singers the chance for echolike sound effects. A classic example is Shakespeare's "Crabbed Age and Youth," which appears in *Measure for Measure:*

> Take, O take those lips away
> > That so sweetly were forsworn,
> And those eyes, the break of day,
> > Lights that do mislead the morn!
> But my kisses bring again,
> > Bring again—
> Seals of love, but sealed in vain
> > Sealed in vain!

The madrigal was characterized not only by the CONVENTIONS noted above but also by CONCEITS and erotic or PASTORAL content. It was usually sung to the accompaniment of a lute, a pear-shaped stringed instrument. (Compare the twentieth-century revival of madrigal singing to the accompaniment of the guitar.) The madrigal enjoyed tremendous popularity in ELIZABETHAN England not only among poets but also among singers, amateur and professional, and composers—especially such court favorites as Edward Fairfax and Thomas Morley. The popularity of the madrigal is reflected in its frequent appearance in poetry anthologies—for example, in *The Bower of Delights* (1591), *The Phoenix Nest* (1593), and in the many editions of Richard Tottel's miscellany *Songs and Sonnets* from 1557 to 1587. The madrigals in Tottel's collection were often unsigned or anonymous, but according to Hebel and Hudson many of them were almost certainly the work of such poets as Edmund Spenser, Philip Sidney, Thomas Lodge, and Thomas Campion.

Madrigals and mock madrigals occur in the operettas of Gilbert and Sullivan. *The Mikado* (1885), for example, contains the mock madrigal beginning "Brightly dawns our wedding day," for four tearful voices.

REFERENCES: E. H. Fellows, ed., *English Madrigal Verse 1588–1632;* H. W. Janson and Joseph Kerman, "The Madrigal," *A History of Art and Music;* J. William Hebel and Hoyt H. Hudson, eds, *Poetry of the English Renaissance (1509–1660);* B. Pattison, *Music and Poetry in the English Renaissance.*

major premise   See SYLLOGISM (opening illustration).

major term   See SYLLOGISM IA.

malapropism   From *mal à propos,* "inappropriate." An inappropriate word or expression that only sounds something like the one intended. Some representative malapropisms: "We stuff your pay envelopes with *incendiaries*" (for *incentives*); "I like the man, but I am *contemptible* of his ideas" (for *contemptuous*); "It's simply *incredulous*" (for *incredible*); "Never had I suffered such *humility!*" (for *humiliation*). Richard Brinsley Sheridan's famed Mrs. Malaprop in *The Rivals* is the classic user of such near-miss words, and Fowler calls her "the matron saint of all those who go wordfowling with a blunderbuss." Except when used deliberately for humor, malapropism results from a careless acquaintance with words or a confusion about their meanings.

manifest story-line   See DRAMATIC STRUCTURE.

manifesto   A credo or position-paper in which the leader of a political or aesthetic movement sets forth tenets and convictions. See DADAISM, FUTURISM, MODERNISM, SURREALISM.

Märchen   Tale or FOLKTALE.

masque   A semidramatic aristocratic entertainment, allegorical in structure, accompanied by music, dancing, elaborate symbolic costume, and stage props. Early masques were usually pantomimes; and even if speaking-lines were added they were subordinated to the spectacle itself. The first court masque, Samuel Daniel's *Vision of the Twelve Goddesses* (1604), was an allegorical celebration of the blessings bestowed on England by the new monarch, James I. The masque was a very perishable art-form, lasting from 1604 only until the closing of the theatres in 1642. For the Jacobean masques Inigo Jones (1573–1652), the artist and architect, designed elaborate costumes and intricate stage sets, some of them with working fountains. Such stage props were often found ready-made, however, when masques were performed on the estates of the wealthy.

Among the conventions of the masque, especially when it was given as part of a garden party, was audience participation, the actors dancing with the guests. (Compare this convention with its counterpart in the IMMEDIATE THEATER.) Another convention was to fill the intermission with an *antimasque,* a playful PARODY of the main plot.

The masque had its origins in agricultural ritual and popular dramatic entertainments like the St. George sword dances and plays, which involved costumed and masked persons, music, sudden appearances of the dancers, and the like. For many years the best masque in English literature was considered to be John Milton's *Comus* (produced in 1634, published in 1637). (The Greek word *komos* means dance, incidentally, and is also the root from which the word *comedy* derives.) Though originally titled "A Masque," Milton's *Comus* is often regarded as a PASTORAL entertainment. Ben Jonson is perhaps the best-known writer of masques. Among his best are *Hymenai* (1606), *The Masque of Beauty* (1608), *The Hue and Cry after Cupid* (1608), *The Masque of Queens* (1609), and *Oberon* (1611).

REFERENCES: Enid Welsford, *The Court Masque;* Allardyce Nicoll, *Stuart Masques and the Renaissance Stage;* J. C. Meagher, *Method and Meaning in Jonson's Masques;* Alan Brody, *English Mummers and Their Plays.*

mass literature   Popular ("pop") and low-brow literature; such popular pieces as comic books, newspaper comic strips, newspapers themselves (with some few exceptions like the *New York Times,* the *Manchester Guardian,* and the *Christian Science Monitor*), magazines like *People* and *Reader's Digest,* and the most superficial paperbacks. Compare KITSCH; contrast TOUGH LITERATURE.

REFERENCES: Bernard Rosenberg and David M. White, eds., *Mass Culture;* Irving and Harriet Deer, eds., *The Popular Arts;* Reuel Denney, *The Astonished Muse;* Kingsley Amis, *New Maps of Hell;* Jules Feiffer, *The Great Comic Book Heroes;* Eugene McNamara, ed., *The Interior Landscape;* Walter Ong, *The Barbarian Within;* Alan Casty, *Mass Media and Mass Man;* Ray Browne, *Icons of Popular Culture;* J. D. Hart, *The Popular Book;* Russel Nye, *The Unembarrassed Muse;* Carl Bode, *The Half-World of American Culture;* Thomas Ohlgren and Lynn Berk, eds., *A Rhetorical Approach to Mass Culture;* Joan Didion, *Slouching Toward Bethlehem.*

mass media   Television, radio, cinema, and the popular press that publishes MASS LITERATURE.

REFERENCES: Marshall McLuhan, *Understanding Media* and *The Medium Is the Massage;* James Agee, *Agee on Film; Media and Methods* magazine.

maxim   A general truth, usually a rule of conduct, expressed concisely; for example, "Care for the pennies, and the dollars will care for themselves." See APHORISM.

medieval romance   See CHIVALRIC ROMANCE.

melodrama   Literally, a "play with music." A crude play, often self-satirizing, that invites the audience to hiss at the villain. The villain usually represents greed, while the heroine represents chastity. Among the other stereotypes of the melodrama are the drunken father, the beautiful daughter, the lecherous mortgage holder, and the heroine's handsome, honest, but penniless fiancé. Virtue ultimately triumphs over Vice. Played in "opera houses" to the accompaniment of a tinny piano in the pit, the melodrama has entertained music-hall London as well as the American frontier since the early 1800s. *East Lynne, The Drunkard,* and *M'Liss* have been among the most popular.

REFERENCES: Frank Rahill, *The World of Melodrama;* Eric Bentley, *The Life of Drama;* David Grimsted, *Melodrama Unveiled;* Peter Brooks, *The Melodramatic Imagination;* A. L. Lazarus and Victor H. Jones, *Beyond Graustark.*

memoirs   See AUTOBIOGRAPHY.

metafiction   See ANTINOVEL.

metaphor   **1.** An utterance treating one thing as if it were something quite different, so that a resemblance not normally assumed is pointed up; a poetic comparison of two apparently unlike things; for example, "A rapier of light pinned him to the wall." Such a comparison draws attention to the similarity between a searchlight *beam* and a *rapier,* so that the reader gets an immediate image of straightness, thinness, length, and sharpness, and an impression of the beam's function in relation to the victim. In *The Meaning of Meaning* I. A. Richards analyzes the metaphor into two terms: the expressed term or *vehicle;* the unexpressed, but intended, term, or *tenor.* Thus in our "rapier of light" metaphor, the rapier is the *vehicle;* the intended term, beam, the *tenor.* Some other examples: "The wind is a whetted knife"; "The wind cuts"; "The man barks"; "The conversation ping-pongs"; "The road was a ribbon of moonlight." The use of metaphor as discovery is of great importance to children, whose quick and natural making of metaphors often astounds their elders. (See Richard Lewis, ed., *Miracles, Poems by Children of the English-Speaking World.*) Children come to understand new things, however inaccurately, by comparing the new to something already known.

But metaphor is not just *any* comparison. To say that a cannon is a giant pistol is hardly metaphor; the two things are too much alike (in structure and function) to begin with. Metaphor occurs when a surprisingly imaginative connection is made between two images that are in actuality dissimilar. (See RIGHT SURPRISE.) The comparison of objects not actually unlike (for example, "The road was S-shaped") is prosaic, not metaphoric. Even "wind" and "knife" in our example have lost much of their original poetic edge and may be considered FADED METAPHOR. Traditionally, metaphor has been distinguished from *simile,* the latter being a comparison using "like" or "as": "The wind cut *like* a knife."

2. Broadly, metaphor is any fresh, imaginative comparison, whether expressed or implied; it is basic to the concrete universal, the essence of poetry. Aristotle said that metaphor is something a poet is born with.

3. In expository prose, a method of defining or explaining; e.g., "A deponent verb is an active wolf in passive sheep's clothing." Unconscious humor results when the writer mixes metaphors (or CLICHÉS); e.g., "Swimming against the tide may pave the road to success."

REFERENCES: Christine Brooke-Rose, *A Grammar of Metaphor;* Archibald MacLeish, "Metaphor," *Poetry and Experience;* Herbert Read, "Metaphor," *English Prose Style;* Owen Thomas, *Metaphor and Related Subjects;* R. W. Winterowd, "Metaphor and Symbol," *Rhetoric: A Synthesis;* George Lakoff and Mark Johnson, *Metaphors We Live By;* Janet Emig, "Children and Metaphor," *Research in the Teaching of English* (Fall, 1972); S. R. Levin, *The Semantics of Metaphor.*

metaphysical poets   A school of seventeenth-century poets, among them Crashaw, Donne, Herbert, and Vaughan, who were inspired by religious as well as secular experiences and who expressed them in intellectual, imaginative, often extended, METAPHORS and PARADOXES. Herbert's "The Pulley" (with God and man at opposite ends) and Donne's compass, in "A Valediction Forbidding Mourning," are examples of the extended intellectual metaphors at the heart of the metaphysical CONCEIT and WIT. The metaphysical poets had a considerable influence on twentieth-century poets, especially T. S. Eliot. The epithet *metaphysical* (literally, "beyond nature") was originally a derogation applied by Samuel Johnson to poets he regarded as too far removed from rational assumptions about Nature and the GREAT CHAIN OF BEING. But the metaphysical poets, intellectual though they were, having failed to find very much rationality in the universe, looked inward and tried to unify themselves, their own sensibilities; or, looking outward, sought more direct, personal, perhaps mystical bonds with the Creator.

REFERENCES: Edwin Honig, ed., *The Major Metaphysical Poets of the Seventeenth Century: An Anthology;* T. S. Eliot, "The Metaphysical Poets," *Selected Essays;* Herbert Grierson, ed., *Metaphysical Lyrics and Poems;* Douglas Bush, *English Literature in the Earlier Seventeenth Century;* Alfred Alvarez, *The School of Donne;* Rosamund Tuve, *Elizabethan and Metaphysical Imagery;* George Williamson, *The Donne Tradition;* J. B. Leishman. *The Monarch of Wit;* Alexander Witherspoon and Frank Warnke, eds., *Seventeenth Century Prose and Poetry;* Hugh Kenner, *Seventeenth Century Poetry;* Stanley Fish, *Self-Consuming Artifacts;* Joan Bennett, *Five Metaphysical Poets.*

meter   The measurement of poetry; the rhythmic patterns resulting from combinations of heavy and light stresses on words and syllables. The simplest basic stress pattern, corresponding in music to a "measure" or "bar," is called a *foot.* The following kinds of feet are generally encountered in English and American poetry:

Name of Foot (Adjectival form in parentheses)	Stresses [˘ = light stress; ´ = heavy]	Examples
Two-syllable feet		
iamb (iambic)		a̮ gaín
trochee (trochaic)		né · ver
spondee (spondaic)		péll-méll
pyrrhic (pyrrhic)		in a
Three-syllable feet		
anapest (anapestic)		in the dárk
dactyl (dactylic)		yés · tĕr · day
amphibrach (amphibrachic)		tŏ · mór · rŏw
cretic (cretic, *also called* amphimacer)		síl · vĕr-tóngues
bacchius (bacchiac)		a̮ deáth · blów
antibacchius (antibacchiac)		críme · fíght · ĕr
molossus (molossic)		greát white chief
tribrach (tribrachic)		and in the

Four-syllable feet

ditrochee (ditrochaic)	fór · tune-téll · ĕr
choriamb (choriambic)	súg · ăr ănd spíce
paeon, 1st class (paeonic)	wóm · an · lĭ · nĕss
paeon, 2nd class	cŏm · pár · ĭ · sŏn
paeon, 3rd class	ăn ĭn · vá · sĭon
paeon, 4th class	ĭn · tŏ thĕ bréach
Ionic major (ionic)	hárd-héad · ĕd · nĕss
Ionic minor	ăt ă snáil's páce
Epitrite, 1st class	thĕ cóld, cóld gróund
Epitrite, 2nd class	é · vĭl-éyed wítch
Epitrite, 3rd class	thréad · báre ănd tórn
Epitrite, 4th class	fúll-léngth nŏv · ĕl

Each *line* of a poem contains a certain number of the above *feet.* A poetic (or "metrical") line can thus be measured or "scanned" for its *number and kind of feet.* The following are representative samplings of metrical lines:

Metrical lines

monometer (one foot)
    Mў Bĕn! (iambic)
    chíldrĕn (trochaic)
dimeter (two feet)
    Tŏ · mór-/ rŏw díes (iambic)
    Márў / Márў / (trochaic)
trimeter (three feet)
    Nŏ táw- / drў rúle / ŏf kíngs (iambic)
    Cáught ĭn thĕ / spéll ŏf thĕ / mél · ŏ · dў (dactylic)
tetrameter (four feet)
    Cŏme líve / wĭth me / ănd bé / mў lóve (iambic)
    Thén thĕ / lít · tlĕ / Hí · ă / wá · thă (trochaic)
    Lĭke thĕ léaves / ŏf thĕ fór- / ĕst whĕn súm- / mĕr ĭs gréen (anapestic)
pentameter (five feet)
    Thĕ cúr- / fĕw tólls / thĕ knéll / ŏf párt- / ĭng dáy
hexameter (six feet)
    Shĕ knélt, / Sŏ púre / ă thíng, / sŏ frée / frŏm mór- / tăl táint
heptameter (seven feet)
    Ăll fún- / nў fél- / lŏws, cŏm- / ĭc mén, / ănd clówns / ŏf prí- / văte lífe
octameter (eight feet)
    Lĕt ĭt / fáll ŏn / Lócks · lĕy / Háll, wĭth / ráin ŏr / háil, ŏr / fíre
        ŏr / snów

Usual combinations of foot-lines

Kinds	Examples
Iambic trimeter	/ Ĭts flĕece/ wăs whīte/ ăs snŏw/
Iambic tetrameter	/ Ăs Ĭ/ wăs wălk/ĭng pắst/ hĕr house/
Trochaic trimeter	/ Lóndŏn/ Brídge ĭs/ brókĕn/
Trochaic tetrameter	/ Lóndŏn/ Brídge ĭs/ fálling/ dówn, ŏh/
Iambic pentameter	/ Shăll Ĭ/ cŏmpáre/thĕe tŏ/ ă súm/mĕr's dáy?

[Note: a pyrrhic is sometimes substituted for an iamb.]

Dactylic hexameter	/ Thís ĭs thĕ/ fórest prĭ/mévăl, thĕ/ múrmŭrĭng/
	pínes ănd thĕ/ hémlŏcks

[Note: a spondee is sometimes substituted for a dactyl or an anapest.]

Anapestic tetrameter	/ Bŭt wĕ lóved/ wĭth ă lóve/ thăt wăs móre/ thăn
	lóve/

[Note: an iamb is sometimes substituted for an anapest.]

The number of lines to a STANZA (bundle of lines) determines, in part, its name—couplet, tercet, QUATRAIN, sestet, and so on.

The examples of metrical lines in these tables represent, for the most part, "pure" patterns; that is, in each line usually only one kind of foot appears. However, in many celebrated poems substitutions have been made—a trochee for an iamb, a spondee for a trochee. The substitutions have generally been regarded not only as acceptable but also as desirable to keep the dominant RHYTHM from sounding monotonous. Variety in sound-effects is also achieved by ending a line, now with a light (*feminine*) stress, now with a heavy (*masculine*) stress; e.g., "éndĭng"; "thĕ énd." Another device for achieving variety in a series of lines is that of carrying forward, from line to line, the sense of a sentence as opposed to ending a sentence at the end of a line of poetry. See ENJAMBEMENT.

Through the years certain meters and lines, along with the typical STANZA forms in which they occur, have enjoyed popularity. Nursery jingles, for example, which comprise perhaps the most popular and memorable verse, tend to use very short lines, whether trochaic ("Síng ă sóng ŏf síxpĕnce"), or iambic ("Ăs Ĭ looked out mў wíndow"), or dactylic ("Híckŏry, díckŏry, dóck"). When iambic tetrameter in the first and third lines is alternated with iambic trimeter in the second and fourth lines, the result is the "common meter" of the BALLAD stanza. Dactylic hexameter was the original meter of the classical EPICS, although some translators have preferred to render them into iambic pentameter. The latter meter, in fact, has proved far and away the most popular of all in English, perhaps because it comes close to sounding like the ordinary speech patterns of English. Iambic pentameter is the meter of the SONNET, the SPENSERIAN STANZA, the HEROIC COUPLET, and BLANK VERSE.

REFERENCES: Clement Wood, *A Rhyming Dictionary;* Alex Preminger *et al.,* eds., *Encyclopedia of Poetry and Poetics;* Morris Halle and Samuel Keyser, "The Iambic Pentameter," in W. K. Wimsatt, ed., *Comparative Prosody;* Samuel Keyser, "The Linguistic Basis of English Prosody," in David Reibel and Sanford Schane, eds., *Modern English Studies;* P. F. Baum, *Principles of English Versification;* Paul Fussell, *Poetic Meter and Poetic Form.*

metonym   An example of METONYMY.

metonymy   Literally, "name-changing." A device of figurative language in which the name of an attribute or associated thing is substituted for the usual name of a thing: *the blue* for *the sky, the White House* for *the President, the press* for *newspapermen, the campus* for *the school, the Crown* for *the King, the devil* for *mischief, the gas* for *accelerator pedal, eye* for *look at, finger* for *touch, stomach* for *digest, hammer* for *pound.* The names of places may be substituted for things associated with those places: *java* for *coffee, bermudas* and *bikini* for certain pieces of *apparel.* The names of people may be substituted for things associated with those people: *quisling* for *traitor, gerrymander* for *unfair political redistricting, boycott* for *deliberate avoidance, Romeo* for *lover, Helen* for *beautiful woman, Milton* for *poet.* Compare EPITHET and ALLUSION.

SYNECDOCHE, a special kind of metonymy, substitutes the name of a part for the name of the whole, or the other way round: *keyboard artist* for *piano player, hand* for *working man, wheels* for *automobile;* the name of a substance for the thing made of that substance: *iron* for *golf club, cotton* for *dress, pigskin* for *football;* or the name of a container for what it contains: drink a *bottle,* smoke two *packs,* count the *house.*

Like other figures of speech, metonymy contributes to semantic change. Words used as metonyms often become the familiar terms for the things they are used to name: *iron* for *device to press clothing, stamp* for *a device that stamps or is stamped.* Compare FADED METAPHOR.

REFERENCE: "Metonymy" in George Lakoff and Mark Johnson, *Metaphors We Live By.*

metrical romance   Also known as **medieval romance**. A medieval narrative poem (sometimes a prose translation from the French) dealing with the chivalric adventures, loves, and famous deeds of Greek, Roman, Saxon, Anglo-Norman, English, and French figures. Familiar heroes of these romances are Alexander, Charlemagne, and Arthur. Among the celebrated titles are *The Romance of Alexander, The Romance of Charlemagne, Tristan and Iseult, Morte d'Arthur, Sir Gawain and the Green Knight,* and *Perceval* (compare the German *Parzifal*). Sometimes in these writings history predominates over romance, although most scholars distinguish between genuine romances and the mere celebration of famous exploits (see GESTES).

REFERENCES: George Ellis, *Specimens of the Early English Metrical Romances;* A. C. Taylor, *An Introduction to Medieval Romance;* Lewis Spencer, *A Dictionary of Medieval Romance and Romance Writers;* W. H. French and C. B. Hale, eds., *Metrical Romances;* Roger Sherman Loomis, *The Development of Arthurian Romance;* W. P. Ker, *Epic and Romance;* J. A. Bennett and G. V. Smithers, eds., *Early English Verse.*

metrics   The art of composition in, or the analysis of, METER.

middle term   See SYLLOGISM 1*a.*

miles gloriosus   The braggart soldier; a stock character in the comedies of ancient Greece and Rome and in those of medieval and Renaissance England.

REFERENCE: Daniel Boughner, *The Braggart in Renaissance Comedy.*

milieu   Political, social, cultural, and intellectual environment, which Hippolyte Taine, in *History of English Literature,* posited as indispensable background to the understanding of an author and certain works. Taine also attributed importance to race and "moment." Most scholars and philological critics of the late nineteenth and early twentieth centuries rooted their interpretations of literature in the milieu and the biography of the author. Louis Bredvold's *Intellectual Milieu of John Dryden,* for example, is a distinguished product of this kind of scholarship. The revolt against milieu was led by the NEW CRITICS, who, committed to the doctrine of AESTHETIC DISTANCE, put more emphasis on the work of art itself than on biographical, historical, and other "external" facts. A middle position—that a reader or critic may "keep one foot in each world," the world of background and the world of the text itself—has been proposed by the poet, playwright, and teacher Archibald MacLeish.

REFERENCES: Theodore Morrison, "Dover Beach Revisited," in Robert W. Stallman and R. E. Watters, eds., *The Creative Reader;* Frederick C. Crews, *The Pooh Perplex;* Archibald MacLeish, *Poetry and Experience.*

mimes   From the Greek for "imitate." Pantomimes or dramatic skits that use gestures and other nonverbal means of communicating, sometimes in humorous imitation or burlesque of well-known people or types of people. See COMMEDIA DELL'ARTE.

mimesis   From the Greek for "imitation." **1.** The imitation of life or "holding the mirror up to nature" in the literal sense that allowed early Greeks to explain "singing" as "imitation of the birds." **2.** In literary criticism, artistic and SELECTIVE REPRESENTATION of reality as opposed to one-for-one representation. Compare, for example, the differences between a photograph (one-for-one representation) and a portrait (selective representation) or between a pedestrian photograph reflecting the photographer's unimaginativeness and an artistic photograph reflecting carefully selected subject and composition. Poets' talents for abstracting from the environment certain nonliteral, metaphorical (and in Plato's notion, spurious) ideas prompted the author of *The Republic* (Book 10) to ban poets from his ideal world and scene. Much friendlier to the arts was Aristotle in his concept of mimesis—and no doubt shrewder. In *The Poetics* (Chapter 4) he exposes Platonic Ideas as missing the point about true universals and addresses himself to mimesis as representation of man's dramatic actions (compare Kenneth Burke's DRAMATISM) as they unfold in the plot (*mythos*) of a drama or in the dramatic elements of a poem. According to Aristotle, the chief way in which artists inventively "make" (*poiein*) is through selecting for their plots and structures universally representative types on a new high order of abstraction. Aristotle's representative types, which modern critics like Eric Auerbach and Northrop Frye equate with ARCHETYPES, were unfortunately vulgarized as stereotypes (that is, as THEOPHRASTAN or STOCK CHARACTERS) by Aristotle's Roman successors. The discriminating modern critic Frye distinguishes between "high mimetic" (EPIC and TRAGEDY) and "low mimetic" (COMEDY and SATIRE), though he contends that tragedy and comedy are ultimately "lenses in one vision" (*Anatomy of Criticism,* 1957).

During the Renaissance the HUMANISTS' notion of mimesis was narrowly rhetorical: imitation of style. Cicero and Vergil, for example, were held up as paragons of style worth imitating. From the Renaissance until the twentieth century, mimesis received an almost incredible contrariety of interpretations, as Eric Auerbach has shown in his monumental study *Mimesis* (1946). Auerbach shows how each age, each culture, develops its own rhetoric or life style. And what is rhetoric or life style if it is not a way of representing one's reality? (Some contemporary linguists, in fact, define grammar as a system for structuring one's reality.) In short, literature is essentially mimetic.

It remained for the twentieth-century critic Kenneth Burke to re-examine Aristotle's mimesis and to gain from it inspiration, perhaps, for his own mimetic theory, which, in *A Grammar of Motives* (1945), he calls DRAMATISM (act, scene, agent, agency, purpose). Viewed in its own right, Burke's mimetic theory may yet accommodate our sensibilities about "where it's at" and "telling it like it is," may yet reconcile the apparent dichotomy in our alleged two cultures ("Pop" vs. Matthew Arnold's "high seriousness"), as Susan Sontag has observed in the essay "The Basic Unit of Contemporary Art Is Not the Idea But the Analysis and Extension of Sensations," in G. E. Stern, ed., *McLuhan: Hot and Cool.*

REFERENCES: Plato, *The Republic,* Book 10; Aristotle, *The Poetics,* Chapter 4; Eric Auerbach, *Mimesis;* Kenneth Burke, *A Grammar of Motives;* Northrop Frye, "The Archetypes of Literature," in James Miller, ed., *Myth and Method;* Mary McCarthy, "The Fact in Fiction," *Partisan Review* (Summer, 1960); Murray Krieger, "The Deceptive Opposition between Mimetic and Expressive ... ," *Theory of Criticism.*

minor premise   See SYLLOGISM 1*d.*

minor sentence   A sentence that makes sense, in its context and situation, without full predication (that is, without a complete subject-verb combination expressed).

Unlike the FRAGMENT, the minor sentence is a rhetorical device that often lends force to a thought, perhaps the force of brevity, as in proverb and maxim: "Easy come, easy go."

Much of conversation consists of minor sentences, each fully acceptable though not complete in predication. (See ELLIPSIS.) Minor sentences are normal in commands ("Sit down!"), in questions ("Anywhere?"), and in exclamations ("No, not in the judge's chair!"). Answers to questions also often take minor sentence form, since the question itself supplies sense-giving context: "Are you ready?" "*In a minute.*"

Many transitional phrases appear as minor sentences, even in the most staid formal writing: *So much for preliminaries. To get back to the story. Now for the main point.* Compare SIGNPOST DEVICES.

To set off a word or phrase as a minor sentence may give extraordinary emphasis to its content, and the device should not be used unless such emphasis is appropriate. Charles Dickens, an effective user of the minor sentence, begins *Bleak House:*

> London. Michaelmas Term lately over, and the Lord Chancellor sitting in Lincoln's Inn Hall. Implacable November weather. As much mud in the streets, as if the waters had but newly retired from the face of the earth, and it would not be wonderful to meet a Megalosaurus, forty feet long or some, waddling like an elephantine lizard up Holborn Hill. Smoke lowering down from chimney-pots, making a soft black drizzle, with flakes of soot in it as big as full-grown snow-flakes—gone into mourning, one might imagine, for the death of the sun.

All predications sufficiently implied. No chance of misreading. Verbs like ostrich heads: unseen, but perfectly inferred.

miracle plays   Medieval plays based on the lives of saints and on the Biblical miracles, presented first in churches, later in churchyards, for the entertainment and edification of the parishioners. When the plays became too complex and elaborate to be offered by the Church, production was taken over by the crafts and trade guilds and sometimes, especially in France, by traveling professional players. The first miracle play, the "Quem Quaeritis" trope, was a brief dialogue sung at the end of the gradual in the mass on Easter Sunday. It re-enacts the story of the three Marys and the angel in front of the tomb after the Resurrection. See TROPE 2.

There has been some controversy over the use of the terms "miracle play" and "mystery play," some scholars preferring to apply the term "miracle play" to plays based on the lives of saints and on martyrdoms (customarily performed on the particular saint's day), while reserving the term "mystery play" for the CRAFT CYCLE PLAYS enacted by craft guilds on Corpus Christi. E. K. Chambers, however, believes that the term "miracle play" was used by the men of the Middle Ages to refer to all outdoor vernacular plays with religious subjects, and so prefers to use it for both plays about saints and the craft cycle plays.

REFERENCES: Alexander Franklin, ed., *Seven Miracle Plays;* E. K. Chambers, *The Medieval Stage;* Hardin Craig, *English Religious Drama;* Karl Young, *Drama of the Medieval Church;* Harold C. Gardiner, *Mysteries' End;* Allardyce Nicoll, *Masques, Mimes and Miracles;* Arnold Williams, *The Drama of Medieval England;* A. P. Rossiter, *English Drama from Early Times to the Elizabethans; Cambridge History of English Literature,* Vol. V.

miscellany   An ANTHOLOGY, or collection, of literary pieces, the most celebrated being *Songs and Sonnets* (1557), selected by Richard Tottel and frequently referred to as *Tottel's Miscellany.* One of the anthologist's chief purposes is to give pleasure by tempting the reader's appetite with a smorgasbord representative of the fare. No sensible anthologist has ever intended such a sampling to replace the main courses.

misplaced modifier   The misplacement of modifying elements causes remarkable trouble in English, even for accomplished writers. The fault produces an unwanted ambiguity, sometimes laughable but at other times simply misleading. Careful writers are constantly alert to the misplaced modifier that causes either laughter or confusion. "Look at that ridiculous lady's hat," writes the careless scribbler, producing what is either slanderous or slovenly. A more careful writer, however, would leave no room for misinterpretation: "Look at that lady's ridiculous hat."

No serious trouble arises from a misplaced modifier that draws a laugh; for the laugh shows that the reader saw around the blunder and knows what was meant: "I want a car like the one I saw driven by the blonde with a convertible top and a flashy paint job." The writer is understood, but ridiculed. When the misplacement draws no laugh, the writer's meaning may be taken wrongly, and communication breaks down. What is a reader to make of "You can't charm a woman with money"?

Misplacement of modifiers is a perilous trap for writers who may know what they intend, but who give no thought to the reader. Even a great writer sometimes nods, as does William Faulkner in this example from *The Bear:* "... and he broke a plate-glass window that cost McCaslin forty-five dollars and hit a negro woman who happened to be passing in the leg...." It was a pistol shot, not the plate-glass window, that hit the woman—and the woman was not "passing in the leg" but hit in the leg. See SQUINTER.

mixed metaphor   The thoughtless use of more than one METAPHOR in a context so that incongruous images are brought to mind; for example, "The critic hammered out a slashing review." Since hammers do not slash, the writer surely has not considered what is being said. Often such mixtures involve CLICHÉS, or FADED METAPHORS, since the thoughtless writer is seldom original. An example from a newscaster's remarks: "Another of the Communists' red herrings has come home to roost."

MLA   Modern Language Association of America, an association founded in 1883 "to promote study, criticism, and research in English and the modern foreign languages and their literatures." With a membership of more than 30,000, the MLA today serves a dual function: to foster and contribute to scholarship and to enrich the teaching of language and literature in colleges and universities. Its prestigious journal, *PMLA,* is published quarterly. The MLA also publishes an annual *International Bibliography,* listing books and articles printed throughout the world on English and American literature, foreign literatures, and linguistics. An MLA *Newsletter* reports to members on national developments in the profession and on matters relative to association activities. The rules for preparation of scholarly manuscripts, including theses, term papers, and dissertations, are set forth in *The MLA Style Sheet* (Second edition, 1970), and these rules are widely observed in the academic world of publishing. The association also publishes the *MLA Handbook for Writers of Research Papers, Theses, and Dissertations* (1977). The MLA headquarters are at 62 Fifth Ave., New York, N.Y. 10011.

mnemonics   Devices for assisting the memory. Mnemonics are often used by students who must remember detailed lists with each item in its proper place or order; for example, students of astronomy remember the order of stellar classifications by the sentence, "Oh, be a fine girl, kiss me right now, smack," in which the initial letters form the sequence O B A F G K M R N S. Mnemonics are also useful in remembering the correct spelling of many English words. See SPELLING.

mock epic   A poem that treats a trivial subject in an EPIC manner. The mock epic ridicules its subject, however fashionable, by contrasting obvious triviality of subject with grandeur of treatment; it is a form of SATIRE. Famous examples are Dryden's *Absalom and Achitophel,* Pope's *Rape of the Lock,* and Butler's *Hudibras.* Chaucer's "Nun's Priest's Tale" also contains elements of the mock epic. A broader synonym of mock epic is *mock heroic* or *high burlesque.*

REFERENCE: Richmond P. Bond, *English Burlesque Poetry 1700–1750.*

mode   **1.** In grammar, a synonym for *mood.* **2.** In literature, a general label for specific categories of treatment, such as romance, COMEDY, TRAGEDY, IRONY, ALLEGORY, POLEMIC, SATIRE. In contemporary literary criticism, mode is distinguished from GENRE, which pertains to such literary forms as NOVEL, PLAY, STORY. **3.** In Northrop Frye's theory of modes, romance, comedy, tragedy, and irony comprise, in that order, a hierarchy of complexity.

REFERENCES: Northrop Frye, *The Educated Imagination;* Arthur M. Clark, *Studies in Literary Modes;* Ashley Brown and J. L. Kimmey, eds., *Modes of Literature* (series); Lawrence S. Hall, "Modes," *A Grammar of Literary Criticism;* Josephine Miles, *Eras and Modes in English Poetry.*

modernism   **1.** Loosely, a synonym of anything contemporary. **2.** Strictly, an international movement in literature and the arts, especially in literary criticism, which began in the late nineteenth century and flourished until the 1950s. Henry James's essay "Art of Fiction" (1884) is generally considered the first modernist MANIFESTO. James insisted that technique is more important than subject; that fiction writers should practice the self-discipline reflected in poets' and composers' attention to structural standards. While not rejecting James's tenets, Ezra Pound added the rallying cry "Make it new!" T. S. Eliot, in his essay "Tradition and the Individual Talent," tried to reconcile Pound and James. Most modernists, however, gravitated toward Pound: Eliot himself along with James Joyce, Ford Madox Ford, Virginia Woolf, e. e. cummings, Auden, Mann, Faulkner, Proust, Gide, Beckett, and Nabokov—to name a few. (Some of those writers are also claimed by critics as adherents of other -isms.) "Modernism was an age of crisis," writes Maurice Beebe, "an age marked by a shared sense of loss, exile, and alienation." Compare EXPATRIATES. Literary critics associated with modernism include Gertrude Stein, Malcolm Cowley, Edmund Wilson, Lionel Trilling, George Steiner, Georg Lukács, Howard Nemerov, Leslie Fiedler, Irving Howe, and Roger Shattuck.

REFERENCES: Maurice Beebe, "What Modernism Was," *Journal of Modern Literature* (July, 1974); Harry Levin, "What Was Modernism?" in his *Refractions;* Hugh Kenner, *The Pound Era;* Ihab Hassan, *Paracriticisms;* Richard Ellman and Charles Feidelson, eds., *The Modern Tradition;* Joseph Chiari, *The Aesthetics of Modernism;* Harold

Bloom, *The Ringers in the Tower;* Geoffrey Hartman, *The Unmediated Vision;* M. L. Rosenthal and Sally Gall, "The Modern Sequence and Its Precursors," *Contemporary Literature;* Alan Wilde, "Modernism and the Aesthetics of Crisis," *Contemporary Literature.*

molossus   See METER.

monologue   An extended speech by one person; a passage or a work written to be spoken by one person only. See DRAMATIC MONOLOGUE.

morality play   A late medieval popular play in which the characters are virtues and vices personified, such as Temperance and Greed. The best-known morality play is *Everyman* (ca. 1500), in which the titular lead represents a common person, just as does Christian in Bunyan's allegory, *The Pilgrim's Progress.* In another morality play, *The Castle of Perseverance,* such characters as World, Flesh, and Devil (along with retinues of minor-vice characters) vie for the Soul (a separate character) of Man (another character).

REFERENCES: E. K. Chambers, *The Medieval Stage;* G. R. Owst, *Literature and Pulpit in Medieval England;* Joseph Quincy Adams, ed., *Chief Pre-Shakespearian Dramas;* A. P. Rossiter, *English Drama from Early Times to the Elizabethans;* G. H. Fisher, ed., *Medieval Literature of Western Europe.*

motif   A recurring symbol, expression, or feature (e.g., the love potion that redeems for humanity a person temporarily bestialized.) See Stith Thompson, *Motif Index of Folk Literature.* Compare THEME.

mummers, mummery   See MASQUE.

muse   In Greek mythology, any of the nine goddesses who preside over the arts and some of the sciences: Calliope (epic poetry), Clio (history), Erato (love lyrics), Euterpe (music and songs), Melpomene (tragedy), Polyhymnia (sacred songs), Terpsichore (dance), Thalia (comedy and pastoral poetry), and Urania (astronomy). See INVOCATION.

mystery play   See MIRACLE PLAY and CRAFT CYCLE PLAYS.

mystery story   See DETECTIVE STORY.

myth   1. A traditional narrative of unknown authorship concerning supernatural persons and events. Different from LEGEND (or debased history) and closer to FOLKLORE, myth tends to concentrate on explanations for natural phenomena (compare ANIMISM). Thus the stories about the Greek god Zeus (also the Roman Jupiter and the Norse Odin) seek to explain thunder and lightning; the stories of Ceres and Gaea, to explain spring and fertility; and the stories of Apollo and Daphne, to explain the sunrise following the dawn. See also ARCHETYPE, especially regarding the seasons. A whole series of myths attempt to account for certain constellations as deifications of former mortal heroes. PERSONIFICATION and ALLEGORY appear in almost all myth, as distinguished from SAGA, which deals with the exploits of more or less historical persons, and as distinguished from FABLE and fairy tale, which are designed to teach a moral lesson.

REFERENCES: Thomas Bullfinch, *Mythology* [Nordic as well as classical]; Robert Graves, ed., *Larousse Encyclopedia of Mythology* [contains myths of many different cultures, especially Oriental]; Edith Hamilton, *Mythology;* Paul Harvey, ed., *The Oxford Companion to Classical Literature;* James Frazer, *The Golden Bough* [a comparative study of different cultures and primitive religions with respect to one major myth and its variations—the myth of the birth, death, and resurrection of fertility, as symbolized in the search for the golden fleece]. The College English Association chapbook *On the Mythological,* edited by Kathleen Raine, contains a "Selected Bibliography of Myth in Literature" by James McPeek.

2. A second kind of myth, more recent than the first, and of identifiable authorship, is the "mythical system" or "mythical world" created mostly in fiction. This kind of world is characterized by moral assumptions (though not necessarily by DIDACTICISM) and its demigods and demigoddesses are endowed with more of the frailties and fewer of the heroic qualities of classical gods and goddesses. In Faulkner's mythical world of Yoknapatawpha County, for example, the Compsons and the Sartorises represent the decadent old aristocracy of the South, while the Snopeses represent first the poor whites, then the social-climbing and callous mercantile whites, lacking in agrarian grace, conscience, and sensibility. Similarly, Al Capp has created in his cartoons the mythical world of Dogpatch County, where L'il Abner and Daisie Mae predominate in the roles of back-country, half-literate satyr and nymph. Perhaps the subtlest creations of mythical worlds are those of J. R. R. Tolkien, a former Oxford professor of philology. In *The Hobbit* (1937) gnomelike creatures act out, almost as in an allegory, the all-too-human struggle between good and evil. Aside from the hierarchy of hobbits, dwarves, elves, trolls, and goblins, Tolkien's mythological worlds (among them "Middle Earth") are recreated out of an ingenious mix of contemporary and medieval language and symbols.

REFERENCES: David Miller, "The Moral Universe of J. R. R. Tolkien," *Mankato Studies in English* (Spring, 1967); John Steinbeck, ed., *The World of L'il Abner;* Malcolm Cowley, "Faulkner's Mythical Kingdom," in the Introduction to *The Viking Portable Faulkner;* John B. Vickery, ed., *Myth and Literature;* Paul Olson, *The Uses of Myth;* Ernst Cassirer, *Philosophy of Symbolic Forms;* Mark Schorer, "The Necessity of Myth," in Richard W. Lid, ed., *Grooving the Symbol;* Emil Roy, *Myth in Nietzsche's Zarathustra;* Mircea Eliade, *Myth of the Eternal Return.*

3. In expository essays, especially those dealing with social and anthropological issues, the term *myth* is often used in a derogatory sense to describe certain popular superstitions—for example, "the myth of progress" and "the myth of success." Indiscriminate use of the term can be explosive, however, since one person's "myth" may be another's religious conviction.

REFERENCES: W. G. Sumner, *Folkways;* Richard Chase, *Quest for Myth;* Claude Levi-Strauss, "Time Regained," *The Savage Mind.*

mythopoetics   1. In poetry and fiction, especially in a series of novels or poems, the creation by an author of a mythical world. The creation of such a mythical world, in which the cultural context helps to explain the behavior, assumptions, and the interrelatedness of the characters, usually requires a broad canvas, the extension of space and time in several novels, stories, or poems. William Faulkner created in his novels and short stories the world of Yoknapatawpha County. Smaller mythical universes have been created by

Edgar Lee Masters (Spoon River), Sherwood Anderson (Winesburg, Ohio), Edwin Arlington Robinson (Tilbury Town), and the cartoonist Al Capp (Dogpatch County). Another kind of mythopoetic world is the complex system which the poet Yeats developed to explain human history and the human place in the universe. This system, which he outlined in *A Vision,* forms the basis of many of his later poems. The mythopoetic world that an author creates almost always reflects a personal social criticism and VISION OF LIFE.

2. In literary criticism mythopoetics is the critic's interpretation *(a)* of the mythical world that an author has created—for example, Faulkner's Yoknapatawpha County; or *(b)* of certain ARCHETYPES consciously or unconsciously re-created—for example, the hero's JOURNEY on a boat or raft through a life of symbolic ordeals, as in *Moby-Dick, The Heart of Darkness,* and *The Adventures of Huckleberry Finn.* Freudian critics tend to interpret literary myths as mechanisms of *individuals'* wish-fulfillments; Jungian critics tend to interpret literary myths as reflections or echoes of the unconscious dreams of the whole human race. (See ARCHETYPE.) In literary criticism an interpreter may also call attention to an author's conscious or unconscious re-creation, in a character, of a classical mythological character. Thus a critic may well call Melville's *Billy Budd* a "modern myth," in which Billy is a re-creation of Apollo. For Billy shares with Apollo such characteristics as youth, physical attractiveness, innocence, aesthetic sensitivity, absolute purity of moral behavior—especially avoidance of vengeance except for automatic involuntary (and deadly) reaction to evil—the need for expiation of guilt-feelings, involuntary magnetism, and qualities of the NOBLE SAVAGE. Another interpreter may compare Billy with Jesus, especially in the final episode, in which Billy is executed and his shipmates take small chips and relics of the crucifix-like yardarm.

REFERENCES: Otto Rank, *The Myth of the Birth of the Hero;* Carl Jung, *Archetypes and the Collective Unconscious;* Northrop Frye, "Archetypes of Literature," in *Fables of Identity;* Norman O. Brown, *Life Against Death;* Richard Chase, *Quest for Myth;* Maud Bodkin, *Archetypal Patterns in Poetry;* J. B. Vickery, ed., *Myth and Literature: Contemporary Theory and Practice;* Hugh Dickenson, *Myth on the Modern Stage;* Henry Nash Smith, *Virgin Land: The American West as Symbol and Myth;* Harry Slochower, *Mythopoesis;* Philip Wheelwright, *The Burning Fountain;* Jan Wojcik and Raymond Frontain, eds., *The David Myth in Western Literature.*

N

name-calling   The pursuit of arguments, campaigns, or advancements by negative means, not by supporting one's own cause so much as by attacking that of an opponent or by attacking the opponent's person. The technique is to "smear" the opponent or opponent's cause by attaching abusive labels: "Friends, don't be *taken in* by the *deceptive appearance* of my *fast-talking* opponent and that *gang* of *henchmen* from *out of town*. They have come *sneaking* down here to *conceal the truth* and *rob* us of all we hold dear." The name-caller may go as far as to label an opponent "Communist," "Fascist," "atheist," "misguided," or anything with an unfavorable connotation. See PROPAGANDA DEVICES.

narration   Storytelling. Perhaps the central method of literature, narration primarily reports action—focusing upon events in their concrete reality. The causes and the meanings of those events are, of course, necessary to the ultimate value of the story; but good narrative *presents* the action and does not merely *tell about* it. See INDIRECT DISCOURSE.

Since no narrative can report all of life's events, narration depends for its success upon the writer's skill in selecting details and organizing them in a clear and meaningful sequence.

From the time of Aristotle the pattern of narration has been much discussed but little changed by writers and critics. It is generally agreed that a good story must have three parts—beginning, middle, and end. In the *beginning* the writer sets the stage and introduces all that the reader needs to know for full appreciation of the story—the EXPOSITION. In the *middle* the writer builds tension and suspense through COMPLICATION. In the *end* the writer resolves the tension, bringing the events to some satisfactory conclusion, or DÉNOUEMENT. See DRAMATIC STRUCTURE.

Effectiveness in narration depends much upon proper choice and maintenance of a POINT OF VIEW—that is, a well-defined "window" through which the reader views the story's events. The window is, more properly, the mind and eye of a narrator—a person who sees and reveals the events of the story, often tempering them by personal attitudes and limitations.

In telling a story, a speaker or writer actually blends with narration some other forms of discourse—DESCRIPTION, EXPOSITION, even ARGUMENTATION occasionally. But always the focus is upon the events themselves in their vivid concreteness, and the descriptions and explanations are designed only to enhance the narrative.

Literary forms whose method is chiefly narration include the ANECDOTE (often the joke), the tale, the SHORT STORY, the NOVEL, the NOVELLA, the NOVELETTE, the narrative poem, the BALLAD, the EPIC, the news report, the historical report, the DIARY, and the BIOGRAPHY, including AUTOBIOGRAPHY. Compare DRAMATIC STRUCTURE.

REFERENCES: Caroline Gordon, *How to Read a Novel;* Gertrude Stein, *Narration;* Robert Scholes and R. Kellogg, *The Nature of Narrative;* Leo Braudy, *Narrative Form in History and Fiction;* J. P. Pusack, *Narrative Situations;* Eric Rabkin, *Narrative Suspense;* John Olmstead, *Design of the Narrative;* W. J. T. Mitchell, ed., *On Narrative.*

narrative hook   A device by which a writer initially catches the interest of the reader. Since a story (with people in action) normally catches interest most effectively of all literary forms, the writer or speaker who begins by relating an incident or ANECDOTE has a head start toward holding attention. The narrative hook is used by public speakers, teachers, ministers, writers of nonfiction—by virtually anyone who has an audience to capture, whether the form of discourse be chiefly NARRATION, EXPOSITION, or ARGUMENTATION. The device is typified (but not shown at its best) by the hackneyed opening, "A funny thing happened to me on my way to the...."

narrator   See FOCUS OF NARRATION.

naturalism   1. In philosophy, the ancient Greek beginnings of scientific realism. 2. In literature, especially fiction, the representation of life in its most depraved and sordid aspects, times, and places. Thus reading a naturalistic novel can sometimes be like riding through a sewer in a glass-bottomed boat. The chief tenet of the literary naturalists is that humans are helpless pawns of their environment, and the primary concern of naturalists is with people from poor and ugly environments. The naturalistic movement in modern times is generally said to have started with the French novelist Emile Zola (1840–1902), author of *Nana* and *Germinal.* The novels of Theodore Dreiser (1871–1945) are prevailingly naturalistic, especially *An American Tragedy* and *Sister Carrie.* Upton Sinclair's *The Jungle* and Frank Norris's *The Octopus* are other celebrated examples. Naturalism is to be distinguished from REALISM, with which it is sometimes confused. Realism, like naturalism, is often concerned with the more sordid sides of human existence, but not exclusively and not for the same reasons. Literary realists try to depict life as it is—both good and bad—and are not necessarily concerned with the causative role of environment. Naturalistic novelists and the more recent secular existentialists believe that environment and universe are indifferent, if not hostile, to humanity. See EXISTENTIALISM and HUMANISM.

REFERENCES: Edward Stone, *What Was Naturalism?* Lars Ahnebrink, *The Beginnings of Naturalism in American Fiction;* Charles Walcutt, *The Rise of Literary Naturalism;* William Kimball, "Naturalism in Some Representative American Authors," *Venture* (April, 1969); Gifford Davis, "The Spanish Debate over Idealism and Realism before the Impact of Zola's Naturalism," *PMLA* (October, 1969); Alfred Kazin, "Revival of Naturalism," *On Native Grounds.*

nature   1. The physical world—mountains, meadows, brooks, woods, birds, and so on—with which such authors as Wordsworth, Emerson, and Thoreau "commune"; also called *external nature*. Wordsworth, like many another romantic idealists, believed that by "communing with Nature," one could discover oneself. Thus he believed in Nature as a kind of teacher, or at least a source of inspiration: "One impulse from a vernal wood / May teach you more of man / Of moral evil and of good / Than all the sages can." In this respect Wordsworth was one of the spiritual mentors of Ralph Waldo Emerson, who says in his essay "Nature": "Give me health and a day, and I will make the pomp of emperors ridiculous." Perhaps the most celebrated literary work in praise of the great outdoors and the simple life is Thoreau's *Walden* (1854). In it he says, "I went to the woods because I wished to live deliberately, to front only the essential facts of life, and see if I could not learn what it had to teach, and not, when I came to die, discover that I had not lived." **2.** For notions related to "human nature," see HUMANISM and NOBLE SAVAGE. **3.** In literary criticism "holding the mirror up to nature" is one aspect of MIMESIS.

REFERENCES: Joseph Warren Beach, *The Concept of Nature in Nineteenth-Century English Poetry;* A. O. Lovejoy, *The Great Chain of Being;* John Arthos, *The Language of Natural Description in Eighteenth Century Poetry;* D. B. Wilson, "Two Modes of Apprehending Nature," *PMLA* (January, 1972).

NCTE   National Council of Teachers of English   A non-profit professional organization of over 80,000 teachers of English—elementary, secondary, and college levels—devoted to the improvement of curriculum in the language arts. NCTE was founded in Chicago in 1911 by a group of high-school teachers and professors in protest against the misguided domination of high schools by universities. The Council holds annual conferences in one or another of the major cities of the United States, and also several regional conferences in collaboration with affiliates. NCTE publications include *Language Arts, English Journal, College English, College Composition and Communication, English Education,* and *Research in the Teaching of English.* Headquarters are at 1111 Kenyon Road, Urbana, Illinois 61801.

REFERENCE: J. N. Hook, *A Long Way Together.*

near-rhyme   Oblique-rhyme, off-rhyme, slant-rhyme. See RHYME.

negative to affirmative   See SYLLOGISM 1*h*.

negative capability   A term introduced by the poet John Keats in a letter to his brothers George and Thomas (December 21, 1817). "I had not a dispute [Keats said] but a disquisition with [Charles] Dilke on various subjects; ... at once it struck me what quality went to form a Man of Achievement, especially in Literature, and which Shakespeare possessed so enormously ... I mean *Negative Capability;* that is, when a man is capable of being in uncertainties, mysteries, doubts, without any irritable reaching after fact and reason...." Thus the term *negative capability* has all too often been misinterpreted to mean "a negative attitude toward ideas." But as Lionel Trilling has observed, Keats used the term to refer to "a way of dealing with life"—"to let the mind be a thoroughfare for all thoughts"; to let the subconscious do its work and not "try too hard in coming at a truth." In a letter to Richard Woodhouse (27 October 1818) Keats said, "A Poet ... has no identity ... he is continually filling some other body." Thus another of Keats's ways of approaching experience—a way closely related to negative capability, as Aileen Ward has observed—was to let go of one's own preconceived notions and to "identify with the object ... to imagine the inner life itself. ..."

REFERENCES: Lionel Trilling, "Introduction," *The Selected Letters of John Keats;* Aileen Ward, *John Keats, The Making of a Poet;* Walter Jackson Bate, *Negative Capability;* Monroe Spears, "The Newer Criticism," *Shenandoah* (Spring, 1970); Thomas Harwelt, ed., *Keats and the Critics.*

Neo-Classicism   The CLASSICISM of the RESTORATION and eighteenth century; a reaction against the extravagant theater and the lyrical brilliance of the RENAISSANCE. The period of Neo-Classicism closed with the beginnings of ROMANTICISM toward the end of the eighteenth century.

One of the chief differences between the classicism of the Renaissance and that of the Restoration and later was that some Restoration writers returned to classical models in an almost slavish imitation. (Renaissance classicists had used classical models as springboards for individualistic departures.) Another difference—and perhaps the fundamental philosophic difference undergirding all others—was in the attitude toward man. Whereas the Renaissance classicists had viewed man idealistically and humanistically as an individual with limitless possibilities, the Restoration and eighteenth-century Neo-Classicists viewed man, somewhat more realistically, as embodying evil and good, idleness and initiative, etc. The Neo-Classicists (among them, Dryden, Pope, and Swift) extolled such virtues—checks and balances—as Order, Discipline, Rules, Reason, Decorum, and Good Taste, on which they did not hesitate to capitalize in their essays and verses. They also discouraged such suspect virtues as imagination, invention, innovation, emotion, and the like. As a consequence, intellect, METAPHYSICAL wit, and so on, in the late 1600s and the early 1700s became popular. Classical models of prose and verse were openly imitated. Interest in design and form gained an ascendancy over interest in IMAGERY and emotional language with some few exceptions.

REFERENCES: Walter Jackson Bate, "Neoclassic Developments and Reactions," *Prefaces to Criticism;* George Sherburn, *The Restoration and the Eighteenth Century;* Louis Bredvold, *The Intellectual Milieu of Dryden;* James R. Sutherland, *A Preface to Eighteenth-Century Poetry;* W. M. Richardson, "Neo-Classicism Reconsidered," *Southern Humanities* (Spring, 1971); Lionel Casson, ed., *Masterpieces of the Classical Age;* Paul Spacks, ed., *18th Century Poetry.*

New Critics   Originally, such American writers as John Crowe Ransom, Allen Tate, R. P. Blackmur, Robert Penn Warren, and Cleanth Brooks (in England, T. S. Eliot, I. A. Richards, and William Empson), who revolted against the nineteenth-century school of biographical critics. Whereas the earlier critics had based their interpretations of literary masterpieces not only on the works themselves, but also on biographical and historical backgrounds (MILIEU) and other external influences, the new critics insisted on interpretations supported mostly by the literary works themselves ("close reading of the text"). The new critics rejected external "facts" and scientific positivism, insisting that a masterwork of literature creates its own facts, logic, and integrity—that form and content interact inextricably. Such criticism is no longer new, of course, and it claims numerous devotees. Nor do these writers regard themselves as "critics" so much as interpreters, "readers," and "explicators." Among the concepts of the new criticism: AESTHETIC DISTANCE, AMBIGUITY, BIOGRAPHICAL FALLACY, DRAMATISM, INTENTIONAL FALLACY, EXPLICATION DE TEXTE, and MYTHOPOETICS.

REFERENCES: John Crowe Ransom, *The New Criticism;* I. A. Richards, *Practical Criticism;* William Elton, *A Glossary of the New Criticism;* Ezra Pound, *The ABC of Reading;* Cleanth Brooks, *The Well-Wrought Urn;* Allen Tate, *On the Limits of Poetry;* R. P. Blackmur, *The Lion and the Honeycomb;* Cleanth Brooks and Robert Penn Warren, *Understanding Poetry* and *Understanding Fiction;* Kenneth Burke, *The Philosophy of Literary Form;* René Wellek and Austin Warren, *Theory of Literature;* Joel Spingarn, "The New Criticism," in B. S. Oldsey and A. O. Lewis, Jr., eds., *Visions and Revisions.*

New Humanism   A short-lived movement (ca. 1910–30) in literary criticism, led by Irving Babbitt, Paul Elmer More, and Norman Foerster, in reaction against NATURALISM, ROMANTICISM, and the kind of realism inspired by Freud and Marx. The patron saint of this movement was Matthew Arnold, especially the nostalgic models provided by "Dover Beach" and *Culture and Anarchy.* One of the leaders of this movement had branded the novels of Dreiser and Dos Passos as "cesspools." The New Humanists argued for a return to restraint and reason, but a humane reason as opposed to the cold reason of science and logical positivism. However, with the advent of the NEW CRITICISM, Freudian and Marxian ideas, and the fiction of the 1940s, 1950s, and 1960s, the New Humanism became hopelessly outmoded and almost forgotten. Compare HUMANISM and EXISTENTIALISM.

REFERENCES: Paul Elmer More, *Shelburne Essays;* Norman Foerster, *American Criticism;* Irving Babbitt, *Rousseau and Romanticism.*

nexus   A connecting-link or TRANSITION.

nihilism   (From the Latin *nihil,* nothing.) A cynical life-view, which regards idealist ideas as absurd or meaningless. The term was popularized by the Russian novelist Turgenev in *Fathers and Sons* (1862) and was taken up by anti-Czarist anarchists during the Russian Revolution of 1917. How nihilism can lead to violence was dramatized by Dostoevsky in his novel *The Possessed* (1867). How nihilism can lead to EXISTENTIALIST despair is reflected in Hemingway's story "A Clean Well-Lighted Place," in which the protagonist substitutes the word *nada* (Spanish for *nothing*) for such words in the Lord's Prayer as *Father, heaven, hallowed, bread,* and *forgive.* While nihilism has motivated anarchists from Kropotkin to Rubin to reject organizations other than their own, some nihilists (like B. F. Skinner, for example) are neither anarchists nor existentialists, preferring to believe that only science can save the world.

REFERENCES: Stepan Stepniak, *Career of a Nihilist;* Vera Figner, *Memoirs;* Edmund Wilson, *To the Finland Station;* Peter Kropotkin, *Revolutionary Pamphlets;* Michael Bakunin, *God and the State;* L. Krimerman and L. Perry, eds., *Patterns of Anarchy;* B. F. Skinner, *Beyond Freedom and Dignity;* Jerry Rubin, *Do It;* J. A. Ogilvy, *Many-Dimensional Man;* W. G. Kay, "Romantics of Nihilism," *Southern Quarterly* (April, 1971); Stanley Cooperman, "The Poetry of Dissent," *Michigan Quarterly* (Winter, 1971); R. B. Hauck, *A Cheerful Nihilism;* John Hagopian, "Nihilism in *The Sound and the Fury,*" *Modern Fiction Studies* (Fall, 1967).

Nobel Prize   Since 1901, an annual prize in literature (among other fields) of about $200,000 awarded by the Swedish Academy in Stockholm to a writer of "idealistic works." The award was established by Alfred Nobel (1833–1896), a Swedish chemist. Notable winners of the literature award include William Butler Yeats (1923), George Bernard Shaw (1925), Thomas Mann (1929), Sinclair Lewis (1930, first American writer to win), Eugene O'Neill (1936), Pearl Buck (1938), Gabriela Mistral (1945), Hermann Hesse (1946), T. S. Eliot (1948), William Faulkner (1949), Bertrand Russell (1950), Ernest Hemingway (1954), Albert Camus (1957), Boris Pasternak (1958; declined), Jean Paul Sartre (1964; declined), Samuel Beckett (1969), Pablo Neruda (1971), Heinrich Böll (1972), Saul Bellow (1976), Isaac Singer (1978), Czeslaw Milosz (1980).

REFERENCES: Warren French, *American Winners of the Nobel Literary Prize;* Marshall McClintock, ed., *The Nobel Prize Treasury;* Horst Frenz, ed., *Nobel Prize Lectures in Literature (1901–1967).*

noble savage   1. The idol of Jean-Jacques Rousseau (1712–78) and certain romantic primitivists, who believed the savage in innocence to be more admirable than the civilized person. 2. A literary cult based on this creed. James Fenimore Cooper seems to have been a devotee of the noble savage, as reflected in *The Last of the Mohicans* and the other *Leatherstocking Tales.* In *Billy Budd* Herman Melville invests Billy with all the virtues of an unspoiled child of nature (Billy was a natural child in more ways than one) and depicts him as a foil against the villainous Claggart, the "civilized" officer unable to accept "natural perfectibility." (Compare and contrast PALEFACE AND REDSKIN.) For a citizen's savage attack on the "noble savage," read Irving Babbitt, *Rousseau and Romanticism.*

REFERENCES: Jean-Jacques Rousseau, *Emile;* Roy Harvey Pearce, *Savagism and Civilization;* Franz Boas, *Mind of Primitive Man;* Claude Levi-Strauss, *The Savage Mind;* Peter Collier, ed., *Crisis: A Contemporary Reader.*

nonce word   A word coined for a specific occasion and not likely to be applicable again; one useful only for the nonce, for the present.

nonfiction   Such prose as articles, autobiography, biography, essays, and history.

nonrestrictive   See RESTRICTIVE and COMMA 7.

non sequitur   A conclusion that does not follow logically from its premises or from the evidence offered to support it. One kind of non sequitur is the POST HOC. See CAUSAL REASONING.

noun-banging   The stringing together of nouns used attributively. "The party platform committee rules argument" is the noun-banger's way of describing an argument over the rules of debate between members of a committee assembled to write the platform of a political party. In the hands of an expert noun-banger, "missile guidance center" may become, progressively, "missile guidance center personnel," "missile guidance center personnel office," "missile guidance center personnel office equipment," and even "missile guidance center personnel office equipment maintenance." Such compounds may be perfectly clear to those knowledgeable in the subject; but often what is gained in conciseness is canceled by an increase in ambiguity. Compare NOUNIFICATION.

nounification   1. The pretentious or thoughtless making of nouns by adding a suffix such as *-ion, -ance, -ment, -ness,* or *-ity* to verbs and other forms; and, generally, the use of more nouns than are needed. "State" becomes "make a *statement*"; "recognize" becomes "give *recognition* to"; "forgive" becomes "extend *forgiveness* to." Often a short noun is made verb by the adding of a suffix and then reconverted into noun by the adding of another suffix: "noun" becomes "nounify," then "nounificate," then "nounification." The habit is characteristic of GOBBLEDYGOOK. **2.** The awkward or ambiguous stringing together of nouns that end in *-ion;* for example, "complication of the production of solutions by the administration." One of the ways of clarifying such an utterance is to use definite agent-subjects and simple verbs; e.g., "Administrators complicate problems when they try to solve them." See AGENT.

novel   A long prose narrative of fifty thousand to one hundred thousand words or more, dramatizing a major character's experiences. Prose narratives, LEGENDS, FABLES, and TALES were written and circulated from the earliest times, but serious development of the novel started in eighteenth-century England with the rise of the mercantile middle class. Henry Fielding, author of *Tom Jones,* defined the novel as a "comic epic romance in prose." By "comic" he implied that it contained not only humor and WIT but also happy resolutions of problems. By "epic" he implied that its hero reflected the culture, customs, and aspirations of a nation or race. (See EPIC.) By "romance" he implied both amorous and heroic adventures. By "prose" he implied *(a)* that romance need not be confined, as it had been in previous centuries, to verse and *(b)* that this new form of fiction contained such nonfiction as essays and philosophic comment. Since the eighteenth century, novels have been more or less true to Fielding's definition, though many have experimented with STREAM OF CONSCIOUSNESS, PSYCHOLOGICAL INTROSPECTION, and so on. See ANTINOVEL.

Novels often nominated as "greatest" include *Tom Jones* (Henry Fielding), *Vanity Fair* (William Makepeace Thackeray), *David Copperfield* (Charles Dickens), *The Scarlet Letter* (Nathaniel Hawthorne), *Moby Dick* (Herman Melville), *Madame Bovary* (Gustave Flaubert), *War and Peace* (Leo Tolstoy), *Crime and Punishment* (Feodor Dostoevsky), *Middlemarch* (George Eliot), *The Return of the Native* (Thomas Hardy), *The Adventures of Huckleberry Finn* (Mark Twain), *The Red Badge of Courage* (Stephen Crane), *The Wings of the Dove* (Henry James), *Sons and Lovers* (D. H. Lawrence), and *Ulysses* (James Joyce).

REFERENCES: Caroline Gordon, *How to Read a Novel;* Bradford Book, "The Novel," in Lewis Leary, ed., *Contemporary Literary Scholarship;* Cleanth Brooks and Robert Penn Warren, *Understanding Fiction;* W. H. Evans, *Introduction to the Novel;* Edward Wagenknecht, *Cavalcade of the English Novel* and *Cavalcade of the American Novel;* Ernest Baker, *The History of the English Novel;* Ian Watt, *The Rise of the Novel;* Dorothy Van Ghent, *The English Novel;* Richard Chase, *The American Novel and Its Tradition;* Joseph Warren Beach, *The Twentieth Century Novel: Studies in Technique;* Frederick Karl, *The Contemporary English Novel;* Chester Eisinger, [American] Fiction of the Forties;* John W. Aldridge, ed., *Critiques and Essays on Modern Fiction;* Philip Stevick, ed., *The Theory of the Novel;* Elizabeth Hardwick, "Reflection on Fiction," *The New York Review of Books* (February 13, 1969); Alain Robbe-Grillet, *For a New Novel: Essays on Fiction;* Georg Lukács, *Theory of the Novel.*

novelette   A short novel (fifteen to fifty thousand words, approximately). A more serious art form than the novella, the novelette blends the unity of effect of the short story with a little more of the scope of the novel and much of its psychological introspection. Among the masterpieces of this form are *Benito Cereno* (Herman Melville), *The Death of Ivan Ilych* (Leo Tolstoy), *A Simple Heart* (Gustave Flaubert), *Notes from Underground* (Feodor Dostoevsky), *Abel Sanchez* (Miguel Unamuno), *The Heart of Darkness* (Joseph Conrad), *The Beast in the Jungle* (Henry James), *The Metamorphosis* (Franz Kafka), *Death in Venice* (Thomas Mann), *The Pastoral Symphony* (André Gide), *The Fox* (D. H. Lawrence), *Agostino* (Alberto Moravia), *The Old Man* (William Faulkner), *The Morning Watch* (James Agee), *The Old Man and the Sea* (Ernest Hemingway), and *Seize the Day* (Saul Bellow). One hesitates to add Katherine Anne Porter's *Noon Wine*. For—as distinguished from such terms as *short stories, long stories, short novels,* and *novels*—the term *novelette* (like the term NOVELLA 2) is controversial and strikes some people as a derogation. Miss Porter, for example, says in the Preface to her *Collected Stories* (1965), "Please do not call my short novels *novelettes* or even worse, *novellas*. *Novelette* is classical usage for a trivial dime-novel sort of thing; *novella* is a slack, boneless, affected word that we do not need to describe anything." Nevertheless, the term *novelette* persists in contemporary currency, for better or worse, as a synonym for *short novel.*

REFERENCES: Leo Hamalian and Edmond Volpe, eds., *Ten Modern Short Novels;* Charles Neider, ed., *Short Novels of the Masters;* R. C. Albrecht, *The World of Short Fiction;* W. H. Gass, *Fiction and the Figures of Life.*

novella   1. In medieval and early Renaissance literature, a piece of fiction (about ten to fifteen thousand words) of Italian or French origin and mostly about adulterous intrigues. Representative collections of such *novelle* that later found their way into English translation are Boccaccio's *Decameron* (1353) and Margaret of Navarre's *Heptameron* (1558). Many a novella from the *Decameron* and the *Heptameron* appeared, for example, in William Painter's collection, *Palace of Pleasure* (1566). 2. In modern literature, a long story of about the same length as its Renaissance prototype (not a condensed novel). That it has "poetic insights" and "treats an unusual occurrence," as Goethe observed, hardly distinguishes it from other fictional genres, and Katherine Anne Porter has suggested abolishing the term altogether. (See NOVELETTE.) Nevertheless, the term persists. In *Hemingway: The Writer as Artist,* for example, Carlos Baker refers to *The Old Man and the Sea* as a novella and to Conrad's "The Heart of Darkness" as "Conrad's most masterly novella."

REFERENCES: Arnold Sklare, ed., *Art of the Novella;* P. and R. Cholakian, eds., *The Early French Novella, an Anthology.*

O

obiter dicta   Casual but sophisticated comments or observations made in passing.

objective correlative   1. The image undergirding a metaphor or literary symbol. 2. That kind of artistic selectivity that re-creates an experience by means of referent objects and images rather than by subjective comment; a term introduced by T. S. Eliot to name a set of objects or chain of events selected by the artist to call up a particular emotion in an audience—an emotion appropriate to (correlative with) these objects. Thus Wordsworth instead of observing, "Oh, what a touching picture that reticent girl makes against that rock!" gives us "a violet by a mossy stone." And Shakespeare gives Lady Macbeth unwashable bloody hands to communicate her state of mind during her sleepwalking scene.

REFERENCES: T. S. Eliot, "Hamlet and His Problems," *Collected Essays;* David De-Laura, "Pater and Eliot: The Origins of the Objective Correlative," *Modern Language Quarterly* (September, 1965).

oblique rhyme   Same as near rhyme. See RHYME.

obscenity   The quality or state of indecency, lewdness, or depravity—or any act or product that, in "the eye of the beholder," has such quality. In literature and the arts a work is often judged obscene if it can be demonstrated to be specifically and commercially designed to incite antisocial sexual acts. A work so judged is classed as pornographic (from the Greek words *porne,* "prostitute," and *graphein,* "to write"). At times and in various places, obscene or pornographic works have been the object of CENSORSHIP or official banning dictated by the courts of law. In court the writer's *intention,* as far as it can be determined or judged, is taken into account. And even when a work is judged obscene it may be saved from banning or censorship if it is adjudged to have "redeeming qualities" of literary accuracy, beauty, or instruction. The court often seeks an answer to the question, "Does this book tend to make the normal reader (as distinguished from the pervert) more human or less human?" The question, echoing a tenet of Aristotle's theory of CATHARSIS and of FREUDIAN repression theory, is extremely difficult to answer. The answer, in fact, varies from time to time, from place to place, depending on the background of the judge; and a decision by one judge does not necessarily set an irreversible precedent.

However, the celebrated decision in 1933 by Judge Woolsey of the United States District Court in New York (Southern District), lifting the ban on

James Joyce's novel *Ulysses,* seems to have set a precedent in the interpretation of such criteria as *intention* and *normal reader.* Judge Woolsey exonerated *Ulysses* on the grounds that *(a)* its intention was "not pornographic—not dirt for dirt's sake" but rather "a serious and sincere attempt to devise a new literary method for the observation and description of mankind"; *(b)* the normal reader is "a person with average sex instincts ... what the French would call *l'homme moyen sensuel* [average sensual man] who plays the same role ... as does the 'reasonable man' in the law of torts...." Judge Woolsey had, moreover, consulted two friends whose literary judgment he respected, and he

was delighted to find [he wrote in his decision] that they both agreed ... that reading *Ulysses* in its entirety, as a book must be read in such a test as this, did not tend to excite ... lustful thoughts but that its net effect on them was only that of a somewhat tragic and very powerful commentary on the inner lives of men and women.

Notice that to the criteria mentioned above there is now added the criterion of a work "read in its entirety" and not of bits and pieces taken out of context. Thus the mere presence of sexual scenes and Saxon four-letter words in a literary work does not by itself necessarily mark the work as a whole obscene.

Another milestone case involving an interpretation of the intention criterion occurred in 1968, when the Supreme Court decided against the editor of *Eros* magazine on the grounds that his advertisements tended toward the obscenity of pandering. But perhaps the most celebrated court decision on the issue of obscenity was handed down in 1946 by Supreme Court Justice William O. Douglas in favor of *Esquire* magazine. Here is a key excerpt from the decision:

Under our present system of government there is an accommodation for the widest varieties of tastes and ideas. What is good literature, what has educational value, what is refined public information, what is good art—each of these considerations varies with individuals as it does from one generation to another. There doubtless would be a contrariety of views concerning Cervantes' *Don Quixote,* Shakespeare's *Venus and Adonis,* or Zola's *Nana.* But a requirement that literature or art conform to some norm prescribed by an official smacks of an ideology foreign to our system.

Basic premises among cultivated people, finally, include the following: (1) The sex act can and should be treated in literature and life with a sense of responsibility. (2) Books and advertisements written specifically and commercially to incite antisocial sex acts are obscene. (3) Written pandering is as obscene as oral pandering. (4) Even more obscene crimes against humanity are bigotry, slavery, murder, genocide, and war.

REFERENCES: Norman Podhoretz, "Our Changing Ideals" and Eric Larrabee, "Pornography Is Not Enough," in Irving and Harriet Deer, eds., *The Popular Arts;* Lee Burress, "Foolish Figleaves," *The English Journal* (January, 1969); Richard Kuh, *Foolish Figleaves;* John Frank and Robert Hogan, *Obscenity, the Law, and the English Teacher;* Charles Rembar, *The End of Obscenity;* Felice Lewis, *Literature, Obscenity, and Law.*

obscurantism   Organized or unorganized opposition to the dissemination of knowledge. Compare CENSORSHIP.

occasional verse   Verse written for a specific occasion; sometimes by prescription, as by a POET LAUREATE on request, sometimes on the poet's own inspiration, as Milton's "Lycidas" or Spenser's "Epithalamion."

octameter   See METER.

ode   A poem in an elevated manner, usually written for a specific occasion. The odes of the ancient Greek poet Pindar were songs intended to celebrate the victories of athletes at the annual games, though these songs also concern themselves with nobility as a concept. They were sung by a choir to Pindar's own music, while dancers performed an intricate ballet. Although these odes consist generally of three parts—strophe, antistrophe, and epode—within the parts they are so complex and varied as to be more like symphonic music than like poems in stanzaic form. The Pindaric ode has been compared (by Horace) to a rushing mountain stream, swollen by rain and overflowing its banks. It is typically emotional, extravagant, bold, energetic, even at times incoherent. By contrast, the odes of Horace are—as befits the Augustan era in which they were written—more regular, quiet, and polished, though they can be moving nonetheless.

Both Horace and Pindar have inspired great odes in English. The seventeenth-century poet Abraham Cowley wrote some odes that his age called Pindaric, though they do not approximate the Greek poet's work in form. From the same period we have Andrew Marvell's beautiful "Horatian Ode upon Cromwell's Return from Ireland." Other celebrated odes include Milton's "On the Morning of Christ's Nativity," Wordsworth's "Ode on the Intimations of Immortality from Recollections of Early Childhood," Shelley's "Ode to the West Wind," and Keats's "Ode on a Grecian Urn."

REFERENCES: George N. Shuster, *The English Ode from Milton to Keats;* Carol Madison, *Apollo and the Nine;* Gilbert Highet, "The Renaissance and Afterwards: Lyric Poetry," *The Classical Tradition;* David Lee Rubin, "Toward a New View of Malherbe," *Papers of the Midwest MLA* (1969).

O.E.D.   Oxford English Dictionary. See DICTIONARIES.

officialese   The woolly, impersonal, pedantic, and prolix style of writing often adopted by those who prepare office bulletins or official announcements. See GOBBLEDYGOOK.

off-rhyme   The same as near-rhyme, oblique-rhyme, slant-rhyme. See RHYME.

omniscience   In fiction, what the narrator knows—theoretically and by definition everything. Actually, however, narrative omniscience occupies a spectrum from totality down to innocence, with several limited degrees in between. For further details and examples, see FOCUS OF NARRATION.

onomatopoeia   A sound-effect of words that sound like what they describe: "The slap, slap, slap, of the lapping pond"; "The moan of doves in immemorial elms / And murmuring of innumerable bees."

open book   **1.** When pronounced / ó pən *búk* /, a FADED METAPHOR meaning "obvious" or "transparent": "That brother of mine is an open book."
2. When pronounced / ó pən-bùk /, with high pitch and heavier stress on *open,* a synonym for "open-ended," or a work full of intentional AMBIVALENCE and AMBIGUITY, open to various interpretations. Compare CLOSED.

operational definition   See DEFINING 4.

ottava rima   A stanza of eight iambic pentameter lines rhyming *abababcc*. It was used by Ariosto in *Orlando Furioso* and by other poets of the Italian Renaissance, though with lines of eleven syllables. In English it has been used by Spenser, Milton, Keats, Byron (in *Don Juan*), and memorably by Yeats in "Sailing to Byzantium":

O sages standing in God's holy fire	*a*
As in the gold mosaic of a wall,	*b*
Come from the holy fire, perne in a gyre,	*a*
And be the singing-masters of my soul.	*b*
Consume my heart away; sick with desire	*a*
And fastened to a dying animal	*b*
It knows not what it is; and gather me	*c*
Into the artifice of eternity.	*c*

outline   A systematic statement of the content of a discourse. The jottings made preliminary to organizing a speech or written work may be a *rough outline,* perhaps loosely indicating the intended relationship and sequence of ideas. But the formal outline is carefully structured.

Outlines are of three types: (1) *topic,* (2) *sentence,* (3) *paragraph.*

1. The *topic outline* indicates the order and relationships of topics within a discourse, doing so by headings and subheadings rather than by full statements.

2. The *sentence outline* is similar in structure to the topic outline, but each of its entries is a complete sentence, affording a fuller development of the subject and the relationships of its parts.

3. The *paragraph outline* follows (or prescribes) the order of paragraphs in a discourse, ordinarily offering as items something very close to the topic sentences of the paragraphs of that discourse. It thus becomes a kind of PRÉCIS.

Each of these types follows a basic system of organization and structure, with topics and subtopics numbered or lettered by rank. Topics of highest rank are assigned Roman numerals I, II, III, ... Then follow items of rank in this order: capital letters, arabic numbers, lowercase letters, arabic numbers in parentheses, lowercase letters in parentheses, lowercase Roman numerals followed by closing parenthesis, and so on.

In skeleton the outline looks like this, each topic of equal rank indented to the same point:

```
                          Topic/Title
I.
  A.
    1.
      a.
        (1)
           (a)
           (b)
        (2)
      b.
    2.
  B.
II.
```

When properly prepared, the formal outline follows a strict PARALLELISM—each of its items is couched in similar grammatical form. The proper outline also divides each topic or subtopic into *at least two* parts (or divides it not at all)—just as an apple cannot be cut into fewer than two parts. Thus, when I appears, II must also appear; when A appears, B must also.

REFERENCE: Ralph Loewe, *The Practical Writer.*

outlining for interpretive exposition   The following is a useful pattern for a short-statement outline:

Thesis statement:
Thesis question:
    Answer I:
        Support A
        Support B
        Support n
    Answer II:
        Support A
        Support B
        Support n
    Answer n:

Filled in, a model outline for a five-hundred-word exposition might look something like this:

Thesis: Lady Macbeth functions less as a believable woman than as Macbeth's own evil self.
Thesis question: How do we know this?
    Answer I: She keeps awakening in him mostly his hitherto unaroused evil desires.
        Support A: "Your face, my thane, is a book where men / May read strange matters."
        Support B: "Was the hope drunk / Wherein you dress'd yourself?"
    Answer II: She keeps egging on only his evil desires once they are aroused.
        Support A: "But screw your courage [to do evil] to the sticking place."
        Support B: "Wouldst thou have that / Which thou esteem'st the ornament of life / And live a coward in thine own esteem?"
    Answer n: She says and does little or nothing else that might identify her particularly as a woman.

overphrasing   See DEADWOOD.

overpredication   See DEADWOOD.

Oxford Movement   A nineteenth-century religious movement that started at Oxford University in 1833. The leaders—John Henry Newman (ultimately a convert to Roman Catholicism, and later a Cardinal), John Keble (author of *The Christian Year*), R. H. Froude (an historian), Charles Mariott, and E. B. Pusey (butt of the EPITHET "Puseyism")—sought to inject new life and spirit into what they regarded as an effete Established Church. They published a series of tracts, *Tracts for the Times,* that aroused much controversy and that led to the synonym "Tractarian" for the movement. Because one of their chief pleas was for a return to some of the aesthetic rituals of the Roman Catholic Church, the members soon became identified as "Anglo-Catholics." Though this movement was primarily religious rather than literary, it did influence directly and indirectly many literary figures, among them (ultimately) T. S. Eliot.

REFERENCES: R. W. Church, *The Oxford Movement;* H. W. Stewart, *A Century of Anglo-Catholicism.*

oxymoron   Contradictory ideas expressed in as few words as possible; an abbreviated PARADOX. An oxymoron consists, usually, of a noun and its modifier; but the modifier seems to give the noun an attribute quite the opposite of what is normally associated with it. To call someone a *delightful bore* is to use oxymoron. Other examples: *acid sweetness, studied carelessness, eloquent silence, living death, cowardly hero.* For best effect the oxymoron's contradictory words should be immediate constituents, for if they are widely separated, they lose their sharp effect; and the Greek derivation (*oxy* = sharp, pointed; *moron* = foolish—that is, pointed foolishness) seems to demand sharpness. The oxymoron may appear as an EPITHET when the attribute normally associated with the thing or person is twisted to an opposite: *all-seeing Milton* (for Milton was blind, though only optically); *Little Old New York* (for the city was among the biggest in the world even when the phrase was first used). See ANTITHESIS.

P

paean   A song praising a person or event. Compare DITHYRAMB.

paeon   See METER.

paleface and redskin   Two polar types of writers, chiefly American, represented on the one hand by Walt Whitman, a "redskin, full of energy," who gloried in his Americanism, and on the other hand by Henry James, an EXPATRIATE, full of sensibility, who was somewhat ashamed of his national origin. Following are tags of the two polarities:

Palefaces	*Redskins*
patrician (highbrow)	plebeian (lowbrow)
civilized	frontier
drawing-room	open-air
lonely	gregarious
disciplined	free-wheeling
conservative	radical
humanistic	naturalistic

REFERENCES: Philip Rahv, "Paleface and Redskin," *Image and Idea;* Leslie Fiedler, *Love and Death in the American Novel.*

palindrome   A word or longer expression that reads the same backward as forward (e.g., *radar*). Though of doubtful value, palindromes and their contrivance have provided parlor games and brainteasers. Among the longest devised in English are "Madam sides reversed is madam" and the well-known "Able was I ere I saw Elba." Compare DICHO. Distinguish from ANAGRAM.

REFERENCE: H. W. Bergerson, *Palindromes and Anagrams.*

palinode   A poem that retracts something of a previous poem—e.g., Chaucer's *Legend of Good Women* retracts slurs in *Troilus and Criseyde.* See note on "Palinode of Stesichorus" in Maurois' *Memoirs.*

pamphleteer   See LETTERS 4.

pantoum   Developed by Malayan poets, a poem of no set length, consisting of quatrains in which the second and fourth lines of one quatrain are recycled as the first and the third lines of the next quatrain, and so forth through the last quatrain. The final line of a pantoum repeats its first line. Pantoums and variations were tried by Baudelaire, Victor Hugo, Austin Dobson, and Brander Matthews.

parable   An ANECDOTE or very SHORT STORY with an implied or expressed moral. The parables of Jesus are examples, especially those of "The Prodigal Son" and "The Wise and Foolish Virgins." A modern master of humorous parables is E. B. White. See, for example, his "The Decline of Sport," in *Second Tree from the Corner.*

REFERENCES: "Prose Forms: Parables," in Arthur Eastman *et al.,* eds., *The Norton Reader;* Joachim Jeremias, *The Parables of Jesus.*

paradox   A seeming contradiction; whatever sounds impossible yet is in fact possible. "It's the little things in life that are colossal," said G. K. Chesterton (1874–1936), the British essayist and master of paradox. A paradox is a play on ideas, side-by-side contraries that seem to clash and reconcile simultaneously. In "Canis Major" Robert Frost calls the Big Dog constellation "that heavenly beast." See OXYMORON.

Paradoxical ideas provide the theme for serious poetry, for poets often set out to show that things are not what they seem—that death is life, that love is hate. Richard Lovelace, in "To Althea, From Prison," writes, "Stone walls do not a prison make"—and in confinement that poet finds freedom. The underlying statement in much poetry is made, and can only be made, by paradox, as Cleanth Brooks observes:

> More direct methods may be tempting, but all of them enfeeble and distort what is to be said.... Many of the important things which the poet has to say have to be said by means of paradox:—most of the language of lovers ... most of the language of religion: "He who would save his life, must lose it"; "The last shall be first."

Perhaps the best-known paradoxes occur in seventeenth-century META-PHYSICAL POETRY, especially that of John Donne. Examples: "that he may raise, the Lord throws down" and "when thou hast done, thou hast not done" (the last word a PUN, of course, on the poet's name).

Paradox brings freshness to otherwise trite truisms: "Youth is wasted on the young," said George Bernard Shaw. "Divorces are made in heaven," says an irreverent character in Oscar Wilde's *Importance of Being Earnest.* Here the shock value underscores the truth as the author sees it.

Nonsensical paradoxes are part of folk sayings, Mother Goose rhymes, riddles, and FOLK SONGS. Among the best-known nonsensical Irish folk paradoxes: "You can't rightly get there from here"; "I would not object to their noise if they would only keep quiet"; "I wouldn't be after parting with it [saucepan] if it wasn't to get money to buy something to put in it."

Paradoxical situations and IRONIES, finally, underlie the structure of great fiction—where, as in the phrasal paradox itself, opposing forces clash.

REFERENCES: Cleanth Brooks, "The Language of Paradox," *The Well-Wrought Urn;* Andrew Wanning, Introduction to the *Laurel Edition of Donne;* Harold Pagliaro, "Aphoristic Paradox," *PMLA* (March, 1964).

paragraph   A group of sentences that relate to a single topic and are joined in meaningful order to support it. Though the ancient Greeks did not break their pages into indented blocks of type as we do today, the word "paragraph" derives from their habit of marking a turn of thought in writing by a short line in a text, a *paragraphos*—literally, "a writing beside." Today an indention serves the same purpose: to make the organization of thought visible on the printed page.

Good paragraphs are a matter of art rather than of rule; but certain principles underlie art. It is generally conceded that a good paragraph has at least these virtues: (1) *unity,* (2) *coherence,* (3) *adequate development.*

1. *Unity* means singleness of purpose. Traditionally, the paragraph is built upon a *topic sentence*—a presentation of the core thought. But that thought may lie hidden, implicit in the paragraph rather than openly stated in a "sentence." Typically, it offers a generalization that is clarified and supported by the rest of the paragraph. Whether it appears first, last, or in the middle is of little import; the idea in the topic sentence must be narrow enough to be developed adequately in brief space and must form an essential part of the complete theme. A topic sentence is to a paragraph what the "thesis" is to the whole paper. Even when a paragraph contains no *stated* topic sentence, it contains or implies a topic question, a central question. And all or most of the statements that a paragraph does contain answer, or should answer, this topic question. As for appropriate length of a paragraph: it should be just long enough to answer the topic question it raises—and no longer.

2. *Coherence* begins with consistency—the holding to one point of view, one attitude, one tense (or a consistency of tenses); it implies an orderly joining of thought elements into a meaningful pattern. Progression of thought may be chronological, carrying the reader through a series of events in time; spatial, carrying the reader from part to part of a structure or landscape; logical, carrying the reader from a cause to its effects, from a generalization to specific cases, from particulars to a generalization, or from the less to the more important. Coherence is strengthened by artful repetition of syntactical structures (PARALLELISM, BALANCE, ANTITHESIS), of words (including substitution of synonyms or of pronouns for nouns), and even of sounds (ALLITERATION, ASSONANCE, CONSONANCE). Further, coherence is enhanced by careful use of words of TRANSITION and conjunction, so that the ideas in the paragraph are tied to one another through their development.

3. Since good paragraphs are the product of art more than of precept, no writer should be inhibited by overzealous adherence to rules of *adequate development.* Yet it is helpful to be aware of some common types of paragraphs designed to do special jobs. Among them are paragraphs of *(a)* definition, *(b)* description, *(c)* comparison, *(d)* contrast, *(e)* illustration (by details or examples), *(f)* explanation of cause and effect, *(g)* argument (by evidence and conclusion), *(h)* classification and analysis (by division or enumeration), *(i)* negative detail (elimination of alternatives to an argument), *(j)* restatement, *(k)* transition (leading from one phase of a theme to another). The writer of effective paragraphs does not fear to mix one or more of these techniques in a single paragraph when to do so serves a purpose without violating unity of topic.

Just as the sentences in an effective paragraph relate to a single topic and are linked coherently, so the paragraphs in a theme relate to the THESIS and are linked to one another like the elephants in a circus parade. Just as each elephant grasps in its trunk the tail of the preceding elephant, good paragraphs pick up the tails of the preceding paragraphs, preserving a parade of thought. Appropriate conjunctions and repeated words and phrases help the writer link paragraphs. Paragraphs so linked contribute to a composition's unity, coherence, and adequate development. As a rule, one starts a new paragraph for each change of speaker, actor, or action.

REFERENCES: C. J. Howard and R. F. Tracz, *The Paragraph Book;* Cleanth Brooks and Robert Penn Warren, *Modern Rhetoric;* Malcolm Moore and Conrad Geller, *Paragraph Development;* D. H. Karrfalt, "Symposium on the Paragraph," *The Paragraph;* Virginia Burke, *The Paragraph in Context;* John Ostrom, *Better Paragraphs;* Richard Larson, *Sentences in Action.*

parallelism   The principle in sentence structure that elements of equal function should have equal form. Parallel structures are usually required for:

1. *Coordinates:*

We have *lecture on Monday* and *lab on Tuesday.*
My sister and *my father* will attend.
Will you *ride* or *walk?*
Most Americans see America *at thirty thousand feet* and *at six hundred miles an hour.*

2. *Correlatives:*

We must either *end the war* or *extend it.*
Vickie not only *cooked the meal* but also *washed the dishes.*
Tom is neither *bright* nor *dull*—just *average.*

3. *Compared elements:*

Horace is more *greedy* than *needy.*
Children like *to play games* as well as *to do chores.*

4. *Contrasted elements:*

Mike is *heavy* but not *fat.*
Marty loves to swim—not *in the lake,* but *in the ocean.*
The bed is *firm,* yet *comfortable.*

5. *Verbal noun complements:*

Reading is *understanding.*
To exercise is *to build* strength.

6. *Verbal appositives:*

The trick is *to hang on, to hold fast.*
Rod went *tumbling, sprawling.*

7. *Elements in series and outlines:*

Nancy, Sue, and *Jackie* are here.
They have *books, pens,* and *notepads.* They expect to *hear lectures* this morning, *join discussions* this afternoon, and *attend the dance* tonight. They always enjoy *listening, talking,* and *dancing.*

Parallelism is both substance and ornament in effective writing and speech. It will be useful to illustrate with a prose passage from Robert Louis Stevenson ("On Some Technical Elements of Style in Literature"):

```
    All our | arts
        and | occupations lie wholly on the surface; it
is on the surface that we perceive their | beauty,
                                          | fitness,
                                      and | significance;
```

```
and|   |to pry below is
    |to be   |appalled| by their emptiness
        and|    |shocked| by the coarseness
of the|  |strings
and   |  |pulleys.
```

Faulty parallelism occurs when the elements joined in such structures, though they are intended to serve equal functions, do not have equal grammatical form. These examples are obviously faulty:

"He is *my friend* and *who will never let me down*." (Noun phrase not parallel with adjective clause.)

"Cheryl tried *to memorize* lines and *repeating* them." "It's better *to get* the work done rather than *letting* it go." (Infinitives not parallel to gerunds.)

"The player *with experience* has advantage over the player *who has none*." (Prepositional phrase not parallel with adjective clause.)

"*Loneliness* is more painful than *being without money*." (Noun not quite parallel with gerund phrase. Improvement: "*Loneliness* is more painful than *poverty*," or "*Being without company* is more painful than *being without money*.")

"Sydney traveled *through Europe, Africa,* and *in Asia*." (Noun not parallel with prepositional phrases. Improvement: "... through *Europe, Africa,* and *Asia*.")

See also ANTITHESIS and BALANCE.

paraphrase   A recasting of a passage so that the meaning and general tone of the original are retained although different words are used. A paraphrase may be useful as a test of understanding the original, but is not intended as an improvement or replacement of the original. Nor is a paraphrase a shortened version like a PRÉCIS, but only a version in different words. Paraphrasing a poem as a device for extracting "meaning" should be handled with extreme caution, as Cleanth Brooks warns in "The Heresy of Paraphrase," *The Well-Wrought Urn.* Susan Sontag, in *Against Interpretation,* disparages the paraphrase altogether.

parentheses   A pair of upright curves, (), used to set off an aside or an insertion having only an indirect connection with the rest of the sentence. Current practice relegates the paired parentheses to infrequent use in standard prose, since careful writing makes necessary very little discontinuous or gratuitous comment. Some informative asides are acceptable (see the examples below—in addition to this one itself), but the cute remark in parentheses is considered a blemish.

1. Enclose grammatically unrelated matter within a larger context, either internal or at the end of the main body, in parentheses. The parentheses do not alter the need for other normal sentence punctuation: "William Shakespeare (1564–1616) had reached popular success long before the year of Elizabeth's death (1603). Most accounts of his affairs (see Chapter IV) are obscure." (When the enclosed matter constitutes a full sentence or several sentences, the terminal period is placed inside the closing parenthesis.)

2. Enclose figures or letters that indicate divisions and are run into the text. In enumerating the reasons for the use of the parentheses, for example, each reason may be prefaced by (1), (2), (3), ...

3. Use a single parenthesis after lowercase Roman numerals in an OUTLINE: i), ii).

4. Enclose the dates of birth and death after a name: "Samuel Johnson (1709–84)."

5. In FOOTNOTES, enclose the place and date of publication; in BIBLIOGRA-PHIES, enclose the dates of periodicals. See DOCUMENTATION.

parody   The mimicking of a literary work or of the style of a well-known artist; for example, Fielding's *Shamela,* which mimics Richardson's *Pamela.* When a performer mimics another performer, it may be a compliment, for the style being imitated is at least a recognized hallmark. Ernest Hemingway's sentences, characteristically "and"-ridden, lend themselves to parody, as do William Faulkner's, which often twist and detour (by means of parentheses) for several pages. A modern parody of Shakespeare's *Macbeth* and at the same time a satire of "warhawks" is Barbara Garson's play *MacBird!* Especially unfortunate victims of parodists have been sentimental poems. Joyce Kilmer's "Trees" begins "I think that I shall never see / A poem as lovely as a tree." In the parody by Ogden Nash, one of America's best-known writers of light verse, the poem becomes a protest against billboards: "I think that I shall never see / A billboard lovely as a tree. / Indeed, unless the billboards fall, / I'll never see a tree at all." A celebrated book of parodies (and something of a hoax) was *Spectra* (1916) by Witter Bynner and Arthur Davison Ficke.

REFERENCES: Charles Kaplan, ed., *The Overwrought Urn;* Dwight Macdonald, ed., *Parodies;* A. L. Lazarus, *Entertainments and Valedictions.*

parsimony   See ECONOMY IN WRITING.

part publication   A method of publishing, popular during the Victorian era, in which novels were issued in twenty paperbound parts, each sold at only a shilling. Dickens, along with other Victorian and later writers, published many novels in this form, and such serialization sometimes influenced the plotting. A different market, the carriage trade, elicited "three-deckers," the more expensive three-volume novels described by the Lauterbachs (below). Comparing those paperbound pieces with the finally revised hardbound books can yield insights into the craft of fiction-writing. See CLOSURE.

REFERENCES: Charles and Edward Lauterbach, "The 19th Century 3-Volume Novel," *Papers of the Bibliographical Society of America* (V. 51, 1957); Paul Herring, "Dickens' Monthly Number Plans for *Little Dorrit,*" *Modern Philology* (1966); Carol Harter, "Revisions in Faulkner's *Delta Autumn,*" *Journal of Modern Literature* (#1, 1970); Robert Mayo, *The English Novel in the Magazines, 1740–1815;* Mary Ellen Chase, *Thomas Hardy from Serial to Novel;* Robert Slack, "The Text of Hardy's *Jude,*" *Nineteenth Century Fiction* (XI); Dorothy Deering, "A Pilot Computer Program for the Victorian Periodicals . . . ," *Victorian Periodicals Newsletter* (Jan., 1970).

Participles Anonymous   A writers' club, most leading writers of fiction belonging to it. Members of Participles Anonymous prefer the finite verb (e.g., *walked*) to the participle (e.g., *walking*) at the beginnings of sentences, however heavily they may indulge in end-of-sentence participial and absolute phrases —absolute phrases, that is, after the main clause. For example, most fiction writers avoid a sentence like this: "Walking across the porch, Tom heard the weathered planks creak under his boots," in preference to a sentence like this: "Tom walked across the porch, the weathered planks creaking under his boots." The last sentence is also an example, incidentally, of RENDERING details *after* the main clause.

REFERENCES: H. W. Fowler, "Participles" and "Sentry Participles," *Modern English Usage,* Second Edition, revised by Ernest Gowers; Francis Christensen, *Notes toward a New Rhetoric;* Caroline Gordon and Allen Tate, *The House of Fiction;* R. V. Cassill, *Writing Fiction.*

pastiche   Literally, "a patchwork." A jumble of literary styles, often a PARODY of the styles of well-known writers; in the play *Mrs. Moonlight,* for example, a serious attempt to imitate the best qualities of style of several master playwrights. James Joyce's *Ulysses* contains a pastiche of famous English prose styles in the chapter beginning "Deshil Holles Eamus," usually referred to as the "Golden Oxen of the Sun" chapter. One of the most entertaining and irreverent pastiches of the 1950s is Peter De Vries's *Tents of Wickedness,* in which the protagonist-author Charles Swallow attempts the styles, respectively, of Dreiser, Faulkner, Fitzgerald, Hemingway, Joyce, Kafka, Marquand, Proust, and Thurber. As against conscious and artful pastiche, there must be mentioned the hazard to young writers of unconsciously adopting and using the styles of respected authors without having created distinctive styles of their own. The effect is that of pastiche—a bit of one's own creation, a bit of Runyon, a bit of Faulkner, and so on.

pastoral   Pertaining to shepherds and the countryside. Most pastoral writing is the city-dweller's idea of country life. See ECLOGUE.

REFERENCES: Renato Poggioli, *The Oaten Flute;* Eleanor Terry Lincoln, ed., *Pastoral and Romance: Modern Essays in Criticism;* Robin Magowan, "A Note on Genre," *College English* (April, 1969); William Empson, *Some Versions of Pastoral;* Richard Cody, *The Landscape of the Mind;* Jon Lawry, *Sidney's Two Arcadias.*

pathetic fallacy   John Ruskin's phrase for the tendency of writers unconvincingly to attribute sympathetic human qualities to inanimate forces in nature; thunder and lightning, for example, warn Caesar's wife Calpurnia (in Shakespeare's *Julius Caesar*) of ominous dangers to his life. (The blizzards of MELODRAMA are not exactly sympathetic; they usually add obstacle and frustration to a heroine about to run for help.) When water is described as "cruel" or "kind," according to the mood of a character, the description is a pathetic fallacy.

REFERENCE: John Ruskin, Chapter VII, *Modern Painters.*

pedagogical novel   See DIDACTIC NOVEL.

pentad   See DRAMATISM.

pentameter   See METER.

Perennialism   See GREAT BOOKS.

period   When a sentence has rounded its full thought, the sentence is a period; that is, in the Greek sense of "a going around" or of coming full circle. The Greeks marked the rounded thought in writing by a dot or small circle. By association the dot itself came to be called a *period,* and the mark used to punctuate the end of a written declarative sentence. Today the period is also used for certain conventional purposes, including the marking of decimals and most abbreviations.

The period is used:

1. To mark the end of a declarative sentence; that is, a sentence that does not command, question, or exclaim.

2. To mark the end of an imperative sentence not intended to be emphatic: "Please turn in the assignment tomorrow." (Stronger commands are emphasized by the EXCLAMATION MARK.)

3. To mark the end of a question whose intent is mildly imperative: "Will you please send us three dozen pairs of nylons."

4. To mark the end of a MINOR SENTENCE the full meaning of which is made clear by context: "Good writing can be acquired only by wide and intelligent reading. And in no other way whatsoever."—David Lambuth.

5. After initials in names: T. S. Eliot, H. G. Wells.

6. To punctuate many, but not all, abbreviations: A.M., Dr., e.g., etc., ibid., M.D., Mrs., St. Louis, U.S.

7. As a decimal point with numbers: 808.4, $43.02.

8. In a group of three (...) to mark an ellipsis.

When a period appears next to an end quotation mark, the period comes first: "Wait and see."

When an abbreviation comes at the end of a sentence, one period serves for the abbreviation and the sentence terminal: "Be here at 8 A.M."

In current established practice, the period is *not* used:

1. After display lines (such as titles, subheadings, or headlines), datelines (in correspondence), or signatures.

2. After most groups of capitalized initials and acronyms that have come into common usage: NATO, TWA, UCLA, UN.

3. After *per cent* (except at the end of a sentence).

4. After Roman numerals.

5. After certain scientific and scholarly abbreviations: H_2O, Fe (and other chemical symbols), MS (manuscript), OE, MHG (and other abbreviations for linguistic eras).

6. After contractions written with the APOSTROPHE: nat'l, sec'y (though these forms should be avoided in formal writing).

7. After 1st, 2nd, 3rd, *n*th.

period fault   See FRAGMENT.

periodic sentence   A sentence that delays its main idea until the end, or period, while presenting the subordinate ideas or modifiers first. The full sense of such a sentence is not realized until the period. The periodic sentence thus contrasts with the LOOSE SENTENCE, whose message comes early, with modifiers and afterthoughts trailing. The periodic sentence may be long or short, simple or complex. It ends with an indispensable main element—a subject, a verb, an object or other complement, or an essential (RESTRICTIVE) modifier.

Carefully handled, the periodic sentence, with its tight structure and delayed statement, is capable of dignity and emphasis. But it should be used with caution: Dignifying or emphasizing every thought shows poor planning just as surely as does emphasizing nothing. The formality and suspense of the periodic sentence may, if not relieved by variety of length and rhythm, seem artificial, even bombastic. "To end sentence after sentence with a thump would lead to maddening monotony," says F. L. Lucas in his classic essay "What Is Style?"

The periodic sentence was cultivated as the basis of a literary style by such eighteenth-century writers as Joseph Addison, Samuel Johnson, Edmund Burke, and Edward Gibbon, all of whom modeled their prose style on the works of the Roman orator Cicero.

Current English tends toward informality and the CUMULATIVE SENTENCE and so shuns the heavily periodic style. (See RHETORIC 4.) Yet the periodic sentence may have both modernity and ease, as in these examples:

Not to be troubled about anything over which one has no control, whether the oppression of tyrants or the peril of earthquakes—on the necessity of this also, Epictetus and I are as one. Yet, close as is the resemblance between our opinions, I could not help feeling, as I read, that Epictetus was wise in holding his opinions and that I, though holding the same opinions, was far from wise.
—ROBERT LYND, "On Not Being a Philosopher," *It's a Fine World.*

peripatetic   1. Pertaining to Aristotle's walking "to and fro" as he taught in the Lyceum at Athens (4th century B.C.). 2. Informal; now here, now there. Compare the use of the term in a column-title "The Peripatetic Reviewer."

peripety   A turning point, usually a severe reversal, in which as a result of an unforeseen incident, but not a mere coincidence, a character moves from ignorance to sudden confrontation with reality. For example, in Sophocles' *Oedipus the King,* an ironic reversal occurs when the Messenger intending to bring Oedipus good news reveals the secret of the king's birth and, hence, incestuous marriage. Compare DISCOVERY 1.

REFERENCE: Caroline Gordon and Allen Tate, *The House of Fiction.*

periphrasis   A roundabout way of communicating, now generally avoided by writers and speakers. A periphrasis of "Our fathers founded a new nation here" might read: "A number of individuals related to us paternally organized a governmental setup here within the geographical bounds of what is now referred to as this country, as a kind of novel experiment, you might say." See DEADWOOD 4.

REFERENCES: James R. Masterson and Wendell B. Phillips, *Federal Prose: How to Write In and/or For Washington;* Dwight D. Eisenhower, "West Point Address," in Dwight Macdonald, ed., *Parodies;* Ezra Pound, "Dichten = Condensare," *ABC of Reading.*

persona   **1.** Originally, a mask (with a megaphone built into the mouth) worn by classical Greek actors during performances in amphitheaters. **2.** A character in a play, one of the *dramatis personae,* as in the plays of Shakespeare and in the dramatic poems of Robert Browning and Ezra Pound. **3.** The "person" mentioned by St. Paul in his various Epistles: "God is no respecter of *persons.* There is neither Jew nor Greek nor Gentile [but that God sees through one's mask (*persona*) to the real person underneath]." Thus the King James scholars translated by transliteration the Greek and Latin word for "mask," *persona.* **4.** Among recent critics influenced by the psychologist Carl Jung the persona is regarded as the special role, or "voice," or "mask," that a poet (especially Browning, Yeats, Eliot, Pound, and Frost) assumes in a given poem, rather than speaking directly to the reader. One of the first questions that a reader or an explicator asks of a poem, then, is "Who is speaking?" or "What is the persona?" The answer is something more than what is on the surface; for instance, in a dramatic monologue like Browning's "My Last Duchess," the obvious speaker is the Duke. But the reader should ask, "What *role* is the Duke playing?" See SPEAKING VOICE.

REFERENCES: John Hall Wheelock, "Four Voices," *What Is Poetry?;* T. S. Eliot, "The Three Voices of Poetry," *Collected Essays;* Walker Gibson, *Persona;* Ingmar Bergman, *Persona* (a film).

personification   A figure of speech attributing human qualities to inanimate objects or abstract ideas. Writers and speakers of earlier centuries often treated such abstractions as Truth (with a capital letter) as if they were sentient beings. For example, Samuel Johnson had Fame tell a tale and Victory hover over a general; and poets often addressed such beings as the *West Wind* or *Melancholy.* (See APOSTROPHE.) Today personification is likely to be indirect, seldom pretending to address the personified thing, yet giving it human capacities: "The boiled *cabbage leered* at him from the table"; "The *tires complained* aloud as he took the curve at high speed." When personification of the abstract is developed at great length in narrative, it may become ALLEGORY. The habit of personification perhaps grew out of a tendency for humans to see all things as comparable to themselves, or perhaps out of a psychological need for company, so that the rocks and trees, doors and chairs, hopes and fears became fellow creatures. When exaggerated and sentimentalized, personification may become an instance of what John Ruskin called PATHETIC FALLACY, a belief that natural objects and phenomena share the feelings of human beings. Personification is common in LEGEND, MYTH, and SAGA.

REFERENCES: C. S. Lewis, *Allegory of Love;* Morton W. Bloomfield, "A Grammatical Approach to Personification Allegory," *Modern Philology* (1962–63).

Petrarchan sonnet   See SONNET.

phenomenology   **1.** A school of thought associated with EXISTENTIALISM and concerned with "pure phenomena," each phenomenon regarded in its derivative Greek sense of "something observed." Unlike empiricists (e.g., laboratory scientists), however, phenomenologists accept intuition in responding to phenomena. The founder of this philosophy was Edmund Husserl (1859–1938).

2. Related to (1), a practice of poets who rely on their intuitions for the impact of one word or image on another. (Compare the "impingements" of STRUCTURALISM.) This practice results in unique schematizations, as in FREE VERSE.

REFERENCES: Albert Camus, *The Myth of Sisyphus;* Harmon Chapman, *Sensations and Phenomenology;* W. V. Spanos, "Charles Olson . . . a Phenomenological Approach," *Contemporary Literature;*Robert Magliola, *Phenomenology and Literature.*

Phi Beta Kappa   A non-profit society that fosters and rewards the highest standards and achievements of scholarship in the humanities, the arts, and the sciences. Founded at the College of William and Mary, Williamsburg, Virginia, in 1776, Phi Beta Kappa remains the oldest honorary Greek-letter society in the United States. The Greek letters stand for "philosophia biou kybernetes"— philosophy the guide of life. The society's publications include the *American Scholar,* a quarterly, and *The Key Reporter,* which is sent to members. Headquarters are at 1811 Q Street N.W., Washington, D.C. 20009.

Philistinism   The worship of materialism; castigated by Schopenhauer, Matthew Arnold, Ralph Waldo Emerson, Henry David Thoreau, and H. L. Mencken. Also the inability to appreciate the more subtle and nonmaterial values of literature and art.

REFERENCE: Matthew Arnold, "Sweetness and Light," *Culture and Anarchy.*

philology   Literally, "love of language"; actually, love of learning, including literature as well as language. Both the term and what is represented were phenomena of the nineteenth century and earlier. A philologist studied Anglo-Saxon for its literature (e.g., *Beowulf*) as well as its language. Most scholars— E. K. Chambers, F. J. Child, George Lyman Kittredge, Walter W. Skeat, Kemp Malone, for example—regarded language and literature as inextricably one whole. Today, because of extreme specialization, scholars tend to regard the study of literature and the study of language as two separate disciplines. The study of language now comes under the heading of "linguistics," a term that has all but replaced "philology."

REFERENCES: Howard Mumford Jones, *One Great Society;* Jacques Barzun, *The House of Intellect;* Albert Marckwardt, *A Common Language.*

philosophic statement   The main idea, thematic predication, or conclusion, more often implied than expressed, to which a literary work leads the reader. In *The House of the Seven Gables* Hawthorne leads the reader to a philosophic statement like: "The sins of the fathers are visited upon the children." A philosophic statement is not always so biblically moral, however, Katherine Anne Porter's story "Theft" leads the reader to a statement like: "A person who does not look out for himself gets stepped on." The philosophic statement expressed or implied in a literary work is likely to reflect the author's VISION OF LIFE. See THESIS STATEMENT.

REFERENCE: Monroe Beardsley, "Predication," *Aesthetics.*

picaresque novel   A novel containing *(a)* a *picaro,* or rogue, as a central character, *(b)* an episodic rather than a dramatic story-line, *(c)* a number of characters whom the rogue ruins, and *(d)* a wide range of adventures in "faraway" settings. Examples of picaresque novels are Thomas Nash's *Unfortunate Traveller, or the Life of Jacke Wilton* (1594), Alain René le Sage's *Gil Blas* (1715), Daniel Defoe's *Moll Flanders* (1722), Henry Fielding's *Jonathan Wild* (1743), Tobias Smollett's *Peregrine Pickle* (1751), Hervey Allen's *Anthony Adverse* (1933), and Saul Bellow's *The Adventures of Augie March* (1953).

REFERENCES: Frederick Monteser, *The Picaresque Element in Western Literature;* Robert Alter, *Rogue's Progress;* Ulrich Wicks, "The Nature of Picaresque Narrative," *PMLA* (March, 1974).

Pindaric ode   See ODE.

pirated edition   **1.** The unauthorized printing of a play or other work. Some of Shakespeare's plays were first published in pirated editions. **2.** In modern times, the unauthorized publication of English books by printers in Russia, China (particularly on Formosa), and other countries that do not subscribe to international agreements on COPYRIGHT. **3.** Any unauthorized publication. The pirating of books has been, since the institution of formal international agreements on copyright, episodic, and in the twentieth century has been limited in America to underground classics which, because of vagaries of American copyright law, could not be formally copyrighted here. D. H. Lawrence, in particular, suffered from pirated American editions of his novels.

plagiarism   The act of appropriating the ideas or writings of other persons and presenting them as one's own. See DOCUMENTATION.

REFERENCE: Peter Shaw, "Plagiary," *The American Scholar* (Summer, 1982).

plain folks   A propaganda device whose aim is to make an audience feel that the speaker (or candidate or product) is down-to-earth, simple, and honest— like the audience itself. The office-seeker who puts on overalls and pitches hay with the farmer-voters is using the plain-folks appeal.

platitude   Any commonplace statement of the dull or obvious. See TRITENESS, BROMIDE, STEREOTYPE, and CLICHÉ.

Platonism   The teachings of Plato (427?–347 B.C.), especially the belief that ultimate reality is to be found not in material particulars but in abstracted Universals: Ideas and Ideals. Thus platonic love, discussed in Plato's *Symposium,* transcends the physical and is to be found in its spiritual manifestation: Beauty. Platonism was adopted and adapted by the early Christians, but the Neoplatonists of the RENAISSANCE preferred to reconcile their respect for Beauty with their love of beautiful persons and things of this world. See IDEALISM.

play   See COMEDY, COMMEDIA DELL'ARTE, DRAMATIC STRUCTURE, INNS OF COURT PLAYS, INTERLUDE, MASQUE, PROBLEM PLAY, THEATRE OF THE ABSURD, TRAGEDY.

Pléiade   A constellation of sixteenth-century French critics including Pierre de Ronsard, Joachim du Bellay, and five others. Ronsard and du Bellay, devotees of PLATONISM, urged French writers to read not only the works of contemporaries but also, and especially, the classical Greeks and Romans. Ronsard borrowed the Pléiade tag from an ancient Alexandrine group of seven poets.

REFERENCES: R. J. Clements, *The Critical Theory and Practice of the Pléiade;* A. W. Satterthwaite, *Spenser, Ronsard, and Du Bellay.*

pleonasm   See DEADWOOD.

plot   See DRAMATIC STRUCTURE.

poem, poetry   1. As distinguished from PROSE, poetry defies generalization. One cannot say that poetry has a special subject matter, for it has not. (In fact, the would-be poets who regard "beauty" and "moral lessons" as the special subject matters of poetry are the first to stultify it.) Nor can one say that emotion and RHYTHM are the preserves of poetry rather than of prose, though formal meters are indeed peculiar to poetry. Expository prose (but not fiction) communicates directly and with relatively little ambiguity, or tries to, whereas a poem suggests much more than it says and is purposefully indirect and ambiguous.

2. As distinguished from DOGGEREL and LIGHT VERSE, a poem is a serious attempt, not necessarily without humor, to re-create an experience. The subject matter of poetry seems to be unrestricted, but the treatment rises above the trivial, transforms the matter, and transports the reader, so that a critic like John Ciardi would ask of a poem not "*What* does it mean?" but "*How* does it mean?" Thematic meaning is rooted in and arises from treatment. Treatment is almost everything. To attain the distinction of being a poem, moreover, the piece bears the unique mark of the poet.

3. The chief kinds of poems are *(a) narrative-dramatic,* including BALLAD, EPIC, METRICAL ROMANCE, and DRAMATIC MONOLOGUE; *(b)* LYRIC, including BALLADE, SONNET, ODE, MADRIGAL, RONDEL, and VILLANELLE; and *(c)* FREE VERSE.

REFERENCES: F. T. Palgrave, *The Golden Treasury; The Oxford Anthology of English Verse;* Donald Hall *et al.,* eds., *New Poets of England and America;* Louis Untermeyer, ed., *Modern American Poetry* and *Modern British Poetry;* Judson Jerome, *Poetry: Unpremeditated Art;* John Ciardi,*How Does a Poem Mean?;* Lawrence Perrine, *Sound and Sense;* John Hall Wheelock, *What Is Poetry;* Cleanth Brooks and Robert Penn Warren, *Understanding Poetry;* Karl Shapiro, ed., *Prose Keys to Modern Poetry; The Poetry Index;* B. Stevenson, ed., *The Home Book of Verse;* Alex Preminger and others, eds., *Encyclopedia of Poetry and Poetics.*

poeticism   A derogatory term applied to the contemporary use (unless in PARODY) of such archaic expressions as "o'er" for "over," "e'er" for "ever," "e'en" for "even," and the like; also such words as anon, azure, beckon, bespeak, bivouac, brow, clime, ecstasy, ethereal, goest, hie, know not, know not whether, Lo, naught, replete, repose, rife, steed, thee, thine, thou, thrall, thy, visage, whilst, and wilt.

poetic justice   In fiction and drama, especially MELODRAMA, the just rewards and punishments that the heroes and villains eventually receive. Though poetic justice prevails as a general rule in the novels of Dickens and the plays of Shakespeare, it fails to materialize in such EXISTENTIALIST novels as those by Dostoevsky, Kafka, and Camus and in such absurdist plays as those by Sartre, Anouilh, Cocteau, Giraudoux, Brecht, Dürrenmatt, and Ionesco.

poetic license   The poet's right to use language in any way to serve a specific purpose; thus the poet may occasionally wish to substitute a SPONDEE for an IAMB, to vary a traditional pattern like the VILLANELLE, or to make such experiments as the logic and structure of each poem dictate. Tennyson's "The blue fly sung in the pane" is an example of poetic license; to have substituted "sang" would have diminished the line poetically.

poet laureate   The poet honored by English royalty as more or less the official favorite. The laureateship lasts for the rest of the so-honored poet's life. The honor is not without its drawbacks, since the laureate is supposed to produce poems for certain occasions, regardless of inspiration. Among the best-known laureates are John Dryden, William Wordsworth, Alfred, Lord Tennyson, and John Masefield. The present Poet Laureate is Sir John Betjeman. Among poets who declined the honor were Thomas Gray and Sir Walter Scott. Rudyard Kipling is said to have been passed over because of the line in his poem "Recessional": "The captains and the kings depart." Most of the laureate poems written for occasions have fallen short of excellence.

point of view   1. The attitude, opinion, or set of values unifying oral or written argumentation. 2. In description, the physical point or vantage ground from which the observer views what is being described. 3. In fiction and other narration, the FOCUS OF NARRATION.

REFERENCES: Percy Lubbock, "Point of View," *The Craft of Fiction;* James Moffett, ed., *Points of View: An Anthology of Short Stories;* Wayne Booth, *The Rhetoric of Fiction.*

polyphonic prose   Literally, "many-sounding." Prose in essays and fiction, especially the fiction of James Joyce, which comes close to (is sometimes undistinguishable from) FREE VERSE. Examples range from the comparatively restrained "He saw the sea of waves, long dark waves rising and falling, dark under the moonless night" (*A Portrait of the Artist as a Young Man*), to the DITHYRAMBIC "O that awful deep down torrent O and the sea the sea crimson sometimes like fire" (*Ulysses*), to the experimental "Don Dom Dombdomb and wee fillyo!" (*Finnegans Wake*).

REFERENCE: W. Y Tindall, *A Reader's Guide to Finnegans Wake.*

polysyndeton   The use of many *ands*—more often than not, too many. Children who relate an adventure ("I went out and I saw Billy and we got our bikes and we rode to the circus and we saw the elephants") use polysyndeton as a natural means of "getting on" with a story. The device may be used deliberately, of course, to create a desired effect. It appears with success in the King James Bible:

> And the earth was without form, and void; and
> darkness was upon the face of the deep. And the
> Spirit of God moved upon the face of the waters....

Polysyndeton is often the rhetoric of the catalogue, as it is in the prose of Ernest Hemingway and in these verses by Walt Whitman:

> The early lilacs became part of this child,
> and grass and white and red morning-glories, and white
> and red clover, and the song of the phoebe-bird....

Although overuse and inappropriate use of polysyndeton produce a noticeable mannerism, it can, like most devices of REPETITION, be used to achieve a tone of simplicity and power—as long as it is used with care. Its contrasting device is ASYNDETON.

pop literature, popular culture   See MASS LITERATURE.

pornography   See OBSCENITY.

portmanteau words   Two or more words telescoped into one; for example, *brunch* (for *breakfast* and *lunch*). Many portmanteau words occur in *Alice in Wonderland*. Compare ACRONYM.

post hoc, ergo propter hoc   Literally, "after this, therefore on account of this." A fallacy in CAUSAL REASONING, asserting that since B follows A, A must have caused B. For example, it is clearly fallacious to assume that because one eats dinner just before the sun sets, the eating of dinner causes the sun to set. See INDUCTIVE REASONING 3.

REFERENCE: Darrell Huff, "Post Hoc Rides Again," in H. Wendell Smith, ed., *Elements of the Essay*.

preamble   An introductory statement preceding a formal document, explaining the document's purpose. The most celebrated example is the Preamble to the Constitution of the United States.

precept   See APHORISM.

précis   A concise summary or digest of any literary work. It is not an outline; in fact, it is a complete composition in itself, with all the elaboration and illustration of the original work cut away. It omits all but the essential. The précis is also called an ABSTRACT. Compare PARAPHRASE.

preface   1. The page or two in which an author tells readers why the book came to be written, for what purpose and audience, and under whose auspices. Among the celebrated, if somewhat longer, prefaces is Samuel Johnson's to his *Dictionary* (1755), in which he observes, "Every other author may aspire to praise; the lexicographer can only hope to escape reproach." For a modern example of a model preface, see Samuel Eliot Morison's Preface to *Admiral of the Ocean Sea*. 2. A kind of informal, often satirical, essay in which the writer pretends to be presenting elementary matters, philosophic appetizers preliminary to a main course, but in fact makes a main course of the appetizers. A typical example is *A Preface to Morals* by Walter Lippman. A synonym for this kind of preface is *prolegomenon*. Compare INTRODUCTION.

REFERENCES: Jacques Barzun, *The Modern Researcher*; H. L. Mencken, *Prefaces*.

prelude   1. In general, a long poem as a preface to a long prose work; e.g., the longer sections of James Russell Lowell's *Vision of Sir Launfal* begin with preludes. **2.** A work complete in itself, an autobiography or aesthetic confession offered to audiences as a kind of introduction to, or explication of, the artist's other works; e.g., Wordsworth's *Prelude*.

premise   See SYLLOGISM (opening paragraph).

preposition at end   The belief that an English sentence should not end with a preposition is what Fowler calls a "cherished superstition." Many who listen to the language through ears of pedantry and prejudice cling to this belief—though their own speech, when candid, may abound with final prepositions. The teacher's enjoinder to avoid the preposition at end probably arose from the common tendency to repeat a preposition unnecessarily—and inelegantly: "He had nothing *in* which to carry the fish *in.*" Also common is the habit of attaching a preposition or an adverb needlessly: "Where have you been at?" When the preposition is not redundant, it falls at the end quite naturally in plain English. Little would be gained by recasting such expressions as these: "Oscar had much to live *for,*" "Always know what you're working *with,*" "She's had no experience to speak *of.*" Fowler's advice is useful: If a preposition falls naturally at the end, keep it there.

Pre-Raphaelites   A school of Victorian writers and artists including Dante Gabriel Rossetti, John Millais, Holman Hunt, Edward Burne-Jones, and William Morris. The Pre-Raphaelite Brotherhood ("PRB") was their club name; *The Germ,* their magazine. In revolt against VICTORIAN academism, they advocated a return to art as they believed it to be before the time of Raphael (1483–1520). Along with their interest in medievalism, they admired hedonistic realism, especially sensuous details. Robert Buchanan attacked their eroticism in "The Fleshly School of Poetry"; John Ruskin came to their defense in letters to the *Times* and in *Pre-Raphaelitism* (1851).

REFERENCES: Jerome Buckley, ed., *The Pre-Raphaelites;* William Gaunt, *The Pre-Raphaelite Tragedy;* John Hunt, *The Pre-Raphaelite Imagination;* Graham Hough, *The Last Romantics;* Robert Hosmon, ed., *The Germ;* James Sainbrook, ed., *Pre-Raphaelitism.*

problem play   **1.** Broadly, any serious play in which certain aspects of the human condition are presented as a problem; e.g., Shakespeare's *King Lear.* **2.** More specifically, a drama of ideas. In *A Doll's House* Henrik Ibsen dramatizes the issue of woman's role in modern society; in *Death of a Salesman* Arthur Miller dramatizes the issue of values in a mercantile society.

REFERENCES: Eric Bentley, *In Search of Theater;* Fred B. Millett and Gerald E. Bentley, *The Art of the Drama;* Frederic Litto, ed., *Plays from Black Africa;* Ernest Schanzer, *Shakespeare's Problem Plays.*

proem   An introductory statement preceding a formal literary work or speech; a FOREWORD, PREFACE, or PRELUDE.

progress   **1.** Pronounced prō´-gress, in Elizabethan England a public procession made by the Queen and her retinue, usually to a house party given by a nobleman (for example, the Earl of Leicester at his Castle Kenilworth in 1575, the background of one of Scott's Waverley novels). **2.** A philosophic concept—"the idea of progress"—that views the history of mankind as a series of gradual improvements interrupted by setbacks only temporarily.

REFERENCE: Charles Beard, "The Idea of Progress," in Cleanth Brooks and Robert Penn Warren, *An Approach to Literature*.

projective verse   Just as speakers in a psychological "projective test" project themselves, through their responses, beyond the stimulus (usually a painting or picture), so speakers in a projective poem project themselves—their thoughts, feelings, "breathing" (Robert Creeley's term) beyond such stimuli and "artificial structures" as METER, LINE, FORM. The Projectivists (Robert Creeley, Charles Olson, Robert Duncan, Denise Levertov, LeRoi Jones, Alfred Hayes, and others) thus reject the doctrine of Marshall McLuhan and of the NEW CRITICS that form or "the medium" is "the message," that form disciplines meaning, that form helps one to "discover one's meaning" (Mark Schorer's theory).

REFERENCE: Donald M. Allen, ed., *The New American Poetry*.

prolegomena   Prefatory remarks.

prolepsis   From the Greek for *anticipation*. Speaking figuratively of some anticipated event as if it had already happened. It may appear as a kind of exaggeration (see HYPERBOLE) in which the status of the moment is projected to its extreme result, as in "I'm frozen to death" or "We have won tomorrow's game." A famed example of prolepsis is Hamlet's remark as he lies wounded: "Horatio, I am dead." Prolepsis occurs also in such phrasing as "knock him flat" or "run her ragged," in which the anticipated result is indicated by an objective complement.

prolixity   See DEADWOOD.

prologue   **1.** A synonym of PRELUDE 1. The best-known examples are Chaucer's Prologue to *The Canterbury Tales,* describing the various members making the pilgrimage to Canterbury, and such prologues as are prefixed to most of the tales, especially those of the Miller, the Reeve, the Cook, the Man of Law, the Shipman, the Prioress, the Monk, the Friar, the Clerk, the Summoner, the Pardoner, and the Wife of Bath. **2.** In drama the prologue is a convention of RESTORATION and eighteenth-century plays, in which the stage manager (or other official) would preface a performance with an explanation of what it was all about. (Compare, in the modern theater, the servant's prologue in Robert Bolt's *Man for All Seasons* and the Stage Manager's in Thornton Wilder's *Our Town.*) The play prologue has its counterpart in the EPILOGUE.

propaganda devices　Methods of gaining advocates for an idea, a cause, a person, or a product—usually through a beguiling association of things. To persuade people that they should support, believe in, or buy, the propagandist (or advertiser or publicist) seeks to associate a particular idea, cause, person, or product with admired things (see GLITTERING GENERALITY, TRANSFER, TESTIMONIAL, PLAIN FOLKS). The propagandist may deal in bias by emphasizing arguments in favor of and ignoring arguments against what is advocated (see CARD-STACKING). The propagandist may persuade many simply by pointing out (or at least asserting) that others hold this view (see BANDWAGON); and may seek support for one view by attacking its opponent (see NAME-CALLING and ARGUMENT AGAINST THE MAN). Other tendentious appeals, most of them covered by the terms already referred to, are known by the Latin terms for certain devices of rhetorical argument (see AD CAPTANDUM, AD HOMINEM, AD IGNORANTIAM, AD MISERICORDIAM, AD POPULUM, AD VERECUNDIAM).

REFERENCE: William Hummel and Keith Huntress, *The Analysis of Propaganda*.

prosaic　A synonym for "dull," "humdrum" or "commonplace"—that is, a derogation, not ordinarily a neutral term. The neutral term pertaining to prose is PROSE: e.g., "prose fiction" or "prose narrative."

prose　Most works that are not POEMS. Prose may be classified as *(a) utilitarian* or *documentary*—letters, bills of notice, legal advertisements, directions, encyclopedic information, news reports, etc.—and *(b) aesthetic* or *lyrical*—FICTION, ESSAYS, certain plays, etc. See EXPOSITION, BELLES LETTRES, and POEM.

REFERENCE: Arthur T. Quiller-Couch, "On the Capital Difficulty of Prose," *The Art of Writing*.

prosody　The theory of versification. See METER and RHYME.

protagonist　Hero or chief character. See DRAMATIC STRUCTURE.

Protestant ethic　See CALVINISM.

provenience, provenance　The origins or sources of a literary work. See INFLUENCE.

proverb　See APHORISM.

pseudonym or **pen name**　The fictitious name that an author uses, for various reasons. Mary Ann Evans used the pen name "George Eliot"; and Aurore Dupin "George Sand" to escape the onetime prejudice against women writers. Samuel Clemens picked up from his pilot days on the Mississippi the "Mark Twain" pen name by which he became widely known. "O. Henry" was really William Sidney Porter. Charles Dickens's early pen name, "Boz," which he soon abandoned, was the nickname of a pet younger brother. Other celebrated pseudonyms: Molière (Jean Baptiste Poquelin), Voltaire (François Marie Arouet), George Orwell (Eric Blair). Other synonyms for pseudonym and pen name are *nom de plume* and *nom de guerre*. See A. Taylor *et al.*, *Anonyma and Pseudonyma*.

psychedelic   Literally, "mind-expanding." **1.** Pertaining to the effects of certain drugs, notably lysergic acid (LSD), upon the consciousness. The vivid colors, fluid lines, and bizarre patterns characteristic of LSD-induced hallucinations have been adopted as the basis of a decorative style now widely disseminated throughout popular culture. The moving strobe-light effects produced on walls and ceilings during light shows are likewise meant to approximate the effects of consciousness-expanding drugs. **2.** Pertaining to contemporary art, cinema, and graphics influenced by the decorative style described in (1).

REFERENCES: Mordecai Marcus and Henry Salerno, eds., "Popular Culture," *Cross Section: Essays on Contemporary America;* "The Aesthetics of the Popular Arts," in Irving and Harriet Deer, eds., *The Popular Arts: A Critical Reader;* Marshall Lee, ed., *Psychedelic Art;* William Sparke and Clark McKowen, *Montage;* R. E. L. Masters and Jean Houston, *Varieties of Psychedelic Experience;* J. B. Hogins and G. A. Bryant, eds., *Juxtaposition.*

psychic distance   In fiction, the use of a generalization like "the man" or "he" (instead of "Harry") and "the woman" or "she" (instead of "Helen") at the beginnings of narratives to attract the attention of the reader-as-bystander before a more intimately rendered characterization is offered. (Compare a movie scene in which the camera eye opens on a long shot, then zooms in for a closeup.) Examples can be found in the opening passages of Henry James's *Beast in the Jungle,* Joseph Conrad's "Lagoon," James Joyce's "Two Gallants," D. H. Lawrence's "Rocking Horse Winner," Katherine Anne Porter's "Noon Wine," Ernest Hemingway's "Snows of Kilimanjaro," and William Faulkner's "Spotted Horses." In "The Lagoon" Conrad's unnamed "white man" leads us to the protagonist, Arsat; similarly, in Chekhov's "Gooseberries" several minor characters lead us to the main character, or to the story about him.

psychoanalysis   **1.** A set of treatments, mostly confession and CATHARSIS, presided over by a psychoanalyst, a physician who studies not only conscious behavior, as do "behaviorist" psychologists, but also subconscious or unconscious human behavior. Such an analyst is a student of certain "depth psychologists," notably Freud, Jung, Rank, and Adler. According to Freud a person's behavior is motivated more by forces hidden beneath the consciousness than by those that are apparent. He called these hidden forces the "id"; the more conscious forces, the "ego" and "superego." To the superego he assigned the role of censor, ever ready to veto impulses originating in the id.

2. In literature, a synonym for "psychological introspection"—the art of the writer who portrays the thoughts and motivations of characters, whether or not the writer echoes Freud or Jung or is even aware of them.

3. In literary criticism, an emphasis of interpretation, chiefly Freudian, developed by such writers as Edmund Wilson, Norman Holland, Lionel Trilling, Steven Marcus, and Leslie Fiedler. The magazine *Literature and Psychology* is the leading American exponent of the psychoanalytic school of literary criticism. See LEVELS OF MEANING.

REFERENCES: Sigmund Freud, *A General Introduction to Psychoanalysis;* Carl Jung, *Psychological Types;* Alfred Adler, *Understanding Human Nature;* Ruth Munroe,

Schools of Psychoanalytic Thought; Carl Jung, *Archetypes and the Collective Unconscious;* Otto Rank, *The Myth of the Birth of the Hero;* Lawrence S. Hall, "Psychological Focus," *A Grammar of Literary Criticism;* Simon O. Lesser, *Fiction and the Unconscious;* Frederick J. Hoffman, *Freudianism and the Literary Mind;* Oscar Cargill, "The Theban Plague," *CEA Critic* (February, 1969); Albert Mordell, *The Erotic Motive in Literature;* Norman N. Holland, *The Dynamics of Literary Response;* Leon Edel, *The Psychological Novel (1900–1950);* Frederick Crews, *Literature and Psycholoy* (MLA booklet); Alan and Sue Stone, eds., *The Abnormal Personality through Literature;* Margaret Church, *Time and Reality.*

pulps   Magazines printed on coarse pulpy paper slightly heavier than newsprint, the coarseness of the paper often matched by the woodenness of the content Perennial pulps include *True Confessions* and *Popular Westerns.* Compare SLICKS.

REFERENCES: Tony Goodstone, *The Pulps: Fifty Years;* Frank Gruber, *The Pulp Jungle;* Robert Weinberg and L. McKinstry, *The Pulp Hero Index.*

pun   A play on words, so that one utterance brings to mind two sound-alikes or two incongruous meanings of the same word. Condemned to death for punning, the court jester won pardon from the king—and greeted the reprieve with the pun, "No noose is good news." A pun need not be "the lowest form of wit"—a view held chiefly by those whose experience with puns has been confined to the shallows. Says Fowler, "The assumption that puns are *per se* contemptible ... is a sign at once of sheepish docility and desire to seem superior. Puns are good, bad, indifferent, and only those who lack wit to make them are unaware of the fact."

Like the two poles of an electrical circuit, the elements of a pun may come together wastefully to make only sparks and sputters—or they may come together usefully to engender power and light. Max Eastman (in *Enjoyment of Laughter*) distinguished three sorts: the *atrocious,* the *witty,* and the *poetic.*

Atrocious (also called bad, lame, or feeble) are of the spark-and-sputter sort. They bring to mind two words, or two meanings of one word, only one meaning relevant, the other "dragged in." The tire manufacturer who advertised that "It's time to retire" has produced such a pun. When that billboard pun was made more graphic (advertisers said "more successful") by the addition of a yawning, pajama-clad boy holding a candle in one hand and a tire in the other, pun connoisseurs still groaned.

Witty puns provide a double relevance: both members of the word-pun bear meaning for those who can bare it. They play not only upon words, but also upon ideas—ideas ranging from the simple/obvious to the complex/obscure. In the simpler range is the advertisement urging you to buy a certain mattress "for the rest of your life." More complex and obscure is this newsclip with comment from England's *Punch* magazine:

Died April 15th 1895, John, the son of Henry and Rachel
Longbottom, at the age of 2 1/2 years.
Vita brevis est, ars longa.

To appreciate that pun requires a good ear, an unsheltered vocabulary, and some knowledge of Latin.

Poetic puns go beyond the merely humorous play upon words, as William Empson observes in *Seven Types of Ambiguity.* From Chaucer to Robert Frost and beyond, the pun has been turned to poetry's uses. In Dylan Thomas's "Do Not Go Gentle into That Good Night" the speaker refers to "grave men near death," a slyness that the running reader may miss altogether.

Punning and its appreciation sometimes depend upon paronyms, words having a common root. Knowledge of etymology provides a special delight in word play as when, for example, James Joyce says of a character, "He was astoneaged." Punning is also called paronomasia. See HOMONYM, HOMOPHONE.

REFERENCES: William Empson, *Seven Types of Ambiguity;* Paul F. Baum, "Chaucer's Puns," *Chaucer, A Critical Appreciation;* Sister Miriam Joseph, *Shakespeare's Use of the Arts of Language;* Bennett Cerf, *Treasury of Atrocious Puns;* A. Moger, *The Complete Pun Book;* Max Eastman, *Enjoyment of Laughter.*

punctuation   A system of signs and symbols to aid the reader in understanding grammatical and syntactical relationships, as well as intonation, as they are represented in written discourse. In the broadest sense even the space between words is a kind of punctuation, for it helps the reader to separate meaningful elements at a glance; in this sense CAPITALIZING, INDENTION, and PARAGRAPH-ING can be considered as kinds of punctuating. But punctuation is more narrowly and commonly considered the use of certain marks to *link, separate,* or *terminate* utterances in writing. In this book each mark of punctuation is treated in its separate article (see APOSTROPHE, BRACKETS, COLON, COMMA, DASH, ELLIPSIS, EXCLAMATION MARK, HYPHEN, PARENTHESIS, PERIOD, QUESTION MARK, SEMICOLON, VIRGULE).

Puritanism   1. A Calvinistic movement that acquired political power in England with the rise of Oliver Cromwell, who ruled the Commonwealth from 1649 to 1659. The Puritans succeeded in closing the London theaters ("pits of iniquity") in 1642, but were themselves suppressed after the RESTORATION of Charles II in 1660. 2. In the New England colonies, the prevailing Calvinist outlook of the settlers and the theocentric forms of government that this outlook inspired, especially under Increase Mather (1639–1723) and Cotton Mather (1663–1726). 3. Broadly, the attitude that unless one represses sexual desire one is doomed to eternal punishment. See CALVINISM.

REFERENCES: Bliss Perry, *Puritanism and Democracy;* Perry Miller, *The New England Mind;* Vernon L. Parrington, *Main Currents in American Thought* (Vol. 1); Roy Harvey Pearce, ed., *Colonial American Writing;* Larzer Ziff, *Puritanism and the American Experience.*

purple passage   Any noticeably florid passage of a written work. The purple passage, or purple patch, differs markedly in tone from its context, making a sudden flourish with elaborate FIGURES OF SPEECH, IMAGERY, or rhetorical devices not congenial to the context. The term ordinarily implies unfavorable criticism, suggesting that the author has written the passage tastelessly.

purpose in communicating   See INTENTION and DRAMATISM.

pyrrhic   See METER.

Q

quatrain   A STANZA or poem of four lines.

question mark   The symbol "?" whose basic use is clearly indicated in its name. It is placed after a direct question, but not after an indirect question; and the writer must know which is which. A direct question is a seeking of information ("Have you read Spinoza?" "What else?" "Was he the topic of your paper?"), but an indirect question is *an utterance about* a question ("We want to know *whether you have read Spinoza*"; "Tell us *what else*"). Direct questions are followed by question marks; the utterances *about* questions are followed by periods. Sometimes the two are combined: a direct question is "quoted" within another utterance ("We asked him, 'What have you told the president?'") or is used appositively within another such utterance ("The burning question, How long will it last? consumed me"). No comma is used after the question mark.

Question marks are also used after items in a question series: "Did you remember your lunch? your money? your tickets?" The question marks, in place of commas, emphasize the items one by one.

If a full question is quoted, the closing quotation marks go outside the question mark ("What's the name of that song?"), but the question mark goes outside the quotation marks if what is quoted is not itself a question ("Have you read 'The Raven'?"). If our example were not itself quoted, it would be punctuated thus: Have you read "The Raven"? See QUOTATION MARKS.

Question marks in parentheses are sometimes used to indicate doubt or uncertainty or to question the accuracy of some bit of information: "John Marston (1575–1634), the dramatist, was born at Coventry(?)." No space is left between the challenged word or number and the parentheses.

Using the question mark in parentheses to convey IRONY may have a childish effect: "He entertained(?) with his color slides." It is one thing to challenge information, quite another to challenge an opinion—even the writer's own.

Question marks are never doubled. If a sentence is a question within a question and both end in the same place ("Did she ask, 'Where's Johnny?'"), one question mark will do. Extra question marks for emphasis ("Can you guess where we went???") may be appropriate in a personal letter, but not in serious EXPOSITION.

quip   A brief, witty remark, often sarcastic; a BON MOT, a JEU D'ESPRIT.

quotation marks   Dictionaries sometimes define quotation marks as pairs of inverted commas (for opening quotes) and pairs of apostrophes (for closing quotes). Journalists call them simply "quotes"—and we have "put quotes around" the word. Quotation marks are used:

1. To enclose directly quoted matter, from a single word to many paragraphs. Direct quotations report the exact words spoken (or, in fiction, supposedly spoken).

"Where are you going?" she asked.
"On private business," he replied.

An indirect quotation is not the exact words of a speaker or writer, but a summary of the words, and is written without quotation marks.

She asked where he was going. He said that is was private business.

Indirect quotations usually appear as noun clauses, like those in the examples. In the formal quotation (as in a research paper) of long passages or of poetry, indention often takes the place of quotation marks. See RESEARCH PAPER.

2. To enclose words that deserve special notice. Quotation marks for this purpose should be used only when the words quoted really deserve the extra attention.

Perry was a "bright" boy, and that was his downfall.

3. Singly, to enclose quotations within quotations.

"Wasn't it Winston Churchill who said, 'We shall never surrender'?" Mary asked.
"Everybody had to memorize Bryant's 'Thanatopsis' or flunk Miss Bisby's English course."

4. To enclose titles of published works that are parts of larger units. Such titles include those of chapters, magazine or newspaper articles, short stories, and poems. Also enclosed in quotation marks are the titles of radio and television shows, songs and other short musical works, paintings and other art works. See TITLE.

When several paragraphs are quoted continuously, opening quotation marks appear at the beginning of each paragraph; but closing quotation marks appear only after the final paragraph.

Closing quotation marks usually appear next to other punctuation, such as COMMA, PERIOD, QUESTION MARK, or EXCLAMATION MARK. These are the patterns followed by most writers and editors:

1. Commas and periods always go inside the end-quotation marks.

"That," he pontificated, "is beyond question."
Write a comment on the Ramon Fernandez in Wallace Stevens's "Idea of Order at Key West."

2. Colons and semicolons always go outside quotation marks.

I saw two reasons for reading "Locksley Hall": it was considered "great literature"; it was sure to be expected on the examination.

3. The question mark and the exclamation mark go inside quotation marks
if what is quoted is a question or an exclamation; otherwise, they go outside.

Shelley asked, "If Winter comes, can Spring be far behind?"
Wasn't that the last line of his "Ode to the West Wind"?
The whole cast sang "Oklahoma!"
How we all enjoyed hearing "Stardust"!

quotations, introducing   In expository essays, long quotations—even those by
celebrated authorities—are better abstracted in the essayist's own words. But if
a brief passage in the celebrity's words seems more appropriate than a paraphrase (perhaps because the revelation may be contrary to popular notions),
the technique with which the writer introduces that direct quotation can
heighten its effectiveness. Other than such introductory expressions as "Here is
Alfred North Whitehead on this point" or "as Alfred North Whitehead has put
it," there is the device of "keynoting"—of first summarizing in a brief statement
the substance of what is about to be quoted so that the quotation corroborates
and reinforces the point that both the writer and the authority are making.
This quotation from the anthropologist (and authority) Franz Boas and the
way in which the critic Richard Chase introduces it may serve as an example:

No people have ever been known to be without a literature. Tales and songs are
worldwide, writes Professor Boas.

The Bushman and the Eastern Eskimo, although poor in the production of art, are
rich in tales and songs, of which they possess a well-nigh inexhaustible treasure.
The poor hunter of the Malay peninsula and the Australian aborigines have their
literature no less than economically advanced people.

—Richard Chase, "Myth as Literature," *The Quest for Myth.*

The critic has introduced the quotation, and at the same time advanced the
logical flow of the essay, with the keynote summary.

R

ratiocination   Often erroneously called "deduction" in reference to the way Sherlock Holmes and other celebrated detectives in fiction solve cases; more accurately, a process of inductive reasoning, since it starts with clues and proceeds from these specific data to "conclusions." Poe called "The Murders in the Rue Morgue" and "The Gold Bug" ratiocinative mysteries.

rationalism   1. The philosophic viewpoint associated with the Age of the Enlightenment in France (eighteenth century)—especially those aspects of the Enlightenment that rejected emotion and the cult of the noble savage, and preferred reason, restraint, and balance. One associates with this viewpoint such writers as Voltaire, Diderot, and Thomas Paine. 2. A philosophic movement, akin to DEISM which rejected, as a foundation for religious beliefs, pure faith unsupported by reason.

REFERENCES: W. E. H. Lecky, *History of the Rise and Influence of the Spirit of Rationalism in Europe;* J. W. Smith, *Theme for Reason;* Phillip Harth, *Swift and Anglican Rationalism;* R. H. Levy, *Rationalism in Boileau's Art of Poetry;* George Santayana, *The Life of Reason.*

realism   1. In scientific philosophy, the belief that when you see or touch a table, the table is there ("it's real"), as distinguished from the belief that it is only your idea of the table that is real (idealism or Platonic realism). (For distinctions among such philosophic concepts as *Platonic realism, scientific realism, social realism, religious realism,* see Herbert E. Cushman, *A Beginner's History of Philosophy.*) 2. In literature, especially fiction, the writer's philosophic emphasis on life-as-it-is rather than life-as-it-might-be. Such early realistic novels as *The Rise of Silas Lapham, Ethan Frome,* and *Washington Square* may thus be contrasted with such romantic novels as *Ivanhoe, The Last Days of Pompeii,* and *The Last of the Mohicans.* Compare NATURALISM.

REFERENCES: Joseph Warren Beach, *The Twentieth-Century Novel;* Walter Lawrence Myers, *The Later Realism;* Everett Carter, *William Dean Howells and the Rise of Realism;* Vernon L. Parrington, *Beginnings of Critical Realism in America (1860–1920);* Harold H. Kolb, Jr., *The Illusion of Life;* Larzer Ziff, *The American 1890s.*

redaction   1. Revision by an editor. 2. A new edition or version of a work. 3. A digest of a longer work or works; for example, Malory's *Morte d'Arthur* is a redaction of several Arthurian legends. Similarly, Homer's *Iliad* is believed to be a redaction of several ancient Grecian legends.

red herring   In ARGUMENTATION, any attempt to draw attention from the main issue by raising another. The name of the device comes from the practice of using a smoked herring to train hunting dogs to follow a scent. If an arguer (or a propagandist) can lure listeners into discussing or considering an irrelevant or false issue, they may forget entirely about the real issue. (Also known as *smokescreen.*)

reductio ad absurdum   A form of conditional argument used to establish or refute a THESIS by arguing that a proposition is true because its contrary is obviously false or absurd, or that a proposition is false because its contrary is obviously true.

To disprove, for example, that I do not exist:

Assume: I do *not* exist.

Deduce: If I do not exist, then I cannot think. But I *can* think (since this argument itself requires thinking).

Conclude: Since I have denied the alternative ("consequent"), I must conclude that the condition does not hold. Therefore, "If I do *not* exist" is false—and "I exist" must be true.

The reductio ad absurdum is more often used to refute an opponent's argument. In defending the accused, an attorney may set out to prove that the client did not commit the crime. By assuming the contrary—that the client *did* commit the crime, the attorney reasons that the client must have been at the scene of the crime; but evidence shows that the client actually was elsewhere at the time. Conclusion: "To have committed the crime, the client had to be in two places at once—a condition that is obviously absurd; therefore the client did *not* commit the crime."

redundancy   See DEADWOOD.

reduplication   The doubling of all or part of a word. In some languages the device has INFLECTIONAL effect, but in English it is used chiefly to indicate a diminutive or affectionate tone—as in *dada* and *mama,* or (the slang) *super-duper* and *whing-ding.* The affectionate tone is often achieved by doubling of names: President Kennedy's infant son was called *John-John.* In RHETORIC reduplication occurs when the end of one structure (word, phrase, clause, or verse) is repeated as the initial element of the next: "Now in the shadows she *lingers, / lingers* in silent repose."

referent   See SEMANTICS 1.

refrain   1. In popular songs, a synonym for "chorus" as distinguished from the seldom sung "introduction." 2. In poetry, especially BALLADS and other narrative verse, a line repeated verbatim or with variation at the end of each stanza. (Compare REPETEND, which usually carries more variation.) The best-known example is Poe's refrain in "The Raven": "Quoth the raven, 'Nevermore!'" Following are the first and last stanzas of William Morris's ballad "Two Red Roses across the Moon":

There was a lady lived in a hall,
Large of her eyes and slim and tall;
And ever she sung from noon to noon,
Two red roses across the moon.

Under the may she stooped to the crown;
All was gold, there was nothing of brown,
And the horns blew up in the hall at noon,
Two red roses across the moon.

reification   The treatment of abstractions as though they were things. Reification helps to make the abstract idea concrete, more easily "realized" by the reader or listener. It often takes the form of METAPHOR ("Truth is a deep well"), though more strictly metaphor compares two concrete things rather than one abstract and one concrete.

Renaissance   1. Generally, any rebirth, the French word having been adopted in preference to the English *renascence*. Compare Italian *rinascimento*.

2. The rebirth of interest in Greek and Roman culture that took place first in Italy during the fourteenth and fifteenth centuries and gradually spread across the Continent, reaching England in the sixteenth and seventeenth centuries. Classical ideas and literary forms had been held up as models throughout the Middle Ages, but without a clear conception of their origins or of the vast differences that separated the ancient Greco-Roman world from the medieval world. To the Middle Ages, Roman aristocrats were "knights"; a TRAGEDY was a story of a high person's fall, rather than a dramatic form; and RHETORIC, which had been such an integral part of public and forensic oratory in the ancient democracies, was a set of rules employed only for writing letters and poetry, since in a feudal society there was little occasion for anyone to write speeches. Classical authors—mainly Latin ones, as few in medieval times knew Greek—were venerated for their antiquity, but the civilization of which they were a part was virtually unknown.

With the Renaissance came a sense of historical perspective, a curiosity about the past, and the excitement of new discoveries: America, the Copernican heavens, a rich earth, and a rich cultural heritage. Italian interest in things classical received impetus in part from Byzantine scholars who fled to Italy at the fall of Constantinople (1453), bringing with them a knowledge of classical Greek texts that had been known previously only through hearsay and a very few scattered translations. But an interest in Greek language and literature was already being felt well before the middle of the fifteenth century, and Greek was becoming available by way of Byzantine and Greek-speaking Arabic visitors. Petrarch (1304–74), for example, had a Byzantine tutor, with whom he studied Homer.

In the arts and in architecture, as well as in literature, the rediscovery of classical masterpieces stimulated the production of new works that were classical in spirit, but original in conception. The architecture of Andrea ("Palladio") di Pietro (1508–80), the inventions and paintings of Leonardo da Vinci (1452–1519), and the paintings and sculpture of Michelangelo Buonarroti (1475–1564) are among the most celebrated products of the Italian Renaissance. This was the age of great private collections of classical art and patronage of contemporary artists by noble families, such as the Medici of Florence.

The emergence of HUMANISM was another feature of the Renaissance. This is the idea that man has a potential for culture which distinguishes him from lower orders of beings, and which he should strive constantly to fulfill. What we now refer to as a "Renaissance man" is a person who, by long and varied training, has fulfilled as many of his potentials for culture as possible and has thereby attained the state of civilization. Michelangelo, for example, was a "universal" or Renaissance man in his ability to write sonnets, paint and sculpt great works of art, and design some of the architecture that has made Rome famous.

Finally, the Renaissance impulse cannot be dissociated from a passion for translation—from Greek into Latin, and from Latin into various vernacular languages. Translation and the invention of the printing press were the chief means by which classical culture was brought within the reach of a wide reading public across Western Europe. In the process of translation many Greek and Latin words found their way into the vernacular languages, particularly into French, English, and Spanish, strengthening and enriching them and making them better vehicles for sophisticated literature and philosophy.

REFERENCES: Gilbert Highet, *The Classical Tradition;* B. L. Ullman, *Studies in the Italian Renaissance;* Roberto Weiss, *The Dawn of Humanism in Italy;* Leonardo da Vinci, *Notebooks;* George F. Young, *The Medici;* John A. Symonds, *The Life of Michelangelo;* Carl J. Burckhardt, *The Civilization of the Renaissance in Italy;* Paul O. Kristeller, *Renaissance Thought: The Classic Scholastic and Humanistic Strains and Studies in Renaissance Thought and Letters;* R. R. Bolgar, *The Classical Heritage and Its Beneficiaries;* Erwin Panofsky, *Renaissance and Renascences in Western Art.*

3. The Renaissance in England is generally held to comprise the ELIZABETHAN and JACOBEAN eras. It was perhaps England's Golden Age, especially in literature. Among the giants were Shakespeare, Spenser, Jonson, Sidney, Marlowe, and Donne. Though the Renaissance is said to have arrived late in England, it was making headway in several fields long before the reign of King James I. Aside from the Italian influence on English art, architecture, and music, the ideals of the Renaissance gentleman as outlined in Castiglione's *The Courtier* (1518, English translation 1561) and other etiquette books were well known enough to become the butt of satire in Elizabethan and Jacobean plays. (See COURTESY BOOKS.) Poets and travelers like Wyatt and Surrey brought back from Italy the Petrarchan sonnet form and other literary souvenirs during the early 1500s. But perhaps one of the basic forces behind the English Renaissance was the classical scholarship of William Grocyn (1446–1519), John Colet (1467–1519), and Thomas Linacre (1460–1524), who made translations possible. Grocyn introduced at Oxford the teaching of Greek. Colet, who studied in Italy and France, on his return collaborated with William Lily, first headmaster of St. Paul's School, and with the celebrated humanist Erasmus and Sir Thomas More in writing grammars and readers. Whatever "little Latin and less Greek" Shakespeare picked up as a schoolboy in Stratford-on-Avon he almost surely got from one or another of the instructional materials prepared by these classical scholars.

REFERENCES: J. V. Cunningham, ed., *The Renaissance in England;* L. E. Elliott-Binns, *England and the New Learning;* Samuel Dresden, *Humanism in the Renaissance;* C. S. Lewis, *English Literature in the Sixteenth Century;* Douglas Bush, *English Literature of the Earlier Seventeenth Century* and *The Renaissance and English Humanism;* J. Willliam Hebel and Hoyt H. Hudson, eds., *Poetry of the English Renaissance (1509–1660);* James Ross and Mary McLaughlin, eds., *The Viking Portable Renaissance Reader;* J. D. Huston and A. B. Kernan, eds., *Classics of the Renaissance Theater.*

4. The American Renaissance was the age of Emerson, Thoreau, Hawthorne, Melville, and Whitman. Except for Whitman, who lived in New York, these writers lived for the most part in New England. Depending on the literary historian, the American Renaissance sometimes includes attention to Mark Twain, who lived most of his life away from the influences of Boston and New York literary circles. The phenomenon consisted chiefly of nineteenth-century New England developments in American literature, characterized by a departure from some few British traditions, by experimentation, and by individuality. Like the Italian and English Renaissances, the American Renaissance was not a movement but a phenomenon of a certain time and place. Though the giants of this era did join one movement or another, such as BROOK FARM, and all of them knew one another, each developed quite independently.

REFERENCES: F. O. Matthiessen, *American Renaissance;* Van Wyck Brooks, *The Flowering of New England;* Vernon L. Parrington, *The Romantic Revolution in America;* Paul Sherman, *Emerson's Angle of Vision;* Edmund Wilson, ed., *The Shock of Recognition.*

rendering   **1.** In narration and description, the art of showing as opposed to telling or reporting; SCENE as opposed to summary; the art of using concrete details, images, and speech. Contrast these examples:

Reporting: Delia became angry with her brother.
Rendering: Delia glowered at her brother: "I hope you break a leg, you overgrown ox!"
Reporting: The waves hit the schooner and splashed over the men.
Rendering: White-capped combers gathered into moving walls, smashed into the hull, and crashed over the decks, soaking the sailors to their skins.

See TEXTURE.

2. In composition for beginners the term "rendering" is sometimes used in its culinary sense of "condensing" or "tightening" or "boiling off the fat and water." See DEADWOOD.

REFERENCES: Hart Day Leavitt and David Sohn, *Stop, Look, and Write;* Walker Gibson, *Seeing and Writing;* Caroline Gordon, *The House of Fiction;* Allen Tate, "Techniques of Fiction," in Bernard Oldsey and Arthur Lewis, Jr., eds., *Visions and Revisions;* J. Patrick Creber, *Sense and Sensitivity;* Wallace Stegner, ed., *The Writer's Art* and *Twenty Years of Stanford Short Stories;* Joseph Conrad, "Preface to *The Nigger of the Narcissus";* Mark Schorer, "Technique as Discovery," in James Miller, ed., *Myth and Method;* Francis Christensen, "The Cumulative Sentence," *Notes toward a New Rhetoric;* Wayne Booth, "The Story-Telling Distinction," *The Rhetoric of Fiction;* Leon Surmelian, *Techniques of Fiction Writing;* R. V. Cassill, *Writing Fiction.*

repartee   See STICHOMYTHY.

repetend   A line of verse repeated, like a REFRAIN, at certain intervals, but each time with a slight variation bent to the context of its own stanza. Thus in Poe's "Annabel Lee," the initial "In a kingdom by the sea" becomes "In this kingdom by the sea" and "In her sepulcher there by the sea." For variety a repetend is sometimes placed irregularly among stanzas of a long narrative poem, as are Coleridge's in "Christabel."

repetition   1. In PROSE, repetition is often needless or awkward. But skillful writers do not hesitate to use repetition deliberately if necessary or appropriate for clarity or force. Where would be the force of Lincoln's Gettysburg Address, for example, had he said "government of, by, and for the people"? 2. In poetry deliberate repetition is used in ALLITERATION, ASSONANCE, CONSONANCE, REFRAIN, RHYME, SESTINA, and so on. Compare CACOPHONY and REDUNDANCY.

research   Studious, diligent investigation aimed at verifying facts and drawing reasonable conclusions. (1) *Pure research* is that done chiefly by students and scholars, having as its aim the extension of knowledge in some limited way. (2) *Applied research* has as its aim the invention of useful products, the prediction of phenomena, the control of disease or of other aspects of the environment.

   Pure research is carried on in three distinct manners: *(a) academic*—investigation of documentary evidence, chiefly in libraries; *(b) scientific*—investigation by laboratory observation and experimentation; *(c) field*—investigation by interview, consensus, or observation of facts outside the laboratory or the library.

   For the student and writer *academic research* is clearly the most common, and the RESEARCH PAPER in literary or humanistic studies is its chief result.

research paper   An extended piece of written EXPOSITION or ARGUMENTATION (or a combination of both) in which the results of investigation and reasoning that support a THESIS are presented. Such a paper almost always includes DOCUMENTATION. The tone and content of a research paper are usually more explanatory than argumentative, though the methods of argumentation are used to present the THESIS. The purpose of the research paper is to bring together old and new information and documented recent opinions that have not previously been brought together, and to use them as evidence in support of a thesis. The research paper, then, is (or should be) more than a rehash of what has been done before—more than a paraphrase of a few encyclopedia articles, though it may synthesize information and opinion from several articles and books.

   Usually, the writer of a research paper follows these steps: (1) selecting a topic; (2) limiting the topic to an aspect that can be feasibly handled in the available time and with the available resources; (3) making a preliminary OUTLINE to guide the investigation; (4) compiling a working BIBLIOGRAPHY of potentially pertinent items from library catalogues, periodical indexes, reference works, and other published bibliographies in the topic field; (5) reading the materials; (6) note-taking, or selecting what is pertinent and useful from the materials; (7) ordering the notes and preparing the final outline; (8) writing the paper, with appropriate REVISING; (9) documenting by means of footnotes and final bibliography.

Note-taking and documenting are generally done at the same time to avoid retracing of steps. Ordering, or adjusting of the outline, may continue even through the step of writing and revising. See DOCUMENTATION, OUTLINE, and REVISING.

REFERENCES: Donald Sears, *Harbrace Guide to the Library and Research Paper;* J. K. Gates, *Guide to the Use of Books and Libraries;* John Nist, "Doing Research," *Speaking into Writing;* Saul Gallin and Peter Spielberg, *Reference Books: How to Select and Use Them;* D. F. Bond, *A Reference Guide to English Studies* [a revision of the bibliographical guide by Tom Peete Cross]; R. B. McKerrow and Henry M. Silver, *On the Publication of Research;* Ben Schneider and H. K. Tjossem, *Themes and Research Papers.*

Restoration   The period of English history from 1660 to 1688 (from the restoration of the Stuarts to the throne at the end of the Puritan Commonwealth and Protectorate) comprising the reigns of Charles II (1660–85) and James II (1685–88). It was an era characterized by the rise of NEO-CLASSICISM and libertinism. Notables of the Restoration were poet-critics John Milton and John Dryden; dramatists Wycherly and Congreve; Restoration wits Rochester, Sedley, Dorset, and Cotton.

REFERENCES: George Sherburn, *The Restoration and Eighteenth Century;* Walter Jackson Bate, *From Classic to Romantic;* Louis Bredvold, *The Intellectual Milieu of John Dryden;* John Loftis, ed., *Restoration Drama: Essays in Criticism;* Alan Downer and A. Kirsch, eds., *Masterpieces of the Restoration;* Brice Harris, ed., *Restoration Plays;* Eric Rothstein, *Restoration Tragedy;* D. S. Berkeley, *The Penitent Rake in Restoration Comedy;* D. M. Vieth, ed., *Complete Poems of John Wilmot;* Alexander Witherspoon and Frank Warnke, eds., *Seventeenth-Century Prose and Poetry.*

restrictive   In a sentence, an essential (or defining) MODIFIER or APPOSITIVE— one that cannot be taken from the context without altering the sense. "The fellow is my roommate" would leave a question—*What fellow?* Therefore a defining modifier seems needed: "The *tall* fellow" or "The fellow *on the diving-board*" or "The fellow *who is about to do a swandive*" (the italicized elements are restrictive modifiers). In "My brother likes poetry" the implication is that the speaker has but one brother; if he has more than one, the sentence needs a restrictive modifier, or a restrictive appositive, for *brother:* "My brother *at college*" (modifier) or "My brother *Ned*" (appositive). Restrictive elements are not set off by commas. See COMMA FAULT 4.

review   **1.** A notice of a literary work. According to the newspaper or magazine in which it appears, a review may be brief or lengthy, journalistic or literary, an expository article or an essay in literary criticism. Most literary journals (e.g., *Blackwood's* and the *Quarterly Review* in England; *The Atlantic, Harper's,* and *The New York Review of Books* in America) carry reviews of current literary works, as do a host of other journals ranging from such weeklies as *The Saturday Review, The Nation, The New Republic,* to such quarterlies as *The Kenyon Review* and the college reviews, from Antioch's to Yale's. Occasionally, a review makes history, as did J. G. Lockhart's review of one of Keats's poems in 1818 in *Blackwood's Magazine* and Poe's review of Hawthorne's *Twice-Told Tales* in the *North American Review.* A good review avoids mere summary, focuses upon one major aspect, and makes a value judgment. See BOOK REVIEW. **2.** A periodical publication that prints reviews as well as other articles of information and comment.

revising   The art of improving a written piece of work without beating it to a fine dust. Writers who compose perfect copy—writers who "get it right" at first draft—are in a very small minority. The majority have revealed in their journals, as well as in various versions of a given literary work, or both, that they return again and again to early drafts, making an improvement here and an improvement there—sometimes rewriting altogether.

There is much to be said for both the nonsystematic and the systematic approaches to revising, though in the end revising is an individual process. But almost every approach demands a "cooling-off" period between the white-hot heat of creating the first draft and that day or hour of reckoning known as the deadline. According to nonsystematic approaches, the writer reads the piece over casually and swiftly, if possible aloud and at one sitting, to test over-all impact. This system will also suggest specific elements that may need revising. In the more systematic approaches, the writer gives the manuscript *several* readings—once for content, once for structure or form, once for mechanics, and so on. Whatever the approach, the serious writer allows as much time as possible between the first and the last drafts. Willingness to revise reflects a practical humility. Here, for example, is the celebrated psychologist Erik Erikson, writing in the second edition of *Childhood and Society*: "In what revision has taken place, then, I have first of all corrected those passages which on rereading I did not quite understand myself."

CUE (Coherence, Unity, Effectiveness) Checklist for Use in Revising

Coherence: Does your composition hang together?
1. Using identification, titles, signposts, transitions, documentation.
2. Using appropriate punctuation and other mechanics; spelling.
3. Generating logical flow; using appropriate illustrations and accurate quotations; introducing quotations coherently; avoiding circular reasoning.
4. Attending to agreement of verbs with subjects, pronouns with antecedents.
5. Recasting dangling and misplaced modifiers.
6. Building appropriate parallelism; clarifying unintended omissions.

Unity: Does your composition generate a central effect?
1. Slanting (but not slouching) toward your audience.
2. Settling on a main purpose; for exposition, outlining.
3. Maintaining a consistent attitude, tone, persona, focus of narration.
4. Sharpening, in exposition, the controlling or thesis statement.
5. Suggesting, in imaginative genres, your own main point or theme.
6. Developing, in each paragraph, a main topic (not necessarily a topic sentence).
7. Recasting shifty definitions, mixed metaphors, and zeugmas (unless deliberately intended ones work successfully).

Effectiveness: Does your composition hook the reader?
1. Tightening; cutting deadwood; recasting whichmires; using appropriate allusions.
2. Using techniques for emphasis.
3. Recasting circumlocutions into direct language; avoiding noun-banging and nounification; using agent-verb constructions; using variety.
4. Using appropriate diction—idioms but not clichés.
5. Rendering with concrete images and objective correlatives; building cumulative sentences and joining Participles Anonymous.
6. Revising and proofreading.

REFERENCES: Louis Zahner *et al.*, "Revise It Yourself! A Checklist for Revising Your Compositions," in *The* [Harbrace] *English Language Series;* Max Shulman, "Ten Tips for Writers" and Joyce T. Smith, "Manuscript Preparation," in A. S. Burack, ed., *The*

Writer's Handbook; MLA Style Sheet; Geneva Hanna, "Proofreading, a Panacea," *English Journal* (October, 1962); Daniel D. and Paula R. Pearlman, *Guide to Rapid Revision;* John Nist, "Checklist for Revisions," *Speaking into Writing;* W. C. Knott, "Rewriting," *The Craft of Fiction;* H. Wendell Smith, "A Guide to Revision," *On Paper;* Ronald A. Sudol, ed., *Revising: New Essays for Teachers of Writing.*

rhetoric   **1.** The art of effective communication in speaking and writing. For the ancient Greeks and Romans rhetoric was the art of the *rhetor* or orator, and since oratory so often lent itself to persuasion, rhetoric came to mean the art of persuasion through effective techniques of ARGUMENTATION. **2.** In Medieval and Renaissance times the emphasis fell upon the more decorative aspects of discourse, so that rhetoric came to mean *elegant discourse,* and it often degenerated into EUPHUISM. **3.** The modern world still shows certain effects of that sense of the term, but the study of rhetoric today, at least in the schools, is the study of composition—the principles of speaking and writing. In addition, rhetoric as a scholarly discipline has recently been reexamined for its contributions to the illumination of all the language arts. The very word *rhetoric* included in a literary or linguistic study today tends to give that study a prestigious aura—as it does in such titles, for example, as *The Rhetoric of Fiction, A Generative Rhetoric of the Paragraph,* and *The Transformational Density of Dickinson's Rhetoric.* Analogous with NEW [literary] CRITICISM and with the new grammars, there are several "new rhetorics" competing for attention, as Daniel Fogarty shows in his *Roots for a New Rhetoric.* Perhaps one of the new rhetorics with promise of permanence is Walker Gibson's, the SPEAKING VOICE. **4.** Depending on the context (e.g., in a discussion of a poet's style) and on whether it is coupled with the derogatory qualifier "mere," the term rhetoric sometimes means "bad writing." See CUMULATIVE SENTENCE, DICTION, SPEAKING VOICE, STYLE.

REFERENCES: Walker Gibson, *Tough, Sweet, and Stuffy;* Francis Christensen, *Notes toward a New Rhetoric;* Dudley Bailey, ed., *Essays on Rhetoric;* Edward Corbett, ed., *Classical Rhetoric for the Modern Student;* Kenneth Burke, *A Rhetoric of Motives;* Richard Weaver, *The Ethics of Rhetoric;* I. A. Richards, *The Philosophy of Rhetoric;* Leo Rockas, *Modes of Rhetoric;* J. E. Connor and Marcelline Krafchick, eds., *Speaking of Rhetoric;* Richard Cook, "Swift as Tory Rhetorician," *Texas Studies in Literature and Language* (Spring, 1962); Walter Ong, *Rhetoric, Romance, & Technology;* Richard Larson, ed., *Rhetoric [a reader].*

rhetorical question   A device (particularly useful in ARGUMENTATION) by which the audience is lured into hearing an answer that the writer or speaker is about to provide—or perhaps into providing an obvious answer for themselves. The asker of the rhetorical question does not expect an overt answer. A famed example is Patrick Henry's "Is life so dear, or peace so sweet, as to be purchased at the price of chains and slavery?"

rhyme, rime   The repetition of sounds, usually at the ends of lines in verse; ordinarily avoided in prose: "make / shake"; "miss / criss." Monosyllabic rhymes are called *masculine* rhymes; disyllabic rhymes—"ranches / branches" —are called *feminine* rhymes. (*Note:* Masculine and feminine *rhymes* are to be distinguished from masculine and feminine *lines.* See METER.) When a rhyme occurs inside a line of verse, it is called *internal* rhyme: "He gave his rain and

Cain." In humorous verse, often by surprise, there occurs a rhyme achieved by a pair of words: "crystal" rhymed with "missed all." The latter is also an example of *near-rhyme* (also called *slant rhyme, oblique rhyme,* and *wrenched rhyme*), a device often used deliberately by a poet wishing to depart from close, "sing-song" rhyme. Emily Dickinson frequently uses slant rhyme, as in "pavement / bereavement" and "crumb/ home."

As language and pronunciation change in time and place, certain words which once rhymed may no longer do so. A case in point is Pope's (eighteenth-century) rhyme "pine / join"; he and his contemporaries, pronounced the second word "jine."

Rhyme schemes are conventionally described by assigning the letters *a, b, c, d,* etc., to the rhyme words at the ends of successive lines. Thus the familiar jingle "Mary had a little lamb" is described as rhyming "*abcb,*" the second and fourth lines (*bb*) rhyming "snow / go," the first and third lines (*ac*) not rhyming.

REFERENCES: Clement Wood, *The Complete Rhyming Dictionary and Poet's Craft Book;* Lawrence Holofcener, *A Practical Dictionary of Rhymes;* J. G. Halkett and R. E. Kuehn, eds., *The Powerful Rime;* X. J. Kennedy, "On Rime," *New York Quarterly* (Summer, 1977); John Hollander, *Rhyme's Reason.*

rhyme royal   A seven-line stanza in iambic pentameter rhyming *ababbcc.* It was used by Chaucer in *Troilus and Criseyde,* among other poems; by Shakespeare in *The Rape of Lucrece;* by William Morris in *The Earthly Paradise;* and by John Masefield in *Dauber.* The following is a representative stanza from *The Earthly Paradise*:

Dreamer of dreams, born out of my due time,	*a*
Why should I strive to set the crooked straight?	*b*
Let it suffice me that my murmuring rime	*a*
Beats with a light wing against the ivory gate,	*b*
Telling a tale not too importunate	*b*
To those who in the sleepy region stay,	*c*
Lulled by the singer of an empty day.	*c*

rhythm   **1.** The occurrence and recurrence of words and word groups, now with strong stress, now with weak stress, in any speech-stream or in written works. As distinguished from METER, rhythm is a cadence not ordinarily measured by speaker or writer, and in that narrow sense rhythm may be considered the raw material of meter. **2.** In a broader sense, rhythm is a pristinely natural and poetic phenomenon, a cyclic recurrence shared by all living creatures (e.g., birth, mating, death) and even by inorganic matter—for example, the tides, the lightning-thunder-rain, the seasons, phenomena contributing to, if not the very stuff of, ARCHETYPE and MYTH.

REFERENCES: George Saintsbury, *A Historical Manual of English Prosody* and *A History of English Prose Rhythm;* P. F. Baum, *The Other Harmony of Prose;* Jacques Barzun and H. F. Graff, "Right Emphasis and Right Rhythm," *The Modern Researcher;* Joost Meerloo, *Along the Fourth Dimension;* David Karrfalt, "Some Comments on the Principles of Rhythm in a Generative Rhetoric," *Journal of English Teaching* (Fall, 1969); T. H. McCabe, "Rhythm as Form in Lawrence," *PMLA* (Jan., 1972); Patricia Spacks, *The Varied God.*

right surprise   In METAPHOR and SIMILE, (comparison of dissimilars) the one element of similarity that works surprisingly well. "The boy looked like a man" does not surprise as much as "The boy looked like a bulldozer."

rococo   **1.** In the fine arts, a style developed in France in the eighteenth century and characterized by graceful, somewhat feminine, curvilinear designs; for example, foliage, scrolls, and shells. This florid style in art (also in music) succeeded the somewhat more masculine baroque of the previous century. **2.** In literature, rococo refers to works, especially those of the eighteenth century, characterized by deft lightness of touch, wit, and a tone at once colloquial and sophisticated; such works, for example, as Pope's "Rape of the Lock," Voltaire's *Candide,* and Laurence Sterne's *Tristram Shandy.* Compare BAROQUE.

REFERENCES: Peter Demetz, "Reflections on the Use of Rococo as a Period Concept," *The Disciplines of Criticism;* Helmut Hatzfeld, *The Rococo.*

rock verse   Popular verse about love, alienation, protest, personal identity, sex, drugs, and problems of adolescence. This verse, full of folksy CLICHÉS, was set to a hybrid music that combined blues, jazz, folk, electronic country Western, and a bravura beat akin to that of Appalachian stomping. One or another of these grafts dominated according to a singer's or a group's characteristic preferences. The best-known groups included The Comets, The Beatles, The Jefferson Airplane, The Momas and the Poppas, The Grateful Dead, The Temptations, The Rolling Stones, and The Supremes. Certain singers, among them Elvis Presley and Bob Dylan, remained unaffiliated with any group. Some composers of rock verse, along with their most popular pieces: Bill Haley (of The Comets), "Rock Around the Clock"; Joe Turner, "Shake, Rattle, and Roll"; John Lennon and Paul McCartney (of The Beatles), the "Sgt. Pepper" songs; Grace Slick (of The Jefferson Airplane), "Somebody to Love"; Bob Dylan, "Blowin' in the Wind"; Mick Jagger (of The Rolling Stones), "Get Off of My Cloud"; Joni Mitchell, "Both Sides Now"; Jimmy Hendrix, "Voice in the Wind"; Carl Perkins, "Blue Suede Shoes" (popularized by the gyrating Elvis Presley); Dionne Warwick, "Walk On By," also popularized by Diana Ross (of The Supremes).

REFERENCES: Lillian Roxon, *Rock Encyclopedia;* Jonathan Eisen, ed., *The Age of Rock;* Richard Goldstein, ed., *The Poetry of Rock;* Linda Eastman, *Rock and Other Four-Letter Words;* Pauline Rivelli and Robert Levine, eds., *The Rock Giants;* Carl Belz, *The Story of Rock;* Mike Jahn, *Rock.*

role playing, game playing   **1.** In rhetoric and psychodrama taking a role or PERSONA and acting it out without a "script." **2.** In literature, games have had a profound influence. They have inspired passwords, incantations, and spells or charms. Many FOLK SONGS and most CAROLS were originally composed to accompany dances or rhythmic stepping and hopping. Maypoles have been played with by both Puritans and witches in Hawthorne's stories. Among a host of card games, tarot was a favorite of Yeats, Eliot, and Joyce, as reflected

in *A Vision, The Waste Land,* and *Finnegans Wake.* According to Arthur
Koestler, game-roles undergird most readers' responses to, and most writers'
re-creation of ARCHETYPES, METAPHOR, MYTH, ALLEGORY, PARADOX, PUNS—
whatever requires a "play of mind." Frost's quip about FREE VERSE, "like
playing tennis with the net down," sums up his feeling that to bypass rules of
form and meter is to bypass the game of writing poetry. This is also the creed
of such formalists as Yeats, Pound, Eliot, Auden, Ransom, Roethke, Lowell,
and X. J. Kennedy. (See the latter's magazine *Counter/ Measures.*) ANTINOVEL-
ists Sarraute and Robbe-Grillet, though rejecting "well-made plots," do not
reject playful improvising with THEMES and MOTIFS. "Love is a game; fiction is
a game," says Robbe-Grillet, who uses the term *ludique* (from *ludo,* I play) to
describe what he is up to. In short, writing and interpreting are games.

REFERENCES: John Huizinga, *Homo Ludens;* Norman O. Brown, *Life Against Death;*
Arthur Koestler, *The Act of Creation;* Margaret Williams, ed., *Word Hoard;* R. D.
Abrahams, *Jump-Rope Rhymes;* C. L. Barber, "May Games ... ," W. Sutton and
R. Foster, eds., *Modern Criticism;* B. B. Rowland, "The Miller's Tale: Game Within
Game," *Chaucer Review* (Fall, 1970); Richard Howard, tr., Roland Barthes' *Critical
Essays;* Robert de Ropp, *The Master Game.*

roman à clef   Literally, "key novel." A popular kind of romance in seven-
teenth- and eighteenth-century France and England in which certain characters
were supposed to be transparencies of prominent people, though "keys" had to
be published as adjuncts to satisfy appetites of readers eager for gossip. These
key novels had their counterparts in *key plays* (*drames à clef*). (Both "*clefs*"
were satirized by Molière in *Les Précieuses Ridicules.*) A very popular key
novel, written by Madeleine and (her brother) George de Scudéry, was *Clélie
... * (1654–60) in ten volumes. Others were Honoré d'Urfé's (anglicized as
Durfey) *Astrée* (1607–19), Mme. de Lafayette's *La Princesse de Clèves* (1678),
Mrs. Mary Manley's *Power of Love* (1720), and Eliza Haywood's *Philidore
and Placentia* (1727), the latter two quite sentimental. Of the more realistic key
novels of the nineteenth century, the most celebrated were Thomas Peacock's
Headlong Hall (1815) and Nathaniel Hawthorne's *Blithedale Romance.* Cer-
tain "key" aspects are attributed to such modern novels as Aldous Huxley's
Point Counter Point, Evelyn Waugh's *The Loved One,* Ernest Hemingway's
The Sun Also Rises, and Simone de Beauvoir's *The Mandarins.*

REFERENCE: Earle Wallridge, *Literary Characters Drawn from Life.*

romance   1. One of the MODES. 2. One of the GENRES. See CHIVALRIC ROMANCE,
GOTHIC NOVEL, METRICAL ROMANCE, ROMAN À CLEF.

romanticism   In English literature, the poetic movement led by Wordsworth,
Coleridge, Keats, Shelley, and Byron between 1795 and about 1830. The Romantic poets were concerned mainly with *(a)* The need to fabricate a new
mythology to explain the universe and the individual's place in it; *(b)* emotion
over reason (in this they had much in common with the German STURM-UND-
DRANG movement of the 1770s); *(c)* spontaneity over "art," although the

Romantic poets' letters, journals, and revisions of poems now being re-examined reveal that they did not entirely resist technique and form; and *(d)* a realistic rather than an idealistic view of nature, even if this approach led such poets as Wordsworth and Shelley into certain tenets of idealism (for example, the idea of progress and ultimate perfectibility).

By 1798, when Wordsworth published his Preface to the *Lyrical Ballads,* a kind of manifesto for the Romantic movement, the concept of the GREAT CHAIN OF BEING seemed no longer adequate to explain the makeup of the universe; the eighteenth-century poetry based on that idea no longer seemed relevant to the turn-of-the-century mood. Eighteenth-century poetry had not assumed progress or ultimate perfectibility; it had been more concerned with the place of abstract "Man" in the "Chain" and with how to live the good life. In contrast to this attitude, the Romantic poet was concerned with self-discovery; looking within and asking, "Who am I?" (One can hardly imagine Samuel Johnson asking such a question.)

Moreover, the Romantic poets, intent on expressing themselves in what Wordsworth called "language really used by men," were less concerned about making contact with their audience than with the need for self-expression; the poet must express the spirit within, audience or not. In turning away from NEO-CLASSICAL notions about "ideal Nature" the Romantics preferred to seek their reality through spontaneous and personal acts of the IMAGINATION. As Keats said in a letter, "I am certain of nothing but the holiness of the heart's affection and the truth of the Imagination." He could not perceive how anything could be known except through "personal identity." (See NEGATIVE CAPABILITY.) They also sought their reality through the RENDERING of personal experience, especially through IMAGERY, the concrete particular ("a violet by a mossy stone," "the lone and level sands," "those caves of ice!"). See OBJECTIVE CORRELATIVE.

Among other characteristics of the Romantics: They preferred the countryside (the Lake Windemere country, for instance) to the materialistic city ("Getting and spending, we lay waste our powers"); preferred longing or mysterious aspiration (as reflected in Keats's "Ode on a Grecian Urn") rather than fulfilled desire. They attempted to connect, indeed to fuse, certain worlds—Truth and Beauty for Keats; the Platonic paradise and the realm of concrete phenomena for Shelley. Wordsworth sought to incorporate the object—the external world of nature—into himself, the subject.

What almost every poet of the Romantic movement shared was a desire to bring nature, God and man, the finite and the infinite, the familiar and the mysterious, into unity through the shaping power of the individual's imagination.

REFERENCES: Meyer Abrams, *The Mirror and the Lamp;* John Livingston Lowes, *The Road to Xanadu;* C. M. Bowra, *The Romantic Imagination;* Clarence D. Thorpe *et al.,* eds., *Major English Romantic Poets;* Frank Kermode, *Romantic Image;* Geoffrey Hartman, *The Unmediated Vision;* Northrop Frye, ed., *Romanticism Reconsidered;*

Marjorie H. Nicolson, *Mountain Gloom and Mountain Glory;* Robert Gleckner and Gerald Enscoe, eds., *Romanticism: Points of View;* David Perkins, ed., *English Romantic Writers;* Lilian Furst, *Romanticism;* Harold Bloom, *The Ringers in the Tower;* E. R. Wasserman, *Shelley: A Critical Reading;* Michael Yetman, "Emily Dickinson ... Romantic Tradition," *Texas Studies in Language and Literature* (Spring, 1973); L. M. Trawick, ed., *Backgrounds of Romanticism;* Roda Roberts, trans., Henri Peyre's *What Is Romanticism?;* Helen Vendler, *On Extended Wings.*

rondeau   A French verse pattern or variations thereon used by many English poets. The traditional rondeau consists of fifteen tetrameter lines divided into three STANZAS, with lines 9 and 15 being short REFRAINS. Except for the refrains there are only two rhymes in the poem. Following is the traditional rhyme scheme, in which *c* represents the refrain lines: *aabba aabc aabbac.* There are also many free variations of the pattern. Perhaps the most celebrated English "Rondeau," a free variation, is this, by Leigh Hunt:

> Jenny kissed me when we met,
>   Jumping from the chair she sat in;
> Time, you thief, who love to get
>   Sweets into your list, put that in;
> Say I'm weary, say I'm sad,
>   Say that health and wealth have missed me,
> Say I'm growing old, but add,
>   Jenny kissed me.

REFERENCE: Nigel Wilkins, ed., *One Hundred Ballades, Rondeaux, and Virelais.*

rondel   A French lyric pattern, or variation on it, something like the RONDEAU, its predecessor; it consists of thirteen or fourteen lines in iambic pentameter. These usually rhyme *abbaabab abbaab,* with the first two and the last two lines REFRAINS. As in most French lyrics like the rondel and rondeau there are no more than three rhymes in the poem, a convention that not only challenges the poet but also tends to predetermine a TOUR DE FORCE. As with the rondeau and other French models, English poets have taken all sorts of liberties, especially in shortening the refrain lines. Chaucer begins but does not finish a rondel ("Now welcome, summer, with thy sun [so] soft") in his *Parliament of Fowls.* Perhaps the best-known "Rondel" in English—quite a free variation on the French form—is this, of Swinburne:

> Kissing her hair I sat against her feet,
> Wove and unwove it, wound and found it sweet;
> Made fast therewith her hands, drew down her eyes,
> Deep as deep flowers and dreamy like dim skies;
> With her own tresses bound and found her fair,
>   Kissing her hair.
>
> Sleep were no sweeter than her face to me,
> Sleep of cold sea-bloom under the cold sea;
> What pain could get between my face and hers?
> What new sweet thing would love not relish worse?
> Unless, perhaps, white death had kissed me there,
>   Kissing her hair?

roundel   A variation of the RONDEAU and RONDEL, running on only two rhymes, with the refrain taken from the first line.

roundelay   A variation of the RONDEL.

run-on sentence   Two or more sentences written without punctuation to separate them. The run-on sentence is normally considered a fault in formal writing—especially in school and in college—since it seems to show that the writer does not know when a sentence has been completed. The term *run-on* is also applied to a pair of sentences written with only a comma (no conjunction) between them, but that error is more often called a COMMA FAULT or comma splice.

S

saga   1. Loosely, a history transmitted orally as well as in writing: "the saga of the American West." Also a series of related novels; for example, *The Forsyte Saga* by John Galsworthy. 2. Old Norse, Icelandic, or Scandinavian folk EPIC in prose or verse with a legendary hero, orally transmitted during the eleventh and twelfth centuries, thereafter written. Among the best known are Snorri Sturluson's *Starlunga Saga* and *Heimskringla* and also *Frithiof's Saga* (thirteenth century), based on an Icelandic myth about a Norwegian king and his beautiful daughter, Ingeborg. Compare LEGEND 2.

REFERENCES: Knut Liestol, *Origin of the Icelandic Family Sagas;* Halvdan Koht, *The Old Norse Sagas;* A. S. Hoffman, *Book of the Sagas;* Loftur Bjarnason, "Land of Song and Saga," *Brigham Young University Studies* (Winter, 1969).

sarcasm   Scornful, taunting, contemptuous language. The word derives from the Greek *sarkazein,* "to tear flesh," and the metaphor is reflected in the expressions "cutting remark" and "biting jibe." A giant like Polyphemus in the *Odyssey* sneers at Ulysses, "you puny, good-for-nothing little runt" (Book IX). Sarcasm may or may not be coupled with IRONY. Ironic sarcasm is often apparent praise that really condemns: "You're the best secretary who ever used to work here," says employer to employee. According to Gilbert Highet, in *The Anatomy of Satire,* sarcasm is irony "whose true underlying meaning is both so obvious that it cannot be misunderstood and so wounding that it cannot be dismissed with a smile."

satire   From *satura,* "a lavish assortment of fruits." A term often misunderstood in literary studies, since it is both a GENRE and a MODE. 1. A genre developed mainly by the Roman poets Horace and Juvenal, and the Roman prose writers Petronius and Lucan. These Roman satires sometimes did, sometimes did not, ridicule the follies of their day. 2. In any genre (poem, play, novel, tract) a mode of literary ridicule, which sets the work's tone and meaning. As a mode, satire works through subtle attack or through biting wit on a person, place, event, issue, philosophy, system, or institution. The satirist's purpose is to correct, being committed to certain moral standards from which the person or institution satirized has departed. The satirist is concerned with showing the incompatibility, in fact, between certain standards ("the good old days," the Roman republic, the Golden Age, or whatever) and the misguided present. Through IRONY, pretended innocence, and other voices, the satirist aims to lead us into seeing familiar phenomena and conditions as if for the first time or as though they were from another planet, another place, another time. These phenomena may be depicted in distorted or even perverted shapes so that we tend to judge and condemn them first, and only later recognize their resemblance to the conditions in our own system of government, our own way of life. This is the method used by Swift in *Gulliver's Travels* (1726), in which the more admirable creatures, a race of rational horses called Houyhnhmns, demonstrate a greater sense of justice than do the vicious and bestial Yahoos, who look very much like human beings.

Another approach, also found in Swift, is to introduce into the actual world some unsophisticated person whose artless comments give us a glimpse of how we look through the eyes of first innocence. The satirist thus strips from the things satirized the veil of familiarity that normally reconciles us to them, and makes us see them as they really are.

Still another approach, one used by Cervantes and especially by Voltaire, is to introduce into the actual world some naive protagonist (Don Quixote or Dr. Pangloss) and ridicule that person's philosophic position. In *Candide,* for instance, Voltaire debunks the naive Pangloss's conviction that "this is the best of all possible worlds." (Dr. Pangloss is generally regarded, incidentally, as a transparency of the German idealist Leibnitz.) In Cervantes' *Don Quixote,* which is at least in part satirical, the protagonist, trying to correct what he regards as social and moral blemishes, tilts against windmills; that is, he fights senseless ("quixotic") battles.

The butts of satire accord with the satirist's VISION OF LIFE. Thus Cervantes and Voltaire satirize romantic idealists, whereas Swift castigates social realists for their lack of humane idealism. But whatever the world-view, and however the satirist tries to restore in us a sense of right reason, the main tool is IRONY. And this irony, which is intended to enlighten and correct, is to be distinguished from SARCASM, which is intended merely to wound. In fact, the Romans distinguished between the ironic, laughing satirist (the "Horation") and the sarcastic, didactic satirist (the "Juvenalian"). Both kinds of satire have afforded the writer a means of expressing irreverence and subversiveness.

The best-known satires, besides those mentioned above, include the medieval *Tyl Eulenspiegel* and *Reynard the Fox* (see FABLES and FABLIAUX); Butler's *Hudibras,* an attack on PURITANISM; Byron's *Don Juan;* Gilbert and Sullivan's operettas, most of them attacks on imperialism; the plays of Oscar Wilde and of George Bernard Shaw, full of attacks on middle-class values; the fiction of Mark Twain, especially *The Mysterious Stranger;* the novels of Sinclair Lewis, especially *Babbitt;* and Barbara Garson's play *MacBird!,* which combines satire with PARODY.

REFERENCES: Gilbert Highet, *The Anatomy of Satire;* W. O. S. Sutherland, *The Art of the Satirist;* Alvin Kernan, ed., *Modern Satire;* Edgar Johnson, ed., *A Treasury of Satire;* David Worcester, *The Art of Satire;* Ian Jack, *Augustan Satire;* Northrop Frye, "The Nature of Satire," *University of Toronto Quarterly* (1944); Maynard Mack, "The Muse of Satire," *Yale Review* (1951); Hugo Reichard, "Pope's Social Satire," *PMLA* (June, 1952); Jacob Adler, *The Reach of Art;* John Tuckey, *Mark Twain's Mysterious Stranger and the Critics;* see also *Satire Newsletter,* a quarterly.

saw   See ADAGE.

scansion   The counting of poetic feet. See METER.

scenario   1. An outline or a summary of the plot of a play or other dramatic work. Compare SYNOPSIS. 2. A fully elaborated script for the making of a motion picture, with dialogue and actions of the actors, descriptions of settings, and directions for photographing.

scene   1. In the theater of ancient Greece the *skene* was the place (literally, the "tent") in or near which an action or DIALOGUE took place. 2. Today the *scene* is the basic building-block in a story, novel, or play; it is the setting as well as the whole of a unified action (including dialogue), whether defined by the rise and fall of curtain or lights—as in a play—or defined by a distinct change of characters or change of locale in any work of fiction. 3. A term in Burke's pentad. See DRAMATISM.

scene and summary   In a typical story or novel, part of what happens is reproduced with a sense of immediacy by means of action and DIALOGUE; part is reported only by one or another of the characters or by the narrator or by the author. In distinguishing between those two major fictional processes, writers and critics refer to the first as scene, to the second, as summary.

schlemihl   An unlucky bungler. The label comes from the Yiddish (literally, beloved of God). A schlemihl (also schlemiel) sometimes lapses into roguery, as does Chamisso's Peter Schlemihl and Bellow's Herzog. Compare ANTI-HERO and THEOPHRASTAN CHARACTERS.

REFERENCES: Ruth Wisse, *The Schlemiel as Modern Hero;* Leslie Field, "Saul Bellow . . ." *Jewish Studies* (Dec., 1978).

science fiction   Short stories and novels that combine fantasy with known and speculative scientific phenomena, adventures into the future and outer space, and propaganda about hypothetical political systems, including UTOPIAS. Science fiction ranges in quality from the pseudo-scientific KITSCH in PULP magazines to the more plausible, scientifically based, works of such authors as Isaac Asimov and Arthur C. Clarke. Plausible science fiction also includes the works of Jules Verne, Edgar Allan Poe, H. P. Lovecraft, H. G. Wells, Ray Bradbury, Robert Heinlein, Theodore Sturgeon, and Kurt Vonnegut. Representative titles are Asimov's *I, Robot* and Bradbury's *Martian Chronicles.* Two of the most popular "sci-fi" movies have been *Star Wars* and *Close Encounters of the Third Kind.*

REFERENCES: B. W. Aldiss, *Billion Year Space: The History of Science Fiction;* August Derleth, ed., *Beyond Time and Space;* Wilson Tucker, ed., *Science Fiction Treasury;* Basil Davenport, *Inquiry into Science Fiction;* Sheila Schwartz, "World of Science Fiction," *English Record* (February, 1971); H. Bruce Franklin, *Future Perfect;* Mark Rose, *Anatomy of Science Fiction.*

selective representation   A term suggested by Aristotle (*Poetics,* I and II) in his MIMESIS ("imitation of life"); the term, still argued by scholars and translators, and perennially reiterated by critics, seeks to distinguish "genuine" art, which is highly selective, from "mere" reporting or photography, which are comparatively less selective, if not always indifferently "random" representation. The dialogue in a literary work—*Sunrise at Campobello,* for example—may *sound* like the speech or dialect of actual persons (for example, the

Roosevelts) but it actually only approximates or suggests it, as comparison with real-life tape recordings reveals. The playwright has thus selected certain utterances, utterance-patterns, pet words and expressions, characteristic pronunciations, etc., of real-life models, assembling *selective* rather than random or photographic representations. *Note*: Because dialects of characters in literary works are selective rather than random representations, many a linguist rejects them, perhaps justifiably, as appropriate data for laboratory study and for purposes of linguistic atlases. For most other purposes, however, the dialects of a Huck Finn or an Eliza Doolittle are not only *selective* but also (on a higher level of abstraction) *faithful* representations of their regional and cultural contexts. Linguists and other scientists sometimes delude themselves about their "objectivity," as C. P. Snow and others have shown. Scientists use subjective as well as objective, deductive as well as inductive processes.

REFERENCES: Erich Auerbach, *Mimesis;* Hazard Adams, "Imitation and Creation," *The Interests of Criticism;* J. D. Boyd, *The Function of Mimesis and Its Decline;* Joyce Cary, *Art and Reality;* Mario Praz, *Mnemosyne.*

semantics   The study of meanings as distinguished from structures, forms, or appearances. Semanticists (much more than linguists, psychologists, and psycholinguists) regard language as a vast resource of meanings, as a source of pluralistic possibilities of meanings, depending on CONTEXT. In this respect several semanticists gravitate toward literary criticism. The main tenets in semantics are: (1) there are countless more things (concrete objects and other "referents") than there are names for them; there are simply not enough words to go around for things; (2) the word is not the same as the thing but only symbolically represents the thing—e.g., the word *desk* is not the actual thing we sit at but only one convenient symbolic representation that we have invented or pulled out of ("abstracted from") the thing-in-itself; (3) for all abstractions there is a staircase or "ladder," going from the *less abstract to the more abstract*, as illustrated below:

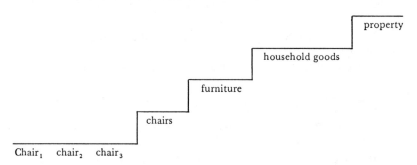

(4) a speaker or writer using a higher-level abstraction indiscriminately runs the risk of sounding irresponsible—for example, condemning all furniture or even all chairs because of the bad performance of one or two chairs; (5) language is thus not only a part of human behavior, it also affects human behavior; (6) language suggests meaning; it almost always suggests more than

it says in so many words. One must therefore read between the lines; one must ask, "What does the total context imply and assume?" (7) utterances, which often tell us more about the speaker than about a person the speaker labels, tend to be *neutral,* or *complimentary,* or *derogatory.* For example, when is an "unemployed person" (neutral) a "man of leisure" (complimentary), and when a "bum" (derogatory)? See ISGS.

REFERENCES: Alfred Korzybski, *Science and Sanity;* Wendell Johnson, *People in Quandaries;* Benjamin Lee Whorf, *Language, Thought and Reality* (ed. J. B. Carroll); Charles Osgood *et al., The Measurement of Meaning;* S. I. Hayakawa, *Language in Thought and Action;* C. K. Ogden and I. A. Richards, *The Meaning of Meaning;* Marshall McLuhan, *Understanding Media;* A. L. Lazarus, "Language-Learning Objectives," in Alton C. Morris *et al.,* eds., *College English: The First Year;* Alfred North Whitehead, *Symbolism, Its Meaning and Effect* [discusses semantics and symbolic logic]; Kelly Thurman, *Semantics;* Donald Hayden and E. P.Alworth, eds., *Classics in Semantics;* Edward Hall, *The Silent Language;* George Steiner, *Language and Silence.*

semicolon   Among the "stop" or "separator" devices of punctuation, the semicolon (;) indicates a separation between elements of equal rank, usually between the independent clauses of a compound sentence. The semicolon is used:

1. To separate the major parts of a compound sentence when no conjunction is used between them.

The victory was in view; none of the generals doubted it.

If *and* were used, the comma would be the normal punctuation.

The victory was in view, and none of the generals doubted it.

2. To separate the major parts of a compound sentence when *however, therefore, hence* (or another conjunctive adverb) is used between them.

They knew we opposed them; moreover, they knew we would defeat them.

3. To separate the major parts of a compound sentence even when *and* (or other such conjunction) is used—if any one of those parts is long and involved or already contains commas.

His attitude, already widely censured, grew more offensive with every session; yet he could not temper it.

4. To separate major items in a series when commas are used within those items.

The Cabinet members present included Artuosi, Labor; Dillahunt, Treasury; Pierce, Commerce; and Nedden, Interior.

5. To set off items of example introduced by *namely, that is, for example* (or other such conventional phrases).

He had many tricks to learn; for instance, how to ask for money without mentioning his poverty.

Inexperienced writers sometimes confuse the semicolon (;) with the colon (:), using it improperly to introduce something (Dear Mr. Smith;) when proper punctuation demands the colon (Dear Mr. Smith:).

Senecan tragedy   English plays with plots hinging on violence; the actions of tyrants; madness, ghosts, poison, suicide, incest, and other striking and spectacular themes, which imitated, or were influenced by, the plays of the Roman writer Seneca. Seneca, though using many of the myths of the Greek dramatists, brought the action indoors; he also made great use of secrecy and concealment. His plays are filled with bloodshed, elaborate description, sententious DIALOGUE, and thunderous diatribe. His main themes are the cares of empire, the fickleness of fortune, the uncertainty of popular favor, the cruelty of war, and the rashness of youth. All these elements appear in *Gorboduc* (1562), the first of the true Senecan tragedies in English. Another famous one was Kyd's *Spanish Tragedy,* which took from Seneca the ghost, the revenge theme, and the soliloquy, elements which were also used to good effect in Shakespeare's *Hamlet.*

REFERENCES: John W. Cunliffe, *The Influence of Seneca on Elizabethan Tragedy;* Howard Baker, *Induction to Tragedy* [qualifies assumptions about Seneca's influence on Elizabethan tragedy]; F. L. Lucas, *Seneca and Elizabethan Tragedy.*

sensibility   **1.** In eighteenth-century literature, an agrarian, anti-urban, and antimercantile life style reflected in sentimental drama (see SENTIMENTALISM), the SENTIMENTAL NOVEL, and the poetry of the "School of Sensibility." Although many a minor poet who belonged willy-nilly to that school wrote odes to sensibility, three of the best-known poems associated with sensibility are Joseph Warton's *Enthusiast; or Lover of Nature* (1744), William Collin's "Ode to Simplicity" (1746), and Thomas Gray's "Elegy Written in a Country Churchyard" (1750)—with its "lowing herds" and "homely joys . . . far from the madding crowd's ignoble strife." Oliver Goldsmith's long poem *The Deserted Village* also celebrates the charms of agriculture and laments the ravages of commercial trade. Similarly, William Cowper's long poem *The Task* (1784), though opening as a TOUR DE FORCE on the evolution of the sofa, shifts into profuse tributes to gardening and the delights of rural life. Because of its emphasis on tender feelings (the boy in the EPITAPH of Gray's "Elegy" "gave to Misery all he had, a tear") and on overt emotional responsiveness as opposed to STOICISM and hard-shelled reticence, eighteenth-century sensibility has usually been regarded as incipient ROMANTICISM. But this notion is perhaps unfair, each movement having an integrity of its own. A revival of eighteenth-century sensibility, along with many of its tenets, can be seen in the work of the BEAT POETS and the Hippie movement and in the poetry of Allen Ginsberg (1926–   ). Ginsberg—unlike Walt Whitman, with whom he is often compared—has been inclined to "howl" against many aspects of mercantilism that Whitman was willing to accept and even celebrate (e.g., in "Carol of Occupations").

2. In twentieth-century literary criticism, sensibility is a synonym for sensitivity or the aesthetic mix of sensuous and intellectual response to experience. In 1921 T. S. Eliot, for example, regretted in Milton's poetry a "dissociation of sensibility," a failure of "unification" or integrity between feeling and thought. Most of Eliot's successors in criticism have rejected Eliot's assumptions, however, as being too simplistic whether or not he misread the psychology of

Remy de Gourmont (1885–1915), an apologist for the SYMBOLISTS. Contemporary critics seem readier to accept the sensitivity theory of Charles Baudelaire (1821–67), a theory that seems to have stood up remarkably well over the years. In his essay "The Painter of Modern Life," in *Romantic Art* (1869), Baudelaire observed that the first-rate artist responds to (and is "drunk with") experience through all the senses, much as a child who discovers something for the first time, although the genius then selectively refines these first impressions and shapes them into "exquisitely sensitive" expression. Modern poets, with a few exceptions, while accepting the truth of Baudelaire's observations, have tended to shy away from letting the public see their "intoxications," whether initial or refined. In fiction, however, the prose that most reflects Baudelairian sensitivity (probably initial as well as refined) is that of Marcel Proust (in *Remembrance of Things Past*, 1913–27) and James Joyce (in *Ulysses*, 1922, and *Finnegans Wake*, 1939).

REFERENCES: Bonamy Dobrée, "The Claims of Sensibility," *Humanitas* (Spring, 1946); F. W. Bateson, "Dissociation of Sensibility," in "Contributions to a Dictionary of Critical Terms," *Essays in Criticism;* William Van O'Connor, *Sense and Sensibility in Modern Poetry;* Northrop Frye, "Towards Defining an Age of Sensibility," *E*(nglish) *L*(iterary) *H*(istory), *XXIII* (1956); George Arms, *The Fields Were Green;* Raymond Williams, *The Country and the City.*

sentence fragment   See FRAGMENT.

sentimental drama   See SENTIMENTALISM 3.

sentimental novel   Also called novel of sensibility. A novel or a work of episodic prose fiction in which the characters overreact emotionally and in which the author bumptiously assumes an extravagant amount of empathy by readers. The classic example is Henry Mackenzie's *Man of Feeling* (1771). In this work the hero, young Harley, becomes ill when he hears that his beloved Miss Walton is about to marry a rival; when she visits him to deny the rumor and declare her love for him, he expires. In Mackenzie's own words:

He seized her hand—a languid color reddened his cheek—a smile brightened faintly in his eye. As he gazed on her, it grew dim, it fixed, it closed. He sighed and fell back.... Miss Walton screamed at the sight—His aunt and the servants rushed into the room— They found them [sic] lying motionless together.—His physician happened to call at that instant. Every art was tried to recover them—With Miss Walton they succeeded.— But Harley was gone forever.

As casual structurally as *The Man of Feeling,* but more sanctimonious in its moral assumptions, *Pamela, or Virtue Rewarded* (1740), Samuel Richardson's EPISTOLARY NOVEL, chronicles the episodes in which Pamela keeps the eligible "Mr. B." chasing her until he is caught in marriage. The agrarian SENSIBILITY and sentimentality of this work, along with its moral hypocrisy, were urbanely satirized in the skit *Shamela; or an Apology for the Life of Mistress Shamela Andrews* (1741), the work almost certainly of Henry Fielding. Fielding made another hit, the next year, with the novel *Joseph Andrews,* of which the first part depicts Joseph escaping attacks on his virtue by Lady Booby (compare the Old Testament Joseph dodging the advances of Potiphar's wife).

Richardson's *Pamela* seemed to elicit a host of sentimental novels, the best known of which included Laurence Sterne's *Tristram Shandy* (1760-67), whose sentimentality is often relieved by humor; Oliver Goldsmith's *Vicar of Wakefield* (1766), which assumed the reader's sentiments to be on the side of huge families and agrarian, as opposed to urban, prejudices; Fanny Burney's *Evelina, or a Young Lady's Entrance into the World* (1778); William Godwin's half-believable *Caleb Williams* (1794); and Maria Edgeworth's melodramatic *Castle Rackrent* (1801).

A death blow to the sentimental novel was intended by Jane Austen in the novels *Sense and Sensibility* (1811) and *Pride and Prejudice* (1813). But her attack proved too subtle—judging from the sentiment that gushed from fiction (to say nothing of MELODRAMA) in England and America during the rest of the 1800s and early 1900s. Even an otherwise great novelist like Charles Dickens indulged in sentimentality, especially in *Oliver Twist* (1837-38).

In the New World, Richardsonian sentimentalism was emulated in the very first American novel, William Hill Brown's *Power of Sympathy* (1789). Other sentimental American novels included Charles Brockden Brown's *Wieland* (1798), which was also one of the first American GOTHIC NOVELS, and Hugh Henry Brackenridge's *Modern Chivalry,* published in installments between 1792 and 1815.

Perhaps the best known, though not necessarily the worst offender, among sentimental fiction writers in America was James Fenimore Cooper (1789-1851). The sentimentalism and other excesses in the Leatherstocking Tales—especially in *The Last of the Mohicans* (1826) and *The Pathfinder* (1840) and most disastrously in *The Deerslayer* (1841)—were mercilessly attacked by Mark Twain in 1895 in an article in the *North American Review* entitled "Fenimore Cooper's Literary Offenses." Like Dickens, however, Cooper had created enough credible people and scenes to win immortality in spite of his sentimentalism.

Although the corrective—novels of REALISM—began to appear in America as early as the 1880s (for example, William Dean Howells's *Rise of Silas Lapham,* 1885), the sentimental novel persisted into the early 1900s with such CLOAK AND SWORD exemplars as George Barr McCutcheon's *Graustark* series, 1901-14. The sentimental novel finally disappeared under the onslaught of realism, NATURALISM, and the fiction of psychological introspection, especially the prolific output of Henry James (1843-1916), which achieved much of its momentum posthumously. See SENSIBILITY, SENTIMENTALISM, MELODRAMA.

REFERENCES: Robert M. Lovett and Helen Hughes, *The History of the Novel in England;* Alan D. McKillop, *The Early Masters of English Fiction;* Ronald Crane, "Suggestions toward a Genealogy of the Man of Feeling," *English Literary History* (Vol. I, 1934); Louis Bredvold, *The Natural History of Sensibility;* Virginia Woolf, "Mr. Bennett and Mrs. Brown," *The Common Reader;* H. R. Brown, *The Sentimental Novel in America;* Mark Twain, "Fenimore Cooper's Literary Offenses," in Edmund Wilson, ed., *The Shock of Recognition;* Leslie Fiedler, "Cross the Border, Close the Gap," *Playboy* (December, 1969); J. D. Yohannan, ed., *Joseph & Potiphar's Wife....*

sentimentalism   **1.** In general, a synonym for sentimentality or overindulgence in emotion. **2.** In particular, an aesthetic flaw in any literary piece that makes extravagant emotional appeals or unwarranted claims on the reader's emotions. Well-known examples in verse are the works of Edgar Guest, James Whitcomb Riley, Thomas Gray, and Oliver Goldsmith. But even a generally restrained and understating poet like Emily Dickinson occasionally indulges in sentimentalism, as in her poem, "If I can stop one heart from breaking." The trouble with sentimentalism is not that it asks us to feel but that it asks us to feel more than what the depicted situation itself elicits. It is as if the author, obtruding between the piece itself and the audience, is persuading us to shed a tear or two. And this persuasion can misfire. Rather than shed a tear we may smile if, in addition to the feeling that we are supposed to be experiencing, we give in to the slightest but stubbornest bit of thinking. For example, even Emily Dickinson unconsciously obtrudes with her word "stop," which in the context of her poem is all too vulnerable to a second meaning—the manipulative ("tear-jerking") device on a pipe organ. MELODRAMAS and similar plays of the nineteenth and early twentieth centuries gained popularity no doubt because their sentimentalism elicited tears from the simple and smiles from the sophisticated. **3.** Eighteenth-century bourgeois tragedy—e.g., Richard Steele's *Conscious Lovers* and George Lillo's *London Merchant; or, The History of George Barnwell*—relied heavily on sentimentality, as did such prose pieces as Laurence Sterne's *Sentimental Journey* and Henry Mackenzie's *Man of Feeling.* Though moods and styles change from time to time, place to place, and audience to audience, it is safe to observe that most literature that has stood the tests of time and place has resisted sentimentalism.

REFERENCES: H. R. Brown, *The Sentimental Novel in America;* Arthur Sherbo, *English Sentimental Drama;* Neil Myers, "Sentimentalism in W. C. Williams' Early Poetry," *American Literature* (1/1966).

sequel   A literary work that continues a narrative from its setting and previous chronology in another work. In Cooper's *Leatherstocking Tales, The Last of the Mohicans* (1826) is a sequel to *The Deerslayer,* though the latter was not published until 1841. Similarly, in Faulkner's mythical Yoknapatawpha County, *Sanctuary* (1931) is a sequel to *The Reivers,* which was not published until many years later.

serials, serialization   See PART PUBLICATION.

series   Three or more items, consecutive and in the same grammatical form, within a sentence; for example: "... government *of the people, by the people,* and *for the people....*" The three or more items may be single words, PHRASES (as in the example), or CLAUSES (independent or subordinate). The series is normally punctuated by a comma after each item except the last (see COMMA 2). It is worth noting that *two* items joined by *and* are not considered a series; no comma is used in "time and tide," but commas would be needed if there were three or more items, as in "time, tide, and temptation."

sesquipedalianism   The use of big words; that is, of words "a foot and a half long." A classic example is *antidisestablishmentarianism.*

sestet   A six-lined stanza. See METER and SONNET.

sestina   A complex French form of poetry now coming back into fashion.
Arnaut Daniel, a twelfth-century poet and TROUBADOUR, is generally credited
with the invention of the sestina. The form was popular in Provence and, in
Italy, became known through the sestinas of Dante and Petrarch. The sixteenth-century English courtiers Wyatt and Surrey imported the form along
with the sonnet. Between then and the twentieth century very few English
poets—with the exception of Swinburne (a Victorian)—wrote sestinas. In the
twentieth century the most distinguished sestinas have been written by Ezra
Pound, T. S. Eliot, and W. H. Auden.

The sestina consists of six six-line STANZAS plus a three-line ENVOI, all in
iambic pentameter. Unlike the VILLANELLE, the sestina has no REFRAIN. In fact,
it uses no RHYME, preferring that the sound-effects emanate from the repeated
end-words. This repetition follows a fixed pattern, as illustrated in the following well-known sestina by W. H. Auden:

Hearing of Harvests Rotting in the Valleys
Hearing of harvests rotting in the valleys
Seeing at end of street the barren mountains
Round corners coming suddenly on water,
Knowing them shipwrecked who were launched for islands,
We honor founders of these starving cities,
Whose honor is the image of our sorrow.

Which cannot see its likeness in their sorrow
That brought them desperate in the brink of valleys;
Dreaming of evening walks through learned cities,
They reined their violent horses on the mountains,
Those fields like ships to castaways on islands,
Visions of green to them that craved for water.

They built by rivers and at night the water
Running past windows comforted their sorrow;
Each in his little bed conceived of islands
Where every day was dancing in the valleys,
And all the year trees blossomed on the mountains,
Where love was innocent, being far from cities.

But dawn came back and they were still in cities;
No marvelous creature rose up from the water,
There was still gold and silver in the mountains,
And hunger was a more immediate sorrow;
Although to moping villagers in valleys
Some waving pilgrims were describing islands.

"The gods," they promised, "visit us from islands,
Are stalking head-up, lovely through the cities;
Now is the time to leave your wretched valleys
And sail with them across the lime-green water;
Sitting at their white sides, forget their sorrow,
The shadows cast across your lives by mountains."

So many, doubtful, perished in the mountains
Climbing up crags to get a view of islands;
So many, fearful, took with them their sorrow
Which stayed them when they reached unhappy cities;
So many, careless, dived and drowned in water;
So many, wretched would not leave their valleys.

It is the sorrow; shall it melt? Ah, water
Would gush, flush, green these mountains and these valleys
And we rebuild our cities, not dream of islands.

Notice the virtuosity with which the poet plays his key end-words (valleys, mountains, water, islands, cities, and sorrow) across his poem. He deliberately creates a shifting to suggest the shifting and flowing of people from one "ideal" place to another. Notice, also, the pattern that the poet contrives—the system of repetition. *Valleys,* the end-word of the first line of the first stanza is repeated in each of the other stanzas, respectively in lines 2, 4, 5, 3, 6; and in the envoi, line 2. *Mountains,* the end-word of line 2 of the first stanza, is repeated in each of the other stanzas, respectively in lines 4, 5, 3, 6, 1; in short, with the exception of the envoi, each stanza uses each of the end-words in a unique position; in each stanza, each end-word occurs in a new line and in a subtly different new light. In the envoi, one finds all six end-words.

setting   The time, place, and MILIEU, or cultural context, in a story, novel, or play. The SHORT STORY, like most dramas, tends to have a single setting, whereas a novel allows for more scope in time and space.

REFERENCE: W. H. Evans, "Setting," *Structure of Literature,* ed. R. Beauchamp.

seven arts, the   (Also called the *classical liberal arts.*) The *trivium* (grammar, LOGIC, and RHETORIC) and the *quadrivium* (arithmetic, astronomy, geometry, and music). During the Middle Ages studying the *trivium* led to the B.A. degree; the *quadrivium,* to the M.A. degree.

seven deadly sins   *Pride, envy, anger, laziness, greed, gluttony,* and *lust.* Each of these takes its hierarchic place in the circles of Hell described by Dante in *The Inferno.* Intellectual pride, including betrayal of friends, is the most deplorable and its punishments the most severe. The seven deadly sins have been assumed as standard realities not only by medieval writers, who personified them in the MORALITY PLAYS, but also by writers as modern as T. S. Eliot (in *The Cocktail Party* and *Murder in the Cathedral*); Graham Greene (in *Brighton Rock, The Heart of the Matter,* and *The End of the Affair*); and Edward Albee (in *Tiny Alice*).

REFERENCES: Angus Wilson, Edith Sitwell, and others, *The Seven Deadly Sins;* Morton Bloomfield, *The Seven Deadly Sins;* Henry Fairlie, *The Seven Deadly Sins Today.*

shifting definition   See EQUIVOCATION.

shock of recognition   The sudden realization that one is in the presence of achievement; originally, one genius's recognition of another. "For genius all over the world," said Melville, "stands hand in hand, and one shock of recognition runs the whole circle round."

REFERENCES: Edmund Wilson, *Shock of Recognition* (anthology); Marvel Shmiefsky, "Yeats and Browning," *Studies in English Literature* (Autumn, 1970).

short-short story   (Also known as *short-short.*) A tightly knit narrative of about a thousand words, with all the strictures and challenges of the SHORT STORY and with even less leeway for RENDERING.

short story   A comparatively short fictional prose narrative (usually about five thousand words, but also as short as three thousand and as long as ten thousand) with a short time-span and very few characters and scenes, in which all the elements—plot, characterization, theme, etc.—aim toward a *single effect* or *impact,* a single mood or emotional atmosphere (Edgar Allan Poe's concept). A short story may also be defined as the RENDERING of an experience, no matter how brief, into feelingful significance. Somerset Maugham demanded of a short story that it have "unity of impression" and that it invite reading within a "single sitting." Though episodic tales were told all over the world and written down for many centuries before the nineteenth, the dramatic narrative containing unity of effect (i.e., a single setting or locale, a single conflict, a single moment of decision or character-change) was predominantly an American enterprise, if not the invention, of such writers as Poe, Hawthorne, Irving, and Melville. Even the prolific French writer Maupassant acknowledged his indebtedness, in this genre, to the Americans.

Before the advent of movies and television, short stories were published in many magazines. But today very few magazines publish fiction. Among the few that do, the best fiction can be read in *The Atlantic, The New Yorker, Mademoiselle,* the LITTLE MAGAZINES, and *Seventeen* (which offers an annual prize for the best story written by a teen-ager). Some of the best collections of short stories are listed below. A glance through the tables of contents of these collections reveals the comparatively few writers well thought of. Among the British: Robert Louis Stevenson, Sir Arthur Conan Doyle, Rudyard Kipling, Joseph Conrad, Katherine Mansfield, Virginia Woolf, D. H. Lawrence, James Joyce, H. G. Wells, Elizabeth Bowen, Somerset Maugham, and Frank O'Connor. Among the Americans: Mark Twain, Bret Harte, O. Henry, Jack London, Henry James, Willa Cather, Sherwood Anderson, Pearl S. Buck, F. Scott Fitzgerald, Ernest Hemingway, William Faulkner, John Steinbeck, William Saroyan, Katherine Anne Porter, Eudora Welty, John O'Hara, Kay Boyle, Herbert Gold, Ralph Ellison, J. D. Salinger, John Cheever, John Updike, Philip Roth, James Baldwin, Flannery O'Connor, Shirley Ann Grau, and Joyce Carol Oates. Compare NOVELLA and NOVELETTE.

REFERENCES: Ralph Singleton, ed., *Two and Twenty;* James Moffett, ed., *Points of View;* Alton C. Morris *et al.,* eds., *College English: The First Year;* Arthur Mizener, ed., *Modern Short Stories;* Barbara McKenzie, ed., *The Process of Fiction;* Robert Scholes, *Elements of Fiction;* J. B. Hall, ed., *The Realm of Fiction: 61 Short Stories;* Jarvis Thurston, ed., *Reading Modern Short Stories;* Robert Penn Warren and Albert Erskine, eds., *Short Story Masterpieces;* Winifred Lynskey, ed., *Reading Modern Fiction;* Edith Mirrielees, *Story Writing;* "The Importance of Irrelevancies," in A. S. Burack, ed., *The Writer's Handbook* (1968); Robert Freier *et al.,* "The Short Story," *Adventures in Modern Literature;* William Abrahams, ed., *The O. Henry Prize Stories Annual;* William Saroyan *et al.,* "International Symposium on the Short Story," *Kenyon Review* (January, 1969); Helmut Gerber, ed., *The English Short Story in Transition* (1880–1920); R. V. Cassill, *Writing Fiction.*

Siamese sentence   See RUN-ON SENTENCE.

signpost devices   Just as signposts on highways are courtesies to travelers, so signposts (also called *guideposts*) in written works are courtesies to the reader. Signposts in their most mechanical form consist of such indispensables as writer's name, title of paper, page numbers, etc. But in the longer expository paper (term paper, library paper, etc.) they also consist of such thoughtful markers as (1) *a statement of the chief purpose,* preferably in the opening paragraph; (2) *summary statements* at the ends of main sections, especially if a contrariety of information and ideas has been presented; (3) *subsidiary statements of purpose* at the beginnings of sections. The latter statements can also serve as TRANSITIONS. For example: "The previous section was devoted to the main characteristics of X.... I now turn to a brief history of their development and a discussion of some of their possible causes." Of course, such signpost statements can be disabused of their tediousness if the writer capitalizes on specific expressions peculiar to that particular paper. And decisions on such matters of style hinge on whether the paper is intended as *(a)* a *record* of research, addressed to one's associates, or *(b)* a *product* of research (i.e., an article or essay) addressed to a broader outside audience, for example, in a magazine.

REFERENCE: "The Question of Audience," *MLA Style Sheet.*

simile   An explicit comparison of *two unlike things,* ordinarily using the words *like* or *as;* for example, in "Auto Wreck" Karl Shapiro writes that the ambulance comes with its "ruby flare / Pulsing out red light *like an artery.*" The light is compared to blood pulsing from an artery; the simile says that the one is *like* the other, not that the two are almost identical—and that is simile's (and metaphor's) distinction from prosaic comparison. Simile draws a comparison between things that are normally not thought of as related or alike. "A child is like a man" is no simile, for the child and the man are too nearly alike in actuality. But the utterance "a child is like a balloon" is indeed simile (and "a child is a balloon" is metaphor), calling our attention to imaginative similarities between two actually unlike entities (child and balloon). Reading similes or creating them calls for imaginative insight—a readiness in sensing similarities and relationships that escape the literal mentality. See EPIC SIMILE and compare METAPHOR.

"single vision, Newton's sleep"   Derogation by the poet William Blake (1757–1827) of a materialistic VISION OF LIFE that he thought was reflected in Newtonian physics. In a letter to his patron Thomas Butts (March 22, 1802) Blake wrote: "May God us keep / from Single vision & Newton's sleep!" Actually Newton was not as materialistic as Blake believed, even if the physicist did subscribe to (anti-Establishment) DEISM. Blake was also anti-Establishment but his heresy excluded both Newtonian "particles of light" and ENLIGHTENMENT rationalism. Blake believed that Newton (1642–1727) had suffered from a blindspot toward mystical vision, the Light of Revelation. In several of his poems, moreover, Blake denied the reality of matter altogether and regarded many an alleged evil (except oppression) as more often than not merely "intellectual error"; humans restrict themselves too much, he said, to "mind-forged manacles." Up to that point Blake sounds like a Christian Scientist. However, unlike most Christians—and as a harbinger of Freud and Walt Whitman—Blake scorned injunctions against the exercise of sexual energy. "Abstinence sows sand ... Desire gratified / plants fruit and beauty.") In short, Blake dismissed one of the Establishment's tenets about "sin," even though he loved Jesus.

Often quoted, "single vision, Newton's sleep" is often misread; as Harold Bloom observes, Blake did not mean to imply a preference for "double vision," for the Judeo-Christian dualism that makes every human a battleground for the war between "the spiritual and the carnal." That assumption, which undergirds most of the world's literature, was not Blake's. He resisted equating "carnal" with "evil," and saw the energy of human desire as wholesome and indispensable to mankind's highest goal: poetic IMAGINATION.

REFERENCES: Algernon Swinburne, *William Blake;* Northrop Frye, *Fearful Symmetry;* Alfred Kazin, "Introduction," *The Portable Blake;* Harold Bloom, "Commentaries," in David Erdman, ed., *Complete Works of William Blake;* Hazard Adams, *William Blake: A Reading of the Shorter Poems;* Irene Chayes, "Little Girl Lost ... ," *Bulletin of the New York Public Library* (November, 1963); Jean Hagstrum, "Blake Rejects the Enlightenment," *Studies on Voltaire and the 18th Century;* Mark Curran, "Review of Roszak's *Where the Wasteland Ends," College English* (April, 1973); [Re: Blake and Whitman, pages 326–27] Justin Kaplan, *Walt Whitman, a Life;* R. S. Westfall, "The Career of Isaac Newton," *American Scholar* (Summer, 1981).

skeltonic verse   Short-lined verse, sometimes racy, sometimes DOGGEREL, originally developed by John Skelton (1460–1529). Among his best-known verses is "Philip Sparrow," which contains this representative stanza:

> When I remember again
> How my Philip was slain,
> Never half the pain
> Was between you twain,
> Pyramus and Thisbe,
> As then befell to me:
> I wept and I wailed
> The tear-es down hailed—
> But nothing it availed
> To call Philip again,
> Whom Gib our cat hath slain.

slanting   1. In poetry, the use of *slant-rhyme* or NEAR-RHYME. 2. In journalism, the bending of an editorial (or even a news report, unfortunately) to influence a particular audience. Some slanting is always with us, though many of the popular media have begun to exercise some self-discipline. In the early 1900s slanting the news was common practice among journalists, particularly the "yellow journalists." 3. In free-lance writing the term has a somewhat less derogatory connotation. When writers speak of their work as "slanted" toward a given "market," they have more often than not "analyzed the market" to see which audience their work seems best directed toward. See AUDIENCE.

slant rhyme   See RHYME.

slapstick   **1.** A stick with a hinged slat that makes a slapping sound when someone is struck with it. In ancient comedies—for example, those of the Greek Menander (343–291? B.C.) and of the Romans Plautus and Terence (second century B.C.)—the hits that a master administered with a walking-stick to a slave or servant (later, king to jester) who talked too cleverly or out of turn or both. **2.** In medieval times, in some of the CRAFT CYCLE PLAYS and MORALITY PLAYS, scenes which contained similar "stage business." Noah's wife, for example, was traditionally portrayed as a shrew who hit him over the head with household objects; the devils in scenes of hell often ran away, vanquished, with firecrackers popping from the rear of their devil-suits. **3.** In modern times, the same kind of humor. In *The End of the Beginning,* a play by Sean O'Casey, two foolish idlers turn a farmhouse into a shambles while trying to tie down a cow with a rope through a fireplace chimney. **4.** In third-rate movies and television programs, such horseplay as pie-throwing and pratfalls.

slash   See VIRGULE.

slicks, the   Journalists' jargon for such magazines as *Harper's, The Atlantic, Saturday Review, Life,* and so on, which were printed on "slick," glossy paper (as opposed to the coarse paper of the PULPS). While the label "slick" carried with it a kind of "sour grapes" connotation (at least when used by writers who wished they could be published in the slicks), it did not include the most sophisticated magazines. Such magazines as *The Nation, The New Republic, The Christian Century,* and so on, even if not slick, published many "think pieces" that editors of the slicks tended to reject.

sock   The low shoe, the conventional attire of actors of ancient comedy; contrasted with the BUSKIN used in tragedy.

solecism   Narrowly defined, any violation of standard usage ("Where's the car at?") or grammar ("They come yesterday"). Broadly defined, a solecism may be any mistake, impropriety, or incongruity in the use of language—CATACHRESIS, MALAPROPISM, MIXED METAPHOR, mispronunciation, DANGLER. It must be remembered, however, that *what is a solecism in one company may be respectable usage in another.*

soliloquy   A solo speech, usually in serious drama, in which a character thinks out loud. The classic examples are in Shakespeare's *Hamlet,* especially the speech beginning "To be or not to be."
REFERENCE: Wolfgang Clemen, *Shakespeare's Soliloquies.*

sonnet   From the Italian *sonetto,* "a little sound or song." A fourteen-line lyric poem in iambic pentameter with a variety of stanza forms and rhyme schemes but generally conforming to the Italian or Petrarchan pattern (an *octave* rhyming *abbaabba* and a *sestet* rhyming *cdecde* or *cdcdcd*) or to the Shakespearian pattern (three *quatrains* and a *couplet* with the rhyme scheme *abab cdcd efef gg*). The label "English sonnet" usually refers to the Shakespearian pattern, but it is somewhat loosely applied since English sonnet forms also embrace the

Spenserian (*abab bcbc cdcd ee*), the Miltonic-Wordsworthian (*abbaabba cdecde*), and variations through the centuries to Dylan Thomas.

In his sonnets to Laura, Petrarch (1304–74) used a *volta*, or turn of thought, between the octave and the sestet, the octave developing a problem that the sestet resolves. An example in an English sonnet is John Milton's "On His Blindness," in the octave of which the speaker expresses a feeling of helplessness, a feeling that is resolved in the sestet, which concludes, "They also serve who only stand and wait." Although Petrarch's work had been known to scholars at the universities, its wider introduction to England is credited to two of King Henry VIII's young ambassadors to Italy—Thomas Wyatt (1503?–42) and Henry Howard, Earl of Surrey (1517?–47). Both courtiers led politically stormy and all too brief lives (Surrey was executed), but their creative vitality is reflected in the large number of their poems posthumously reprinted in *Tottel's Miscellany* (1557). Aside from scores of other poems (including Surrey's BLANK VERSE), Wyatt had translated ten of Petrarch's sonnets, for example, and had composed twenty-one of his own. Although he retained the Petrarchan octave, he experimented—within the sestet—with a closing couplet. Surrey introduced the pattern that was to be adopted by Shakespeare in his sequence of one hundred and fifty-four sonnets dedicated to a "W. H." This is the sequence that begins "From fairest creatures we desire increase / That thereby beauty's rose might never die." and ends "Love's fire heats water, water cools not love." It is the sequence that contains one of the most poignant love sonnets—number seventy-three:

> That time of year thou mayst in me behold
> When yellow leaves, or none, or few, do hang
> Upon those boughs which shake against the cold,
> Bare ruin'd choirs, where late the sweet birds sang.
> In me thou seest the twilight of such day
> As after sunset fadeth in the west;
> Which by and by black night doth take away,
> Death's second self, that seals up all the rest.
> In me thou seest the glowing of such fire
> That on the ashes of his mouth doth lie,
> As on the death-bed whereon it must expire,
> Consumed with that which it was nourished by.
>> This thou perceiv'st, which makes thy love more strong,
>> To love that well which thou must leave ere long.

Other sixteenth-century and early seventeenth-century poets who seemed to have been as taken as were Wyatt and Surrey with the possibilities of the sonnet were Philip Sidney (1554–86); Edmund Spenser (1552–99), who invented the Spenserian form described above; and John Donne (1572–1631), whose "crown" of seven "Holy Sonnets" used the last line of each of the first six sonnets as the first line of each succeeding sonnet. But toward the end of the seventeenth century—after Milton, who died in 1674—and for most of the eighteenth century the sonnet suffered a decline—with some few exceptions like those of Cowper, Gray, and Warton.

It took a giant like William Wordsworth (1770–1850) to revive interest in the form. He wrote over five hundred sonnets, of which at least three seem destined for immortality: "Milton! thou shouldst be living at this hour," "The world is too much with us," and "Earth has not anything to show more fair." Two other romantic poets—Percy Bysshe Shelley (1792–1822) and John Keats (1795–1821)—wrote considerably fewer sonnets but have done better than Wordsworth as far as ratios of anthologized titles are concerned. For Shelley's "Ozymandias" and Keats's "On First Looking into Chapman's Homer" continue to be the two sonnets most widely reprinted.

The best-known nineteenth-century English sonnets include Elizabeth Barrett Browning's "How do I love thee? Let me count the ways," Matthew Arnold's "Shakespeare," Dante Gabriel Rossetti's "A sonnet is a moment's monument," and Gerard Manley Hopkins's "God's Grandeur" (which uses that poet's SPRUNG RHYTHM).

The best-known twentieth-century English sonnets include Thomas Hardy's "If but some vengeful god would call to me," William Butler Yeats's "Leda and the Swan," Rupert Brooke's "The Soldier," and Dylan Thomas's "Altarwise by owl-light in the halfway house" (with its TRANSFERRED EPITHETS).

The best-known American sonnets include Henry Wadsworth Longfellow's "Three Silences"; Edwin Arlington Robinson's "Calvary"; Robert Frost's "The Silken Tent," "Acquainted with the Night," and "Once by the Pacific"; Edna St. Vincent Millay's "Euclid alone has looked on Beauty bare"; e. e. cummings's "I like my body when it is with your / body"; Merrill Moore's "The Noise That Time Makes" (one of a thousand in his book *M*); and X. J. Kennedy's "Nothing in Heaven Functions As It Ought." See also SONNET SEQUENCE.

REFERENCES: Robert Bender and Charles Squier, eds., *The Sonnet: A Comprehensive Anthology of British and American Sonnets from the Renaissance to the Present;* Arthur Quiller-Couch, ed., *The Oxford Book of Sonnets;* William Wiatt, "Sir Thomas Wyatt's Word Play," *Annuale Mediaevale.*

sonnet sequence   Also called **sonnet cycle.** A series of sonnets developing a single theme or addressed to one person. In most of these sequences each sonnet retains its independence even though it may appear like a stanza in the longer literary work to which it contributes. The prototype was Petrarch's *Sonnets to Laura in Life* (ca. 1330). The best-known English sonnet sequences include Philip Sidney's *Astrophel and Stella* (1584); Edmund Spenser's *Amoretti* (1595); Shakespeare's *Sonnets* (1609); John Donne's "Holy Sonnets" (1633); William Wordsworth's *Ecclesiastical Sonnets* (1822); Elizabeth Barrett Browning's *Sonnets from the Portuguese* (1850); and Dante Gabriel Rossetti's *House of Life* (1881). Best-known American sequences include Henry Wadsworth Longfellow's "Divina Commedia" (1867), a sequence of six Petrarchan sonnets added to his translation of Dante's *Divine Comedy;* Arthur Davison Ficke's *Sonnets of a Portrait Painter* (1914); William Ellery Leonard's *Two Lives* (1925); Elinor Wylie's *One Person* (1928); Edna St. Vincent Millay's *Fatal Interview* (1931).

REFERENCE: L. C. John, *Elizabethan Sonnet Sequences.*

sound-effects   Devices of repetition or imitation in the sounds of language. Most of these devices are treated in separate articles in this glossary. See ALLITERATION, ASSONANCE, CACOPHONY, CONSONANCE, DISSONANCE, EUPHONY, ONOMATOPOEIA, and RHYME.

sorites   See SYLLOGISM 1*j*.

Southern gothic   A style of fiction associated with certain writers from the southern United States, among whom are Carson McCullers, Shirley Ann Grau, and Flannery O'Connor. Short stories and novels in this mode deal with themes of incest, insanity, sexual perversion, religious manias, and various other extreme psychological disturbances. The characters are frequently concerned with family history, and they live in houses that echo with reminders of the family's past. See GOTHIC NOVEL.

speaker   A narrator or a person; to be distinguished from PERSONA or SPEAKING VOICE.

speaking voice   In the new rhetoric (see RHETORIC 3), the role that the speaker assumes or "makes like"—reporter, novelist, teacher, preacher, lawyer, doctor, and so on. Whatever a speaker says in a given role controls the rhetoric, the style or manner, of saying it. Even in such a tour de force as the reading of names from a telephone directory the assumed role of the speaker, the speaking voice, can be projected and understood. In the EXPLICATION of poetry the teacher usually asks not only "Who is speaking?" but also "What is the speaking voice—the role—in this particular poem?" Compare VOICE 1.

REFERENCES: Walker Gibson, *Tough, Sweet, and Stuffy;* Yvor Winters, "Problems for the Modern Critic of Literature," *Hudson Review* (Autumn, 1956); Wayne Booth, "The Author's Many Voices," *The Rhetoric of Fiction;* Edith Wylder, *The Voice of the Poet: Emily Dickinson's Manuscripts;* James Moffett, "Writing, Inner Speech, and Meditation," *College English* (March, 1982).

spelling   Arranging the right letters in the right order. Such arrangement is a matter of custom and may thus vary from time to time and place to place, although spelling tends toward permanence because of its being in print. Spoken language varies much more than written language, and variant forms of speech are more widely accepted than variant spellings. What is accepted by the majority of editors and writers eventually works its way into dictionaries. To those familiar with dictionary spelling, any writing with misspelled words *looks* illiterate and can retard one's social and economic progress—though there is the exception of the successful who can hire others to spell for them.

Learning to spell remains an individual enterprise. Those who learn by sight tend to do better than those who vocalize, since the correspondence between sounds and correct spelling is notoriously unreliable. And some of the traditional rules of spelling are not only unreliable but also vulnerably complicated; their many exceptions do have explainable causes, but those causes are often more difficult to master than the words themselves. Still, it does remain practical to memorize a few of the rules—the most reliable and the least complicated. Here are the most useful:

1. *The IE/EI rule.* Place *i* before *e* except after *c* (*believe, piece, niece, chief, siege, relief, friend, mischievous;* but *receive, deceive, conceit.*) The relatively few exceptions—for the most part, words whose pronunciation has

undergone historical change—include *seize, neither, leisure,* and *neighbor* ("Seize neither leisure nor neighbor!"). Notice that *neighbor* has a long A sound, a clue to why the *e* goes before the *i,* as it does in *weight, freight,* and *sleigh.*

2. *The final Y rule.* Form the plural of words ending in *-ey (turkey, odyssey)* by adding *s (turkeys, odysseys)*. To form the plurals of words ending in *consonant + y (baby, story)* drop the *y* and add *ies (babies, stories)*. Similarly, to indicate the tense of verbs ending in *consonant + y (try, cry)* drop the *y* and add *ies (tries, cries)* for the present tense; *-ied* for the past tense *(tried, cried)*. Proper names ending in *y (Kennedy, Murphy)* add only *s* to form their plurals (the *Kennedys,* the *Murphys*).

3. *The dis-/mis- prefix rule.* Do not omit from, or add any letters to, the main stem-word *(appear, disappear; satisfied, dissatisfied; spell, misspell; section, dissection)*.

4. *The word-families rule.* Keep *ant/ance* and *ent/ence* words in their own families *(entrant, entrance; absent absence; resistant, resistance; existent, existence)*.

5. *The -able/ible rules. (a)* Since many more of the frequently used words end in -able than in -ible, it is useful to memorize the most frequent *-ibles (accessible, possible, incredible, sensible, permissible, intelligible, irresistible,* and *eligible)* and to use *-able* for all others. *(b)* But you may use a more reliable rule if you know one or another of the Romance languages. Words derived from *-ar* verbs *(amar, peccare)* take *-able (amiable, impeccable)*; all others take *-ible (credere, credible; sentire, sensible)*. *(c)* In adding *-able* to words ending in *-e* (place, engage) keep the *e (placeable, engageable)* if omitting it would result in an unintended meaning or sound. Compare *placeable* (capable of being placed) with *placable* (appeasable). Notice the *gag*-sound in *gagable* as distinguished from *engagable.*

So much for useful rules. Many good spellers rely instead upon mnemonics (memory-devices) to help them over the trouble-spots in commonly misspelled words. The more ridiculous and outrageous the mnemonic, say psychologists, the more effective—and the ones you invent for yourself will prove the most effective for you. Here are some of the commonly misspelled words along with some model mnemonics, which you can no doubt improve upon.

Words and Trouble-Spots	*Mnemonic Models*
acciden**tally**	Tally ho! AccidenTALLY ... accidentally
a**cc**o**mm**odate	CC ... MM ... aCCoMModate ... accommodate
ac**q**uaintance	We CQ (seek you) for an acquaintance.
a**cross**	One cross ... A cross ... across
a**dd**ress	There's an AD for this DRESS ... AD DRESS ... address
advi**ce**, advi**se**	The noun rhymes with ICE; the verb, with WISE
affect, **e**ffect	How does the news affect you? Has it a weird effect? Hard work effects (produces) wealth.
all right	Two words: all + right

Words and Trouble-Spots	Mnemonic Models
altogether, all together	We're altogether unbeatable when we all pull together.
angel, angle	She's a heavenly angel, viewed from any angle.
apologize	POLO ... a POLO gize ... apologize
argument	Drop the e from argue ... argument
article	Icicle ... -icle ... artICLE ... article
athlete	Two syllables only ... ATH .. LETE... athlete
attendance	DANCE AT TEN. AT TEN DANCE ... attendance
bargain	GAIN from the deal ... barGAIN ... bargain
beautiful	He's her BEAU ... BEAUtiful ... beautiful
beginning	NN ... begiNNing ... beginning
benefited	ED keeps FIT. BENE! BENE FIT ED ... benefited
bicycle	CYCLE ... BI ... BI CYCLE ... bicycle
bulletin	LET IN a little BULL ... BULL E TIN ... bulletin
business	BUS into town on BUS I NESS ... business
calendar	CAL END AR ... calendar
capital, capitol	TAL for the area, TOL for the DOME: the capital city, the capitol building
cemetery	E, E, E ... cEmEtEry ... cemetery
changeable	ABLE + CHANGE (not chang) ... CHANGE ABLE, changeable (See Rule 5c.)
competition, repetition	PET words: comPETition, rePETition
compliment, complement	comPLEment COMPLETES ... complement; comPLIment butters up as in a LINE ... compliment
conscience	SCIENCE ... conSCIENCE ... conscience
conscientious	con SCIENT I ous ... conscientious
convenience	VENI ence ... con VENI ence ... convenience
courteous	COURT E ous ... courteous
curious, curiosity	-OUS becomes -OSITY ... CURI OSITY curious, curiosity; porous, porosity; monstrous, monstrosity
definitely	FINITE ... deFINITEly ... definitely
description	DES cription ... description
desert, dessert	One dry s in deSert; two juicy ss in deSSert-deSSert takes a second helping of s
despair	DES pair ... despair
disappear, disappoint, dissatisfy	(See Rule 3.)
disastrous	AST rous + DIS ... DIS ASTrous ... disastrous
disciple, discipline	CIP ... disCIPle; CIP ... dis CIP line, discipline
eighth	eight + H ... eightH ... eighth
embarrassed	RR ... Railroad a RR into embaRRaSSed, embarrassed
environment	IRON ... Put an IRON into envIRONment, environment
exaggerate	GG! exaGGerate ... exaggerate
except, accept	EX is out; AC is in ... except: rule out; accept: take in
exhausted	H ... Hausted ... exHausted ... exhausted
exhilarate	H ... HilArate ... exhilarate

Words and Trouble-Spots	Mnemonic Models
foreign	REIGN ... FO ... FO REIGN ... foreign
government	GOVERN + MENT ... government
guarantee	GUARD your GUARantee ... guarantee
hindrance	HIND + RANCE ... hindrance
indispensable	He's IN DIS PEN because he stole a SABLE ... IN DIS PEN SABLE ... indispensable
irrelevant	IR REL E VANT ... irrelevant
irresistible	IR RESIST -ible ... irresistible
its, it's	It + is = it's ... It's a nice day. Possessive *its* takes no apostrophe. What gives this cat its silky coat?
leisure	LEI (from Hawaii) + SURE ... leisure
license	LICE (plural of *louse*) ... License
loose, lose	footLOOSE and fancy free, win or LOSE
maintenance	MAIN idea is to put TEN in the middle ... MAIN TEN ANCE ... maintenance
mischievous	Three syllables only: MIS CHIEV OUS
mortgage	Hi, MORT! How's your GAGE? MORT GAGE ... mortgage
necessary	CESS ... Is this CESSpool necessary? NE CESS ary
ninety, ninth	At NINETY you deserve to have your E's (ease)
noticeable	NOTICE + ABLE ... noticeable. (See Rule 5c.)
obstacle	not TIC but TAC ... obsTACle ... obstacle
occasion	CC ... S ... OCCaSion ... occasion
occurrence	CC ... RR ... Ence ... occurrence
original	ORIGIN + al ... original
parallel	If you're up to par you can give your all ... PAR ALL EL ... parallel
pastime	pa's time, not ma's ... PAS TIME ... pastime
personal, personnel	NEL is on the payroll; she's a person, a member of the PERSON NEL ... personnel; in her locker she keeps her PERSONAL belongings.
possess	SS ... SS ... poSSeSS ... possess
precede, proceed	PRE + CEDE ... precede (go before) PRO + CEED ... proceed (go ahead)
prejudice	DICE ... PREju ... PRE ju DICE ... prejudice. The only D is in the Dice.
principal, principle	PAL is chief ... principal amount; our principal; LE as at the end of ruLE principLE
psychology	PSY (the Greek letter) + chology
quiet, quite	Library sign: QUIET, please! Have we said QUITE enough?
recommend	C ... MM ... One C and you'll say MM! reCoM-Mend
rhythm	rHy,tHm; rHy, tHm; rHy, tHm ... rhythm
ridiculous	RID ... get RID of any vowel but i in the first syllable ... RID ic u lous ... ridiculous
secretary	SECRET. Your secret is safe with your SECRETary.
separate	A. You rate an A when you put an A before the RATE.
similar	LAR. Don't make a liar out of simiLAR.

Words and Trouble-Spots	Mnemonic Models
stationary, stationery	STANDing still is stationARY ... stationary. What writER puts pEN to is stationERY.
supersede	S ... Sede ... superSede
than, then	My father is taller THAN yours ... THEN answers to WHEN.
there	THERE answers to WHERE.
they're	THEY'RE = THEY + ARE ... They're now arriving.
their	THEIR, tHEIR, shows possession that falls to an HEIR ... their
to, too	TO market, TO market! If you come TOO, it won't cost TOO much.
tragedy	DY gets the only D in trageDy ... tragedy
truly	Drop the e from true ... truly
unnecessary	Necessary + UN ... UN Necessary ... unnecessary
village, villain	The VILLage vilLain has lain for years ... LAIN ... vil LAIN ... villain
weird	WE ... aren't WE all WEird ... weird (an exception to the "i before e" rule)
woman, women	One woMAN ... two or more woMEN
your, you're	YOUR is the possessive—It's YOUR turn, now YOU'RE = YOU + ARE ... You're getting a surprise.

REFERENCES: H. Wendell Smith, "A Guide to Accurate Spelling," *On Paper;* Rozanne Knudson and A. L. Lazarus, "The Purdue Survey on Spelling," NCTE *Councilgram* (November, 1967); Joseph Mersand, *Spelling Your Way to Success;* J. N. Hook, *Spelling 1500;* P. and C. Norback, *The Misspeller's Dictionary;* Donald W. Emery, *Variant Spellings in Modern American Dictionaries.*

Spenserian stanza   The nine-line STANZA popularized by Edmund Spenser (1552–99) in *The Faerie Queene.* The first eight lines are iambic pentameter; the last line is an ALEXANDRINE (iambic hexameter). The rhyme scheme is *ababbcbcc:*

It was a hill placed in an open plain,
That round about was bordered with a wood
Of matchless height, that seemed th'earth to disdain,
In which all trees of honor stately stood,
And did all winter as in summer bud,
Spreading pavilions for the birds to bower,
Which in their lower branches sung aloud;
And in their tops the soaring hawk did tower,
Sitting like king of fowls in majesty and power.

Among the celebrated poems subsequently written in Spenserian stanza are Robert Burns's "The Cotters' Saturday Night," Shelley's "Adonais," Keats's "The Eve of St. Agnes," and Byron's "Childe Harold."

split infinitive   The infinitive in English consists ordinarily of two words: *to prepare, to ask, to follow.* When something is put between the *to* and its verb-like form, the structure is split—and is called a split infinitive: "One must learn *to* properly *prepare* his lessons"; "It is courteous *to* always *ask* permission"; "What is worse than *to* blindly *follow* an unworthy leader?"

Whether the split infinitive is a fault depends always upon the specific utterance—its rhythm and its meaning. Some splits are awkward; others tax the understanding; some few are needful, being the best way to say what is intended. "*To prepare* his lessons properly" is quite an improvement; "*to follow* an unworthy leader blindly" is not much better than "*to* blindly *follow*"; and "*to ask* permission always" distorts the meaning of "*to* always *ask* permission."

What can be done with the split infinitive in "I am expected *to* really *do* my best"? Placed elsewhere, the adverb *really* will drift from its proper work. What is most effective here is to keep the infinitive split.

It is generally considered weak, however, to split the infinitive too broadly asunder: "Don't forget *to* (when you get to London next week) *write* us all about it," or "He made it a ritual *to* every morning before breakfast *take* a swim"—these are simply slipshod. Attention to the natural rhythms of English and to the problems readers have in mentally knitting up a raveled thought will help the writer avoid unfortunate splitting.

spondee   See METER.

spoonerism   By a slip of the tongue the sounds of a phrase may be transposed: "He's back in the outyard growing the mass" for "He's out in the backyard mowing the grass." This kind of slip is called a spoonerism, named for The Rev. William A. Spooner (1844–1930) of New College, Oxford, in whose speech such transpositions were frequent. Spoonerisms have become a device of conscious word-play for humorous effect, whole stories and essays being written (or revised) for the fun of spoonerisms—such as "The Pea Little Thrigs" and "How to Sty a Frake in Your Own Outfire Doorplace," which the humorist contends, is not so difficult as some thinkle seem to peep.

sprung rhythm   1. Loosely, any ACCENTUAL VERSE. 2. Specifically, the term Gerard Manley Hopkins (1844–1889) invented for his own accentual verse; in Hopkins' system sprung rhythm counts only the heavily, not the lightly, stressed syllables. Hence in practice, where two or two and a half *trochees* (heavily stressed syllables) surprise the reader in an otherwise *iambic* line, the effect is tantamount to syncopation. In one of Hopkins' best-known poems, "God's Grandeur," the reader begins the iambic line "And all is seared with trade ..." and is suddenly surprised with the *epitrite* "bleared, smeared, with toil." (See METER.)

REFERENCES: Gerard Manley Hopkins, "Preface" to *Poems* (1876–1889) and his "Letters" (especially those to R. W. Dixon) in William H. Gardner, ed., *The Penguin Poets Series;* Todd Bender, *Gerard Manley Hopkins.*

squinter   A disconcerting utterance that looks two ways at once; the receiver cannot be sure which way is meant. For example: "Girls who cry *often* get little sympathy." (Do they often *cry,* or do they often *get little sympathy?* Avoiding that kind of squinter takes a less ambiguous placement of the modifier: "Girls who often cry" or "Often, girls who cry....") Another example: "Danley decided *when the war was over* not to enlist again." (Did he decide after the war was over, or did he decide earlier?) The careful writer would shift the *when* clause to the very beginning or very end of the sentence. Compare MISPLACED MODIFIER, DANGLER, and REFERENCE OF PRONOUNS.

stanza   In poetry, a bundle of lines—two lines, a couplet; three lines, a triplet or tercet; four lines, a quatrain; six lines, a sestet; eight lines, an octet or octave, and so on. See METER and METRICS; also BALLAD stanza, BURNS STANZA, OTTAVA RIMA, SPENSERIAN STANZA, and TERZA RIMA.

statement   1. A synonym for declarative assertion. See SENTENCE. 2. In the SYLLOGISM, a *premise* or *conclusion* in one or another of several forms. See SYLLOGISM 1c.

statement of fact   Any assertion, true or false, that can be operationally tested; for example: *(a)* "There are thirteen eggs in this carton." *(b)* "There are five major stresses in this line of the poem." *(c)* "Nat Turner had been promised his freedom."

statement of opinion   Any assertion, true or false, that cannot be operationally tested but that may well be supported by argumentation. (See THESIS STATEMENT.) For example: *(a)* "Shakespeare was a realist." *(b)* "T. S. Eliot writes tough poetry." *(c)* "William Styron's *Confessions of Nat Turner* is an incendiary novel."

statistical induction   See INDUCTIVE REASONING 2.

stereotype   In language, any conventional usage, whether a salutation in a letter ("Dear Sir") or ready-made phrase ("It may interest you to know" or "hale and hearty"). The stereotype is thus a kind of triteness. Compare CLICHÉ. In literature, the stereotype extends to characters and plots that offer only the conventional and expected. A stereotyped character is one whose attitudes, actions and reactions, words, and dress fall in with a widely held idea of what such a "type" of person is like; one who does not grow, change, or do the unexpected thing. Similarly, a stereotyped plot is one in which the story-line is conventional and known to most readers. (See Hollis Cate and Delma Presley, "Beyond Stereotype ..." *Notes on Mississippi Writers,* Fall, 1970).

stichomythy, stichomythia   1. In Greek drama, quick dialogue; brief sentences exchanged in rapid sequence by two characters, often in the form of questions and answers. Elements of IRONY and of the riddle are characteristic of tragic stichomythy. 2. In the theater generally, from ancient to modern times, any fast repartee or conversational ping-pong. SENECAN TRAGEDY was especially fond of stichomythy, using it as a means of heightening suspense. In comedy stichomythy has always lent itself to PUNS and other word play. Here is an example from George Farquhar's *Beaux' Stratagem* (1707):

CHERRY: Then, friend, good night.
ARCHER: I hope not.
CHERRY: You may depend upon't.
ARCHER: Upon what?
CHERRY: That you're very impudent.
ARCHER: That you are very handsome.
CHERRY: That you're a footman.

REFERENCES: George Thomson, *Aeschylus in Athens;* Allardyce Nicoll, *Development of the Theatre;* Kenneth Macgowan, *A Primer of Playwriting.*

stipulative definition   See DEFINING 8.

stock character   In a story or a play, a character with very few individualistic and many stereotyped traits; e.g., the braggart soldier, the gossiping maid, the overbearing butler, and so on.

stock epithet   See EPITHET 3.

Stoicism   1. The teachings of Zeno (fourth century B.C.) and the "porch philosophers" popularized in the works of Seneca. 2. Dogged coping with hardships; indifference to pleasure or pain.

stream of consciousness   A narrative technique in which a character seems not only to be thinking out loud, but also to be manifesting symptoms of subconscious experience. In creating this illusion the novelist dispenses with normal sentences and punctuation and instead runs words, notions, feelings, images, and vestiges from deep within the psyche's past together in one continuous stream, a technique also called "interior monologue." Perhaps the best-known example is Molly Bloom's monologue (the "Penelope" passage) at the end of James Joyce's *Ulysses*. Other users of this technique have been Virginia Woolf, in *The Waves;* William Faulkner, in *The Sound and the Fury;* and Dorothy Richardson, in *Pilgrimage,* a series of novels written between 1915 and 1938.

In examining Joyce's novel *Ulysses* for legal purposes, preparatory to deciding whether or not it violated OBSCENITY laws, Judge John Woolsey keenly analyzed the stream-of-consciousness technique:

Joyce has attempted [observed Judge Woolsey] ... to show how the screen of consciousness with its ever-shifting kaleidoscopic impressions carries ... not only what is in the focus of each man's observation of the actual things about him, but also in a penumbral zone, residua of past impressions, some recent and some drawn up by association from ... the subconscious. He shows how each of these impressions affects the life and behavior of the character he is describing ... what he seeks is not unlike the results of a double or ... a multiple exposure on a cinema film which would give a clear foreground with a background visible but somewhat blurred and out of focus in varying degrees ... and [Joyce reveals] an honest effort to show exactly how the minds of the characters operate.

REFERENCES: Robert Humphrey, *Stream of Consciousness in the Modern Novel;* R. A. Brower, "Virginia Woolf," *The Fields of Light;* T. S. Eliot, *Introducing James Joyce;* Frederick Karl, *The Contemporary English Novel;* Melvin J. Friedman, *Stream of Consciousness: A Study in Literary Method;* Leon Edel, *The Psychological Novel, 1900–1950;* Morris Beja, "Matches Struck in the Dark [Virginia Woolf]," *Critical Quarterly* (Summer, 1964).

strophe   See ODE.

structuralism   1. In linguistics, a system that classifies elemental sounds (*phones*) and their combination into groups of similar sounds (*phonemes*), meaningful units (*morphemes*), and sentences or other patterns.

2. In literary criticism, systems of analysis practiced by Continental critics, especially in France. The structuralists follow a few of the practices of the NEW CRITICS, including "close reading of texts"; but, whereas the New Critics focus on a work as self-contained, structuralists seek for *relationships* between a work and its social-literary heritage. Borrowing from anthropologists and psychologists like Levi-Strauss and Jung, the structuralists explore a work's

cultural and mythological patterns (ARCHETYPES), both empirical and subconscious, both explicit and implicit. Such theorists or critics as Jean Piaget and Roland Barthes, for example, identify bundles of myth patterns (*mythemes*) in a work, studying not only its historical ("diachronic") but also its contemporary ("synchronic") themes.

Structuralists often pursue such cultural-literary patterns as appear in folk and fairy tales (conventional openings, defeat of monsters, happy endings for protagonists). Such critics identify those basic patterns ("paradigms") in a work and interpret their symbolic implications.

James Joyce's *Ulysses* has offered perhaps more treasure to the structuralists than has any other novel. The exploits of Joyce's Stephen Dedalus are compared with those of certain characters in Homer's *Odyssey*. The characterization of Stephen, the structuralists say, has "impinged on" Homer's characterization of Telemachus. With humorous variations Bloom is patterned after Ulysses, Molly Bloom after Penelope. The picaresque wanderings of Stephen and Bloom into public baths and the parlors of Circe-like women are, say the structuralists, patterned after several episodes in the *Odyssey*.

How the structuralists see the relationships among works whose images "impinge" on one another may be seen in a structuralist explication of the poem "Kalispera"—at least its first seven lines:

> On Crete, one night, at the Palace Theatre,
> anti-climax to more genuine ruins,
> I saw a Bondish movie with Mycenean titles
> in which the lovely Hellene spy, after fruitless
> encounters with the agent, finally offers
> herself (flash/flesh) like a bowl of muscats.
> Whereupon out of the winedark audience ...

The contemporary (synchronic) and dilapidated movie palace of popular culture is contrasted with the more hallowed palaces of bygone (diachronic) Cretan royalty, while the term of contrast "anti-climax" still lives in the ongoing world of drama and the theater. The phrase "fruitless encounters" both puns and impinges upon the spy's "bowl of muscats," a voluptuousness characteristic of female spies in James Bond movies and of grape-growing, DYONYSIAN Crete itself. The grapes impinge upon the "winedark audience," a sea of swarthy grape-pickers and suntanned tourists. ("Winedark" is an EPITHET used by classical Greek poets, Homer among them, to describe seas like those that wash the shores of Crete.)

REFERENCES: Claude Levi-Strauss, *Totemism;* Jean Piaget, *Structuralism;* Roland Barthes, *Mythologies;* Northrop Frye, "Archetypal Criticism: Theory of Myths," *Anatomy of Criticism;* Vladimir Propp, *Morphology of the Folktale;* Richard and Fernande de George, eds., *Structuralists from Marx to Levi-Strauss;* John Sturrock, ed., *Structuralism from Strauss to Derrida;* Richard Macksey, ed., *The Languages of Criticism;* Anthony Burgess, *Joysprick: An Introduction to the Language of James Joyce;* Robert Scholes, *Structuralism in Literature;* Michael Lane, *Introduction to Structuralism;* Jonathan Culler, *Structural Poetics;* Alan Purves, *Formal Structure in Kubla Khan;* Sarah Youngblood, "Structure and Imagery in K. A. Porter's 'Pale Horse, Pale Rider'," *Modern Fiction Studies* (Winter, 1960); A. L. Lazarus "Kalispera," *New Republic* (Dec. 6, 1969); Dorothy Selz, "Structuralism for the Non-Specialist: A Glossary and a Bibliography," *College English* (Oct., 1975). *Note:* The October, 1975, issue of *College English* is given over to "Structuralism for Teachers of English."

Sturm und Drang   Literally, "storm and stress." A romantic youthful movement of the 1770s in revolt against traditional classicism. Founded by J. G. Herder (1744–1803), the movement attracted such artists as Goethe (d. 1832) and Richard Wagner (d. 1883). In the novel *The Sorrows of Young Werther* Goethe recognized in the younger generation of his time an attitude of *Weltschmerz,* or satiety with life, brought on, he felt, by the suppression of individuality, the requirement that all forms of thought be useful and practical, and the general restraint that eighteenth-century society imposed upon youthful enthusiasm. The problem, as Goethe saw it, was youth's lack of any object in which to have faith. The RATIONALISM of the age had seemingly explained away all aspects of religion that could not be supported by logic, and with them much of the emotional and intuitive satisfaction of Christianity. Goethe's hero Werther turned to affairs of the heart for the spiritual satisfaction that had been denied him in rationalistic religion. His combination of physical attraction with spiritual love stood in marked contrast to the established attitudes of the time, which placed physical attraction in the category of frivolity. The adherents of this movement let their emotions run hard, as did Goethe in *Werther,* which was later satirized by Thackeray in *The Yellowplush Papers* (1838).

REFERENCES: Goethe's Letters to Herder in Thomas Mann, ed., *The Permanent Goethe;* Roy Pascal, *Storm and Stress;* Stanley Vogel, *German Literary Influences on American Transcendentalists.*

style   **1.** Graphic mechanics as described in the "style book" of a newspaper, printing press, or publisher; the *MLA Style Sheet* of the Modern Language Association and *The Chicago Manual of Style* of the University of Chicago Press are pre-eminent examples. Certain periodicals, such as the Kansas City *Star* and *The New Yorker* magazine, have from time to time issued style sheets for the private use of their staff members. The style sheet of the Kansas City *Star,* for example, is reputed to have nurtured Hemingway on succinct sentences, active verbs, and economy of vocabulary. (See Charles Fenton, *The Apprenticeship of Ernest Hemingway.*)

2. A subjective label for "literary elegance" or the lack of it. "Style is the man himself," said the French naturalist and critic Buffon (1707–88). "I am not satisfied to let it go with the aphorism that style is the man," said Robert Frost. "Rather, his style is the way he carries himself toward his ideas and deeds.... It is the mind skating circles round itself as it moves forward" ("Letter to Louis Untermeyer" in Lawrance Thompson, ed., *Selected Letters of Robert Frost,* p. 299). William Golding, author of *Lord of the Flies,* said at the NCTE Conference in San Francisco in 1963 that style is the end result of "pristine clarity" and cited as examples the closing sentences of Richardson's *Clarissa.* Many NEW CRITICS—among them Allen Tate and Robert Penn Warren—refer again and again to the French novelist Flaubert as a master stylist insofar as narrative RENDERING is concerned.

3. An attempt at objective analysis of style has been made by John Carroll, among others, in order to "program" computers and accommodate other devices of "quantifying." Among the measurements Carroll has proposed (in Sebeok, cited below) are the following:

number of paragraphs	number of verbs
number of sentences	number of transitives
sentence length(s)	number of intransitives
clause complexity	number of actives
number of noun clauses	number of passives
number of adjective clauses	number of copulatives
number of adverbial clauses	mean tense
number of parenthetical phrases	entropy of tense
number of appositives	number of proper nouns
number of phrases	number of common nouns
number of words to a sentence	number of determiners
number of words to a phrase	number of definite articles
number of words to a clause	number of indefinites
number of syllables in word(s)	number of pronouns
number of words with Latin affixes	number of personal pronouns
number of verbal modifiers	number of impersonals
number of attributive adjectives	number of prepositions
number of complements	number of numbers

Carroll then lists some "subjective" measures of style, which he hopes can ultimately be either "quantified" or else described operationally enough to be useful to stylistic analysis:

meaningful—meaningless	personal—impersonal
precise—vague; clear—hazy	masculine—feminine
profound—superficial (trivial)	varied—monotonous
subtle—obvious	complex—simple
concrete—abstract	rational—emotional
succinct—wordy	vivid—pale
graceful—awkward	ordered—chaotic
vigorous—flaccid	opinionated—impartial
lush—austere	original—trite
earnest—flippant	pleasant—unpleasant
intimate—remote	good—evil
elegant—uncouth	strong—weak
natural—affected	interesting—boring

REFERENCES: Richard Bridgman, *The Colloquial Style in America;* Monroe Beardsley, "Style: Semantic and Phonetic," *Aesthetics;* Thomas Sebeok, ed., *Style in Language;* Northrop Frye, "Manual of Style," *The Well-Tempered Critic;* F. L. Lucas, "What Is Style?" in Barnet Kottler and Martin Light, eds., *The World of Words;* Paul C. Wermuth, ed., *Modern Essays on Writing and Style;* Arthur Eastman, ed., "An Album of Styles," *The Norton Reader;* Glen Love and Michael Payne, eds., *Contemporary Essays on Style;* Anna Balakian, "Style and the New Economy," in H. Mitgang, ed., *American at Random;* Carl Klaus, *Style in English Prose;* Donald Hall, ed., *The Modern Stylists;* W. F. Irmscher, *Ways of Writing;* Frederick Candelaria, *Perspectives on Style;* Raymond Queneau, *Exercises in Style;* John Knott and R. Parker, eds., *The Triumph of Style;* Gregory Cowan and Elisabeth McPherson, *Plain English, Please;* Charles Bazerman, "A Relationship between Reading and Writing . . ." *College English* (Feb., 1980); L. T. Miles, *Style and Stylistics, an Analytical Bibliography.*

subordination   The couching of less important ideas in less important structures of language. Subordination is a device both for EMPHASIS and ECONOMY, helping to push secondary matters into the background and to reduce wordage. In terms of sentence structure, *subordinate* contrasts with *independent; what* ever is put into a structure other than an independent clause is *subordinated*. In order of importance, the subordinating structures are (1) subordinate clause, (2) absolute phrase, (3) phrase, (4) word, (5) segmental morpheme.

To illustrate: in the context "The little duck that belonged to the girl had no mother, and it died," one of the two clauses may be made subordinate: "Because the little duck that belonged to the girl had no mother, it died." Further, the adjective clause may be reduced to the possessive: "The *girl's* little duck." The phrase *little duck* may be reduced by the *-ling* morpheme for *little*: "The girl's *duckling*." The revision with its several subordinations: "Because the girl's duckling had no mother, it died."

Beyond the sentence structures, subordination may be achieved by placement of elements—the least important ideas being treated in less emphatic position. The end of a context is normally the most emphatic position, the beginning the next most emphatic, and the middle the least emphatic. What is to be subordinated, then, may well be placed in the middle of a sentence, of a paragraph, or of a larger work.

surrealism   Just as in the antirational paintings of Salvador Dali legs are apt to grow out of eyes or ears, fingers out of furniture, and so on, so in certain contemporary poetry and fiction there can be seen, from time to time, similarly incongruous IMAGES and scenes. Though hardly any writer creates these "automatically," as some critics have claimed, the writer may operate as a kind of medium to dreams, the subconscious, even to hallucinations (not necessarily induced by drugs). Such depth imagery (compare DEEP IMAGES) is not exactly unrealistic, since it does create an ILLUSION OF REALITY. But it is not conventionally realistic either. It has come to be called *sub*realistic or, more often, surrealistic, a term invented in 1917 by the French poet and painter Guillaume Apollinaire (1880–1918). The two best known surrealist poets are René Char of France and Pablo Neruda of Chile. There are also elements of surrealism in the fantasy-folklore-fiction of the British writer J. R. R. Tolkien; in Dylan Thomas's *Portrait of the Artist as a Young Dog* and *Adventures in the Skin Trade;* and in the Walpurgis night episode of James Joyce's *Ulysses.* The United States can claim several well-known surrealist poets, among them Kenneth Patchen, Michael McClure, and Kenneth Koch, as well as many poets who occasionally write surrealist poems. Nathaniel West's *Dream Life of Balso Snell* is an example of surrealist fiction, as are the stories of Kenneth Patchen. Surrealist elements are also present in Carson McCullers's short novel *Reflections in a Golden Eye,* and in Djuna Barnes's novel *Nightwood.*

REFERENCES: Roger Shattuck, "Guillaume Apollinaire," *The Banquet Years;* André Breton, *Manifestoes of Surrealism;* Herbert Gershman, *The Surrealist Revolution in France;* J. H. Matthews, *Surrealism and the Novel;* Ferdinand Alquie, *The Philosophy of Surrealism;* Pablo Neruda, *A New Decade: Poems 1958-1967* [translated by Ben Belitt and Alastair Reid]; Mary Ann Caws, *Surrealism and the Literary Imagination.*

sweeping generalization   An emotional assertion frequently unsubstantiated by, and contrary to, factual evidence, yet asserted as though a statement of fact: e.g., "Women drivers are the world's worst." (*Note*: Insurance statistics show that most reckless driving is done by males in their early twenties.) Such generalizations ("All Jews are...." "All Catholics are...." "All blacks are....") suffer from failure to discriminate among individuals. Sweeping generalizations are also known colloquially as *sweepers* and are usually derogatory, as contrasted with GLITTERING GENERALITIES.

REFERENCE: Lionel Ruby, "Are All Generalizations False?" *The Art of Making Sense.*

syllabication   Strictly, the dividing of words into syllables; here considered for its importance in the dividing of words between one line and the next in writing and printing. For printers the problem is momentous, since typesetters must *justify,* or space out, each line to a predetermined, uniform length, as is done in this book. For the writer in script or at the typewriter, the problem is less, for a ragged right margin may be used. Thus the writer may avoid the problem of dividing words altogether.

For compositors, who must meet the problem, and for writers who choose to do so, there are a number of rules that are of help. The fundamental rule is *divide between syllables.* What is or is not a syllable then becomes the critical problem. In American English, a syllable is determined by the pronunciation and not, as in England, by the etymology. Pronunciation, even without a dictionary, will usually provide a correct syllabication, but there need be no doubt if a good dictionary is consulted, for every dictionary of value indicates syllabication.

Knowledge of syllabication alone, however, will not be sufficient to determine whether a word *may* be divided in composition. A cardinal principle is that the initial component of the divided word should accurately reflect both the desired pronunciation and the expected sense; in short, the part left at the end of the line should suggest the whole word. For example, "I pro-duce this prod-uce" and "We pro-ject for this proj-ect." The rules given here are intended to be applied in conjunction with the use of a dictionary, and are mostly negative elaborations of the basic rule.

1. Never divide a one-syllable word: *touched, through, shipped, prism.*

2. Never divide a word of fewer than six letters, regardless of the number of syllables: *unity,* not *uni-ty; party,* not *par-ty; iota,* not *io-ta.*

3. Never leave a single-letter syllable on the first line: *usu-ally,* not *u-sually; imag-inary,* not *i-maginary.*

4. Never leave fewer than three letters on the second line: *pointed,* not *point-ed; mother,* not *moth-er; related,* not *relat-ed; em-panel,* not *empan-el; emer-gency,* not *emergen-cy.*

5. Never divide within a prefix or suffix; divide after the prefix or before the suffix: *over-optimistic,* not *overop-timistic; inter-act,* not *in-teract; super-natural,* not *su-pernatural; celes-tial,* not *celesti-al; reli-gious,* not *religi-ous.*

6. Never divide abbreviations or contractions: A.M., not A.-M.; *haven't,* not *have-n't; doesn't,* not *does-n't.*

7. Never divide month and day from year in dates.

8. Never divide proper names or separate initials from a surname.

9. Never divide the last words of more than two successive lines

10. Never divide the last word of a paragraph.

11. Divide words already containing a hyphen only after the hyphen; never insert a second hyphen in such words: *cross-section,* not *cross-sec-tion; tax supported,* not *tax-sup-ported.*

12. When a vowel alone forms a syllable, divide after the vowel: *credu-lous,* not *cred-ulous; exhila-rate,* not *exhil-arate.*

13. When a syllable has a silent vowel, do not leave that syllable standing alone: *prin-ciple,* not *princi-ple; chuckle,* not *chuc-kle; bristle,* not *bris-tle.*

14. Never divide a number of less than 10,000 and avoid dividing larger numbers; if the division is unavoidable, divide after a comma: 1,873,–974.

syllabus   A brief statement or listing of the main points to be covered in a course of study. Some syllabi include a list of books to be read and dates by which the student should have read them. The very idea of a syllabus has been rejected or resisted by the "bored school" of educationists. (See, for example, Neil Postman and Charles Weingartner, *Teaching as a Subversive Activity.*)

syllepsis   The use of a word to do double duty within an utterance so that it appears to shift its meaning unexpectedly. Syllepsis is ordinarily effective (in English, at least) only as humor. Some examples (with the shifty words in italics): "We *shot* one deer and lots of photographs"; "He writes *with* enthusiasm and red ink"; "Walter *ran for* the relay team and class prexy"; "She's *engaged* for the evening and to Charles." As the examples show, syllepsis is not the same thing as a pun, in which the word-play depends more upon sound than upon mere shifting of idiom or usage. Compare ZEUGMA.

syllogism   A formal argument chiefly in DEDUCTIVE REASONING, couched in rigid form and observing rules that ensure the validity of the conclusion. A typical syllogism consists of three statements, as follows:

   a) Major premise—e.g., All cows are females.
   b) Minor premise—e.g., Bessie is a cow.
   c) Conclusion—e.g., Bessie is a female.

In this article the following kinds of syllogism will be discussed: (1) *categorical,* (2) *conditional,* (3) *alternative,* and (4) *disjunctive.*

1. *The categorical syllogism* is so called because each of its statements is categorical, or absolute, with no *ifs* or other limitations. Understanding the principles of valid reasoning in the categorical syllogism requires a knowledge of the parts of the syllogism—their names, their aspects, and their functions.

   (a) Term: each of the things named in a syllogism. In the syllogism about Bessie the cow, the *terms* are *cows, females,* and *Bessie.* Every categorical syllogism has three terms: the *major term* (the term in the predicate of the conclusion), the *minor term* (the term in the subject of the conclusion), and the *middle term* (the term that appears in both premises but not in the conclusion).

(b) Class: each term refers to (or names) a group whose members share certain characteristics. *Cows* are a *class; females* are a *class; Bessie* is a *class*—this time a class with but one member, or "a class of one."

(c) Statement: a subject-predicate assertion; every syllogism contains three. Each *statement* contains two terms—one the *subject* of the statement, the other the *predicate-complement* of the statement. The two terms are linked by a verb—usually a state-of-being verb like *is* or *are*. When some other verb appears, the statement usually can be translated into an *is* or *are* statement; for example, if we assert that "All cows give milk," we must understand that *milk* is not a term in the statement, but *milk-giving animals* is the correct term, and we translate the statement as, "All cows *are* milk-giving animals." Statements in the syllogism do not imply equality. "All cows are females" does not assert that cows *equal* females; it asserts, rather, that the class called cows is *included* in the class called females. Syllogistic statements *include* or *exclude;* they do not equate.

(d) Premises: the first two statements in a syllogism, the major premise containing the major term the minor premise containing the minor term.

(e) Conclusion: the final statement in a syllogism. It draws an inference based upon the two premises—and, when valid, justified by them.

(f) Four forms of statement. To understand how statements work in the categorical syllogism, we must consider two special aspects—*quality* and *quantity.*

In the context of deductive logic, *quality* concerns whether a statement is affirmative or negative. The statement "Bessie is a cow" is *affirmative;* it *affirms* that Bessie is a cow. The statement "No cats are cows" is *negative;* it *denies* that cats are cows.

In the context of deductive logic, *quantity* concerns whether a statement is universal or particular. The statement "All cows are females" is *universal;* it refers to *all* of its subject class—*all* cows. The statement "Some birds are robins" is *particular;* it refers to only part of its subject class—*some* birds.

These aspects make possible *four forms of statement,* designated by the symbols as A, E, I, O:

"A" form: the universal-affirmative (*All X is Y*)
"E" form: the universal-negative (*No X is Y*)
"I" form: the particular-affirmative (*Some X is Y*)
"O" form: the particular-negative (*Some X is not Y*)

These four forms of statement may be combined in several patterns to produce a syllogism—as long as their combination does not produce any violation of the rules of validity.

(g) Distribution: the *all* or *some* aspect of a term. Terms refer to classes of things; but when a term appears in a statement, it may refer to *all* members of a class or only to *some* members of the class. A term that refers to *all* members of its class is a *distributed* term; a term that refers only to *some* members of its class is an *undistributed* term. It is helpful to know the pattern of distribution of terms in the four forms of categorical statement:

Forms of Categorical Statement
in Deductive Syllogisms

Statement		Distribution	
		Subject	Predicate
"A" form:		D	U
"E" form		D	D
"I" form		U	U
"O" form		U	D

Reference to the diagrams will show that a term whose circle is entirely shaded or entirely unshaded is a *distributed* term; a term whose circle is *partly* shaded is an *undistributed* term.

In the statement "All cows are females" we are discussing *all* cows; *cows* is a *distributed* term. But we are not discussing all females—only a few of them, the females that are also cows; therefore, *females* is an *undistributed* term. A few moments of study with the diagrams as aid will clarify the matter of distribution of terms.

   (h) Fallacy: an error in the form or process of a syllogism. The most common fallacies in the categorical syllogism are these:

   (1) *Undistributed middle.* The middle term in a categorical syllogism must be distributed *once*—and only once. Consider:

   All *x* is *y*.
   All *z* is *y*.
   Therefore ... ?

No valid conclusion is possible, since the middle term, y, is undistributed in both of its appearances: It never refers to *all* members of its class. Also consider:

> All p is q.
> No r is p.
> Therefore ... ?

Again, no valid conclusion is possible, since the middle term, p, is distributed both times it appears.

(2) *Four terms.* Every syllogism must have *three* terms, and *only* three. Consider:

> All c is d.
> All e is f.
> Therefore ... ?

No conclusion is possible, since the minor premise is entirely irrelevant to the major premise.

(3) *Two particulars.* Every syllogism must have at least one *universal* premise. Consider these:

> Some Americans are men.
> Some girls are Americans.
> Therefore ... ?

It is invalid to conclude that some girls are men, since girls may be among the Americans not mentioned in the first premise. Neither premise is a *universal* statement.

(4) *Two negatives.* Every syllogism must have at least one *affirmative* premise. Consider these:

> No mothers are men.
> Some grandparents are not men.
> Therefore ... ?

It would be invalid to conclude any relationship between grandparents and mothers. Neither premise is an *affirmative* statement.

(5) *Particular switched to universal.* If either premise is a particular, the conclusion must also be a particular. Consider:

> All natives are citizens at birth.
> Some natives are of foreign parentage.
> Therefore, all who have foreign parentage are citizens at birth.

The conclusion is invalid, for it is an *all* statement when one of the premises was a *some* statement.

(6) *Negative switched to affirmative.* If either premise is negative, the conclusion must also be negative. Consider:

> No voters are aliens.
> Some citizens are voters.
> Therefore, some citizens are aliens.

The conclusion is invalid, for it is affirmative although one of the premises was negative. The conclusion becomes valid if we convert it to negative: "Some citizens are *not* aliens."

(7) *Undistributed switched to distributed.* Any term that is undistributed in a premise must also be undistributed if it appears in the conclusion. Consider:

Some Texans are Democrats.
No Democrats are Republicans.
Therefore, some Republicans are not Texans.

The conclusion is invalid, for the term *Texans* is distributed in the conclusion although it was undistributed in the major premise. The conclusion becomes valid if we convert it to "some Texans are not Republicans," leaving the term *Texans* in undistributed form.

(i) *Enthymeme*: an elliptical syllogism. A valid conclusion may be drawn although not all the stages of syllogistic reasoning have been made explicit. Consider:

All lazy students are underproducers;
Therefore, Tim is an underproducer.

The argument has moved directly from a major premise to a conclusion, omitting the minor premise, "Tim is a lazy student."

(j) *Sorites*: a series of interlaced syllogisms in which the conclusion of one syllogism becomes a premise of another, so that the chain leads to a conclusion connecting the subject of the first statement to the predicate of the last.

2. The *conditional syllogism* is so called because its initial premise is introduced by an "if" clause—a conditional clause. This "if" clause (called the *antecedent*) is followed by a "then" clause (called the consequent):

If he goes to the game, then he cannot study.
    (*antecedent*)   (*consequent*)

Conditional arguments depend for their validity upon the proper application of a second premise, which must be in one of two modes:

(a) *affirming the antecedent (modus ponens)*, in which the second premise affirms that the "if" clause, the condition, is true: "He goes to the game";

(b) *denying the consequent (modus tollens)*, in which the second premise denies that the "then" clause is true: "He can study."

Either of these forms will produce a valid conclusion:

If he goes to the game, then he cannot study.
He goes to the game (*modus ponens*).
Therefore, he cannot study.

If he goes to the game, then he cannot study.
He can study (*modus tollens*).
Therefore, he does not go to the game.

Fallacies of the conditional syllogism occur when either of these modes is violated. The fallacies are *affirming the consequent* and *denying the antecedent*. For example, a second premise saying "He cannot study" would not permit a conclusion that "he does not go to the game"—because it is possible that he cannot study, *for other reasons.* And a second premise saying "He does not go to the game" would not permit a conclusion that "he can study"—because the initial premise did not say anything about what might happen if he does not go to the game. See also REDUCTIO AD ABSURDUM.

3. *The alternative syllogism* offers in its major premise an alternative in the "either-or" form: "Either we eat, or we starve." One of the alternatives *must* be true; therefore, if we show that one of them is false, we prove that the other is true. A valid argument reads:

Either we eat, or we starve.
We do not starve.
Therefore, we eat

The major premise is an alternative (*either-or*) statement. The minor premise and the conclusion are both categorical statements, the minor premise *denying* one of the alternatives and the conclusion *affirming* the other. If the minor premise *affirms* an alternative ("we eat"), a fallacy appears:

Either we eat, or we starve.
We eat.
Therefore, we do not starve.

Odd as it may seem in the given context, the conclusion is not valid, for there is nothing in the premises to assure us that we cannot eat and *also* starve. The second premise commits the fallacy of *affirming an alternative*.

4. *The disjunctive syllogism* has a major premise in the "not both ... and ..." form: "Men are *not both* dishonest *and* happy." One of the two conditions *must* be false; therefore, if we show that one of them is true, we show that the other must be false. A valid argument reads:

We cannot both eat our cake and have it;
We have eaten our cake;
Therefore, we cannot have it.

The major premise is disjunctive; the minor premise and the conclusion are both categorical—the minor premise *affirming* one of the two disjunctive conditions. If the minor premise denies one of those conditions, the argument commits the fallacy of *denying a disjunctive*.

REFERENCES: John Sherwood, *Discourse of Reason: A Brief Handbook of Logic and Semantics;* Morris Raphael Cohen, *Introduction to Logic.*

symbol   **1.** In general, and loosely, a synonym for *sign;* e.g., the dollar sign ($), a proofreader's mark (#), a musical notation (⌒), a mathematical notation (+), and the like, usually translatable with a single meaning.

2. In SEMANTICS, which defines language as symbolic process, any word at all (e.g., *furniture*) is symbolic in the sense that it is only more or less representative of, and has been abstracted from, a comparatively more concrete object or REFERENT (e.g., *table* or *chair*) and hence cannot be the object itself, but only a symbol of it.

3. In RHETORIC and in some literature, a symbol shares the characteristics of definitions 1 and 2 above, but in addition carries a *conventional* or broadly accepted and understood representation, especially in PROVERB and CLICHÉ. For example, in the expression "The pen is mightier than the sword," the sword has conventionally symbolized or stood for war or violence; the pen, peace or conciliation or arbitration and the like. Similarly, in the expression "Every man has his cross to bear," cross by ALLUSION as well as by convention symbolizes painful burden or misery or misfortune and the like. Well-known rhetorical and literary symbols with conventional representations include the *cellar* (of bottomness), the *woods* (of inextricability; but compare its non-conventional representations in a poem like Frost's "Stopping by Woods"), the *cornucopia* (of plenty), the *tower* (of strength), the *wheel* (of fortune), the *spiral* (of gradations, as in Dante, Yeats, and Eliot), and the *mountain* (as an object of conquest; but compare the nuances of even that kind of mountain in Dante's *Divine Comedy,* Mann's *Magic Mountain,* and Hemingway's "Snows of Kilimanjaro").

4. In literature and literary criticism, an *unconventional* symbol is any object or image capable of representing several different ideas or experiences, even within one context, and often with diametrically different emotional values and impacts for different characters and readers. For example, the Christian cross may represent the hope of salvation or the power of the church for characters wearing that symbol, whereas the same symbol may represent oppression to the victims in a poem, drama, or narrative about a pogrom or inquisition, to say nothing of a crucifixion. (For the victim of a crucifixion the cross can ambivalently represent oppression *and* salvation.) In short, an unconventional literary symbol is "an object or image outside ourselves, which represents something inside ourselves," as Erich Fromm observes; it generates a variety of sensory and emotional responses. One of the memorable examples of an unconventional symbol in literature is the white whale in Melville's *Moby-Dick.* The reader may well remember the variety of emotional responses and associations that this whale elicits, not only as whale, but also as symbol to Captain Ahab, as distinguished from its meanings for other members of the crew. There is of course the danger of "reading in" more symbolic meanings than an author may have intended. There is also the misguided practice of jumping so far ahead to find symbolic representations as to leap-frog over very important literal representations; for example, in *Moby-Dick,* the whale is a whale and the rope is a guideline or instrument of safety, as Terence Martin has observed.

REFERENCES: Erich Fromm, "The Nature of Symbolic Language," in Richard W. Lid, ed., *Grooving the Symbol, A Contemporary Reader;* Maurice Beebe, ed., *Literary Symbolism;* J. E. Cirlot, *A Dictionary of Symbols;* Monroe Beardsley, "Representation and Abstraction," *Aesthetics;* Kenneth Burke, "Symbolic Action," *The Philosophy of Literary Form;* R. Z. Temple, *The Critic's Alchemy;* Mary McCarthy, "Settling the Colonel's Hash," in R. E. Knoll, ed., *Contrasts;* Terence Martin, *The Instructed Vision;* Barbara Seward, *The Symbolic Rose.*

symbolism   A literary movement that developed first in France in the 1800s and that extended the revolt of ROMANTICISM against REALISM. Such French *symbolistes* as Baudelaire, Rimbaud, Mallarmé, and Verlaine—and, later, such English symbolists as Yeats, Joyce, and Eliot—made poetry "even more a matter of the senses than did the Romanticists," said Edmund Wilson in the "symbolism" chapter of *Axel's Castle.* But sensory experience and the use of imagery are not, of course, the special preserve of symbolist poets. (Almost all poets suggest more than they say directly, and almost all of them appeal to the emotions through IMAGES and SYMBOLS.) What does come closer to pinpointing the symbolist vision, the special symbolist use of imagery and sensory experience, is perhaps best understood in Yeats's discussion of "Dove or Swan" in *A Vision* (Book 5) and in Baudelaire's *Flowers of Evil,* especially in the poem "Correspondences": "Nature is a temple from whose living columns / Commingling voices emerge at times; / Here man wanders through forests of symbols / Which seem to observe him with familiar eyes / ... Colors, scents, and sounds correspond. / There are fragrances fresh as the flesh of children, / .. Possessing the pervasiveness of everlasting things / ... Which the raptures of the senses and the spirit sing." [Translated by Kate Flores, *The Anchor Anthology of French Poetry,* Doubleday, 1958.] For the symbolists another world—either imagined (as by Baudelaire) or constructed (as by Yeats)—exists beyond the world ordinarily visible. And the symbolist poet tries to make that world known by means of images and image-clusters that stand for, that translate, that world. The early symbolist movement was carried on by the French poets Corbière and Laforgue (who in turn influenced T. S. Eliot), by the playwright Maurice Maeterlinck, by the composer Debussy, by the critic Remy de Gourmont, and by such writers as Marcel Proust, James Joyce, and Gertrude Stein. Compare IMAGIST, OBJECTIVE CORRELATIVE.

REFERENCES: Angel Flores, ed., *The Anchor Anthology of French Poetry from Nerval to Valéry;* W. B. Yeats, "The Symbolism of Poetry," *Essays and Introductions;* René Wellek and Austin Warren, "Image, Metaphor, Symbol, Myth," *The Theory of Literature;* Enid Starkie, *Baudelaire and Arthur Rimbaud;* C. M. Bowra, *The Heritage of Symbolism;* Arthur Symons, *The Symbolist Movement in Literature;* Nicholas Perella, *The Kiss Sacred and Profane;* Bernice Slote, ed., *Myth and Symbol;* Jerome Christensen, "The Symbol's Errant Allegory: Coleridge and His Critics," *E*[nglish] *L*[iterary] *H*[istory] (Winter, 1978–79).

symbolists, symbolistes   See SYMBOLISM.

syncope   The compression of a word by the dropping of a letter, sound, or syllable from the middle: "ne'er" for "never," "gen'ral" for "general," "e'er" for "ever." See CLIPPED FORM, POETICISM.

synecdoche   See METONYMY.

synesthesia   In IMAGERY, the use of one sense to convey the experience of another sense; for example, the image "coolness of blue" contains a transfer appeal between the senses of sight and touch. Compare also "piercing yellow," "loud necktie," "salty music."

synopsis   A brief and general overview of a long literary work, usually of a novel. Compare PRÉCIS.

synthesis   See DIALECTIC 3.

T

table of contents   A list (or main topic outline) of the sections or chapters of a book, with the numbers of the pages on which these begin.

tale   **1.** Loosely, a synonym for narrative or story. **2.** Strictly, a folk form, especially the *tall tale,* such as those narrating the exploits of Paul Bunyan, Johnny Appleseed, Pecos Bill, John Henry, and so on.

REFERENCES: Martha Pappas, ed., *Heroes of the American West;* Milton Rugoff, ed., *A Harvest of World Folk Tales;* Stith Thompson, ed., *One Hundred Favorite Folk Tales.* See also the references under FOLKLORE.

tanka   A classic Japanese verse form in five unrhymed lines of, respectively, five, seven, five, seven, and seven syllables. Like the HAIKU, the tanka is characterized by a tight unity of mood, event, and imagery. The chief difference between the two, aside from form, is that the tanka usually builds on an event that would be too difficult to encompass in the three-line haiku. Another difference is that a season is less likely to be established in the tanka. An example of a tanka by Saigo Hoshi:

> Now we know, alas,
> that when we said "Remember,"
> when we vowed as much,
> it was in "We must forget"
> our true hearts had their meeting.
> > Translated by Tadami Takenori

REFERENCE: Sanford Goldstein and Seishi Shimoda, trans., *Tangled Hair.*

tautological argument   See BEGGING THE QUESTION 3.

tautology   **1.** Unnecessary repetition: "bibliography of books," "vocabulary words." See DEADWOOD. **2.** In LOGIC, a statement necessarily valid by its logical structure alone: "Either it is snowing or it is not snowing."

technique   **1.** Loosely, a synonym for STYLE. **2.** In general, an artist's working method—in fiction, drama, poetry, and the other arts—which is at the same time a kind of control. One of Vladimir Nabokov's techniques in *Lolita* is the "diary first-person." In Joyce's *Ulysses* the symbolic journey is one of the chief techniques. **3.** In particular, one such device that may not be chief but only incidental, as is the STREAM-OF-CONSCIOUSNESS technique in *Ulysses.* Similarly, in the play *Strange Interlude,* O'Neill uses the technique of the above-the-stage voice to represent a character's thinking.

According to Mark Schorer, techniques—or a given one—may well become the discipline that leads writers to discover what they have to say. As Marshall

McLuhan has put it, what the artist has to say is largely the way it is said ("the medium is the message").

REFERENCES: Mark Schorer, "Technique as Discovery," *The Hudson Review* (Spring, 1948); Marshall McLuhan, *Understanding Media;* Allen Tate, "Techniques of Fiction," in B. S. Oldsey and A. O. Lewis, Jr., eds. *Visions and Revisions;* X. J. Kennedy, "Fenced-in Fields," *Counter Measures* #1.

tenor   See METAPHOR.

tension   1. In ARGUMENTATION, the force gravitating between an argument and its rebuttal; a proposition and its opposite; a THESIS and its ANTITHESIS (see DIALECTIC). 2. In a literary work, the emotional atmosphere, now serious, now comic, generated by two dynamic opposing forces, meanings, or values—much like counterpoint in music. Examples: the literal vs. the symbolic; a character vs. a FOIL; a plot and its subplot; a GENRE vs. its PARODY; strophe and antistrophe (see ODE); MASQUE and antimasque; HYPERBOLE vs. UNDERSTATEMENT; rhetoric vs. silence; CONSONANCE vs. DISSONANCE; the DONNÉE and the implied; the fact vs. the METAPHOR; form and content. Each force by itself is only a kind of cloud until it clashes with its opposite—to make lightning. Compare ANTINOMIES.

REFERENCES: Allen Tate, "Tension in Poetry," *Essays of Four Decades;* Peter Viereck, *Dream and Responsibility;* Claudia Johnson, *The Productive Tension of Hawthorne's Art.*

term   See SYLLOGISM 1*a.*

term paper   See RESEARCH PAPER.

terza rima   The iambic pentameter, three-lined stanza of Dante's *Divine Comedy,* with the "chain riming" *aba, bcb, cdc,* etc. According to John Ciardi, Dante managed to preserve in the terza rima the flavor of the spoken language. Terza rima was introduced into English by Thomas Wyatt (sixteenth century). It was used by Shelley in "Ode to the West Wind," from which we quote the first two stanzas (*aba, bcb*):

> O wild West Wind, thou breath of Autumn's being,
> Thou, from whose unseen presence the leaves dead
> Are driven, like ghosts from an enchanter fleeing.
>
> Yellow, and black, and pale, and hectic red,
> Pestilence-stricken multitudes: O thou,
> Who chariotest to their dark wintry bed ...

Terza rima has been used by Milton, Byron, Browning, Eliot, MacLeish, and Auden.

testimonial   The argument that, because a well-known person praises, uses, or advocates a thing or idea, the thing or idea must be worthy. The sceptical consumer will ask, "Is the person who is making the testimonial an expert in this particular field?" See PROPAGANDA DEVICES.

tetrameter   See METER.

text   1. The actual written or printed form of a literary work, as established by text experts. 2. In the view of some critics, the literary work before it is experienced by a reader. See LEVELS OF MEANING.

REFERENCE: Andrew Ettin, "Teaching the Textual," *College English* (February, 1980).

texture   1. In RHETORIC, the "transformational density" of an utterance; that is, the measure of succinct modifiers that have been embedded in it and of the specifiers that have been added. For example, in a rich-textured sentence like "Ulysses sailed the wine-dark sea," there is embedded the modifier "wine-dark," which derives consciously or intuitively from some such utterance as "the sea was wine-dark." (That last utterance was reduced to its essence, "wine-dark," and was then embedded as a modifier in the sentence "Ulysses sailed the sea.") As an example of add-ons—especially of absolute phrases (noun-participle, noun-adjective, and so on)—the texture of the sentence "Ulysses sailed the wine-dark sea" may be enriched by such end-phrases as "the men working the oars, the water washing from the wood," one phrase riding piggyback on its predecessor. Although nineteenth- and twentieth-century critics disparaged the Latinate absolute phrase (which almost always occurred at the beginning rather than at the end of a main clause), they seem to have had a blind spot about the position of word groups. Except for a generalization like "the best words in their best order" (Coleridge), these critics' observations on style, especially on texture, are now eclipsed by the observations and insights of contemporary rhetoricians and linguists. The texture-enriching absolute phrase is used extensively by the most celebrated writers, as Francis Christensen has shown—especially by Conrad, Joyce, Faulkner, and Hemingway. These writers have preferred to use it as a terminal add-on, however, rather than as a front-door sentry. (The "sentry participle" was disparaged by Fowler even if it did not dangle. See "participles" in Fowler's *Modern English Usage*.) Using the absolute phrase add-on gives an utterance a cumulative texture similar to that of the LOOSE SENTENCE. See RENDERING.

2. In literature, the depth or richness of a literary piece (as measured by its LEVELS OF MEANING) as opposed to nontexture or flimsiness. A flimsy piece tends to have only one meaning—the literal or surface meaning—and tends to communicate prosaically. A sentimental poem like Emily Dickinson's "If I can stop one heart from breaking," for example, noble as its sentiment may be, is said to have a thin texture because its meaning is communicated directly from the surface and because it has no deeper layers of meaning. In contrast, the same poet's "I Heard a Fly Buzz When I Died" can be said to have a rich texture because much of its meaning is signaled indirectly and beneath what is given literally. (Of course, all literary pieces have to start with some "given," as Henry James observes in "The Art of Fiction.") Similar contrasts are evident between such fiction as Conrad's "Youth" (thin-textured) and *The Heart of Darkness* (rich-textured); between Melville's "Bartleby" (thin-textured) and *Benito Cereno* (rich-textured).

REFERENCES: Francis Christensen, *Notes toward a New Rhetoric;* Laurence Perrine, "Bad Poetry," *Sound and Sense;* Wyndham Lewis and Charles Lee, *The Stuffed Owl;* Henry James, "The Art of Fiction," in James Miller, ed., *Myth and Method;* Owen Thomas, *The Very Press of Imagery* [Texture in Dickinson's poetry]; John Crowe Ransom, *The World's Body.*

Theater of the Absurd   The drama of Samuel Beckett, Eugene Ionesco, Edward Albee, Jack Gelber, Harold Pinter, Jean Genêt, Bertolt Brecht, and other contemporary playwrights, whose attempts to show the absurdities, inconsistencies, and bewildering complexities of twentieth-century life have resulted in extravagant symbolical plays. These defy traditional stage conventions of time, place, plot, and characterization; hence, they are occasionally termed *anti-plays*. The attempt to show human beings as irrational, solitary, and incapable of understanding their condition often divorces the stage action from any context of conventional reality. The dialogue—often absurd and full of CLICHÉS and gibberish—frequently contradicts the action. The very title of Arthur Kopit's *Oh Dad, Poor Dad, Mama's Hung You in the Closet and I'm Feeling So Sad* is representative of the Absurdist language. The characters often lack individuality and consistency, no doubt intentionally so. Midway in Beckett's *Waiting for Godot,* the master and the slave suddenly reverse their roles. (Beckett is, of course, trying to tell us something here.) The laws of nature are disregarded, denied existence, or are even satirized. In Ionesco's *Amédée* a corpse offstage suddenly enlarges until a mammoth foot crashes through the door onto the stage—suggesting, perhaps, that academic circles pay too much attention to the dead, and not enough to the living. The characters in Arthur Adamov's *Ping-Pong* argue the economics and aesthetics of pinball machines with almost religious fervor. The themes of these plays often seem senseless to all but the most confirmed secular EXISTENTIALISTS. In terms of conventional dramatic structure, the anti-play has no beginning or end—no rising action, CLIMAX, or DÉNOUEMENT (see DRAMATIC STRUCTURE). The audience is kept in suspense, not by the progressive unraveling of a problem to its final solution, as in traditional drama, but rather by successive, apparently random, clues as to the "meaning" of the play—the meaning almost always left open-ended. See IMMEDIATE THEATER.

REFERENCES: Martin Esslin, *Theatre of the Absurd;* Jan Kott, *Theatre Notebook: 1947–1967;* George Kernodle, *Introduction to the Theater;* Karen Stein, "Metaphysical Silence in Absurd Drama," *Modern Drama* (Feb., 1971); C. J. Gianakaris, "Absurdism Altered," *Drama Survey* (Winter, 1968–1969); A. P. Hinchcliffe, *The Absurd.*

theme   1. A unifying idea, MOTIF, or archetypal experience in a literary work—for example, the theme of alienation, of "the biter bitten," of the lady killer; the latter, also known as the Don Juan theme, is central to such works as Byron's *Don Juan,* Shaw's *Man and Superman,* Shadwell's *The Libertine,* Molière's *The Stone Banquet,* Browning's *Fifine at the Fair,* not to mention many other works by Hesse, Kierkegaard, Hoffman, Espronceda, Tellez, and Zorrilla. 2. The unifying statement, expressed or implied, in a literary work—for example, "In this grisly world a person has to look out for himself" (K. A. Porter's "Theft"); in that sense, theme being synonymous with "philosophic statement." 3. Loosely, an essay or composition.

REFERENCES: Palmer Bovie, "The Amphitryon Theme from Plautus to Pinter," *Minn. Review* (Fall, 1967); Michael Allen, "The Chase ... a Renaissance Theme," *Comparative Literature* (Fall, 1968); Ruth Todasco, "Theme and Imagery in *The Golden Bowl,*" *Texas Studies* (Summer, 1962); Evon Nossen, "The Beast-Man Theme . . . Steinbeck," *Ball State Forum* (Spring, 1966); Ora Williams, "Theme of Endurance in *As I Lay Dying,*" *La. Studies* (Summer, 1970); Elizabeth McKensie, "Above All Shadows Rides the Sun," *Tolkien Journal* (Winter, 1970); Barbara Lecker, ". . . . Theme of Fancy in *Dombey & Son*," *Dickensian* (Jan., 1971); Robert Baylor and B. Stokes, eds., *Fine Frenzy: Enduring Themes in Poetry*.

Theophrastan characters   Character sketches of conventional types of people in conventional walks of life, broadly generalized if not stereotyped: "The Scolemaster," "the milkmaid," "The Scrivener," the bore, the flatterer, etc. Best-known collections: Joseph Hall, *Characters of Vertues and Vices* (1608) and Thomas Overbury, *A Wife and Twenty-one Other Characters* (1614). The name "Theophrastan" was adopted in recognition of the third-century B.C. character-sketch writer Theophrastus. Aside from influencing Washington Irving (compare "The Morose Scolemaster" and "Ichabod Crane"), these sketches are often cited as contributing to the early development of English prose fiction.

REFERENCES: C. N. Greenough, *A Bibliography of the Theophrastan Character in English;* P. A. Smith, *Our English Seneca;* Wilbur Cross, *History of the English Novel;* "Prose Forms: Characters," in Arthur Eastman *et al.*, eds., *The Norton Reader;* Warren Anderson, *The Characters of Theophrastus*.

thesis   **1.** A formal paper, *term paper,* or RESEARCH PAPER for an academic degree (Bachelor of Arts, Master of Arts, etc.); also a "dissertation," the synonym usually preferred for the Ph.D. opus. **2.** An idea or statement-of-opinion, usually with an argumentative edge or an original interpretation, which the writer or speaker proposes to develop or defend. See DIALECTIC 4.

REFERENCES: Monroe Beardsley, "Interpretation of Literature," *Aesthetics;* Sheridan Baker, "Thesis," *The Practical Stylist;* Edgar Roberts, *Writing Themes about Literature;* William J. Brandt *et al.*, *The Craft of Writing*.

thesis question   A question like "How do we know this?" or "In what ways?" or "What *are* these?" A question one puts to a THESIS STATEMENT to elicit answers. The answers thus elicited serve as main heads in an OUTLINE and main points in an article or expository essay.

REFERENCE: Harry H. Crosby and George Estey, "The Controlling Concept," *The Rhetorical Imperative*.

thesis statement   The statement of the major idea in an article or expository essay; it answers the question, "What do I want to say here—mainly?" or "What is the central point of this essay—what does it add up to?" An interpretive essay related to a study of *Macbeth,* for example, may yield a thesis statement like the following: "Lady Macbeth functions less as a believable woman than as Macbeth's own evil other self." Characteristics of viable thesis statements: (1) They are statements, not topics or questions. (2) They are statements of opinion rather than of fact—they do not rehash what is already given (DONNÉE) in the primary work being interpreted. Thus, if the statement goes something like this: "Lady Macbeth keeps egging Macbeth on," it is too factual—too close to what is given in the play—to qualify as a statement of opinion, even if later this statement of fact may be quite usable as a supporting point. (3) They go out on a limb of commitment. (4) They can be supported by details in the primary text. See THESIS QUESTION.

REFERENCES: Sheridan Baker, *The Practical Stylist;* W. J. Brandt *et al., The Craft of Writing;* Gary Tate and E. P. J. Corbett, eds., *Teaching High School Composition;* Edgar Roberts, *Writing Themes about Literature;* Alan Casty and D. J. Tighe, *Staircase to Writing and Reading;* Richard Dodge and George Wykoff, *Handbook of College Composition;* Bernard Cohen, *Writing about Literature.*

three-decker   Three-volume novel. See PART PUBLICATION.

tightening   See ECONOMY IN WRITING.

title   The name given to a specific piece of writing. Since the title is ordinarily what a reader sees first, it ideally performs one or more of the following functions: (1) attracts attention, (2) establishes the topic, (3) hints at the THEME, (4) predicts MODE and TONE, (5) serves as a memorable name for the work.

Some writers fail to distinguish between a title and a *label:* "My Vacation" or "Food Preparation," for example, will not do; the one is too vague, the other too general, and both are too trite. The vacation piece might be titled, "Where the Bears Are," and as for food preparation a title such as "How to Cook an Armadillo" would at least attract some attention. Literary titles are often ALLUSIONS: *For Whom the Bell Tolls, Gone With the Wind, That Evening Sun.*

Titles referred to in RESEARCH PAPERS have special typographical requirements. Titles of major works (books, plays, operas, magazines, newspapers, pamphlets, and movies) are printed in ITALICS, and indicated in a manuscript by UNDERLINING. Titles of shorter works (usually included within the major ones), such as articles, short stories, chapters, and poems, are in roman type and are enclosed within QUOTATION MARKS. See DOCUMENTATION and RESEARCH PAPER.

tone   1. A synonym for "tone of voice," or the attitude of the speaker or of the writer toward the material or audience. **2.** More strictly, the attitude of the author toward the material or subject—an attitude that will then determine the material's MODE (SATIRE, COMEDY, TRAGEDY, ROMANCE, etc.). **3.** Loosely, a synonym for *voice, mask,* or PERSONA—"the way the poet takes himself" (Robert Frost's definition). Tone is directly or indirectly tied to the author's purpose— to inform or instruct; to entertain, delight, or amuse; to convince or persuade; to inspire; etc. **4.** Tone in ESSAYS is largely linguistic and tied to usage. Essays can thus usually be distinguished as either "formal in tone" (expository essays); or "informal in tone" (imaginative, personal, familiar essays).

REFERENCES: Richard D. Altick, "Tone," *Preface to Critical Reading;* Laurence Perrine, "Tone," *Sound and Sense;* Walker Gibson, *Tough, Sweet, and Stuffy;* Edward M. White, ed., *The Writer's Control of Tone.*

topic outline   See OUTLINE.

topic sentence   See PARAGRAPH.

tough literature   A contemporary label for high-quality imaginatively rendered literature—mostly poetry, drama, and fiction; the opposite of "pop" or low-brow and of mass (or middle-brow) literature, which tend to be superficial and ephemeral. The word "tough" suggests in part its informal sense of "difficult" but even more so its formal sense of complexity, especially complexity of TEXTURE. Besides being rich in texture, tough literature tends to be multi-dimensional in one or another of such features as LEVELS OF MEANING, DRA-MATIC STRUCTURE, ARCHETYPES, SYMBOLISM, IRONY, PARADOX, PERSONA, or in a combination of these aspects. Nor does tough literature consist exclusively of the CLASSICS (literature that has survived the centuries); it includes many modern works (works less than a century old). Certain tough novels by such writers as Dostoevsky, Flaubert, Melville, Mark Twain, Henry James, Conrad, Joyce, Faulkner, and Hemingway, for example, have become the subjects of lifelong studies by scholars and of book-length EXPLICATIONS by critics. Contrast MASS LITERATURE.

REFERENCES: Leslie Fiedler, "The Discovery of High Culture," *The Art of the Essay;* Henry James, "The Art of Fiction" and Joseph Conrad, "Preface to *The Nigger of the Narcissus,"* in James Miller, ed., *Myth and Method;* John Ciardi, *How Does a Poem Mean?;* George Boas, *Vox Populi: Essays in the History of an Idea;* Walker Gibson, *Tough, Sweet, and Stuffy.*

tour de force   1. An ingenious, sometimes farfetched, feat by an author or artist. In this sense the term is derogatory. 2. A remarkable achievement unlikely to be equaled; for example Melville's *Moby Dick* or Laurence Durrell's *Alexandria Quartet.*

Tractarian movement   See OXFORD MOVEMENT.

tradition   See CONVENTION 3.

tragedy   1. A major MODE. 2. A drama in which the PROTAGONIST falls from happiness to misfortune as a result of a "hamartia" or TRAGIC FLAW. According to Aristotle, in *The Poetics,* the falling protagonist who elicits from the audience most pity and terror occupies from the beginning a high station of authority. But Aristotle's and his contemporaries' ethos was in this respect the opposite of that of today's audiences, who rather enjoy seeing the mighty fall and who identify more compassionately with the common folk, as for example, the protagonist in Arthur Miller's *Death of a Salesman.* Ancient Greek tragedy (ca. sixth century B.C.) whose religious origins are not fully known, reached its literary glory in the fifth century B.C. in the works of Aeschylus, Sophocles, and Euripides. *The Complete Greek Tragedies,* edited by David Grene and Richmond Lattimore, contains seven plays by Aeschylus (including the Oresteian trilogy of *Agamemnon, The Libation Bearers,* and *The Eumenides*); seven plays by Sophocles (including *Oedipus the King, Electra,* and *Antigone*); and nineteen plays by Euripides (including *Medea, Iphigenia in Taurus, Helen, The Trojan Women,* and *The Bacchae*). Many more Greek tragedies, among them some prize-winners in the annual competitions, are now lost to us; we know of them chiefly through references by historians. Greek tragedy was characterized by adherence to the UNITIES of time, place, and action; by tragic heroes who usually sacrificed themselves (e.g., Oedipus) to salvage posterity; by a CHORUS that made philosophic comments, sometimes serving as the playwright's mouthpiece; by a fatalistic VISION undergirding themes of retribution and the displeasure of the gods; above all, by formal and poetic language.

When compared with Greek tragedy, Roman tragedy seems second-rate—especially the blood-and-thunder tragedies of Seneca, even if they did follow the unities and certain other mechanics. In the Middle Ages tragedy practically disappeared except for elements in certain of the MIRACLE PLAYS (those concerned, for example, with the Passion of Christ).

Tragedy rose to prominence again during the English RENAISSANCE. The first English tragedy was *Gorboduc* (1562) by Sackville and Norton. During the reign of the Tudors such tragedies as those by Kyd (*The Spanish Tragedy*), by Marlowe (*The Jew of Malta*), and by Shakespeare (*Hamlet, Othello, King Lear, Macbeth*) carried forward some conventions of the Greek tragic hero (e.g., high station) and further developed certain distinctions between those who sacrificed themselves (Hamlet) and those who fought life forces and were overcome by them (Macbeth). But Elizabethan tragedy dared to depart from the classical unities and added COMIC RELIEF—an element that the ancient Greek playwrights would no doubt have considered incongruous in tragedy.

In the seventeenth century, classical tragedy was revived in France by the playwrights Corneille (d. 1684) and Racine (d. 1699). But during the Neoclassical seventeenth and eighteenth centuries in England such "heroic tragedies" as those by John Dryden (*All for Love*), Thomas Otway (*Venice Preserved*), and Joseph Addison (*Cato*) reflected only a slavishness to classical mechanics. In fact, in some of these plays—especially in Otway's *Orphan*—there can be seen the beginnings of melodrama. See MELODRAMA and SENTIMENTALISM.

In modern times tragedy seems to have waned as a dramatic form. Popular preferences have gravitated more to comedy, perhaps as an escape from the real-life tragedy all around us (war, hunger, disease, ignorance, air pollution, water pollution, and so on). Nevertheless, some notable exceptions are the tragedies of J. M. Synge (*Riders to the Sea*), Sean O'Casey (*The Plough and the Stars*), Eugene O'Neill (*Mourning Becomes Electra*), and Arthur Miller (*The Crucible*). See CATHARSIS, DRAMATIC STRUCTURE, TRAGIC FLAW, SENECAN TRAGEDY, PERIPETY.

REFERENCES: David Grene and Richmond Lattimore, eds., *The Complete Greek Tragedies;* Aristotle, *The Poetics;* Lily Bess Campbell, *Shakespeare's Tragic Heroes, Slaves of Passion;* Friedrich Nietzsche, *The Birth of Tragedy;* Herbert J. Muller, *The Spirit of Tragedy;* Richard Levin, ed., *Tragedy: Plays, Theory, and Criticism;* H. D. Saunder, ed., *Man and the Gods;* Cleanth Brooks, ed., *Tragic Themes in Western Literature;* Oscar Mandel, *A Definition of Tragedy;* Geoffrey Brereton, *Principles of Tragedy;* Clifford Leech, *Tragedy;* M. E. Pryor, *The Language of Tragedy;* George Steiner, *The Death of Tragedy;* Virginia Floyd, *Toward a Definition of Hubris.*

tragic flaw   A tragic PROTAGONIST's key trait, such as jealousy, greed, overweening ambition, credulousness, because of which the protagonist is brought down. See DRAMATIC STRUCTURE.

tragic irony   See IRONY.

transcendentalism   1. In philosophy, a belief in *noumena* or intuitions transcending proofs of sense experience, as Emerson explained in his essay, "The Transcendentalist": "The Idealism of the present day [1842] acquired the name Transcendental from ... Immanuel Kant in reply to the skeptical ... Locke, [who] insisted that there was nothing in the intellect which was not previously in the experience of the senses."

2. In literature, a movement that flourished in New England in the 1800s. Emerson, disenchanted with "the sterility of pure RATIONALISM," embraced the transcendentalists' more romantic attitude toward NATURE and the individual as "reflecting God's immanence." Under his leadership the Transcendentalist Club (1836–1860) attracted such writers as Henry Thoreau, Margaret Fuller, Bronson Alcott, Theodore Parker, and George Ripley—the latter a founder of BROOK FARM. Although not a member, Walt Whitman was a kindred spirit, a "romantic transcendentalist" and an "oafish" disciple of Emerson's, as Justin Kaplan observes in *Walt Whitman, a Life*. The Transcendentalists' papers were published by Elizabeth Peabody in her magazine *The Dial* (1840–1844).

REFERENCES: Perry Miller, ed., *The Transcendentalists: An Anthology;* George Whicher, ed., *The Transcendentalist Revolt against Materialism;* F. O. Matthiessen, *American Renaissance;* Van Wyck Brooks, *The Flowering of New England;* M. Simon and T. Parsons, eds., *Transcendentalism and Its Legacy;* O. M. Casale, "Poe on Transcendentalism," *Emerson Society Quarterly* (#50, 1968); Joel Porte, "Transcendental Antics," in Harry Levin, ed., *Veins of Humor;* Joel Myerson, *The New England Transcendentalists and the "Dial."*

transfer   A propaganda device that works upon the theory that favorable attitudes toward one thing may be transferred to another thing if the two are shown or named together. Since people readily form their opinions by association of ideas or symbols, a propagandist or an advertiser may win favor for a particular cause or product by linking it, through words or pictures, with things already held in esteem by the public. See PROPAGANDA DEVICES.

REFERENCES: William Hummel and Keith Huntress, *The Analysis of Propaganda;* J. B. Hogins and G. A. Bryant, eds., *Juxtaposition.*

transferred epithet   See EPITHET.

transition   The leading from one phase to another within a discourse; the bridging between sentences, groups of sentences, paragraphs, and larger sections of a work. Transitional words and phrases show the relationships among those elements—relationships of time, space, cause and effect, part and whole. Among transitional devices are conjunctions, especially the conjunctive adverbs *therefore, consequently, hence, thus, accordingly, however, nevertheless, furthermore, finally, in the same way, on the contrary, moreover.* Transitions between paragraphs may also be achieved by (1) repetition at the beginning of a paragraph of a word or phrase used at the end of the preceding paragraph; (2) use of demonstrative pronouns or demonstrative adjectives *this, that, these, those, such;* these words are best used not alone (leaving their reference broad and uncertain), but with some repetition or summary of the things they refer to: "These victories [already named in preceding paragraph] led to new ambitions on the part of military commanders"; (3) summarizing in a subordinated phrase or clause an idea already established: "*Because none of the battles had been wholly successful so far,* the command sought a new strategy for the remaining campaign."

For addition: *again, also, and, and then, besides, equally, first (second, etc.), finally, further, furthermore, in addition, in conclusion, last, likewise, moreover, next, similarly, then*

For contrast: *and yet, after all, at the same time, although, but, for all that, however, in contrast, nevertheless, nonetheless, notwithstanding, on the contrary, on the other hand, still, yet*
For comparison: *in like manner, in the same way, likewise, similarly*
For purpose: *for this reason, for this purpose, to this end, therefore*
For illustration: *for example, for instance, indeed, incidentally, in fact, in other words, to illustrate, that is*
For result: *accordingly, as a consequence, as a result, consequently, hence, then, therefore, thus*
For passage of time: *afterward, before that, at length, immediately, in the meantime, meanwhile, soon, then, thereafter, while, in maturity*
For summary: *in brief, in short, on the whole, to sum up, to summarize*

Usually considered weak and ineffective are the transitional "numbering" devices—*first, in the first place, secondly, next, and then, finally*—though these are preferable to no transitions at all.

translation   The art of rendering a work in a language other than its original. The RENAISSANCE on the Continent and in England was a golden age of translation. Italian interest in Greek classics received impetus from the Byzantine scholars who fled to Italy at the fall of Constantinople (1453), bringing with them the knowledge and enthusiasm that generated many a translation from the Greek and Arabic. A list of more indigenous Italian translators would be headed by Poggio Bracciolini (1380–1459), who translated from the Latin the works of Lucretius and of Quintilian. In England, Shakespeare borrowed freely from Lord North's translations of Plutarch's lives (1579), from Sir John Harington's translation of Ariosto's *Orlando Furioso* (1591), and from John Florio's translation of Montaigne's *essais* (1603). Perhaps the most celebrated translation of all times remains the Authorized Version of the King James Bible (1611). Based on previous translations of the (Hebrew) Old Testament and the (Greek) New Testament, the Authorized Version was produced by many scholars under the inspired and persistent supervision of King James I. In the face of the large number of translators, the King James Bible remains remarkable for its poetic qualities.

During the eighteenth and nineteenth centuries, controversy persisted over whether such EPICS as Homer's *Iliad* and *Odyssey* should be translated into verse or prose. The argument for prose was that it alone could render the original most intelligibly; for verse, that it alone could render the original most faithfully. Despite the controversy—and whether in verse or prose—eminent translations of Homer include Alexander Pope's in verse (1720 and 1726) and Henry Butcher and Andrew Lang's in prose (1879). John Keats's praise was elicited by a seventeenth-century verse translation by George Chapman (1616). Keats's sonnet "On First Looking Into Chapman's Homer" is well-known.

In modern times, widely distributed American authors whose works have been translated into European languages include Edgar Allan Poe, Mark Twain, and Ernest Hemingway. Fiction and nonfiction (e.g., history and biography) tend to present translators with fewer challenges than do poetry or poetic drama. In the translation of any genre, however, the chief challenge is how does one remain faithful to the original. "Much is lost in translation" is more than a mere quip. "Between an original text and its translation, there is a gap—a 'middle kingdom' of unknowns and equivalences—which the translator traverses alone," observes Ben Belitt, the distinguished translator of Lorca, Neruda, and Borges. Indeed, a tug of war is perennially waged between the literalists (those who would at all costs adhere to the letter) and the free spirits (those who would sacrifice the literal for a radical/liberal rendering). Vladimir Nabokov, in his translation of Pushkin's *Eugene Onegin,* espouses the literal; William Arrowsmith, in his translation of Aristophanes' *The Clouds,* often takes bold (but successful) liberties. Because Arrowsmith and Nabokov are not only scholars, however, but also poets, both of them brilliantly capture the spirit of the originals.

REFERENCES: Edwin Honig, "A Note on the Poetics of Translation," *Modern Poetry Studies;* Roger Shattuck, "Introduction" [to his translation of] *Selected Writings of Apollinaire;* Vladimir Nabokov, "Foreword," *Pushkin's Eugene Onegin;* Ben Belitt, *Adam's Dream: A Preface to Translation;* Rosemarie Waldrop, ed., "Women in Translation," *PSA Bulletin* (Winter, 1982).

travesty   A work that treats a lofty theme trivially.

Tribe of Ben   Nickname for the group of young poets and playwrights who regarded Ben Jonson (1573–1637) as their master. See CAVALIER POETS.

tribrach   See METER.

trilogy   A group of three literary works treating one continuous theme. For example, Aeschylus's *Oresteia (Agamemnon, The Libation Bearers,* and *The Eumenides);* Shakespeare's *King Henry VI* (which consists of three parts); John Dos Passos's *U.S.A. (The 42nd Parallel, Nineteen Nineteen,* and *The Big Money);* James T. Farrell's *Studs Lonigan (Young Lonigan, The Young Manhood . . . ,* and *Judgement Day);* Sigrid Undset's *Kristin Lavransdatter (The Bridal Wreath, The Mistress of Husaby,* and *The Cross);* J. R. R. Tolkien's *Lord of the Rings.*

trimeter   See METER.

triolet   An eight-lined poem rhyming *abaaabab* (only two rhymes) the first two lines repeated as the last two. The best-known example is Austin Dobson's "The Kiss":

> Rose kissed me today,
>   Will she kiss me tomorrow?
> Let it be as it may,
>   Rose kissed me today.
> But the pleasure gives way
>   To a savor of sorrow;
> Rose kissed me today—
> *Will* she kiss me tomorrow?

triteness   Staleness of expression. Whatever lacks freshness of expression is *trite.* Even original ideas may be couched in trite phrasing that robs them of sparkle. When triteness becomes more noticeable than mere lack of freshness, we may call the style *hackneyed*—for to travel by hackney cab is to hire a readymade conveyance, not to go on one's own; and the extremely hackneyed usage may be called *threadbare.* For special sorts of trite phrasing, see CLICHÉ, BROMIDE, PLATITUDE, STEREOTYPE.

trochee   See METER.

trope 1. In rhetoric, any figure of speech or figurative use of a word. (See FIGURATIVE LANGUAGE.) This term has also had the more specialized meaning apparent in the Greek *tropos*, "a turn." A trope is thus a "turn of speech" or a turning of a word to uses it does not ordinarily have. For instance, trope attaches an adjective to a noun that the adjective does not logically modify: "*ripe* October" is so described because October's *crops* are ripe; "*dreamy* night" declares that people are dreamy on such a night; and Horace Walpole mentions "the gentleman with the *foolish* teeth"—not because the teeth were foolish but rather because the *grin* (or the gentleman himself) was foolish. In this sense, a trope is much the same as a transferred EPITHET.

2. In medieval drama, a term for a musical interpolation in Gregorian chants—words added to the wordless series of notes which were sung on the last syllable of the last Alleluia in the mass. These verbal additions or "turns" became a form of dialogue, an important step in the development of liturgical drama. The earliest trope was the dramatic dialogue "Quem Quaeritis" sung on Easter Sunday. In this trope the three Marys come to Christ's tomb, where they find angels. "*Quem quaeritis?*" ("Whom are you seeking?"), the angels ask The Marys reply, "*Jesum Nazarenum crucifixem*" ("Jesus of Nazareth who was crucified"). "*Non est hic; surrexit, sicut praedixerat*" ("He is not here; he is risen just as he foretold"), the angels tell them.

REFERENCE: Joseph Quincy Adams, "Sources of the Liturgical Drama," *Chief Pre-Shakespearian Dramas.*

troubadours From Old French *trobar,* "to seek or invent." Inventive lyric poets of Provence during the twelfth and thirteenth centuries. Many troubadours were attached to the royal courts. See COURTLY LOVE. Other troubadours, like the ROCK lyricists of the 1960s, were wandering minstrels and satirists. See GOLIARDIC VERSE. For representative troubadour lyrics, see Anthony Bonner, ed., *A Troubadour Anthology.*

REFERENCES: Maurice Valency, *In Praise of Love;* F. V. Grunfeld, "The Troubadours," *Horizon* (Summer, 1970); James Wilhelm, *Seven Troubadours;* Ezra Pound, *The Spirit of Romance;* Robert Briffault, *The Troubadours.*

truism A statement of obvious or self-evident truth. One may assert, "Blind men do not see"—but the assertion is hardly worth the effort. An essay that begins, "There are many different kinds of animals," usually has little to say that is cogent. Truisms are often tautological (see TAUTOLOGY), either explicitly ("Poison is dangerous because it can kill you") or implicitly ("Nobody can swim across the Pacific from the mainland to Hawaii"). For some fine distinction of terms see AXIOM, BROMIDE, PLATITUDE, STEREOTYPE, and TRITENESS.

tu quoque Literally, "You, too." The phrase is used to indicate the device of extenuating guilt by spreading it to the accuser or to the audience. "If I am guilty, you are guilty too," says the *tu quoque* arguer. In its baldest form the *tu quoque* argument appears in the well-known Third Knight's speech in T. S. Eliot's *Murder in the Cathedral,* in which the knight rationalizes the killing of Becket: "We have been instrumental," he says to the audience, "in bringing about the state of affairs that you approve. We have served your interests; we merit your applause; and if there is any guilt whatever in the matter, you must share it with us."

U

ubi sunt   Literally, "Where are they [now]?" A perennial motif in POEMS and SHORT STORIES that ask directly or implicitly the nostalgic question, "Where are the . . . of times now past?" (Supply *girls, boys, men, women, heroes, leaders, places, things.*) The best-known poem built on this motif is Dante Gabriel Rossetti's "Ballad of Dead Ladies," a translation of François Villon's BALLADE containing the refrain "But where are the snows of yester-year?" A humorous takeoff on this MOTIF is George Starbuck's poem "Water under the Bridge."

underlining   In preparing manuscripts for print (or for submission to teachers), use underlining to indicate matter to be printed in ITALICS. Italics are used for:

1. Emphasis, especially in calling attention to a portion of matter being quoted:

That is *exactly* what I wanted to hear.
Note the unusual use of words by Edmund Waller in the line, "When I *resemble* her to thee."

Note: Good writers avoid indiscriminate emphasis.

2. Words, letters, and figures used as names of themselves:

A misplaced *only* may twist your meaning.
Are there two *l*'s in *tranquillity?*
There are two *2*'s in *220*.

3. Titles of books, plays, newspapers, periodicals, pamphlets, long poems (printed separately), motion pictures, and television programs:

Absalom, Absalom   *Hiawatha*
Cat on a Hot Tin Roof   *Citizen Kane*
The New York Times   *High Noon*
Toledo *Blade*   *The Dick Cavett Show*
Fortune magazine

Exceptions: Do not underscore: Bible, or books of the Bible; Koran; Prayer Book, Book of Common Prayer, or other books of worship; Constitution, Declaration of Independence, Magna Carta, statute books, or other books of acts and legislative enactment.

4. Operas, operettas, and symphonies:

Rigoletto   *Harold in Italy*
The Student Prince   Prokofiev's *Classical Symphony*

Exceptions: Do not underscore the names of songs, short musical compositions, or other works identified only by number or key.

5. Foreign words and expressions:

Her singing is full of *joie de vivre*.
It is a matter of *chacun à son gout*.
The concept of *Der Ubermensch* has wrought terror in the modern world.

6. Latin abbreviations used in documentation and in running text:

cf.	*loc. cit.*
et al.	*N.B.*
et seq.	*op. cit.*
ibid.	*q.v., qq.v.*
id., idem.	*v.*

Exceptions: Do not underscore i.e., e.g., etc., viz.

7. The names of ships, airplanes, and spacecraft:

S.S. *United States*	*Spirit of St. Louis*
U.S.S. *Enterprise*	*Yankee Clipper*

Exceptions: Do not underscore such things when known by model or serial designations: DC–3, Boeing 747, Apollo 11.

8. Subheadings, usually at the beginnings of paragraphs, but sometimes as separate lines above sections of a manuscript.

underscoring   See UNDERLINING.

understatement   The saying of less than what is merited by the facts of the case; a way of "playing down" or underemphasizing a statement. However, if the statement clearly implies the full meaning—without actually stating it— understatement is a device for achieving especially strong emphasis. It is thus a kind of psychological approach that works by stirring the imagination of the reader or listener—often more effective than any statement the writer or speaker could possibly make. The victorious athlete who passes off a success by saying "I was lucky" may show modesty, but also effectively emphasizes the extent of the achievement. The remarkable contrast between an event and the understated report of it (the first flight to the moon referred to as "an excursion") invariably says more than a report that bears a host of strong adjectives. Exaggeration (see HYPERBOLE) tends to lose effectiveness, and understatement tends to gain effectiveness—perhaps because people appreciate being treated as intelligent enough to understand. Understatement may serve to soften a harsh or offensive idea. (See EUPHEMISM.) Understatement often involves IRONY (*asserting* the opposite of what is intended) and LITOTES (*denying* the opposite of what is intended). Understatement is as common in good literature as it is absent in bad literature. Shakespeare, a master of all the tricks, often makes little things and words carry great weight. In the midst of the terrors in *King Lear* the ragged and crazy Tom enters and says "Poor Tom's a-cold"—it is enough to make the audience, aware of so much more than the damp chill of the countryside, actually shiver.

undistributed middle   A fallacy in the deductive SYLLOGISM in which the middle term ("sports cars" in the example below) is undistributed (that is, it does not refer to *all* of its class) in both of its appearances. Given, for example, the syllogism:

> All Mustangs are sports cars
> All Ferraris are sports cars.
> Therefore Ferraris are Mustangs.

The absurdity of the conclusion is obvious with respect to sports cars. But alas for less obvious conclusions!

unities   **1.** Aristotle's three unities—of time place, and action—described the Greek playwrights' practice of limiting, in most of their plays, the time to one day, the place to one city-state or even one palace, and the action to one unified story-line (with a beginning, rising action, middle or climax, falling action, and end). Although Aristotle had emphasized only the unity of action, several of his successors extended and rigidified the other two unities (see DRAMATIC STRUCTURE). **2.** Poe's "unity of effect," as expounded in his critical review of Hawthorne's *Twice-Told Tales,* posits the theory that everything in a SHORT STORY—the story-line, the SETTING, the characterization, the mood, or tone, the very words—should lead to *one effect:* e.g., horror or beauty.

REFERENCES: Monroe Beardsley, "Unity and Related Concepts," in *Aesthetics;* Daniel Schwarz, "Unity of Eliot's Gerontion," *Bucknell Review* (Spring, 1971).

unity   The quality of singleness of purpose and treatment in a literary work. Unity depends first upon the selection of *one* topic, then upon the treatment of ᵗhat topic in a coherent and self-contained work without digression into ırrelevancy. See UNITIES.

University Wits, the   Tudor English intellectuals like Marlowe, Lyly, Lodge, and Greene. The term *wit* meant *knowledge* or *sophistication* rather than cleverness. See WIT.

unreliable narrator   A narrator who wittingly or unwittingly misinforms other characters and the readers. For example, in Jorge Luis Borges's story "The Garden of Forking Paths" the narrator deliberately misinforms the readers about Captain Richard Madden. Compare IRONY 3.

utilitarian writing   Lists, inventories, receipts, applications, memoranda, class notes, social notes, business letters, classified advertisements, etc., mainly devoted to personal order and growth, and to carrying forward the world's work. Compare EXPOSITION.

REFERENCES: E. Glenn Griffin, *Effective Business Writing;* Herman Estrin, ed., *Technical and Professional Writing;* J. S. Krey *et al., Effective Writing for Business;* Leo Bogart and W. F. Massy, *Strategy in Advertising;* Erwin Steinberg, *Communication in Business and Industry.*

Utopia   1. The title of a book (1516) by Sir Thomas More. In this political romance with specifications for an ideal state, the setting is an imaginary island Utopia. 2. Hence, any ideal state, wherein everything is perfect, as the author envisions perfection, in people, government, education, health, and general welfare. The connotation of a "never-never land" is implicit in the derivation of *utopia*—from the Greek *ou,* not, and *topos,* place. The best-known utopias are described in the following books: Plato's *Republic* (ca. 400 B.C.), St. Augustine's *City of God* (A.D. 411), Dante's *On Monarchy* (ca. 1300), Campanella's *City of the Sun* (1623), Bacon's *New Atlantis* (1627), Butler's *Erewhon* (1874), Bellamy's *Looking Backward* (1888), William Morris's *News from Nowhere* (1890), H. G. Wells's *Modern Utopia* (1905), Aldous Huxley's *Brave New World* (1932), and B. F. Skinner's *Walden Two* (1948). See FUTURISM.

REFERENCES: Frederic R. White, ed., *Famous Utopias of the Renaissance;* Karl Mannheim, *Ideology and Utopia;* J. W. Johnson, ed., *Utopian Literature, a Selection;* Sylvia Bowman, "Edward Bellamy" in *An American Prophetic Influence;* Sheila Schwartz, "World of Science Fiction," *English Record* (February, 1971); William H. Evans and Mary Ellen Chase, *Values in Literature.*

V

vagueness   Generally, imprecision of meaning, haziness, lack of clarity. But that definition leaves vagueness nearly synonymous with AMBIGUITY—and the terms need to be distinguished. To distinguish them, Monroe Beardsley (in *Thinking Straight*) has offered a more useful definition: "In vagueness, you know what the sense is, all right; but you don't know *how much* there is of the quality referred to." Thus *hot* and *cold* are vague words: *how* hot? *how* cold? *Long, heavy, good, bad, wet, populated, rare, common*—all these are vague words, their meanings being matters of unspecified degree. But vagueness has its benefits: It keeps us from having to be precise when precision is of no useful consequence. We may refer to a "crowded room" without finding it necessary to specify the size of the room or the number of persons in it. When the need to be specific is great, as it often is in scholarly work, vagueness may destroy the worth of a writer's THESIS.

variety   Even a good thing too often repeated or too long continued loses its hold upon the mind, and variety is among the spices of language as well as of life. In writing or speech the notable style arises not from relentless insistence upon one manner (sentence pattern, length, rhythm, or structure), but upon a variety in which one manner dominates and is made continually delightful by the differences that set it off. Effective writing achieves variety of: (1) DICTION—not switching indiscriminately from one level of diction to another, but always selecting the appropriate yet unexpected word; (2) sentence structure and length; (3) word order and sentence pattern—varying position of subjects, objects, complements, and modifiers; (4) RHETORIC—avoiding any overuse of such devices as BALANCE, PARALLELISM, PERIODIC SENTENCES, IMAGERY, and FIGURATIVE LANGUAGE; (6) sound and rhythm. Variety, however, should not be sought for its own sake. What is simple and natural can be repeated more readily than what is remarkable and contrived: A simple "he said" is better repeated than varied to "he bellowed" and "he pointed out." The fault to be avoided is often called ELEGANT VARIATION—the precious searching for needless SYNONYMS and cute EPITHETS.

vehicle   See METAPHOR.

verbiage   See DEADWOOD.

verbosity   See DEADWOOD.

verisimilitude   A striking illusion of reality achieved by the writer's painstaking selection and description of details that give the reader the sensation "you are there." A classic example is Defoe's *Journal of the Plague Year* (1722), which is primarily fiction, though based on historical facts.

REFERENCES: Monroe Beardsley, "Phenomenal Objectivity" and "Representation and Abstraction," *Aesthetics;* Benedetto Croce, "The Probable," *Aesthetics;* Erich Auerbach, *Mimesis.*

verse   1. A term generally used for non-PROSE writing. Even if it rhymes and scans (has METER), verse does not come up to the quality of serious poetry. Verse is more informal than poetry in TONE and language. Usually called "verse" rather than "poetry" are *nursery rhymes, jingles, limericks,* and other humorous lines *(light verse).* Compare POEM; see LIGHT VERSE. 2. A single line of poetry.

REFERENCE: Wyndham Lewis and Charles Lee, eds., *The Stuffed Owl: An Anthology of Bad Verse.*

verse paragraphs   Units of blank verse (as in Milton's *Paradise Lost* and Wordsworth's *The Prelude*) set off on the basis of logical flow; as distinguished from STANZAS, which are set off on the basis of rhyme scheme.

vers de société   See LIGHT VERSE.

vers libre   See FREE VERSE.

Victorian   1. Pertaining to the era (1837–1901) when Queen Victoria reigned in England. 2. Pertaining to the artifacts, customs, morals, and pastimes of that period. 3. Sometimes a derogatory EPITHET—especially when prefaced by "mid"—suggesting *strait-laced, prim, prudish,* etc. Among the best-known poets of the Victorian era: Robert Browning (1812–89) and his wife, Elizabeth (1806–61); Alfred, Lord Tennyson (1809–92); Dante Gabriel Rossetti (1828–82) and his sister Christina (1830–94); William Morris (1834–99); Algernon Swinburne (1837–1909); Gerard Manley Hopkins (1844–89); Francis Thompson (1859–1907); Rudyard Kipling (1865–1936) (also famous for his fiction); and A. E. Housman (1859–1936). In this era there were also scores of minor poets famous for one or two memorable poems.

Among the best-known novelists: Charles Dickens (1812–70), George Eliot (1819–80) William Makepeace Thackeray (1811–63), Robert Louis Stevenson (1850–94), George Meredith (1828–1909), and Thomas Hardy (1840–1928), who now seems to be emerging also as a major poet.

Among the major essayists: Thomas Carlyle (1795–1881), whose reputation seems to have suffered an eclipse; T. B. Macaulay (1800–59); Matthew Arnold (1822–88), also a poet and the critic who remains the giant of his age; John Ruskin (1819–1900); John Henry (Cardinal) Newman (1801–90); John Addington Symonds (1840–93); and Andrew Lang (1844–1912).

Among the best-known playwrights: Oscar Wilde (1856–1900); James M. Barrie (1860–1937); Arthur W. Pinero (1855–1934); and the team of William

S. Gilbert (1836–1911) and Arthur Sullivan (1842–1900), who wrote satirical light operas. (George Bernard Shaw was born in 1856, but he did not produce his major plays until after the turn of the century.)

REFERENCES: William Irvine, *Apes, Angels, and Victorians;* W. E. Houghton, *The Victorian Frame of Mind;* Lytton Strachey, *Emminent Victorians;* Gordon Haight, ed., *The Portable Victorian Reader;* G. B. Woods, ed., *Poetry and Prose of the Victorian Period;* A. W. Ward and Alfred Waller, eds., *The Cambridge History of English Literature,* Vols. 12–14; Bonamy Dobrée, *The Victorians and After;* Philip Appleman et al., *1859: Entering an Age of Crisis;* Austin Wright, ed., *Victorian Literature: Modern Essays in Criticism;* George Levine and William Madden, eds., *The Art of Victorian Prose;* Vineta Colby, *The Singular Anomaly;* G. Kauvar and G. Sorensen, eds., *The Victorian Mind;* Masao Miyoshi, *The Divided Self;* J. G. Nelson, *The Sublime Puritan.*

villanelle   An intricate French verse pattern of nineteen lines (five *tercets* and a final four-line STANZA) with only two rhymes throughout—*aba aba aba aba aba abaa*—and at least eight of the nineteen lines repeating a REFRAIN. Some celebrated villanelles (or adaptations) include Auden's "If I Could Tell You," Roethke's "The Waking," and Dylan Thomas's "Do Not Go Gentle." Austin Dobson (1840–1921) is generally credited with introducing into England the villanelle, the BALLADE, and the RONDEL. His "On a Nankin Plate" reflects the playful tone and the metrics of the villanelle:

> *On a Nankin Plate*
>
> "Ah me, but it might have been!
> Was there ever so dismal a fate?"
> Quoth the little blue mandarin.
>
> Such a maid as was never seen!
> She passed, though I cried to her "Wait"—
> Ah me, but it might have been!
>
> I cried, "O my Flower, my Queen,
> Be mine!" "'Twas precipitate"—
> Quoth the little blue mandarin—
>
> But then . . . she was just sixteen,
> Long-eyed—as a lily straight—
> Ah me, but it might have been!
>
> As it was, from her palankeen,
> She laughed—"You're a week too late!"
> (Quoth the little blue mandarin.)
>
> That is why, in a mist of spleen,
> I mourn on this Nankin Plate.
> "Ah me, but it might have been!"
> Quoth the little blue mandarin.

virgule   Hardly another mark of punctuation (/) has so many names—*slant line, slash, bar, shilling sign.* And even though it is not a mark of sentence punctuation, it has more miscellaneous uses than it has names. The virgule is used:

1. To indicate addition or alternative, meaning *and* or *or:* "He traveled on the Continent in 1842/43." *Note:* The use of "and/or" is shunned by grammarians of logical mind.

2. To abbreviate certain much-used words and phrases: *c/o,* for *in care of;* *w/o,* for *without;* *N/A,* for *not available* or *not applicable.*

3. To mark the end of a line of poetry when part of a poem is quoted in run-on format: "Note the irony in the Shakespearean lines: 'If this be error and upon me proved, / I never wrote, nor no man ever loved.'"

4. To separate numerator and denominator in rational numbers: 2/3, 5/8, 15/32.

5. To signify dates reckoned by different calendars, the Old Style (Julian) and the New Style (Gregorian): "George Washington was born on February 11/22, 1732."

6. To signify year-dates reckoned from different New Year's days: "The charter of Massachusetts Bay dates from March 4, 1628/29."

7. To indicate shillings in the sterling monetary system: 10/6.

8. To separate proofreading symbols that refer to errors in a single line on a printer's proof: tr/#/cap

9. In pairs, to enclose symbols in phonemic transcription: In New York City, *bird* is not pronounced "boyd," but /bəyd/.

vision of life   An author's philosophic attitude toward the material; this attitude is usually conscious, though it may also be unconscious. It is sometimes consistent, if not systematic, throughout the author's works, but it more usually varies from work to work. Theodore Dreiser consistently reflects in all his novels one vision of life—NATURALISM. In Faulkner's novels, though many of the characters and actions are morally degraded, there is enough "saving grace" to support Faulkner's view that "man will prevail," that the best human qualities will "endure." The works of Shakespeare, on the other hand, do not reflect a single view of life, so that the reader can only say that in play "X" the vision is REALISTIC; in play "Y" the vision is ROMANTIC; in play "Z" the reflection is of a tragic vision of life.

REFERENCES: Ruben A. Brower, "The Twilight of the Double Vision," *The Fields of Light;* Richard Chase, *The Democratic Vista;* B. S. Oldsey and A. O. Lewis, eds., *Visions and Revisions;* Donald Watt, "Vision and Symbol in Huxley's *Island,*" *Twentieth Century Literature* (October, 1968); Northrop Frye, *Fearful Symmetry.*

voice   In literature there are, according to T. S. Eliot and John Hall Wheelock, at least three distinguishable voices. (1) The first voice is the PERSONA, or mask-voice, that a poet wears for a particular poem. This voice at its most recognizable level may belong to a character-narrator like the Duke in Browning's "My Last Duchess," and is thus removed from the poet. More often, the persona-voice is not that far away from the poet, is in fact only one of many voices, one aspect of a personality. Thus, the flame-snatching rebel voice of the speaker in Frost's "Canis Major" is in quite a different key from the chastened voice of the speaker in "Stopping by Woods...." In short, the persona-voice expresses TONE or mood or attitude in one particular poem or story. (But in Hawthorne's story "My Kinsman Major Molineux" the major protests to Robin, "May not a man have several voices?") (2) The second kind of voice is more cumulative; it is the trademark voice we have come to recognize and associate with a celebrated poet—the conversational voice of Frost, the understatement of Emily Dickinson, the rhetoric of Whitman, and so on. This voice is one of the key characteristics of a poet's style and is so well known as to make itself the easy butt or adulation of PARODY. It can also be heard as a derivative echo in the first attempts of prospective poets. (3) Finally, there is the rarest, least artful voice—something eternal and universal that comes almost effortlessly from the poet's psyche. This is the ARCHETYPAL voice, for which the poet has only served as a kind of medium. Two examples that come to mind are Coleridge's "Kubla Khan" and Yeats's "Sailing to Byzantium," poems for which these poets served as "compulsive midwives," as Northrop Frye has put it. Dante called this voice the anagogical, or mystical (*The Banquet*, I, 1). It is a quality that has no doubt assured the immortality of "The Song of Songs" and of Shakespeare's sonnet "That time of year thou mayst in me behold."

REFERENCES: T. S. Eliot, *The Three Voices of Poetry;* John Hall Wheelock, *What Is Poetry?* (*Note:* Mr. Wheelock divides the above-mentioned three into four voices.) Lillian Feder, "Voices from Hades . . . Ezra Pound," *Ancient Myth in Modern Poetry;* Mary Sullivan, *Browning's Voices in the Ring and the Book.*

volta   See SONNET.

vulgate   1. A Latin translation of the Bible, made by St. Jerome in the fourth century; the authorized version of the Roman Catholic Church. 2. Old French romances in prose, from which Malory borrowed for the *Morte d'Arthur* (1471).

W

W's, the five   The *who, what, when, where,* and *why* that guide a writer, particularly a journalistic reporter, in providing essential information in a story. The five W's (and often the H—*how*) are the central elements of a good LEAD in traditional newspaper reporting. Rudyard Kipling emphasized their importance to a writer:

> I keep six honest serving-men
> (They taught me all I knew);
> Their names are What and Why and When
> And How and Where and Who.

Walpurgisnacht   **1.** Walpurgis Night, the night preceding May 1, the Feast of St. Walpurga (710?–777), an English missionary nun who helped St. Boniface in Germany. **2.** Witches' annual holiday on the Brocken in the Harz Mountains, an extravagant celebration at midnight with bonfires and elaborate religious and sexual rites. In Goethe's *Faust,* Part I, Mephistopheles conducts Faust to a Walpurgisnacht. Similarly, the Devil conducts Hawthorne's Goodman Brown to a comparable, if less elaborate, witches' sabbath. **3.** More broadly, a satirical term for any wild or extravagant midnight ball or party.

REFERENCES: Jules Michelet, *Satanism and Witchcraft;* George Lyman Kittredge, *Witchcraft in Old and New England.*

Wanderjahre   See GRAND TOUR.

Weltanschauung   Literally, "world view." **1.** A comprehensive conception of the world and events in which all is viewed within a consistent philosophical system to explain purpose and meaning. **2.** In a more restricted sense, VISION OF LIFE.

Weltschmerz   World-weariness; satiety with life. See STURM UND DRANG.

which, that   Aside from the grammatical function of these pronouns, each signals a subtly contrastive meaning, as E. B. White observes in his *Elements of Style. Which* almost always signals NONRESTRICTIVES (e.g., "This ticket, which I had to fight for, will cost you ten dollars") and a voice-drop or more interruptive pause than does *that. That* almost always signals RESTRICTIVES (e.g., "The ticket that I had to fight for will cost you more than the ticket that I did not have to fight for.") Frequently a *that* can be eliminated altogether (e.g., "The ticket I had to fight for. . . .") In fact, *which, that,* and *who* all too often clutter, as Ken Macrorie observes in *Telling Writing:* "Good writers remove excessive whichery, thatery, and whooery."

whichmire   James Thurber's term for overly long sentences bogged down in their own *which* clauses; for example, "In this old house, which we owned, which was in a town, which had a name, which I shall not mention...." The chief remedy for a whichmire is to recast completely, perhaps into two or more sentences. If only two *which* clauses are involved, one of them can be recast into an appositive: "In this old house, our very own" or "In this old house of ours."

Whitsunday   See HOLIDAYS.

wit   1. Cleverness or brilliance. A witty person or character is quick with words. (Thus the expression "quick-witted" is a redundancy even if it is accepted idiom.) Dr. Samuel Johnson (1709–84) defined wit as "the discovery of occult resemblances in things apparently unlike." 2. In Shakespeare's works and in those of his contemporaries, wit usually means *sophistication* or *knowledgeability*, a definition close in meaning to the Anglo-Saxon and German roots *witan* and *wissen*, "to know." See METAPHYSICAL POETS and CONCEIT.

REFERENCES: James B. Leishman, *The Monarch of Wit*; Charles Brooks, "On the Difference between Wit and Humor," *Chimney-Pot Papers*.

who, whom   1. The subject and the object forms, respectively, of the relative pronouns corresponding to the personal pronouns. In choosing between *who* and *whom*, try substituting *he* or *him*. For example, in the utterance "Kazantzakis is one author _____ [who, whom] I must read next," you reject "I must read *he*" in favor of "I must read *him*"—hence, "*whom* I must read." That test is faithful, incidentally, to its Latin models, as reflected in the "Quem Quaeritis" TROPE, in which the object *queM* translates as *whoM* ("Whom are you looking for?"). Nevertheless, contemporary speakers abandon such Latinate formality, preferring the more informal "Who are you looking for?" *especially in questions.* In an utterance like "The author of *Zorba the Greek* is an artist _____ [who, whom] Phoebe Adams feels is a genius," you reject "*him* is a genius" in favor of "*he* is a genius"—hence, "*who* (Phoebe Adams feels) is a genius." Notice the temporary bypass of a parenthetical expression like "Phoebe Adams feels." 2. What is perhaps more important, contemporary writers and speakers drop *who* and *whom* altogether wherever the sense allows—as it does in utterances like "Kazantzakis is one author I must read next" and "He is an artist Phoebe Adams feels is a genius."

REFERENCES: Margaret Bryant, *Current American Usage*; Bergen and Cornelia Evans, *Dictionary of Contemporary American Usage*; Mary Whitten, *Harbrace College Handbook*; Janet Emig, "Bibliography," *The Composing Process ...* ; also her "Uses of the Unconscious in Composing," *CCC Journal* (2/1964); Charles Billiard, "How Language Is Sampled," *The Volume Library*.

women's liberation   A revival, in the 1970s, of a movement begun over a century ago to free women from social, sexual, political, and economic discrimination. Champions of these goals include the following: Mary Wollstonecraft, author of *A Vindication of the Rights of Women* (1792); John Stuart Mill, author of *The Subjection of Women* (1869) and cofounder, in England, of the Women's Suffrage Society, alluded to in plays of George Bernard Shaw and the fiction of D. H. Lawrence; Henrik Ibsen, whose play *A Doll's House* (1879) stimulated reexamination of the thesis "woman's place is in the home"; Susan B. Anthony, author of *History of Woman Suffrage* (1881–1887) and leader of the movement in the United States; and Virginia Woolf, author of *A Room of One's Own* (1933). The movement has called attention to such inequities as the sexual double standard, lower wages and salaries for women than for men performing the same jobs, drudgeries of parenthood and housework not shared by husbands.

REFERENCES: Simone de Beauvoir, *The Second Sex;* Margaret Mead, *Male and Female;* Kate Millett, *Sexual Politics;* Germaine Greer, *The Female Eunuch;* Robin Morgan, ed., *Sisterhood Is Powerful;* Mary Ellman, *Thinking About Women;* Elaine Showalter, ed., *Women's Liberation and Literature;* Elsie Adams and M. L. Briscoe, eds., *Up Against the Wall, Mother;* Elizabeth Hampsten, "A Woman's Map of Lyric Poetry," *College English* (May, 1973); Eva Figes, *Patriarchal Attitudes;* Beth Schneiderman, ed., *By and About Women.*

wordiness   The use of more words than necessary; verbosity. See DEADWOOD and ECONOMY IN WRITING.

working bibliography   See DOCUMENTATION and RESEARCH PAPER

wrenched rhyme   The same as slant rhyme. See RHYME.

Z

Zeitgeist   "Spirit of the times." In literary criticism, the assumption that even the most original artist cannot escape reflecting in a work certain influences, modes, manners, and the like, of the times.

REFERENCES: Hippolyte Taine, *History of English Literature;* William Barrett, *Time of Need;* Emil Roy, *British Drama Since Shaw;* also his "World View in Shaw," *Drama Survey* (Winter, 1965); Priscilla Tyler, ed., *Writers on the Other Side of the Horizon.*

Zen   A Buddhist philosophy based on the central belief that enlightenment comes through the renunciation of materialism and through the concentration on things of the spirit. The three "pillars" of Zen, undergirding Salvation (*Gedatsu*) are (1) work (*Samu*), (2) dialogue (*Monto*), and (3) contemplation (*Meiso*), in that order, although the practice properly begins and ends in *Meiso.*

REFERENCES: Philip Kapleau, ed., *The Three Pillars of Zen;* William Barrett, ed., *Zen Buddhism: Selected Writings of D. T. Suzuki;* Alan Watts, *Beat Zen, Square Zen, and Zen.*

zeugma   Literally, "yoking." "Her hair is red, her eyes blue" conveys meaning clearly enough, but causes the grammarian's eyebrow to go up, for it seems to imply "her *eyes is* blue." The fault is an example of zeugma, a construction in which the writer has too optimistically assumed that one predicate or modifier is going to do double duty, when it really cannot. The result is inadvertent, often bumptious, nonsense. Other examples (with the offending constructions in italics): "The silly girl has her head *filled* with straw and her *face* with paint," "No *amount of* money or *people* can influence me," "Did you *drink* all the milk and *the sandwiches*?" Zeugma may not always be a fault; it is sometimes a deliberate feat, as it is in Alexander Pope's line: "feared to stain her honor or her new brocade." Compare SYLLEPSIS.

Index of Authors